Frommer's®

Toronto

2004

by Hilary Davidson

Here's what the critics say about Frommer's:

"Amazingly easy to use. Very portable, very complete."
—*Booklist*

"Detailed, accurate, and easy-to-read information for all price ranges."
—*Glamour Magazine*

"Hotel information is close to encyclopedic."
—*Des Moines Sunday Register*

"Comprehensive and includes information about the many festivals—from beer to literature—that Toronto hosts each year."
—*The Washington Post*

WILEY

Wiley Publishing, Inc.

P9-EDB-076

About the Author

Toronto native **Hilary Davidson** now calls New York City home, thanks to her persuasive Manhattan-born husband, Daniel. She is a contributing editor at *Chatelaine* magazine and writes for *Martha Stewart Weddings, Executive Traveler, Wedding Bells, Glow, Discover,* and *Pages*. She is also a contributor to *Frommer's Canada*. She can be reached at hcdavidson@excite.com.

Published by:

Wiley Publishing, Inc.

111 River St.
Hoboken, NJ 07030-5744

Copyright © 2004 Wiley Publishing, Inc., Hoboken, New Jersey. All rights reserved. No part of this publication may be reproduced, stored in a retrieval system or transmitted in any form or by any means, electronic, mechanical, photocopying, recording, scanning or otherwise, except as permitted under Sections 107 or 108 of the 1976 United States Copyright Act, without either the prior written permission of the Publisher, or authorization through payment of the appropriate per-copy fee to the Copyright Clearance Center, 222 Rosewood Drive, Danvers, MA 01923, 978/750-8400, fax 978/646-8600. Requests to the Publisher for permission should be addressed to the Legal Department, Wiley Publishing, Inc., 10475 Crosspoint Blvd., Indianapolis, IN 46256, 317/572-3447, fax 317/572-4447, E-Mail: permcoordinator@wiley.com.

Wiley and the Wiley Publishing logo are trademarks or registered trademarks of John Wiley & Sons, Inc. and/or its affiliates. Frommer's is a trademark or registered trademark of Arthur Frommer. Used under license. All other trademarks are the property of their respective owners. Wiley Publishing, Inc. is not associated with any product or vendor mentioned in this book.

ISBN 0-7645-4060-2
ISSN 1047-7853

Editor: Myka Carroll
Production Editor: Bethany André
Cartographer: John Decamillis
Photo Editor: Richard Fox
Production by Wiley Indianapolis Composition Services

Front cover photo: A view of Toronto's skyline and harbor
Back cover photo: Hockey Hall of Fame statue

For information on our other products and services or to obtain technical support, please contact our Customer Care Department within the U.S. at 800/762-2974, outside the U.S. at 317/572-3993 or fax 317/572-4002.

Wiley also publishes its books in a variety of electronic formats. Some content that appears in print may not be available in electronic formats.

Manufactured in the United States of America

5   4   3   2   1

Contents

List of Maps   vi

What's New in Toronto   1

1   The Best of Toronto   3

1 Frommer's Favorite Toronto
Experiences 3

2 Best Hotel Bets 7

3 Best Dining Bets 8

The Best of Toronto Online 9

2   Planning Your Trip to Toronto   12

1 Visitor Information 12

2 Entry Requirements &
Customs 13

3 Money 14

*The Canadian Dollar, the U.S. Dollar
& the British Pound* 15

What Things Cost in Toronto . . .17

4 When to Go 18

Toronto Calendar of Events 18

Jump Up! 22

5 Travel Insurance 23

6 Health 24

The SARS Story 25

7 Specialized Travel Resources . . .25

*Wedded Bliss for Gay &
Lesbian Couples* 27

8 Planning Your Trip Online 28

9 The 21st-Century Traveler 30

*Frommers.com: The Complete
Travel Resource* 30

Online Traveler's Toolbox 32

10 Getting There 33

11 Packages for the Independent
Traveler 37

12 Tips on Accommodations 38

13 Recommended Reading 39

3   Getting to Know Toronto   40

1 Orientation 40

Underground Toronto 44

The Neighborhoods in Brief 44

2 Getting Around 46

Fast Facts: Toronto 50

4   Where to Stay   54

1 Downtown West 55

2 Downtown East 65

Family-Friendly Hotels 66

3 Midtown West 68

4 Uptown 71

5 The East End 71

6 At the Airport 72

5 Where to Dine   75

1 Restaurants by Cuisine 80

2 Downtown West 84

Family-Friendly Restaurants 93

3 Downtown East 96

Savory Surfing 98

4 Midtown West 100

Great Greasy Spoons 107

5 The East End 108

Sleepless in Toronto: What to Do When the Midnight Munchies Attack 109

6 Uptown 110

Vegetarian Delights 114

7 North of the City 115

6 What to See & Do   117

Suggested Itineraries 117

1 The Top Attractions 118

Great Toronto Vistas 126

Where to Eat When You're Going to 130

2 More Museums 131

Pssst . . . Want in on a Secret? 132

3 Exploring the Neighborhoods 133

4 Architectural Highlights 135

5 Historic Buildings 138

6 For Sports Fans 140

7 Markets 141

8 Parks, Gardens & Cemeteries 141

9 Especially for Kids 142

10 Organized Tours 144

11 Outdoor Activities 146

Spas & the City 148

12 Spectator Sports 151

7 City Strolls   153

Walking Tour 1: Chinatown & Kensington Market 153

Walking Tour 2: Harbourfront 158

Walking Tour 3: The Financial District 160

Walking Tour 4: St. Lawrence & Downtown East 166

8 Shopping   171

1 The Shopping Scene 171

2 Great Shopping Areas 171

3 Shopping A to Z 172

The Best Bargains 180

Same Time Next Year 191

9 Toronto After Dark   196

1 The Performing Arts 196

2 The Club & Music Scene 206

3 The Bar Scene 210

Cueing Up 210

Hotel Bars 213

4 The Gay & Lesbian Scene ...214

5 Cinemas & Movie Houses 215

6 Coffeehouses 215

Sweet Treats: Toronto's Dessert Cafes 216

10 Side Trips from Toronto   218

1 Stratford 218

2 Niagara-on-the-Lake &
Niagara Falls 227

*Touring Niagara-on-the-Lake
Wineries* 228

A Family Adventure 238

*Niagara Parkway Commission
Restaurants* 240

3 The Muskoka Lakes 240

Rest, Relax, Recharge 247

4 Hamilton 248

Appendix: Toronto in Depth   252

1 History 101 252

Dateline 252

2 Toronto Today 260

Index   261

General Index 261

Accommodations Index 271

Restaurant Index 271

List of Maps

Metropolitan Toronto   4

Underground Toronto   42

The TTC Subway System   47

Where to Stay in Downtown
West   57

Where to Stay in Downtown
East   59

Where to Stay in Midtown &
Uptown   60

Where to Dine in Downtown   76

Where to Dine in Midtown West &
Uptown   78

Where to Dine from Chinatown to
Bloor Street   81

What to See & Do in
Downtown   120

What to See & Do in
Midtown   122

Walking Tour 1: Chinatown &
Kensington Market   155

Walking Tour 2: Harbourfront   160

Walking Tour 3: The Financial
District   163

Walking Tour 4: St. Lawrence &
Downtown East   167

Midtown Shopping: Bloor/
Yorkville   173

Downtown Shopping: Queen Street
West & West Queen West   174

Downtown After Dark   198

After Dark from Chinatown to
Bloor Street   201

Side Trips from Toronto   219

Stratford   221

Niagara-on-the-Lake   229

Niagara Falls   239

The Muskoka Lakes Region   241

Hamilton   249

Acknowledgments

Many, many thanks to my editor, Myka Carroll, whose talent, wit, and good sense made working on this book a pleasure. Thanks are also owed to the rest of the Frommer's team, who worked their usual magic in transforming a manuscript into a book. I am also grateful to my mother, Sheila Davidson, who is always ready to help and yet never makes me feel guilty for taking advantage of her highly skilled—yet unpaid—labor. Finally, I owe a heartfelt thanks to my husband, Dan, whose sense of humor and tireless enthusiasm carried me throughout this project.

An Invitation to the Reader

In researching this book, we discovered many wonderful places—hotels, restaurants, shops, and more. We're sure you'll find others. Please tell us about them, so we can share the information with your fellow travelers in upcoming editions. If you were disappointed with a recommendation, we'd love to know that, too. Please write to:

Frommer's Toronto 2004
Wiley Publishing, Inc. • 111 River St. • Hoboken, NJ 07030-5744

An Additional Note

Please be advised that travel information is subject to change at any time—and this is especially true of prices. We therefore suggest that you write or call ahead for confirmation when making your travel plans. The authors, editors, and publisher cannot be held responsible for the experiences of readers while traveling. Your safety is important to us, however, so we encourage you to stay alert and be aware of your surroundings. Keep a close eye on cameras, purses, and wallets, all favorite targets of thieves and pickpockets.

Other Great Guides for Your Trip:

Frommer's Canada
Frommer's Montréal & Quebec City
Frommer's Nova Scotia, New Brunswick & Prince Edward Island
Frommer's Ottawa with Kids
Frommer's Toronto with Kids

Frommer's Star Ratings, Icons & Abbreviations

Every hotel, restaurant, and attraction listing in this guide has been ranked for quality, value, service, amenities, and special features using a **star-rating system.** In country, state, and regional guides, we also rate towns and regions to help you narrow down your choices and budget your time accordingly. Hotels and restaurants are rated on a scale of zero (recommended) to three stars (exceptional). Attractions, shopping, nightlife, towns, and regions are rated according to the following scale: zero stars (recommended), one star (highly recommended), two stars (very highly recommended), and three stars (must-see).

In addition to the star-rating system, we also use **seven feature icons** that point you to the great deals, in-the-know advice, and unique experiences that separate travelers from tourists. Throughout the book, look for:

Finds	Special finds—those places only insiders know about
Fun Fact	Fun facts—details that make travelers more informed and their trips more fun
Kids	Best bets for kids and advice for the whole family
Moments	Special moments—those experiences that memories are made of
Overrated	Places or experiences not worth your time or money
Tips	Insider tips—great ways to save time and money
Value	Great values—where to get the best deals

The following **abbreviations** are used for credit cards:

AE	American Express	DISC	Discover	V	Visa
DC	Diners Club	MC	MasterCard		

Frommers.com

Now that you have the guidebook to a great trip, visit our website at **www.frommers.com** for travel information on more than 3,000 destinations. With features updated regularly, we give you instant access to the most current trip-planning information available. At Frommers.com, you'll also find the best prices on airfares, accommodations, and car rentals—and you can even book travel online through our travel booking partners. At Frommers.com, you'll also find the following:

- Online updates to our most popular guidebooks
- Vacation sweepstakes and contest giveaways
- Newsletter highlighting the hottest travel trends
- Online travel message boards with featured travel discussions

What's New in Toronto

Toronto—or "Hollywood North," as some wags would have it—is brimming with energy these days. Here's a quick look at what's happening now.

PLANNING YOUR TRIP While there are some new discount airlines flying into Toronto, such as **WestJet** (www.westjet.ca) and **JetsGo** (www.jetsgo.net), **Air Canada** (www.aircanada.ca) is still the major player. It's Canada's only national airline, and it operates direct daily flights from most major U.S. cities and from many smaller ones. Air Canada's response to the discount competition has been to launch a new division called **Tango** (www.flytango.com). It's a cheaper, no-frills service that operates from Toronto's Pearson International Airport, but it only flies to Canadian cities.

Speaking of the **airport,** there are major changes afoot: The grand new terminal is almost complete, and when it opens for business in late 2003, it will replace the gloomy Terminals 1 and 2. In the meantime, try to ignore the messy rerouting of traffic at the airport. See "Orientation" in chapter 3 for complete details on transportation from the airport to downtown Toronto.

WHERE TO STAY Toronto's fine selection of hotels has just gotten better: Two gorgeous new boutique hotels opened for business in 2003. The **SoHo Metropolitan Hotel,** 318 Wellington St. W. (© **800/668-6600**), is a serene spot that blends elegance and technology (not an easy feat). The **Hôtel Le Germain,** 30 Mercer St. (© **866/345-9501**), is the chic and glamorous offering from the Québec-based Groupe Germain. Both offer top-notch service that will make you want to come back again and again. See chapter 4 for full reviews.

And good news for spa-lovers: Some of the very best spas in the city are located in hotels, such as the **Victoria Spa** at the Crowne Plaza, the **Stillwater Spa** at the Park Hyatt, and the **Elizabeth Milan Hotel Day Spa** at the Fairmont Royal York. See "Spas & the City" in chapter 6 for details.

WHERE TO DINE Foodies, take note: 2003 was a banner year for restaurant openings in Toronto. My personal favorite is **Brassaii,** 461 King St. W. (© **416/598-4730**), a bistro that blends excellent food with fine service and a stunning setting—and its prices are quite reasonable.

Other new notables include **Xacutti,** 503 College St. (© **416/323-3957**), which is adding a dash of Indian spice in Little Italy; **Blowfish Restaurant & Sake Bar,** 668 King St. W. (© **416/860-0606**), for top-notch sushi; **Wish,** 3 Charles St. E. (© **416/935-0240**), an inspiring little gem of a bistro; the **Colony Kitchen,** 157 Bloor St. W. (© **416/591-9997**), an Asian-inspired restaurant located in—you won't believe it—the basement of Club Monaco's flagship store; and **Lolo,** 619 Mount Pleasant Rd. (© **416/483-8933**) a down-to-earth bistro with heavenly food. See chapter 5 for full reviews.

WHAT TO SEE & DO There's good and bad news. On the positive side, some Toronto museums are expanding so that they can show off more of their fantastic collections. The bad news is that much of the renovation work will be done in 2004. The most notable is the **Royal Ontario Museum,** which is staying open throughout the year but with a limited number of galleries. The **George R. Gardiner Museum of Ceramic Art** will be closed for much of the year.

By the way, Toronto-bound parents will find lots to keep small fry entertained if they consult a new website: **www.helpwevegotkids.com**. See chapter 6 for more information.

SHOPPING The Canadian dollar is still on the weak side, which is a boon to U.S. and overseas shoppers. Not that you should need further inducement to stop in at the unique local shops, including only-in-Toronto spots like **Peach Berserk** and **Fashion Crimes** (for women's fashions), **Decibel** (for men's), **Mink** (for jewelry and accessories), and **Mabel's Fables** (for children's books and toys).

If you only have a short time to shop while you're in town, turn your sights to **West Queen West,** an up-and-coming neighborhood where you'll find independent clothing boutiques, housewares shops, and antiques boutiques. See chapter 8 for details.

AFTER DARK Toronto has recently gained some new places to keep itself (and you!) entertained. One is the newly revived **Carlu** theater on the seventh floor of College Park. The long-awaited **Yonge-Dundas Square**—a new venue for open-air concerts right in the heart of downtown—opened up. Another attraction is **The Distillery Historic District,** which is now home to the Dancemakers and the Native Earth performing arts groups. See chapter 9 for complete details.

SIDE TRIPS One of the most exciting destinations in Ontario is the **Muskoka** region, which is just 90 minutes away from Toronto. It boasts excellent resorts, fine food, outdoor sports (golf and boating are the two most popular), and soothing spas. See chapter 10 for complete details.

The Best of Toronto

Chances are that even if you've never set foot in Toronto, you've seen the city a hundred times over. Known for the past decade as "Hollywood North," Toronto has stood in for international centers from European capitals to New York—but rarely does it play itself. Self-deprecating Torontonians embody a paradox: Proud of their city's architectural, cultural, and culinary charms, they are unsure whether it's all up to international snuff.

After spending a single afternoon wandering around Toronto, you might wonder why this is a question at all. The sprawling city boasts lush parks, renowned architecture, and excellent galleries. There's no shortage of skyscrapers, particularly in the downtown core. Still, many visitors marvel at the number of Torontonians who live in houses on tree-lined boulevards that are a walk or a bike ride away from work.

Out-of-towners can see the fun side of the place, but Torontonians aren't so sure. They recall the stuffiness of the city's past. Often called "Toronto the Good," it was a town where you could walk down any street in safety, but you couldn't get a drink on Sunday.

Then a funny thing happened on the way through the 1970s. Canada loosened its immigration policies and welcomed waves of Italians, Greeks, Chinese, Vietnamese, Jamaicans, Indians, Somalians, and others, many of whom settled in Toronto. Political unrest in Quebec drove out Anglophones, many into the waiting arms of Toronto. The city's economy flourished, which in turn gave its cultural side a boost.

Natives and visitors alike enjoy the benefits of this rich cultural mosaic. More than 5,000 restaurants are scattered across the city, serving everything from simple Greek souvlaki to Asian-accented fusion cuisine. Festivals such as Caribana and Caravan draw tremendous crowds to celebrate heritage through music and dance. Its newfound cosmopolitanism has made Toronto a key player on the arts scene, too. The Toronto International Film Festival in September and the International Festival of Authors in October draw top stars of the movie and publishing worlds. The theater scene rivals London's and New York's.

Toronto now ranks at or near the top of any international urban quality-of-life study. The city has accomplished something rare, expanding and developing its daring side while holding on to its traditional strengths. It's a great place to visit, but watch out: You might just end up wanting to live here.

1 Frommer's Favorite Toronto Experiences

- **Dining Alfresco on One of the City's Endless Patios:** Any piece of sidewalk might be appropriated for open-air dining at any time. If you can't beat 'em, join 'em. See chapter 5.
- **Cafe Hopping at Trattorias in Little Italy:** Several magazines

Metropolitan Toronto

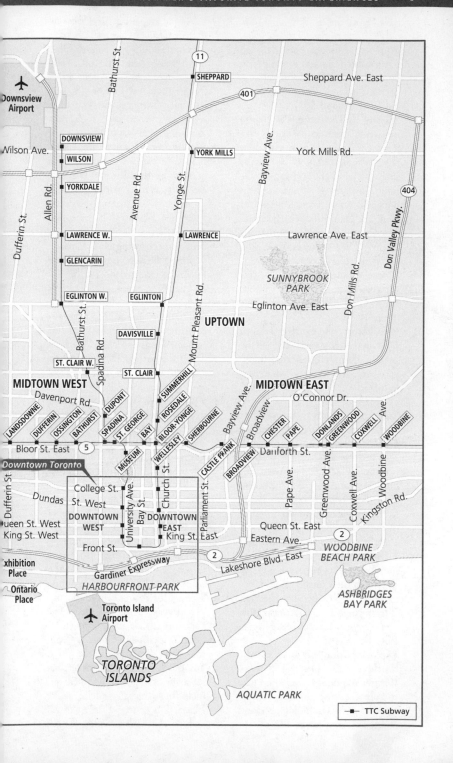

have zeroed in on this neighbor-hood as one of the *haute*-est spots in North America. Trendy, yes, but it's also a fun area for stopping by the many cafes and wine bars, and for dining on outstanding food. See chapter 5.

- **Staying Up Until the Wee Hours in Greek Tavernas:** No one's say-ing that Toronto is a city that never sleeps, but you can make such a claim about lively-at-all-hours Greektown. At 4am, upbeat bouzouki music can still be heard along the Danforth. See chapter 5.
- **Hanging Out at Harbourfront Centre:** There's always something going on—the International Festi-val of Authors, art exhibits, cul-tural celebrations, and the Toronto Music Garden, just to name a few. See p. 180
- **Picnicking on Centre Island:** Hop on the ferry and escape to the islands. From across the water, you'll see the city in a whole new light. See "The Toronto Islands" on p. 44.
- **Swinging from the Henry Moore Sculptures at the Art Gallery of Ontario:** The British sculptor Henry Moore so loved Toronto that he bestowed his greatest works on this museum. Kids have been known to swing from the gigantic works in front of the gallery. See p. 124.
- **Viewing the World from the Top of the CN Tower:** Most Toronto natives say they've never gone to the top of their most famous land-mark. It's a pity, because the view is inspiring. On any reasonably clear day, you can see Niagara Falls. See p. 125.
- **Exploring the Wonders of the World at the Ontario Science Centre:** You don't have to be a tyke to appreciate the amazing interac-tive displays about biology, ecology, and technology. See p. 128.

- **Taking in a Game at SkyDome or the Air Canada Centre:** SkyDome is home base for the Toronto Blue Jays baseball team. The Air Canada Centre is where the Maple Leafs (hockey) and the Raptors (basket-ball) play. Torontonians love their teams and come out to support them in droves. See p. 140.
- **Wandering Through the Riverdale Farm:** In case you need more proof that Toronto is a very green city, it has a working farm in its midst. Cows, sheep, pigs, goats, and other critters call it home. See p. 144.
- **Treasure Hunting for Vintage Clothing in Kensington Market:** How can one small area have a dozen vintage-clothing vendors? And how do they keep prices low and quality good? Haphazard Kensington Market is a joy for bargain hunters. See "Walking Tour: Chinatown & Kensington Market" in chapter 7 and p. 192 in chapter 8.
- **Shopping (or Window-Shopping) in Chic Yorkville.** Once home to the city's bohemian community, Yorkville is an enclave of exclusive shops, art galleries, and upscale cafes. See "Great Shopping Areas" in chapter 8.
- **Checking Out Local Theater:** Toronto likes its blockbuster shows: *Show Boat* and *Ragtime* got their start here before heading to Broadway. Offerings from the CanStage Company, the Tarragon Theatre, and the Lorraine Kimsa Theatre for Young People are con-sistently excellent, too. See "The Performing Arts" in chapter 9.
- **Busting a Gut at a Comedy Club.** Maybe it's something in the water: Toronto has produced more than its share of top-notch comedians, including the shagadelic Mike Myers, Jim Carrey, Dan Aykroyd, and the late John Candy. Check

Impressions

In the eyes of the rest of the country Toronto is a kind of combination Sodom and Mecca.

—Pierre Berton (1961)

out local talent or international stand-up stars at one of the many comedy clubs. See "The Club & Music Scene" in chapter 9.

- **Day-Tripping for Festivals and Falls:** Niagara-on-the-Lake is Ontario's wine country, and home of the Shaw Festival; it's less than a half-hour drive away from Niagara Falls. Picturesque Stratford has its own theater festival. See "Stratford" and "Niagara-on-the-Lake & Niagara Falls" in chapter 10.

<h2 style="background:black;color:white">2 Best Hotel Bets</h2>

- **Best Historic Hotel:** The (gloved) hands-down winner is Le **Royal Meridien King Edward,** 37 King St. E. (© **800/543-4300**), which was built in 1903 and in the past few years has been restored to its former glory. The lobby, with its pink marble columns and ornate frescoes, has seen the crème de la crème of society trot through over the years. In the 1960s, the Beatles holed up in the King Eddy while 3,000 fans stormed the lobby. See p. 66.
- **Best for a Stylish Stay:** The **Hôtel Le Germain,** 30 Mercer St. (© **866/345-9501**), one of Toronto's new boutique hotels, is a stunner, with its dramatic design and lots of artwork in public and private spaces alike (even the elevators!). See p. 55.
- **Best for Tech-Lovers:** The **SoHo Metropolitan Hotel,** 318 Wellington St. W. (© **800/668-6600**), makes the best use of technology I've ever seen at a hotel. It's as if the designers compiled a list of all of the most frustrating aspects about staying in a hotel room and resolved to fix them. And they succeeded! See p. 56.
- **Best for a Romantic Rendezvous:** The **Park Hyatt Toronto,** 4 Avenue Rd. (© **800/233-1234**),

has it all: a beautifully renovated Art Deco building, top-notch service, and one of the best views in the city from the rooftop terrace lounge. This is the place to relax and let yourself be pampered. See p. 69.

- **Best for Families:** The **Delta Chelsea,** 33 Gerrard St. W. (© **800/243-5732**), is a longtime family favorite, and in 2003 it further enhanced its standing by introducing the Family Fun Zone, which includes a playroom with live bunnies and fish, a video arcade, and a waterslide. It also offers children's programs, a daycare center, and kid-friendly restaurants. There are two pools, one for tykes and one for adults, and many rooms have refrigerators or kitchenettes. See p. 64.
- **Best for Business Travelers:** The **Metropolitan Hotel,** 108 Chestnut St. (© **416/977-5000**), is just a few minutes from the Financial District, and its amenities are competitive with those of its pricier competitors. Features include a 24-hour business center and in-room amenities such as fax/modem hookups, large work desks, and cordless two-line phones. The restaurants, Hemispheres and Lai Wah Heen, are

favorite sites for business lunches. See p. 58.

- **Best Moderately Priced Hotel:** Given the location and amenities, it's hard to beat the **Delta Chelsea,** 33 Gerrard St. W. (© **800/243-5732**), for price. Close to the Eaton Centre, Chinatown, and the Financial District, double rooms start at C$129 (US$90) per night. See p. 64.

- **Best Budget Accommodations: Victoria University,** 140 Charles St. W. (© **416/585-4524**), rents out its student residences from mid-May to late August. It's in an excellent location, with simple rooms and great facilities, including tennis courts and a pool. All this for C$66 (US$46) a night. See p. 71.

- **Best Service:** At **The Sutton Place Hotel,** 955 Bay St. (© **800/268-3790**), ask and you shall receive. The high staff-to-guest ratio means that there's always someone around to do your bidding. See p. 70. You also won't lack attention at the **Four Seasons Hotel Toronto,** 21 Avenue Rd. (© **800/268-6282**; p. 68), or the **Park Hyatt Toronto,** 4 Avenue Rd. (© **800/233-1234**; p. 69).

- **Best Hotel Dining:** This is a three-way tie: The Hilton Toronto's very grand dining room, **Tundra** (© **416/860-6800**; p. 86), is a treat for all the senses. But so are the Fairmont Royal York's new offering, **Epic** (© **416/860-6949**; p. 88), and the Park Hyatt's restaurant, **Annona** (© **416/924-5471**; p. 101).

- **Best Gay-Friendly Hotel:** Everyone comes to the **Howard Johnson Selby Hotel & Suites,** 592 Sherbourne St. (© **800/387-4788**). In a Victorian building in a predominantly gay neighborhood, this hotel draws gay, lesbian, and straight travelers with Belle Epoque style and individually decorated rooms. See p. 70.

- **Best for Travelers with Disabilities:** The **Fairmont Royal York,** 100 Front St. W. (© **800/441-1414**), looks monolithic but it pays a lot of attention to accessibility. The adaptations accommodate wheelchair users, the visually impaired, and the hearing impaired. See p. 58.

3 Best Dining Bets

- **Best New Restaurant:** 2003 saw some stiff competition for the title, with lots of new restaurants opening for business, but the winner is **Brassaii,** 461 King St. W. (© **416/598-4730**), a stylish bistro with excellent food, top-notch service, and wallet-friendly prices. See p. 90.

- **Best for a Business Lunch:** A sure bet is **Canoe Restaurant & Bar,** in the Toronto Dominion Tower, 66 Wellington St. W. (© **416/364-0054**), a see-and-be-seen spot for local and visiting power brokers. See p. 85.

- **Best for a Celebration:** The atmosphere at **Blowfish Restaurant &** **Sake Bar,** 668 King St. W. (© **416/860-0606**), is lively every night. The mix of the glamorous dining room, fine sushi, and a cool crowd gives the restaurant its edge. See p. 87.

- **Best for a Romantic Dinner:** I'm the first to admit that I'm biased, but the **Rosewater Supper Club,** 19 Toronto St. (© **416/214-5888**), is my idea of perfect romance (this restaurant was where my husband proposed to me). Relax and let the pampering begin. See p. 97.

- **Best Decor: Monsoon,** 100 Simcoe St. (© **416/979-7172**), has an award-winning interior design by Toronto firm Yabu Pushelberg.

The brown-on-black setting steals attention from the impressive kitchen. See p. 86. Upstart **Rain,** 19 Mercer St. ((C) **416/599-7246**), is easy on the eye, but good luck getting in—even pop diva Nelly Furtado couldn't do it. See p. 89.

- **Best View:** Forget the obvious choice (**360 Revolving Restaurant,** in the CN Tower, 301 Front St. W.; p. 86). Instead, dine at **Scaramouche,** 1 Benvenuto Place ((C) **416/961-8011**), which has a far more elegant perspective. Its floor-to-ceiling windows overlook the downtown skyline. See p. 111.
- **Best Wine List:** The international selection **Centro,** 2472 Yonge St. ((C) **416/483-2211**), is hard to beat. The basement is a wine bar with Italian, Californian, and Australian vintages by the glass; upstairs, the dining room boasts more than 600 bottles from around the world. Prices range from C$32 (US$22) into four figures. See p. 110.
- **Best Bistro:** Bistros often do well with comfort foods, but **Biff's,** 4 Front St. E. ((C) **416/860-0086**), serves up modern takes on classic dishes; its setting goes beyond comfortable to luxury. See p. 96.
- **Best Italian: Il Posto Nuovo,** 148 Yorkville Ave. ((C) **416/968-0469**), serves fine modern Italian cuisine in elegant digs—and the efficient, knowledgeable wait staff makes everyone feel at home. See p. 101.
- **Best Portuguese:** Standing alone on Italian-dominated College Street, **Chiado,** 484 College St.

The Best of Toronto Online

How did anyone ever plan a trip without the help of the Internet? It's hard to imagine now, given the wealth of information available online. But not all sites are created equal, so before you get ensnared in the Web, point and click on these gems.

- **Toronto.com** (www.toronto.com) boasts articles on arts and culture as well as a hotel directory, restaurant reviews, community news, and events listings. One of its best features is its extensive use of photographs.
- **City of Toronto** (www.city.toronto.on.ca) is the official municipal guide to Toronto, a straightforward source of practical information peppered with profiles of fun places to visit and announcements of festivals, free concerts, kids' events, and more.
- **Girl Talk Toronto: A Mini City Guide** (www.journeywoman.com/girltalk/toronto.html) runs the gamut from the serious (transit safety) to the frivolously fun (the best places to shop for shoes). This user-friendly site also highlights arty spots, off-the-beaten-path attractions, and the best places for brunch, all from a female perspective.
- **Green Tourism Association** (www.greentourism.on.ca) is an excellent resource for eco-friendly travelers. There's information about car-free transportation, outdoor activities and sports, and healthy dining.
- *Toronto Life* (www.torontolife.com) has extensive restaurant listings, as well as links for events, activities, and nightlife.
- *Toronto Star* (www.thestar.com) includes everything from theater and concert reviews to local news and weather conditions.

(© 416/538-1910), serves modern Portuguese cuisine. The seafood is flown in daily. See p. 88.

- **Best Greek:** The cooking at **Pan on the Danforth,** 516 Danforth Ave. (© 416/466-8158), will convince you that Pan was *really* the god of food. This is Greek cuisine updated with panache; see p. 108. Watch out for the midtown restaurant **Gus** (1033 Bay St.; © 416/923-8159) as a challenger; see p. 103.

- **Best Out-of-Towner:** Talk about catching on like wildfire—the new restaurant **Wildfire,** at Taboo Resort up in the Muskoka region (© 705/687-2233), is a work of art. Give yourself over to the genius chef by having one of the four-, five-, or 11-course tasting menus. See p. 246.

- **Best People-Watching:** Across from the Sutton Place Hotel is **Bistro 990,** 990 Bay St. (© 416/ 921-9990), where everyone in Toronto but me has made a celebrity sighting. (I'm too busy enjoying the delicious food.) See p. 100.

- **Best Value:** Once again, first prize to **Brassaii,** 461 King St. W. (© 416/598-4730), a stylish new bistro that's got it all. An honorable mention goes to **Messis,** 97 Harbord St. (© 416/920-2186), which has been a training ground for some of the best chefs in Toronto. See p. 90 and 104.

- **Best for Kids: Millie's Bistro,** 1980 Avenue Rd. (© 416/481-1247), is a family favorite with sunny dining rooms and a special children's menu; see p. 112. A more casual choice would be the deli-style **Shopsy's** (33 Yonge St.; © 416/365-3333); see p. 100.

- **Best Steak House: Barberian's,** 7 Elm St. (© 416/597-0335), has boosted the level of protein in Torontonians' diets since 1959.

It also serves great martinis and desserts, but what everyone comes here for is the meat. See p. 84.

- **Best Pizza:** A cubbyhole-size eatery in midtown, **Serra,** 378 Bloor St. W. (© 416/922-6999), makes thin-crust pizzas laden with gourmet ingredients. See p. 107.

- **Best Sushi: Hiro Sushi,** 171 King St. E. (© 416/304-0550). Chef Hiro Yoshida offers up classically prepared sushi as well as a few unique specialties; see p. 97. But there is competition from **Blowfish Restaurant & Sake Bar,** 668 King St. W. (© 416/860-0606); see p. 87.

- **Best Afternoon Tea:** A very tough call. Afternoon tea in the lobby lounge at the **Le Royal Meridien King Edward Hotel,** 37 King St. E. (© 416/863-3131), has been called the most authentic English tea, and it is divine; see p. 66. But I am partial to the phenomenal lavender-and-rose-infused Rooibos Provence tea that you'll find at **Annona at the Park Hyatt,** 4 Avenue Rd. (© 416/924-5471). See p. 101.

- **Best Alfresco Dining:** The lovely patio at **Biff's,** 4 Front St. E. (© 416/860-0086), is just about perfect. Set well back from the street, it affords terrific people-watching possibilities. See p. 96.

- **Best If You Have Only One Meal in Toronto and Price Is No Object:** While I hate to go along with the crowd, the common wisdom is on the money with **North 44,** 2537 Yonge St. (© 416/487-4897). Great food, great staff, great setting. See p. 111.

- **Best If You Have Only One Meal in Toronto and Price *Is* an Object:** Look no further than **Brassaii,** 461 King St. W. (© 416/ 598-4730). For all of the reasons listed above in "Best New Restaurant." See p. 90.

- **Best Chinese: Lai Wah Heen,** at the Metropolitan Hotel, 110 Chestnut St. (© **416/977-9899**), serves deluxe Cantonese and Szechwan specialties, including a variety of shark's fin soups and abalone dishes. It features several good-value prix-fixe specials at lunch and dinner. See p. 89.

- **Best Brunch:** Who needs bacon and eggs when you can have *torta rustica* with layers of ricotta, mozzarella, leeks, peas, and smoked trout? This and other glamorous offerings are available at **Agora,** at the Art Gallery of Ontario, 317 Dundas St. W. (© **416/977-0414**). See p. 87.

- **Best Desserts:** Dufflet Rosenberg bakes up a storm at **Dufflet Pastries,** 787 Queen St. W. (© **416/ 504-2870**). You'll find her name on the dessert list at some of the city's top restaurants. See "Sweet Treats: Toronto's Dessert Cafes" on p. 216.

2

Planning Your Trip to Toronto

Whether you're traveling on a whim or charting your course months in advance, it's important to do some planning to make the most of your trip. You may already be asking how you'll get there and how much it will cost. There are many different sides of Toronto, so you'll need to figure out what kind of trip you want. This chapter will help you find the answers.

1 Visitor Information

FROM NORTH AMERICA

The best source for Toronto-specific information is **Tourism Toronto, Metro Toronto Convention & Visitors Association,** 207 Queens Quay W., Suite 590, Toronto, ON M5J 1A7 (© **800/363-1990** from North America, or 416/203-2600; www.toronto tourism.com). Call before you leave and ask for the free information package, which includes sections on accommodations, sights, and dining. Better yet, visit the website, which includes all of the above plus up-to-the-minute events information.

For information about traveling in the province of Ontario, contact **Tourism Ontario,** P.O. Box 104, Toronto, ON M5B 2H1 (© **800/ ONTARIO** or 416/314-0944; www. travelinx.com), or visit the travel center in the Eaton Centre on Level 1 at Yonge and Dundas streets. It's open Monday through Friday from 10am to 9pm, Saturday from 9:30am to 6pm, and Sunday from noon to 5pm.

Canadian consulates in the United States do not provide tourist information. They will refer you to the offices above. Consular offices in Buffalo, Detroit, Los Angeles, New York, Seattle, and Washington, D.C., deal with visas and other political and immigration issues.

FROM ABROAD

The following consulates can provide information or refer you to the appropriate offices. Consult Tourism Toronto (see "From North America," above) for general information. For a list of Canadian consular offices around the world, visit **www.dfait-maeci. gc.ca/world/embassies/cra-en.asp**.

U.K. and Ireland: The **Canadian High Commission,** MacDonald House, 1 Grosvenor Sq., London W1X 0AB (© **0207/258-6600;** fax 0207/258-6333).

Australia: The **Canadian High Commission,** Commonwealth Avenue, Canberra, ACT 2600 (© **02/6273-3844**), or the **Consulate General of Canada,** Level 5, Quay West, 111 Harrington St., Sydney, NSW 2000 (© **02/9364-3000**). The consulate general also has offices in Melbourne and Perth.

New Zealand: The **Canadian High Commission,** 3rd floor, 61 Molesworth St., Thomdon, Wellington (© **04/473-9577**).

South Africa: The **Canadian High Commission,** 1103 Arcadia St., Hatfield 0083, Pretoria (© **012/422-3000**). The commission also has offices in Cape Town and Johannesburg.

2 Entry Requirements & Customs

ENTRY REQUIREMENTS

Only a passport is required for entry into Canada—no visas or proof of vaccinations are necessary. Canadian airports have been screening travelers for SARS, but this is done via a non-invasive thermal scan.

Safeguard your passport in an inconspicuous, inaccessible place like a money belt and keep a copy of the critical pages with your passport number in a separate place. If you lose your passport, visit the nearest consulate of your native country as soon as possible for a replacement.

FOR U.S. RESIDENTS Whether you're applying in person or by mail, you can download passport applications from the U.S. State Department website at **http://travel.state.gov**. For general information, call the **National Passport Agency** (℗ 202/647-0518). To find your regional passport office, either check the U.S. State Department website or call the **National Passport Information Center** (℗ 900/225-5674); the fee is 55¢ per minute for automated information and $1.50 per minute for operator-assisted calls.

FOR U.K. RESIDENTS To pick up an application for a standard 10-year passport (5-year passport for children under 16), visit your nearest passport office, major post office, or travel agency or contact the **United Kingdom Passport Service** at ℗ 0870/521-0410 or search its website at www.ukpa.gov.uk.

FOR RESIDENTS OF IRELAND You can apply for a 10-year passport at the **Passport Office,** Setanta Centre, Molesworth Street, Dublin 2 (℗ 01/671-1633; www.irlgov.ie/iveagh). Those under age 18 and over 65 must apply for a €12 3-year passport. You can also apply at 1A South Mall, Cork (℗ 021/272-525) or at most main post offices.

FOR AUSTRALIAN RESIDENTS You can pick up an application from your local post office or any branch of Passports Australia, but you must schedule an interview at the passport office to present your application materials. Call the **Australian Passport Information Service** at ℗ 131-232, or visit the government website at www.passports.gov.au.

FOR NEW ZEALAND RESIDENTS You can pick up a passport application at any New Zealand Passports Office or download it from their website. Contact the **Passports Office** at ℗ 0800/225-050 in New Zealand or 04/474-8100, or log on to www.passports.govt.nz.

CUSTOMS
WHAT YOU CAN BRING INTO CANADA

Most customs regulations are generous, but they get complicated when it comes to firearms, plants, meat, and pets. Fishing tackle poses no problem (provided the lures are not made of restricted materials—specific feathers, for example), but the bearer must possess a non-resident license for the province or territory where he or she plans to use it. You can bring in free of duty up to 50 cigars, 200 cigarettes, and 200 grams of tobacco, provided you're at least 18 years of age. You are also allowed 40 ounces (1.14ml) of liquor or 1.5L of wine as long as you're of age in the province you're visiting (19 in Ontario). There are no restrictions on what you can take out. But if you're thinking of bringing Cuban cigars back to the United States, beware—they can be confiscated, and you could face a fine.

For a clear summary of **Canadian** rules, write for the booklet *I Declare,* issued by the **Canada Customs and Revenue Agency** (℗ 800/461-9999 in Canada, or 204/983-3500; www.ccra-adrc.gc.ca).

WHAT YOU CAN TAKE HOME

Returning **U.S. citizens** who have been away for at least 48 hours are allowed to bring back, once every 30 days, $800 worth of merchandise duty-free. You'll be charged a flat rate of 4% duty on the next $1,000 worth of purchases. Be sure to have your receipts handy. On mailed gifts, the duty-free limit is $200. With some exceptions, you cannot bring fresh fruits and vegetables into the United States. For specifics on what you can bring back, download the invaluable free pamphlet *Know Before You Go* online at **www.customs.gov**. (Click on "Travel," and then click on "Know Before You Go.") Or contact the **U.S. Customs Service,** 1300 Pennsylvania Ave. NW, Washington, DC 20229 (© **877/287-8867**) and request the pamphlet.

U.K. citizens returning from a non-EU country have a customs allowance of: 200 cigarettes; 50 cigars; 250 grams of smoking tobacco; 2 liters of still table wine; 1 liter of spirits or strong liqueurs (over 22% volume); 2 liters of fortified wine, sparkling wine or other liqueurs; 60cc (ml) perfume; 250cc (ml) of toilet water; and £145 worth of all other goods, including gifts and souvenirs. People under 17 cannot have the tobacco or alcohol allowance. For more information, contact **HM Customs & Excise** at © **0845/010-9000** (from outside the U.K., 020/

8929-0152), or consult their website at www.hmce.gov.uk.

The duty-free allowance for **Australian citizens** is A$400 or, for those under 18, A$200. You can bring in 250 cigarettes or 250 grams of loose tobacco, and 1,125 milliliters of alcohol. If you're returning with valuables you already own, such as foreign-made cameras, you should file form B263. A helpful brochure available from Australian consulates or Customs offices is *Know Before You Go*. For more information, call the **Australian Customs Service** at © **1300/363-263,** or log on to www.customs.gov.au.

The duty-free allowance for **New Zealand** is NZ$700. Citizens over 17 can bring in 200 cigarettes, 50 cigars, or 250 grams of tobacco (or a mixture of all 3 if their combined weight doesn't exceed 250g); plus 4.5 liters of wine and beer, or 1.125 liters of liquor. New Zealand currency does not carry import or export restrictions. Fill out a certificate of export, listing the valuables you are taking out of the country; that way, you can bring them back without paying duty. Most questions are answered in a free pamphlet available at New Zealand consulates and Customs offices: *New Zealand Customs Guide for Travellers, Notice no. 4.* For more information, contact **New Zealand Customs,** The Customhouse, 17–21 Whitmore St., Box 2218, Wellington (© **04/473-6099** or 0800/428-786; www.customs.govt.nz).

3 Money

CURRENCY

Canadians use **dollars** and **cents,** but with a distinct advantage for U.S. visitors—the Canadian dollar has been fluctuating between 65 and 70¢ in U.S. money, give or take a couple of points' daily variation. In effect, your American money gets you 30% more the moment you exchange it for local currency, and because the nominal

prices of many goods are roughly on par with those in the United States, the difference is real, not imaginary. Sales taxes are higher, though you should be able to recoup at least part of them (see "Taxes" under "Fast Facts: Toronto," in chapter 3).

Paper currency comes in $5, $10, $20, $50, and $100 denominations. (The $1,000 bill is being phased out.)

Coins come in 1-, 5-, 10-, and 25-cent, and 1- and 2-dollar denominations. The gold-colored $1 coin is a "loonie"—it sports a loon on its "tails" side—and the large gold-and-silver-colored $2 coin is a "toonie." If you find these names somewhat, ah, colorful, just remember that there's no swifter way to reveal that you're a tourist than to say "one-dollar coin."

It's a good idea to exchange at least some money—just enough to cover airport incidentals and transportation to your hotel—before you leave home, so you can avoid the less-favorable rates you'll get at airport currency exchange desks. Check with your local American Express or Thomas Cook office or your bank. American Express cardholders can order foreign currency over the phone at © **800/807-6233.**

It's best to exchange currency or traveler's checks at a bank, not a currency exchange, hotel, or shop.

ATMS

The easiest and best way to get cash away from home is from an ATM (automated teller machine). The **Cirrus** (© 800/424-7787; www.mastercard.com) and **PLUS** (© 800/843-7587; www.visa.com) networks span the globe; look at the back of your bank card to see which network you're on, then call or check online for ATM locations at your destination. Be sure you know your personal identification number (PIN) before you leave home and be sure to find out your daily withdrawal limit before you depart. Also keep in mind that many banks impose a fee every time a card is used at a different bank's ATM, and that fee can be higher for international transactions (up to $5 or more) than for domestic ones. On top of this, the bank from which you withdraw cash may charge its own fee.

TRAVELER'S CHECKS

Traveler's checks are something of an anachronism from the days before the ATM made cash accessible at any time. However, keep in mind that you will likely be charged an ATM withdrawal fee if the bank is not your own, so if you're withdrawing money every day, you might be better off with traveler's checks—provided that you don't mind showing identification every time you want to cash one.

You can get traveler's checks at almost any bank. **American Express** offers denominations of $20, $50, $100, $500, and (for cardholders only) $1,000. You'll pay a service

---

The Canadian Dollar, the U.S. Dollar & the British Pound

The prices quoted in this guide are in Canadian dollars, with the U.S. equivalent in parentheses. The exchange rate we've used is $1.40 Canadian to $1 American. The conversion rate for the British pound is $2.20 Canadian.
Here's a quick table of equivalents:

C $	U.S. $	British £
1.00	.70	.45
5.00	3.50	2.25
10.00	7.00	4.50
20.00	14.00	9.00
50.00	35.00	22.50
80.00	56.00	36.00
100.00	70.00	45.00

Tips Spending American Cash

If you spend American money at Canadian establishments, you should understand how the conversion is calculated. Many times, especially in downtown Toronto, you'll see a sign at the cash register that reads U.S. CURRENCY 50%. This 50% is the "premium," which means that for every U.S. greenback you hand over, the cashier will consider it $1.50 Canadian. For example, for a $15 tab you need pay only $10 in U.S. currency.

---

charge ranging from 1% to 4%. You can also get American Express traveler's checks over the phone by calling ☏ **800/221-7282;** Amex gold and platinum cardholders who use this number are exempt from the 1% fee.

Visa offers traveler's checks at Citibank locations nationwide, as well as at several other banks. The service charge ranges between 1.5% and 2%; checks come in denominations of $20, $50, $100, $500, and $1,000. Call ☏ **800/732-1322** for information. AAA members can obtain Visa checks without a fee at most AAA offices or by calling ☏ **866/339-3378. MasterCard** also offers traveler's checks. Call ☏ **800/ 223-9920** for a location near you.

Foreign currency traveler's checks are useful because they're accepted at locations such as bed-and-breakfasts where dollar checks may not be, and they minimize the amount of math you have to do at your destination. American Express, Visa, and MasterCard all offer checks in Canadian dollars.

If you choose to carry traveler's checks, be sure to keep a record of their serial numbers separate from your checks in the event that they are stolen or lost. You'll get a refund faster if you know the numbers.

CREDIT CARDS

Credit cards are a safe way to carry money, they provide a convenient record of all your expenses, and they generally offer good exchange rates. You can also withdraw cash advances (often with an astronomical interest rate) from your credit cards at banks or ATMs, provided you know your PIN. If you've forgotten yours, or didn't even know you had one, call the number on the back of your credit card and ask the bank to mail it to you—it usually takes 5 to 7 business days. Your credit-card company will likely charge a commission (1% or 2%) on every foreign purchase you make, but don't sweat this small stuff; for most purchases, you'll still get the best deal with credit cards when you factor in things like ATM fees and higher traveler's check exchange rates.

Some credit card companies recommend that you notify them of any impending trip abroad so that they don't become suspicious when the card is used numerous times in a foreign destination and your charges are blocked. Even if you don't call your credit-card company in advance, you can always the card's toll-free emergency number if a charge is refused—a good reason to carry the phone number with you. But perhaps the most important lesson here is to carry more than one card with you on your trip; a card might not work for any number of reasons, so having a backup is the smart way to go.

WHAT TO DO IF YOUR WALLET IS LOST OR STOLEN

Be sure to block charges against your account the minute you discover a credit card has been lost or stolen; almost every credit-card company has an emergency toll-free number to call. They may be able to wire you a cash advance off your credit card immediately, and in many places, they can deliver an emergency credit card in a day or two. The issuing bank's toll-free number is usually on the back of your credit card—though of course, if your card is gone, that won't help you unless you recorded the number elsewhere.

Citicorp Visa's U.S. emergency number is ✆ 800/336-8472. American Express cardholders and traveler's check holders should call ✆ 800/221-7282. MasterCard holders should call ✆ 800/307-7309. Otherwise, call the toll-free number directory at ✆ 800/555-1212.

After you've contacted your credit-card company, be sure to file a police report. Odds are that if your wallet is gone, the police won't be able to recover it for you. However, it's still worth informing the authorities. Your credit-card company or insurer may require a police report number or record of the theft.

If you need emergency cash over the weekend when all banks and American Express offices are closed, you can have money wired to you via **Western Union** (✆ 800/325-6000; www.westernunion.com).

Identity theft or fraud are potential complications of losing your wallet, especially if you've lost your driver's license along with your cash and credit cards. Notify the major credit-reporting bureaus immediately; placing a fraud alert on your records may protect you against liability for criminal activity. The three major U.S. credit-reporting agencies are **Equifax** (✆ 800/766-0008; www.equifax.com), **Experian**

What Things Cost in Toronto	US$
Taxi from the airport to downtown	24.50
Subway/bus from the airport to downtown	6.80
Local telephone call	.17
Double at the Park Hyatt (very expensive)	158.00–349.00
Double at the Delta Chelsea (moderate)	90.00–238.00
Double at Victoria University (inexpensive)	46.00
Two-course lunch for one at Stork on the Roof (moderate)*	15.00
Two-course lunch for one at Kalendar (inexpensive)*	10.60
Three-course dinner for one at North 44 (very expensive)*	50.40
Three-course dinner for one at Goldfish (moderate)*	28.30
Three-course dinner for one at the Rivoli (inexpensive)*	16.30
Pint of beer	3.50
Coca-Cola	1.00
Cup of coffee	1.00
Roll of ASA 1100 Kodacolor film, 36 exposures	5.40
Admission to the Royal Ontario Museum	6.80
Movie ticket at a Silver City multiplex	7.50
Ticket for the Royal Alexandra Theatre	17.00–85.00
Includes tax and tip, but not wine.	

(℡ 888/397-3742; www.experian. com), and TransUnion (℡ 800/680-7289; www.transunion.com). For more information about identity theft and how to protect yourself, check the Federal Trade Commission's website at www.ftc.gov or www.consumer.gov/ idtheft.

Finally, if you've lost all forms of photo ID, call your airline and explain the situation; they might allow you to board the plane if you have a copy of your passport or birth certificate and a copy of the police report you've filed.

4 When to Go

THE CLIMATE

Paris may be most delightful in springtime, but Toronto is truly sublime in the fall. It's my favorite time of year for a number of reasons: The climate is brisk but temperate, the skies are sunny, the countless city parks are a riot of color, and the cultural scene is in full swing. Another great time to see the city—if you don't mind some snow—is December, with nonstop holiday festivities. I can also make good arguments for visiting in spring or summer, but I do feel it's my duty to warn you away in January: The temperature can be unbearably cold, and there's less to do.

Never mind what the calendar says; these are Toronto's true seasons: **Spring** runs from late March to mid-May (though occasionally there's snow in mid-Apr); **summer,** mid-May to mid-September; **fall,** mid-September to mid-November; **winter,** mid-November to late March. The highest recorded temperature is 105°F (41°C); the lowest, –27°F (–33°C). The average date of first frost is October 29; the average date of last frost is April 20. The wind blasts from Lake Ontario can be fierce, even in June. Bring a light jacket or cardigan.

Toronto's Average Temperatures °F (°C)

	Jan	Feb	Mar	Apr	May	June	July	Aug	Sept	Oct	Nov	Dec
High	30 (1)	31 (1)	39 (4)	53 (12)	64 (18)	75 (24)	80 (27)	79 (26)	71 (22)	59 (15)	46 (8)	34 (1)
Low	18 (8)	19 (7)	27 (3)	38 (3)	48 (9)	57 (14)	62 (17)	61 (16)	54 (12)	45 (7)	35 (2)	23 (5)

HOLIDAYS

Toronto celebrates the following holidays: New Year's Day (Jan 1), Good Friday and Easter Monday (Mar or Apr), Victoria Day (Mon following the third weekend in May), Canada Day (July 1), Civic Holiday (first Mon in Aug), Labour Day (first Mon in Sept), Thanksgiving (second Mon in Oct), Remembrance Day (Nov 11), Christmas Day (Dec 25), and Boxing Day (Dec 26).

On Good Friday and Easter Monday, schools and government offices close; most corporations close on one or the other, and a few close on both. Only banks and government offices close on Remembrance Day (Nov 11).

TORONTO CALENDAR OF EVENTS

January, February, March, and April are dominated by trade shows, such as the International Boat and Automobile shows, Metro Home Show, Outdoor Adventure Sport Show, and more. For information, call **Tourism Toronto** (℡ **800/363-1990** or 416/203-2600; www.torontotourism.com).

January

Chinese New Year Celebrations, downtown. 2004 is the year of the monkey. Festivities include traditional and contemporary performances of Chinese opera, dancing, music, and more. For **Harbourfront** celebration information, call ℡ **416/973-3000** or visit www. harbourfront.on.ca; for **SkyDome,**

Tips Don't Forget the Sunscreen

Because of Canada's image of a land of harsh winters, many travelers don't realize that summer can be scorching. "The UV index goes quite high, between 7 and 10, in Toronto," says Dr. Patricia Agin of the Coppertone Solar Research Center in Memphis. "It's the same as in New York, Boston, Chicago, or Detroit." A UV index reading of 7 can mean sunburn, so don't forget to pack your sunscreen and a hat, especially if you're planning to enjoy Toronto's many parks and outdoor attractions.

---

call ☏ **877/666-3838** or check www.skydome.com. The new year starts on January 22.

February

Winterfest, Nathan Phillips Square, Yonge and Eglinton, and Mel Lastman Square. This 3-day celebration spreads over three neighborhoods. It features ice-skating shows, snow play, midway rides, performances, ice sculpting, arts-and-crafts shows, and more. For information, call ☏ **416/338-0338** or visit www.city.toronto.on.ca. Usually around Valentine's Day.

Toronto Festival of Storytelling, Harbourfront. Now in its 26th year, this event celebrates international folklore, with 60 storytellers imparting legends and fables from around the world. For information, call ☏ **416/973-3000** or check www.harbourfront.on.ca. Last weekend of February.

March

Canada Blooms, Metro Toronto Convention Centre. At this time of year, any glimpse of greenery is welcome. There are 2.5 hectares (6 acres) of indoor garden and flower displays, seminars with green-thumb experts, and competitions. For information, call ☏ **416/593-0223** or visit www.canadablooms.com. Usually the second week of March.

St. Patrick's Day Parade, downtown. Toronto's own version of the classic Irish celebration. For information, call ☏ **416/487-1566.** March 17.

April

Blue Jays Season Opener, SkyDome. Turn out to root for your home-away-from-home team. For information, call ☏ **416/341-1000** or visit www.bluejays.ca; for tickets, which usually aren't too hard to get, call ☏ **888/654-6529.** Mid-April.

The Shaw Festival, Niagara-on-the-Lake, Ontario. This festival presents the plays of George Bernard Shaw and his contemporaries. Call ☏ **416/690-7301** or 905/468-2172 or visit www.shawfest.com. Mid-April through October.

Sante—The Bloor-Yorkville Wine Festival, Yorkville. This 4-day gourmet event brings together award-winning Ontario vintages, food by top-rated chefs, and live jazz. For information, call ☏ **416/504-3977.** Last weekend in April.

May

Milk International Children's Festival, Harbourfront. This is a 9-day celebration of the arts for kids—from theater and music to dance, comedy, and storytelling. For information, call ☏ **416/973-3000** or visit www.harbourfront.on.ca. Usually starts on Mother's Day (second Sun in May).

The Stratford Festival, Stratford, Ontario. Featuring a wide range of contemporary and classic plays, this festival always includes several works by Shakespeare. Call © **800/ 567-1600** or 416/364-8355 or check www.stratford-festival.on.ca. Early May through October.

June

Harbourfront Reading Series, Harbourfront. Now in its 30th year, this festival celebrates the best of Canadian literature. Top writers such as Timothy Findley, Anne Michaels, and Barbara Gowdy read from their latest works. For information, call Harbourfront at © **416/ 973-3000;** for tickets, call © **416/ 973-4000** or go to www.harbour front.on.ca. Readings go on through most of June.

North by Northeast Festival, citywide. Known in the music biz as NXNE, the 3-day event features rock and indie bands at 28 venues. For information, call © **416/469- 0986** or visit www.nxne.com. June 10 through 12, 2004.

Toronto International Festival Caravan, citywide. This popular 9-day event is North America's largest international festival. It features more than 40 themed pavilions, craft demonstrations, authentic cuisine, and traditional dance performances by 100 cultural groups. For information, call © **416/977- 0466.** Usually the third and fourth weekends of June.

Symphony of Fire, Ontario Place. This international fireworks competition is set to music and draws 2 million people to the waterfront. Six shows take place, on several Saturdays and Wednesdays. For information, call © **416/442- 3667;** for tickets for waterfront seating, call © **416/870-8000.** Mid-June through July.

Taste of Little Italy, College Street between Euclid and Shaw streets. Restaurants, craftspeople, musicians,

and other performers put on displays during this 2-day festival for the whole family. For information, call © **416/531-9991.** Mid-June.

International Dragon Boat Festival, Centre Island. More than 160 teams of dragon-boaters compete in the 2-day event, which commemorates the death of the Chinese philosopher and poet Qu Yuan. For information, call © **416/598-8945** or visit www.dragonboat.com. Third weekend in June.

Gay & Lesbian Pride Celebration, citywide. A week of events, performances, symposiums, and parties culminates in an extravagant Sunday parade. For information, call © **416/92-PRIDE** or 416/927- 7433, or visit www.pridetoronto. com. Late June.

Downtown Jazz Festival, citywide. Sponsored by tobacco giant du Maurier until 2003, when federal legislation prohibited the company from further involvement, the future of this Toronto tradition is uncertain at press time. Hopefully another sponsor will step in to support this 10-day festival that showcases international artists playing every jazz style—blues, gospel, Latin, African, traditional—at 60 venues. For information, check out **www.tojazz.com.** Late June.

July

Canada Day Celebrations, citywide. July 1, 2004, marks the nation's 137th birthday. Street parties, fireworks, and other special events celebrate the day. For information, contact Tourism Toronto (© **800/363-1990** or 416/203- 2600; www.torontotourism.com). Weekend of July 1.

The Fringe—Toronto's Theatre Festival, citywide. More than 90 troupes participate in this 10-day festival of contemporary and experimental theater. Shows last no more than an hour. For information, call ℂ **416/534-5919** or visit www.fringetoronto.com. First week of July.

Great Canadian Blues Festival, Harbourfront Centre. Toronto shows that it's got soul in this 3-day festival of Canada's best blues musicians. In case the rhythm isn't enough to catch you, the Blues Festival coincides with a lip-smacking BBQ fest, also at Harbourfront. For information, call Harbourfront at ℂ **416/973-3000;** for tickets, call ℂ **416/973-4000** or visit www.harbourfront.on.ca. Second weekend in July.

Molson Indy, the Exhibition Place Street circuit. One of Canada's major races on the IndyCar circuit. Away from the track, you'll find live music and beer gardens. For information, call ℂ **416/922-7477** or visit www.molsonindy.com. Third weekend in July.

Caribana, citywide. Toronto's version of Carnaval transforms the city. It's complete with traditional foods from the Caribbean and Latin America, ferry cruises, picnics, children's events, concerts, and arts-and-crafts exhibits. Call ℂ **416/465-4884** for more information or check www.caribana.com. Late July through early August.

August

Festival of Beer, Fort York. More than 70 major Ontario breweries and microbreweries turn out for this celebration of suds. There's also a wide selection of food from local restaurants and live music of the blues, swing, and jazz persuasions. For information, call ℂ **416/698-7206.** First weekend in August.

Canadian National Exhibition, Exhibition Place. One of the world's largest exhibitions, this 18-day extravaganza features midway rides, display buildings, free shows, and grandstand performers. The 3-day Canadian International Air Show (first staged in 1878) is a bonus. Call ℂ **416/393-6000** for information or visit www.theex.com. Mid-August through Labour Day.

Tennis Masters Canada/Rogers AT&T Cup, National Tennis Centre at York University. These two international tennis championships (the former is for men, the latter for women) are important stops on the pro tennis tour. They attract players such as Sampras, Agassi, Seles, and the Williams sisters. In 2004, the men play in Toronto and the women in Montréal. In 2005, they'll alternate. For information, call ℂ **416/665-9777** or visit www.tenniscanada.com. Mid- to late August.

September

Toronto International Film Festival, citywide. The stars come out for the second-largest film festival in the world. More than 250 films from 70 countries are shown over 10 days. For information, call ℂ **416/968-FILM** or log on to www.e.bell.ca/filmfest. Early September.

PGA Tour Canadian Open, Glen Abbey Golf Club, Oakville. Canada's national golf tournament (ℂ **905/844-1800**) has featured the likes of Greg Norman and Tiger Woods in recent years. It's almost always held at Glen Abbey, though Montréal played host in 1997. First or second weekend of September.

Word on the Street, Queen Street West between Simcoe Street and Spadina Avenue. This street fair celebrates the written word with readings, discounted books and magazines, and children's events. Other major Canadian cities hold similar events on the same weekend. For information, call © **416/ 504-7241.** Last weekend in September.

Muskoka Autumn Studio Tour, Muskoka region, Ontario. This year marks the 26th anniversary of this 2-day arts festival, which invites travelers to visit the studios of local artists and craftspeople. For information, check out **www.muskoka. com/tour.** Late September.

October

Oktoberfest, Kitchener–Waterloo, about 1 hour from Toronto. This famed 9-day drinkfest features cultural events plus a pageant and parade. For information, call © **519/ 570-4267** or visit www.oktoberfest. ca. Mid-October.

International Festival of Authors, Harbourfront. This renowned 11-day literary festival is the most prestigious in Canada. It draws more than 100 authors from 25 countries to perform readings and on-stage interviews. Among the literary luminaries who have appeared are Salman Rushdie, Margaret Drabble, Thomas Kenneally, Joyce Carol Oates, A. S. Byatt, and Margaret Atwood. For information, call Harbourfront at © **416/973- 3000;** for tickets, call © **416/973- 4000** or visit www.harbourfront. on.ca. Third weekend of October.

Toronto Maple Leafs Opening Night, Air Canada Centre. Torontonians love their hockey team, so securing a ticket will be a challenge. For information, call © **416/216- 1700;** for tickets, call © **416/872- 5000** or visit www.torontomaple leafs.com. Mid-October.

The Old Clothing Show & Sale, Exhibition Place. Everything from Jazz Age flapper frocks to Austin Powers–like '60s suits, all under one roof. For information, call © **416/410- 1310.** Third weekend of October.

November

Royal Agricultural Winter Fair and Royal Horse Show, Exhibition Place. The 12-day show is the

---

Moments Jump Up!

One of the undisputed highlights of summer in Toronto is the annual Caribana festival. Created in 1967 as a community heritage celebration to tie in with Canada's centennial, Caribana has become North America's largest street festival, drawing more than a million visitors from North America, Britain, and the Caribbean each year. Originally based on Trinidad's Carnival, the festival now draws on numerous cultures— Jamaican, Guyanese, Brazilian, and Bahamian, to name a few—for its music, food, and events.

During the 2 weeks that it runs, you will see the influence of Caribana around the city. It starts with a bang (literally, as there are steel drums involved) at Nathan Phillips Square in front of Toronto City Hall, with a free concert that features calypso, salsa, and soca music. In the days that follow, there are boat cruises, dances, and concerts; the King and Queen Extravaganza, which showcases some of the most amazing costumes you could hope to see; and an arts festival. The highlight is the Caribana Parade, which brings together masquerade and steel-drum bands, dancers, and floats for a memorable feast for all the senses. This is one party you just can't miss.

largest indoor agricultural and equestrian competition in the world. Displays include vegetables and fruits, crafts, farm machinery, livestock, and more. A member of the British royal family traditionally attends the horse show. Call © **416/393-6400** or check www. royalfair.org for information. Mid-November.

Santa Claus Parade, downtown. A favorite with kids since 1905, it features marching bands, floats, clowns, and jolly St. Nick. American visitors are usually surprised that the parade's in November, but it's better than watching Santa try to slide through slush. For information, call © **416/ 249-7833** or visit www.city.toronto. on.ca. Third Sunday of November.

One-of-a-Kind Craft Show & Sale, Exhibition Place. More than 400 craft artists from across Canada display their unique wares at this 11-day show. For information, call © **416/ 960-3680** or visit www.oneofakind show.com. Last weekend in November through early December.

Cavalcade of Lights, Nathan Phillips Square. During this holiday celebration, lights decorate trees in and around Nathan Phillips Square, parties and performances take over the skating rink, and ice sculptures decorate the square. Visit **www.city. toronto.on.ca** for more information. Late November through December 31.

Canadian Aboriginal Festival, SkyDome. More than 1,500 Native American dancers, drummers, and singers attend this weekend celebration. There are literary readings, an arts-and-crafts market, and traditional foods. Call © **519/751-0040** or visit www.canab.com. Last weekend in November.

December
First Night Toronto and New Year's Eve at City Hall. First Night is an alcohol-free family New Year's Eve celebration. A button (C$8/US$5.60) admits you to a variety of musical, theatrical, and dance performances at downtown venues. In Nathan Phillips Square and in Mel Lastman Square in North York, concerts begin at around 10pm to usher in the countdown to the new year. Visit **www.city.toronto.on.ca** for more information. December 31.

5 Travel Insurance

Check your existing insurance policies and credit-card coverage before you buy travel insurance. You may already be covered for lost luggage, cancelled tickets or medical expenses. The cost of travel insurance varies widely, depending on the cost and length of your trip, your age, health, and the type of trip you're taking.

TRIP-CANCELLATION INSURANCE Trip-cancellation insurance helps you get your money back if you have to back out of a trip, if you have to go home early, or if your travel supplier goes bankrupt. Allowed reasons for cancellation can range from sickness to natural disasters to the State Department declaring your destination unsafe for travel. (Insurers usually won't cover vague fears, though, as many travelers discovered who tried to cancel their trips in October 2001 because they were wary of flying.) In this unstable world, trip-cancellation insurance is a good buy if you're getting tickets well in advance—who knows what the state of the world, or of your airline, will be in 9 months? Insurance policy details vary, so read the fine print—and especially make sure that your airline or cruise line is on the list of carriers covered in case of bankruptcy. For information, contact one of the following insurers: **Access America** (© 866/807-3982; www.accessamerica.com); **Travel Guard International** (© 800/826-4919; www.travelguard.com); **Travel Insured International** (© 800/243-3174; www.travelinsured.com); and **Travelex Insurance Services** (© 888/457-4602; www.travelexinsurance.com).

MEDICAL INSURANCE Most health insurance policies cover you if you get sick away from home—but check, particularly if you're insured by an HMO. With the exception of certain HMOs and Medicare/Medicaid, your medical insurance should cover medical treatment—even hospital care—abroad. However, most out-of-country hospitals make you pay your bills up front, and send you a refund after you've returned home and filed the necessary paperwork. And in a worst-case scenario, there's the high cost of emergency evacuation. If you require additional medical insurance, try **MEDEX International** (© 800/527-0218 or 410/453-6300; www.medexassist.com) or **Travel Assistance International** (© 800/821-2828; www.travelassistance.com; for general

information on services, call the company's Worldwide Assistance Services, Inc., at © **800/777-8710**).

LOST-LUGGAGE INSURANCE On international flights (including U.S. portions of international trips), baggage is limited to approximately $9.07 per pound, up to approximately $635 per checked bag. If you plan to check items more valuable than the standard liability, see if your valuables are covered by your homeowner's policy, get baggage insurance as part of your comprehensive travel-insurance package or buy Travel Guard's "Bag-Trak" product. Don't buy insurance at the airport, as it's usually overpriced. Be sure to take any valuables or irreplaceable items with you in your carry-on luggage, as many valuables (including books, money and electronics) aren't covered by airline policies.

If your luggage is lost, immediately file a lost-luggage claim at the airport, detailing the luggage contents. For most airlines, you must report delayed, damaged, or lost baggage within 4 hours of arrival. The airlines are required to deliver luggage, once found, directly to your house or destination free of charge.

6 Health

While Toronto has excellent doctors and some fine hospitals, it's common sense to prepare for the trip as you would for any other. Although the World Health Organization declared that SARS had been contained in summer 2003, it's still advisable to avoid Toronto hospitals except in cases of emergency (the only cases of SARS transmission in Toronto were in hospitals and other health-care centers).

BEFORE YOU GO
If you worry about getting sick away from home, consider purchasing **medical travel insurance** and carry your ID card in your purse or wallet. In

most cases, your existing health plan will provide the coverage you need. See the section on travel insurance above for more information.

If you suffer from a chronic illness, consult your doctor before your departure. For conditions like epilepsy, diabetes, or heart problems, wear a **Medic Alert Identification Tag** (© **800/825-3785**; www.medicalert.org), which will immediately alert doctors to your condition and give them access to your records through Medic Alert's 24-hour hot line.

Pack **prescription medications** in your carry-on luggage, and carry prescription medications in their original

The SARS Story

SARS hit Toronto hard in 2003, though not in the way most people think. The tourism industry was devastated by the World Health Organization warning against travel to the city, and by the many conferences and performances that were cancelled in its wake. While Toronto was undoubtedly the hardest-hit city outside of Asia, the SARS outbreak was limited to health-care facilities. Not a single person picked it up at a restaurant, at the theater, on the subway, or in any other spot a visitor might frequent. Furthermore, at the time of this writing, Toronto's number of SARS cases was under review, as it was discovered that several people with pneumonia had been grouped in with the SARS stats.

This is a drawn-out way of saying that the SARS story in Toronto was blown completely out of proportion. It's one of the safest cities you could visit in North America. And while the famous folks who cancelled their trips got the media attention, many stars came to Toronto despite the SARS hysteria. These levelheaded luminaries include Colin Farrell, Sophia Loren, Gene Hackman, Ray Romano, and Amy Tan. A special mention should go to Toronto's own Mike Myers, who turned serious on a *Tonight Show* appearance last May to encourage Americans to visit his hometown.

containers, with pharmacy labels—otherwise they won't make it through airport security. Also bring along copies of your prescriptions in case you lose your pills or run out. Don't forget an extra pair of contact lenses or prescription glasses. Carry the generic name of prescription medicines, in case a local pharmacist is unfamiliar with the brand name.

Contact the **International Association for Medical Assistance to Travelers (IAMAT)** (© **716/754-4883** or, in Canada, 416/652-0137; www.iamat. org) for tips on travel and health concerns and lists of local doctors. If you get sick, consider asking your hotel concierge to recommend a local doctor—even his or her own. You can also try the emergency room at a local hospital; many have walk-in clinics for emergency cases that are not life-threatening. You may not get immediate attention, but you won't pay the high price of an emergency room visit.

7 Specialized Travel Resources

FOR TRAVELERS WITH DISABILITIES

Toronto is a very accessible city. Curb cuts are well made and common throughout the downtown area; special parking privileges are extended to people with disabilities who have special plates or a pass that allows parking in "No Parking" zones. The subway and trolleys are not accessible, but the city operates **Wheel-Trans,** a special service for those with disabilities. Visitors can register for this service. For information, call © **416/393-4111** or visit www.city.toronto.on.ca/ttc.

The **Community Information Centre of Metropolitan Toronto,** 425 Adelaide St. W., at Spadina Avenue,

Toronto, ON M5V 3C1 (© **416/392-0505**), may be able to provide limited information and assistance about social-service organizations in the city. It does not have specific accessibility information on tourism or hotels. It's available weekdays from 8am to 10pm, and weekends from 10am to 10pm.

Other organizations that offer assistance to disabled travelers include **MossRehab** (www.mossresourcenet.org), which provides a library of accessible-travel resources online; the **Society for Accessible Travel and Hospitality** (© **212/447-7284**; www.sath.org; annual membership fees $45 adults, $30 seniors and students), which offers a wealth of travel resources for all types of disabilities and informed recommendations on destinations, access guides, travel agents, tour operators, vehicle rentals, and companion services; and the **American Foundation for the Blind** (© **800/232-5463**; www.afb.org), which provides information on traveling with Seeing Eye dogs.

FOR SENIORS

Mention the fact that you're a senior citizen when you make your travel reservations. Some hotels and many city attractions grant senior discounts; bring a form of photo ID.

Members of **AARP,** 601 E St. NW, Washington, DC 20049 (© **800/424-3410** or 202/434-2277; www.aarp.org), get discounts on hotels, airfares, and car rentals. AARP offers members a wide range of benefits, including *AARP The Magazine* and a monthly newsletter. Anyone over 50 can join.

Also look into the fun courses offered in the Toronto region at incredibly low prices by **Elderhostel** (© **877/426-8056**; www.elderhostel.org). Elderhostel arranges study programs for those 55 and over (and a spouse or companion of any age); many courses include airfare, accommodations in university dormitories or modest inns, meals, and tuition.

Another great resource is **Wired Seniors** (www.wiredseniors.com). Travelers aged 50 and over will appreciate this site, which lists accommodations and tours geared toward mature visitors (click on "Senior Friendly Web Sites" and enter "Toronto" in the search box). The discounts section (in "Seniors Discount Mall") lists special savings and deals.

FOR FAMILIES

The family vacation is a rite of passage for many households, one that in a split second can devolve into a *National Lampoon* farce. But in Toronto, a city that boasts a plethora of family-friendly sites, such as the Ontario Science Centre, the Children's Own Museum, and the Toronto Zoo, you'll find that a family trip really can offer something for everyone.

For more suggestions on family and kid-oriented entertainment in Toronto, see "Frommer's Favorite Toronto Experiences" in chapter 1 and "Especially for Kids" in chapter 6, or pick up a copy of *Toronto Life,* a local magazine that has an excellent kid's section and events listing.

Other helpful features in this guide include "Family-Friendly Hotels" (p. 66) and "Family-Friendly Restaurants" (p. 93). The "Shopping" chapter includes great suggestions for children's clothes and toys, and Indigo Books Music & More (p. 179) often offers events for kids. For even more tips, pick up a copy of *Frommer's Toronto with Kids.*

Familyhostel (© **800/733-9753**; www.learn.unh.edu/familyhostel) takes the whole family, including kids ages 8 to 15, on moderately priced domestic and international learning vacations. Lectures, field trips, and sightseeing are guided by a team of academics.

You can find good general vacation advice on the Internet from sites like the **Family Travel Network** (www.familytravelnetwork.com); **Traveling**

Internationally with Your Kids (www.travelwithyourkids.com), a comprehensive site offering sound advice for long-distance and international travel with children; and **Family Travel Files** (www.thefamilytravelfiles.com), which offers an online magazine and a directory of off-the-beaten-path tours and tour operators for families.

FOR STUDENTS

The key to securing discounts and other special benefits is to arm yourself with an **International Student Identity Card (ISIC),** which offers substantial savings on rail passes, plane tickets, and entrance fees. It also provides you with basic health and life insurance and a 24-hour help line. The card is available for $22 from **STA Travel** (✆ **800/781-4040,** and if you're not in North America there's probably a local number in your country; www.statravel.com), the biggest student travel agency in the world. If you're no longer a student but are still under 26, you can get a **International Youth Travel Card (IYTC)** for the same price from the same people,

which entitles you to some discounts. (***Note:*** In 2002, STA Travel bought competitors **Council Travel** and **USIT Campus** after they went bankrupt. It's still operating some offices under the Council name, but it's owned by STA.) **Travel CUTS** (✆ **800/667-2887** or 416/614-2887; www.travelcuts.com) offers similar services for U.S. residents. Irish students should turn to **USIT** (✆ **01/602-1600;** www.usitnow.ie).

If you'd like to meet other students, you've come to the right place. Toronto has several major colleges in addition to the sprawling **University of Toronto.** The largest university in Canada, with more than 50,000 students (41,000 full-time), the University of Toronto offers many year-round activities and events that any visitor can attend—lectures, seminars, concerts, and more. U of T Day is usually celebrated in the middle of October. The university holds an open house for the community and celebrates with a children's fair and the annual homecoming football game and parade. Call ✆ **416/978-8342** for more information, call

Wedded Bliss for Gay & Lesbian Couples

Because same-sex marriage became legal in Ontario in 2003, Toronto is a popular spot for gay and lesbian couples to marry (in fact, the Gay Pride celebrations in June 2003 included many newlywed couples). If you want to get married in Toronto, it's pretty simple: Go with your partner to the Registrar General's office at 900 Bay St. (at Wellesley), bring ID (including your passport and birth certificate), pay a small fee, and the marriage license will be yours; there's no residency requirement. See **www.city.toronto.on.ca** for details and an application form that you can download. For help organizing a wedding beyond the confines of City Hall, check out the wedding planner pages at www.toronto.com.

If you're traveling from the U.S. to tie the knot, you should be aware that although Canada and the U.S. have a reciprocal treaty that specifically agrees to recognize marriages that take place in either country, the treaty predates the recent changes in Ontario that made gay marriage legal. At this point, it's unknown what the legalities really mean in practice when a newlywed gay American couple returns home to Texas.

416/978-5000 for campus tours, or visit www.utoronto.ca.

FOR WOMEN

Women Welcome Women World Wide (5W) (© 203/259-7832; www.womenwelcomewomen.org.uk) works to foster international friendships by enabling women of different countries to visit one another (men can come along on the trips; they just can't join the club). It's a big, active organization, with more than 3,000 members from all walks of life in some 70 countries.

Safety and Security for Women Who Travel, by Sheila Swan Laufer and Peter Laufer (Travelers' Tales, Inc.), offers commonsense advice and tips on safe travel. **Journeywoman** (www.journeywoman.com) is a lively travel resource, with a "GirlTalk Guide" to Toronto, and a free e-mail newsletter.

FOR GAY & LESBIAN TRAVELERS

Toronto has a large gay population, estimated at about 250,000. Community life is centered north and south of the intersection of Church and Wellesley streets.

Gay and lesbian travelers can pick up a copy of the biweekly *Xtra!* It's available free at many bookstores, including the **Glad Day Bookshop,** 598A Yonge St., second floor (© 416/961-4161; www.gladdaybookshop.com). It's open Monday to Wednesday from 10am to 6:30pm, Thursday and Friday from 10am to 9pm, Saturday from 10am to 6pm, and Sunday from noon to 6pm. To receive a copy of *Xtra!* ahead of time, write to 491 Church St., Suite 200, Toronto, ON M4Y 2C6 (© 416/925-6665; www.xtra.ca).

For information on upcoming events, call **Tel-Xtra** (© 416/925-9872). Another resource is **Gay Toronto** (www.gaytoronto.com), which lists gay-friendly restaurants, bars, nightclubs, guesthouses, travel agencies, and other businesses and organizations.

The International Gay & Lesbian Travel Association (IGLTA) (© 800/448-8550 or 954/776-2626; www.iglta.org) is the trade association for the gay and lesbian travel industry, and offers an online directory of gay- and lesbian-friendly travel businesses; go to their website and click on "Members."

8 Planning Your Trip Online

SURFING FOR AIRFARES

The "big three" online travel agencies, **Expedia.com, Travelocity.com,** and **Orbitz.com** sell most of the air tickets bought on the Internet. (Canadian travelers should try Expedia.ca and Travelocity.ca; U.K. residents can go for Expedia.co.uk and Opodo.co.uk.) Each has different business deals with the airlines and may offer different fares on the same flights, so it's wise to shop around. Expedia and Travelocity will also send you **e-mail notification** when a cheap fare becomes available to your favorite destination. Of the smaller travel agency websites, **Side-Step** (www.sidestep.com) has gotten the best reviews from Frommer's

authors. It's a browser add-on that purports to "search 140 sites at once," but in reality only beats competitors' fares as often as other sites do.

Also remember to check **airline websites,** especially those for low-fare carriers, whose fares are often misreported or simply missing from travel agency websites. Even with major airlines, you can often shave a few bucks from a fare by booking directly through the airline and avoiding a travel agency's transaction fee. But you'll get these discounts only by **booking online:** Most airlines now offer online-only fares that even their phone agents know nothing about. For the websites of airlines that fly to

> **Tips Air Canada CyberDeals**
>
> One site that's particularly worth checking out is **Air Canada** (www.air
> canada.ca). On Wednesday, it offers deeply discounted flights to Canada for
> that weekend. You need to reserve on Wednesday or Thursday to fly on Fri-
> day (after 7pm only) or Saturday (all day) and return on Monday or Tuesday
> (all day). Once you register with Air Canada's Web Specials page, you'll
> receive an e-mail every Wednesday about available discounts.

and from your destination, go to "Getting There," later in this chapter.

Great **last-minute deals** are avail-able through free weekly e-mail services provided directly by the airlines. Most of these are announced on Tuesday or Wednesday and must be purchased online. Most are only valid for travel that weekend, but some can be booked weeks or months in advance. Sign up for weekly e-mail alerts at airline websites or check mega-sites that com-pile comprehensive lists of last-minute specials, such as **Smarter Living** (www. smarterliving.com). For last-minute trips, **site59.com** in the U.S. and **last minute.com** in Europe often have bet-ter deals than the major-label sites.

If you're willing to give up some con-trol over your flight details, use an **opaque fare service** like **Priceline** (www.priceline.com; www.priceline.co. uk for Europeans) or **Hotwire** (www. hotwire.com). Both offer rock-bottom prices in exchange for travel on a "mys-tery airline" at a mysterious time of day, often with a mysterious change of planes en route. The mystery airlines are all major, well-known carriers—and the possibility of being sent from Philadel-phia to Chicago via Tampa is remote; the airlines' routing computers have gotten a lot better than they used to be. But your chances of getting a 6am or 11pm flight are pretty high. Hotwire tells you flight prices before you buy; Priceline usually has better deals than Hotwire, but you have to play their "name our price" game. If you're new at this, the helpful folks at **Bidding**

ForTravel (www.biddingfortravel.com) do a good job of demystifying Price-line's prices. Priceline and Hotwire are great for flights within North America and between the U.S. and Europe. But for flights to other parts of the world, consolidators will almost always beat their fares.

SURFING FOR HOTELS

Shopping online for hotels is much eas-ier in the U.S., Canada, and certain parts of Europe than it is in the rest of the world. If you try to book a Chinese hotel online, for instance, you'll proba-bly overpay. Also, many smaller hotels and B&Bs—especially outside the U.S.—don't show up on websites at all. Of the "big three" sites, **Expedia** may be the best choice, thanks to its long list of special deals. **Travelocity** runs a close second. Hotel specialist sites **hotels.com** and **hoteldiscounts.com** are also reliable. An excellent free pro-gram, **TravelAxe** (www.travelaxe.net), can help you search multiple hotel sites at once, even ones you may never have heard of.

Priceline and Hotwire are even bet-ter for hotels than for airfares; with both, you're allowed to pick the neigh-borhood and quality level of your hotel before offering up your money. Price-line's hotel product even covers Europe and Asia, though it's much better at getting luxury lodging for moderate prices than at finding anything at the bottom of the scale. *Note:* Hotwire overrates its hotels by one star.

SURFING FOR RENTAL CARS

For booking rental cars online, the best deals are usually found at rental-car company websites, although all the major online travel agencies also offer rental-car reservations services. Priceline and Hotwire work well for rental cars, too; the only "mystery" is which major rental company you get, and for most travelers the difference between Hertz, Avis, and Budget is negligible.

9 The 21st-Century Traveler

INTERNET ACCESS AWAY FROM HOME

Travelers have any number of ways to check their e-mail and access the Internet on the road. Of course, using your own laptop—or even a PDA or electronic organizer with a modem—gives you the most flexibility. But even if you don't have a computer, you can still access your e-mail and even your office computer from cybercafes.

WITHOUT YOUR OWN COMPUTER

It's hard nowadays to find a city that *doesn't* have a few cybercafes. Although there's no definitive directory for cybercafes—these are independent businesses, after all—three places to start looking are at **www.cybercaptive. com**, **www.netcafeguide.com**, and **www.cybercafe.com**. See also "Internet Access" under "Fast Facts: Toronto" in chapter 3.

Aside from formal cybercafes, most **youth hostels** nowadays have at least one computer you can use to get onto the Internet. And most **public libraries** across the world offer Internet access free or for a small charge. Avoid **hotel business centers,** which often charge exorbitant rates.

Most major airports now have **Internet kiosks** scattered throughout their gates. These kiosks, which you'll also see in shopping malls, hotel lobbies, and tourist information offices around the world, give you basic Web access for a per-minute fee that's usually higher than cybercafe prices. The kiosks' clunkiness and high price means they should be avoided whenever possible.

To retrieve your e-mail, ask your **Internet Service Provider (ISP)** if it

---

Frommers.com: The Complete Travel Resource

For an excellent travel-planning resource, we highly recommend **Frommers.com** (www.frommers.com). We're a little biased, of course, but we guarantee that you'll find the travel tips, reviews, monthly vacation giveaways, and online-booking capabilities thoroughly indispensable. Among the special features are our popular **Message Boards,** where Frommer's readers post queries and share advice (sometimes even our authors show up to answer questions); **Frommers.com Newsletter,** for the latest travel bargains and insider travel secrets; and **Frommer's Destinations Section,** where you'll get expert travel tips, hotel and dining recommendations, and advice on the sights to see for more than 3,000 destinations around the globe. When your research is done, the **Online Reservations System** (www.frommers.com/book_a_trip) takes you to Frommer's preferred online partners for booking your vacation at affordable prices.

has a Web-based interface tied to your existing e-mail account. If your ISP doesn't have such an interface, you can use the free **mail2web** service (www.mail2web.com) to view and reply to your home e-mail. For more flexibility, you may want to open a free, Web-based e-mail account with **Yahoo! Mail** (http://mail.yahoo.com). (Microsoft's Hotmail is another popular option, but Hotmail has severe spam problems.) Your home ISP may be able to forward your e-mail to the Web-based account automatically.

If you need to access files on your office computer, look into a service called **GoToMyPC** (www.gotomypc. com). The service provides a Web-based interface for you to access and manipulate a distant PC from anywhere—even a cybercafe—provided your "target" PC is on and has an always-on connection to the Internet (such as with Road Runner cable). The service offers top-quality security, but if you're worried about hackers, use your own laptop rather than a cybercafe to access the GoToMyPC system.

WITH YOUR OWN COMPUTER

Major Internet Service Providers (ISP) have **local access numbers** around the world, allowing you to go online by simply placing a local call. Check your ISP's website or call its toll-free number and ask how you can use your current account away from home, and how much it will cost.

If you're traveling outside the reach of your ISP, the **iPass** network has dial-up numbers in most of the world's countries. You'll have to sign up with an iPass provider, who will then tell you how to set up your computer for your destination(s). For a list of iPass providers, go to **www.ipass.com** and click on "Reseller Locator." Under "Select a Country" pick the country that you're coming from, and under "Who is this service for?" pick "Individual". One solid provider is **i2roam**

(*©* **866/811-6209** or 920/235-0475; www.i2roam.com).

Wherever you go, bring a **connection kit** of the right power and phone adapters, a spare phone cord, and a spare Ethernet network cable. The electrical current is the same as in the United States—110 volts, 50 cycles AC.

Most business-class hotels throughout the world offer dataports for laptop modems, and a few thousand hotels in the U.S. and Europe now offer high-speed Internet access using an Ethernet network cable. You'll have to bring your own cables either way, so **call your hotel in advance** to find out what the options are. Many business-class hotels in the U.S. also offer a form of computer-free Web browsing through the room TV set. We've successfully checked Yahoo! Mail and Hotmail on these systems.

If you have an 802.11b/**Wi-fi** card for your computer, several commercial companies have made wireless service available in airports, hotel lobbies, and coffee shops, primarily in the U.S. **T-Mobile Hotspot** (www.t-mobile. com/hotspot) serves up wireless connections at more than 1,000 Starbucks coffee shops nationwide. **Boingo** (www.boingo.com) and **Wayport** (www.wayport.com) have set up networks in airports and high-class hotel lobbies. IPass providers (see above) also give you access to a few hundred wireless hotel lobby setups. Best of all, you don't need to be staying at the Four Seasons to use the hotel's network; just set yourself up on a nice couch in the lobby. Unfortunately, the companies' pricing policies are byzantine, with a variety of monthly, per-connection, and per-minute plans.

Community-minded individuals have also set up **free wireless networks** in major cities around the world. These networks are spotty, but you get what you (don't) pay for. Each network has a home page explaining how to set up your computer for their

Online Traveler's Toolbox

Veteran travelers usually carry some essential items to make their trips easier. Following is a selection of online tools to bookmark and use.

- **Visa ATM Locator** (www.visa.com), for locations of PLUS ATMs worldwide, or **MasterCard ATM Locator** (www.mastercard.com), for locations of Cirrus ATMs worldwide.
- **Intellicast** (www.intellicast.com) and **Weather.com** (www.weather.com). Gives weather forecasts for Toronto and other cities around the world.
- **Mapquest** (www.mapquest.com). This best of the mapping sites lets you choose a specific address or destination, and in seconds, it will return a map and detailed directions.
- **Universal Currency Converter** (www.xe.com/ucc). See what your dollar or pound is worth in more than 100 other countries.
- **Travel Warnings** (http://travel.state.gov/travel_warnings.html, www.fco.gov.uk/travel, www.voyage.gc.ca, www.dfat.gov.au/consular/advice). These sites report on places where health concerns or unrest might threaten American, British, Canadian, and Australian travelers. Generally, U.S. warnings are the most paranoid; Australian warnings are the most relaxed.

particular system; start your explorations at **www.personaltelco.net/index.cgi/WirelessCommunities**.

USING A CELLPHONE

The three letters that define much of the world's **wireless capabilities** are GSM (Global System for Mobiles), a big, seamless network that makes for easy cross-border cellphone use throughout Europe and dozens of other countries worldwide. In the U.S., T-Mobile, AT&T Wireless, and Cingular use this quasi-universal system; in Canada, Microcell and some Rogers customers are GSM, and all Europeans and most Australians use GSM.

If your cellphone is on a GSM system, and you have a world-capable phone such as many (but not all) Sony Ericsson, Motorola, or Samsung models, you can make and receive calls across civilized areas on much of the globe, from Andorra to Uganda. Just call your wireless operator and ask for "international roaming" to be activated

on your account. Unfortunately, per-minute charges can be high—usually $1 to $1.50 in Western Europe and up to $5 in places like Russia and Indonesia.

World-phone owners can bring down their per-minute charges with a bit of trickery. Call up your cellular operator and say you'll be going abroad for several months and want to "unlock" your phone to use it with a local provider. Usually, they'll oblige. Then, in Toronto, pick up a cheap, prepaid phone chip at a mobile phone store and slip it into your phone. (Show your phone to the salesperson, as not all phones work on all networks.) You'll get a local phone number in Toronto—and much, much lower calling rates.

Otherwise, **renting** a phone is a good idea. While you can rent a phone from any number of overseas sites, including kiosks at airports and at car-rental agencies, we suggest renting the phone before you leave home. That way you can give loved ones your new number, make sure the phone works, and take the phone wherever you go. But phone rental isn't cheap: You'll usually pay $40 to $50 per week, plus airtime fees of at least a dollar a minute. Be sure to shop around.

Two good wireless rental companies are **InTouch USA** (© **800/872-7626;** www.intouchglobal.com) and **Road-Post** (© **888/290-1606** or 905/272-5665; www.roadpost.com). Give them your itinerary, and they'll tell you what wireless products you need. InTouch will also, for free, advise you on whether your existing phone will work overseas; simply call © **703/ 222-7161** or go to http://intouch global.com/travel.htm.

For trips of more than a few weeks spent in one country, **buying a phone** becomes economically attractive, as many nations have cheap, no-questions-asked prepaid phone systems. Stop by a local cellphone shop and get the cheapest package; you'll probably pay less than $100 for a phone and a starter calling card. Local calls may be as low as 10¢ per minute, and in many countries incoming calls are free.

10 Getting There

BY PLANE

Wherever you're traveling from, always shop the airlines and ask for the lowest fare. You'll have a better chance of landing a deal if you're willing to be flexible about when you arrive and leave.

You may be able to fly for less than the standard advance (APEX) fare by contacting a ticket broker or consolidator. These companies, which buy tickets in bulk and sell them at a discount, advertise in the Sunday travel sections of major city newspapers. You may not be able to get the lowest price they advertise, but you're likely to pay less than the price quoted by the major airlines. Tickets purchased through a consolidator are often non-refundable. If you change your itinerary after purchase, chances are you'll pay a stiff penalty.

FROM THE U.S. Canada's only national airline, **Air Canada** (© **888/ 247-2262;** www.aircanada.ca), operates direct flights to Toronto from most major American cities and many smaller ones. It also flies from major cities around the world and operates connecting flights from other U.S. cities.

Among U.S. airlines, **American** (© **800/433-7300;** www.aa.com) has daily direct flights from Chicago, Dallas, Miami, and New York. **United** (© **800/241-6522;** www.united.com) has direct flights from Chicago, San Francisco, and Washington (Dulles); it's a code-share partner with Air Canada. **US Airways** (© **800/428-4322;** www.usairways.com) operates directly into Toronto from a number of U.S. cities, notably Baltimore, Indianapolis, Philadelphia, and Pittsburgh. **Northwest** (© **800/225-2525;** www. nwa.com) flies direct from Detroit and Minneapolis. **Delta** (© **800/221-1212;** www.delta.com) flies direct from Atlanta and Cincinnati.

FROM ABROAD There's frequent service (direct and indirect) to Toronto from around the world.

Several airlines operate from the United Kingdom. **British Airways** (© **0845/773-3377;** www.ba.com) and **Air Canada** (© **08705/247-226**) fly direct from London's Heathrow airport. Air Canada also flies direct from Glasgow and Manchester. **Virgin Atlantic** (© **01293/747-245;** www. virgin-atlantic.com) has direct flights out of Gatwick airport.

In Australia, **Air Canada** (© **02/ 9286-8900**) has an agreement with Qantas and flies from Sydney to

Toronto, stopping in Honolulu. From New Zealand, **Air Canada** (© 09/379-3371) cooperates with Air New Zealand, scheduling on average three flights a week from Auckland to Toronto, via Honolulu, Fiji, or both.

From Cape Town, South Africa, **Delta** (© 011/482-4582 in South Africa) operates via New York; **Air Canada** (© 011/875-5800) via Frankfurt; and **South African Airways** (© 021/254-610; www.saa.co.za) via Miami or New York. Several airlines fly from Johannesburg, including **British Airways** (© 011/441-8600) via Heathrow and **South African Airways** (© 011/333-6504) via Miami or New York.

GETTING THROUGH THE AIRPORT

With the federalization of airport security, security procedures at U.S. airports are more stable and consistent than ever. Generally, you'll be fine if you arrive at the airport **2 hours** before an international flight; if you show up late, tell an airline employee and you'll probably be whisked to the front of the line.

Bring a **current, government-issued photo ID** such as a driver's license or passport; you'll need to show it at the security checkpoint, and your ID at the ticket counter or the gate. (Children under 18 do not need photo IDs for domestic flights, but the adults checking in with them need them.)

Security lines are getting shorter, but some doozies remain. If you have trouble standing for long periods of time, tell an airline employee; the airline will provide a wheelchair. Speed up security by **not wearing metal objects** such as big belt buckles or clanky earrings. If you've got metallic body parts, a note from your doctor can prevent a long chat with the security screeners. Keep in mind that only **ticketed passengers** are allowed past security, except for

folks escorting disabled passengers or children.

Federalization has stabilized **what you can carry on** and **what you can't.** The general rule is that sharp things are out, nail clippers are okay, and food and beverages must be passed through the X-ray machine—but security screeners can't make you drink from your coffee cup. Bring food in your carry-on rather than checking it, as explosive-detection machines used on checked luggage have been known to mistake food (especially chocolate, for some reason) for bombs. Travelers in the U.S. are allowed one carry-on bag, plus a "personal item" such as a purse, briefcase, or laptop bag. Carry-on hoarders can stuff all sorts of things into a laptop bag; as long as it has a laptop in it, it's still considered a personal item. The Transportation Security Administration (TSA) has issued a list of restricted items; check its website (www.tsa.gov) for details.

In 2003, the TSA phased out **gate check-in** at all U.S. airports. Passengers with E-tickets and without checked bags can still beat the ticket-counter lines by using **electronic kiosks** or even **online check-in.** Ask your airline which alternatives are available, and if you're using a kiosk, bring the credit card you used to book the ticket. If you're checking bags, you will still be able to use most airlines' kiosks; again call your airline for up-to-date information. **Curbside check-in** is also a good way to avoid lines, although a few airlines still ban curbside check-in entirely; call before you go.

At press time, the TSA is also recommending that you **not lock your checked luggage** so screeners can search it by hand if necessary. The agency says to use plastic "zip ties" instead, which can be bought at hardware stores and can be easily cut off.

FLYING FOR LESS: TIPS FOR GETTING THE BEST AIRFARE

Passengers sharing the same airplane cabin rarely pay the same fare. Travelers who need to purchase tickets at the last minute, change their itinerary at a moment's notice, or fly one-way often get stuck paying the premium rate. Here are some ways to keep your airfare costs down.

- Passengers who can book their ticket **long in advance,** who can **stay over Saturday night,** or who **fly midweek** or **at less-trafficked hours** will pay a fraction of the full fare. If your schedule is flexible, say so, and ask if you can secure a cheaper fare by changing your flight plans.
- You can also save on airfares by keeping an eye out in local newspapers for **promotional specials** or **fare wars,** when airlines lower prices on their most popular routes. You rarely see fare wars offered for peak travel times, but if you can travel in the off-months, you may snag a bargain.
- Search **the Internet** for cheap fares (see "Planning Your Trip Online," earlier in this chapter).
- **Consolidators,** also known as bucket shops, are great sources for international tickets, although they usually can't beat the Internet on fares within North America.

Start by looking in Sunday newspaper travel sections; U.S. travelers should focus on *The New York Times, Los Angeles Times,* and *Miami Herald.* For less-developed destinations, small travel agents who cater to immigrant communities in large cities often have the best deals. *Beware:* Bucket shop tickets are usually nonrefundable or rigged with stiff cancellation penalties, often as high as 50% to 75% of the ticket price, and some put you on charter airlines with questionable safety records.

Several reliable consolidators are worldwide and available on the Net. **STA Travel** (© 800/781-4040; www.statravel.com) is now the world's leader in student travel, thanks to their purchase of Council Travel. It also offers good fares for travelers of all ages. **Flights.com** (© 800/TRAV-800; www.flights.com) started in Europe and has excellent fares worldwide. **Air Tickets Direct** (© 800/778-3447; www.airticketsdirect.com) is based in Montréal and leverages the currently weak Canadian dollar for low fares; it'll also book trips to places that U.S. travel agents won't touch, such as Cuba.

- Join **frequent-flier clubs.** Accrue enough miles, and you'll be rewarded with free flights and elite status. It's free, and you'll get the

---

Travel in the Age of Bankruptcy

At press time, a major U.S. airline was struggling in bankruptcy court and most of the rest weren't doing very well either. To protect yourself, **buy your tickets with a credit card,** as the Fair Credit Billing Act guarantees that you can get your money back from the credit-card company if a travel supplier goes under (and if you request the refund within 60 days of the bankruptcy.) **Travel insurance** can also help, but make sure it covers against "carrier default" for your specific travel provider. And be aware that if a U.S. airline goes bust mid-trip, a 2001 federal law requires other carriers to take you to your destination (albeit on a space-available basis) for a fee of no more than $25, provided you rebook within 60 days of the cancellation.

best choice of seats, faster response to phone inquiries, and prompter service if your luggage is stolen, your flight is canceled or delayed, or if you want to change your seat. You don't need to fly to build frequent-flier miles—**frequent-flier credit cards** can provide thousands of miles for doing your everyday shopping.

BY TRAIN

Amtrak's "Maple Leaf" service links New York City and Toronto via Albany, Buffalo, and Niagara Falls. It departs daily from Penn Station. The journey takes 11¾ hours. From Chicago, the "International" carries passengers to Toronto via Port Huron, Michigan, a 12½-hour trip. Note that these lengthy schedules allow for extended stops at customs and immigration checkpoints at the border. Both trains arrive in Toronto at Union Station on Front Street, 1 block west of Yonge Street, opposite the Fairmont Royal York Hotel. The station has direct access to the subway.

To secure the lowest round-trip fares, book as far in advance as possible, and try to travel midweek. Seat availability determines price levels; the earlier you book, the more likely you are to land a lower fare. Sample fares (for use as guidelines only), depending on seat availability: from New York, US$65 to $99 one-way or US$130 to $198 round-trip; from Chicago, US$98 one-way, US$108 to $196 round-trip. Prices do not include meals. Always ask about the availability of discounted fares, companion fares, and any other special tickets. Call **Amtrak** at ✆ **800/USA-RAIL** or 800/872-7245, or visit www.amtrak.com.

BY BUS

Greyhound (✆ **800/231-2222;** www.greyhound.com) is the only bus company that crosses the U.S. border. You can travel from almost anywhere in the United States. You'll arrive at the Metro Coach Terminal downtown at 610 Bay St., near the corner of Dundas Street.

The bus may be faster and cheaper than the train, and its routes may be more flexible if you want to stop along the way. Bear in mind that it's more cramped, toilet facilities are meager, and meals are taken at somewhat depressing rest stops.

Depending on where you are coming from, check into Greyhound's special unlimited-travel passes and discount fares. It's hard to provide sample fares because bus companies, like airlines, are adopting yield-management strategies, causing prices to change from day to day.

BY CAR

Crossing the border by car gives you a lot of options—the U.S. highway system leads directly into Canada at 13 points. If you're driving from Michigan, you'll enter at Detroit–Windsor (I-75 and the Ambassador Bridge) or Port Huron–Sarnia (I-94 and the Bluewater Bridge). If you're coming from New York, you have more options. On I-190, you can enter at Buffalo–Fort Erie; Niagara Falls, N.Y.–Niagara Falls, ON; or Niagara Falls, N.Y.–Lewiston. On I-81, you'll cross the Canadian border at Hill Island; on Rte. 37, you'll enter at either Ogdensburg–Johnstown or Rooseveltown–Cornwall.

From the United States you are most likely to enter Toronto from the west on Hwy. 401 or Hwy. 2 and the Queen Elizabeth Way. If you come from the east via Montréal, you'll also use 401 and 2.

Here are approximate driving distances to Toronto: from Boston, 911km (566 miles); Buffalo, 155km (96 miles); Chicago, 859km (534 miles); Cincinnati, 806km (501 miles); Detroit, 379km (236 miles); Minneapolis, 1,564km (972 miles); New York, 797km (495 miles).

Be sure you have your driver's license and car registration if you plan to drive your own vehicle into Canada. It isn't a bad idea to carry proof of automobile liability insurance, either.

If you are a member of the American Automobile Association (AAA), the **Canadian Automobile Association (CAA)** Central Ontario Branch in Toronto (© **416/221-4300;** www.caa.ca) provides emergency road service.

11 Packages for the Independent Traveler

Before you start your search for the lowest airfare, you may want to consider booking your flight as part of a travel package. Package tours are not the same thing as escorted tours. Package tours are simply a way to buy the airfare, accommodations, and other elements of your trip (such as car rentals, airport transfers, and sometimes even activities) at the same time and often at discounted prices—kind of like one-stop shopping. Packages are sold in bulk to tour operators—who resell them to the public at a cost that usually undercuts standard rates.

One good source of package deals is the airlines themselves. Most major airlines offer air/land packages, including **American Airlines Vacations** (© 800/321-2121; www.aavacations.com), **Delta Vacations** (© 800/221-6666; www.deltavacations.com), **Continental Airlines Vacations** (© 800/301-3800; www.coolvacations.com), and **United Vacations** (© 888/854-3899; www.unitedvacations.com). Several big **online travel agencies**—Expedia.com, Travelocity.com, Orbitz.com, Site59.com, and Lastminute.com—also do a brisk business in packages. If you're unsure about the pedigree of a smaller packager, check with the **Better Business Bureau** in the city where the company is based, or go online at www.bbb.org. If a packager won't tell you where it's based, don't fly with them.

Travel packages are also listed in the travel section of your local Sunday newspaper. Or check ads in the national travel magazines such as *Arthur Frommer's Budget Travel Magazine, Travel & Leisure, National Geographic Traveler,* and *Condé Nast Traveler.*

Package tours can vary by leaps and bounds. Some offer a better class of hotels than others. Some offer the same hotels for lower prices. Some offer flights on scheduled airlines, while others book charters. Some limit your choice of accommodations and travel days. You are often required to make a large payment up front. On the plus side, packages can save you money, offering group prices but allowing for independent travel. Some even let you add on a few guided excursions or escorted day trips (also at prices lower than if you booked them yourself) without booking an entirely escorted tour.

Before you invest in a package tour, get some answers. Ask about the **accommodations choices** and prices for each. Then look up the hotels' reviews in a Frommer's guide and check their rates for your specific dates of travel online. You'll also want to find out what **type of room** you get. If you need a certain type of room, ask for it; don't take whatever is thrown your way. Request a nonsmoking room, a quiet room, a room with a view, or whatever you fancy.

Finally, look for **hidden expenses.** Ask whether airport departure fees and taxes, for example, are included in the total cost.

12 Tips on Accommodations

Toronto has a wealth of great places to stay. Major chains such as Hyatt, Fairmont, Four Seasons, Marriott, Sheraton, Westin, Holiday Inn, and Ramada are all represented, and there are several smaller boutique hotels as well. The only difficulty is in getting a deal, particularly in the downtown core. Here are some ways to ensure that you get the best price possible.

SAVING ON YOUR HOTEL ROOM

The **rack rate** is the maximum rate that a hotel charges for a room. Hardly anybody pays this price, however. To lower the cost of your room:

- **Ask about special rates or other discounts.** Always ask whether a less expensive room than the first one quoted is available, or whether any special rates apply to you. You may qualify for corporate, student, military, senior, or other discounts. Mention membership in AAA, AARP, frequent-flier programs, or trade unions, which may entitle you to special deals as well. Find out the hotel policy on children— do kids stay free in the room or is there a special rate?
- **Dial direct.** When booking a room in a chain hotel, you'll often get a better deal by calling the individual hotel's reservation desk than at the chain's main number.
- **Book online.** Many hotels offer Internet-only discounts, or supply rooms to Priceline, Hotwire, or Expedia at rates much lower than the ones you can get through the hotel itself. See "Planning Your Trip Online," earlier in this chapter, for more information.
- **Remember the law of supply and demand.** Business hotels in downtown locations are busiest during the week, so you can expect big discounts over the weekend. Resort hotels are most crowded and therefore most expensive on weekends, so discounts are usually available for midweek stays. Many hotels have high-season and low-season prices, and booking the day after "high season" ends can mean big discounts.
- **Look into group or long-stay discounts.** If you come as part of a large group, you should be able to negotiate a bargain rate, since the hotel can then guarantee occupancy in a number of rooms. Likewise, if you're planning a long stay (at least 5 days), you might qualify for a discount. As a general rule, expect 1 night free after a 7-night stay.
- **Avoid excess charges and hidden costs.** When you book a room, ask whether the hotel charges for parking. Use your own cellphone, pay phones, or prepaid phone cards instead of dialing direct from hotel phones, which usually have exorbitant rates. And don't be tempted by the room's minibar offerings: Most hotels charge through the nose for water, soda, and snacks. Finally, ask about local taxes and service charges, which can increase the cost of a room by 15% or more. If a hotel insists upon tacking on a surprise "energy surcharge" that wasn't mentioned at check-in or a "resort fee" for amenities you didn't use, you can often make a case for getting it removed.

LANDING THE BEST ROOM

Somebody has to get the best room in the house. It might as well be you. You can start by joining the hotel's frequent-guest program, which may make you eligible for upgrades. A hotel-branded credit card usually gives it owner "silver" or "gold" status in frequent-guest programs for free. Always ask about a corner room. They're often larger and quieter, with more windows and light, and they often cost the same as standard rooms. When you make your reservation, ask if the hotel is renovating; if it is, request a room away from the construction. Ask about nonsmoking rooms, rooms with views, rooms with twin, queen- or king-size beds. If you're a light sleeper, request a quiet room away from vending machines, elevators, restaurants, bars, and discos. Ask for one of the rooms that have been most recently renovated or redecorated.

If you aren't happy with your room when you arrive, say so. If another room is available, most lodgings will be willing to accommodate you.

13 Recommended Reading

Though it hasn't always played itself in the movies (doubling often as other major cities instead), Toronto does have quite a literary legacy to call its own. It's the hometown of authors Margaret Atwood, Michael Ondaatje, and media theorist and writer Marshall McLuhan. Famous for saying "The medium is the message," McLuhan's works include *Understanding Media: The Extensions of Man,* and *War & Peace in the Global Village.* There's also a volume called *The Essential McLuhan* to consider if you're a fan.

Atwood's *The Robber Bride* pays homage to her hometown with a story that covers 3 decades of life in the city. Some of her other novels, such as *The Edible Woman, Cat's Eye,* and *The Blind Assassin* also use Toronto as a backdrop. *In the Skin of a Lion* by Michael Ondaatje, the celebrated author of *The English Patient,* is a moving love story that brings the city's landmarks to life. Carol Shields, who died in 2003, set her final novel *Unless* in Toronto's streets.

Another notable novel is *Cabbagetown* by Hugh Gardner, the story of the fight to survive in a Toronto slum in the 1930s. (Cabbagetown was famous as the largest Anglo-Saxon slum in North America). For those more interested in possible futures than the past, there's an Afrofuturist/sci-fi novel called *Brown Girl in the Ring* by Nalo Hopkinson. Some other books to consider: *Noise* and *How Insensitive* by Russell Smith; *Headhunter* by Timothy Findley; *The Origin of Waves* by Austin Clarke; and *Lost Girls* by Andrew Pyper. (While you're at it, you might want to pick up the Booker Prize–winning *Life of Pi* by Yann Martel and *Martin Sloane* by Michael Redhill; while not set in Toronto, these novels are by local authors).

If you're interested in architecture, an especially good read is *Emerald City: Toronto Revisited,* by John Bentley Mays. *Emerald City* explores all of Toronto's special places, from the majesty of Casa Loma to the colorful bedlam of Kensington Market. Speaking of craziness, another nonfiction book to check out is *In the Mad Water: Two Centuries of Adventure and Lunacy at Niagara Falls* by T.W. Kriner. Finally, travel writer Jan Morris is always a delight to read, and her book *O Canada! Travels in an Unknown Country* is no exception.

3

Getting to Know Toronto

Toronto is a wonderful city in which to get lost. Start anywhere in the downtown core and walk in any direction for no more than 15 minutes. You'll see eclectic modern buildings side by side with neo-Gothic and Art Deco architecture, catch a fair glimpse of the city's ethnic spectrum, and walk right into a pleasing patch of greenery.

This is a happy coincidence because the layout and organization of the city mean you *will* get lost at least once during your stay. Streets have names,

not numbers, and they have a crazy-making habit of changing their monikers as they go along. In Mid-town, the must-see Avenue Road, for example, turns into Queen's Park Crescent and then into University Avenue as you head south, and into Oriole Parkway if you go north. My best advice: Relax and enjoy the ride. In this chapter, you'll find information on the highways, byways, and services that make Toronto tick.

1 Orientation

ARRIVING

BY PLANE

Most flights arrive at **Pearson International Airport,** in the northwest corner of Metro Toronto, approximately 30 minutes from downtown. The trip takes 10 to 15 minutes longer during the weekday morning rush (7–9am). A few (mostly commuter) flights land at the **Toronto Island Airport,** a short ferry ride from downtown.

Pearson serves more than 50 airlines. At press time, the most impressive of its three terminals is the **Trillium Terminal 3** (© 905/612-5100). This airy, modern facility has moving walkways, a huge food court, and many retail stores. However, there is an even grander terminal currently under construction that will replace the existing **Terminals 1 and 2.** (Terminal 1 has the distinction of being the gloomiest, ugliest airport terminal this travel writer has ever seen.) Its opening has been delayed, but it should be open for business in late 2003.

To get from the airport to downtown, take Highway 427 south to the Gardiner Expressway East. A **taxi** costs about C$36 (US$25). A slightly sleeker way to go is by flat-rate **limousine,** which costs around C$40 (US$28). Two limo services are **Aaroport** (© 416/745-1555) and **AirLine** (© 905/676-3210). You don't need a reservation. Most first-class hotels run their own **hotel limousine** services; check when you make your reservation.

The convenient **Airport Express bus** (© 905/564-6333) travels between the airport, the bus terminal, and major downtown hotels—the Westin Harbour Castle, Fairmont Royal York, The Sheraton Centre Toronto, and the Delta Chelsea—every 20 minutes, from 4:55am to 12:55am, with one extra run around 2:30am. The adult fare is C$13 (US$8.75) one-way, C$22 (US$16) round-trip; children under 11 accompanied by an adult ride free.

The cheapest way to go is by **bus and subway,** which takes about an hour. From Terminal 2, take the #58 bus to Lawrence West station, the #192 "Airport Rocket" bus to Kipling station, or the #307 bus to Eglinton West station. Only the #192 bus serves Terminal 3; there are no public buses from Terminal 1 (though there is a shuttle that will drop you off at Terminal 2 or 3). The fare of C$2.25 (US$1.60) includes free transfer to the subway. It doesn't matter which bus you use; they all take roughly the same amount of time. (The Airport Rocket reaches the subway fastest, but the subway ride to downtown is twice as long as from the other stations.) For more information, call the **Toronto Transit Commission,** or TTC (© **416/393-4636**).

BY TRAIN
Trains arrive at Union Station on Front Street, 1 block west of Yonge Street, opposite the Fairmont Royal York hotel. The station has direct access to the subway, so you can easily reach any Toronto destination.

VISITOR INFORMATION
For hotel, dining, and other tourist information, head to (or write to) **Tourism Toronto,** 207 Queens Quay W., Suite 590, Toronto, ON M5J 1A7 (© **800/363-1990** or 416/203-2600; www.torontotourism.com). It's in the Queen's Quay Terminal at Harbourfront, and is open Monday to Friday from 9am to 5pm. Take the LRT (light rapid transit system) from Union Station to the York Street stop. The website has up-to-the-minute city calendar and events information.

More convenient is the drop-in **Ontario Visitor Information Centre** (© **416/314-5901**), in the Eaton Centre, on Yonge Street at Dundas Street. It's on Level 1 (one floor below street level) and is open Monday to Friday from 10am to 9pm, Saturday from 9:30am to 6pm, and Sunday from noon to 5pm.

To pick up brochures and a map at **Pearson International Airport,** stop by the **Transport Canada Information Centre** (© **905/676-3506** or 416/247-7678). There's one in each terminal. A staff fluent in a dozen languages can answer questions about attractions, ground transportation, and more.

PUBLICATIONS & WEBSITES
Toronto has four daily newspapers: the *Globe and Mail,* the *National Post,* the *Toronto Star,* and the *Toronto Sun.* All have some local listings, but the best are in the *Star,* which lists events, concerts, theater performances, first-run films, and the like.

Even better bets are the free weeklies *Now* and *Eye,* both published on Thursday and available in news boxes and at cafes and shops around town. *Xtra!* is another weekly freebie; it lists events, seminars, and performances, particularly those of interest to the gay and lesbian community. A free annual directory called *The Pink Pages* targets Torontonians, but out-of-towners will find the information about gay- and lesbian-friendly restaurants, bars, and other businesses quite useful. It's available at shops, restaurants, and bars along Church Street.

Where Toronto is a glossy monthly magazine that lists events, attractions, restaurants, and shops; it's available free at most hotels in the city and at some restaurants in the Theater District. *Toronto Life* is an award-winning lifestyle magazine that has excellent listings of kids' events, theater, speeches, and art exhibitions; the April issue contains a dining guide. *Toronto Life Fashion* magazine will be of interest to serious shoppers.

Toronto.com (www.toronto.com), operated by the *Toronto Star,* offers extensive restaurant reviews, events listings, and feature articles. *Toronto Life's* website

Underground Toronto

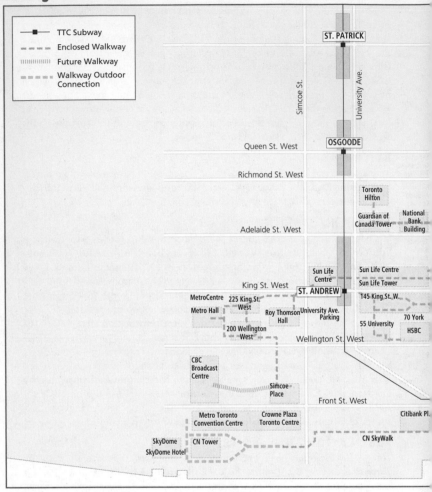

(www.torontolife.com) is another popular choice, particularly for its restaurant reviews and contests. It includes events, shopping, and services listings.

CITY LAYOUT

Toronto is laid out in a grid . . . with a few interesting exceptions. **Yonge Street** (pronounced *Young*) is the main north-south street, stretching from Lake Ontario in the south well beyond Highway 401 in the north. Yonge Street divides western cross streets from eastern cross streets. The main east-west artery is **Bloor Street,** which cuts through the heart of downtown.

"Downtown" usually refers to the area from Eglinton Avenue south to the lake, between Spadina Avenue in the west and Jarvis Street in the east. Because this is such a large area, I have divided it into five sections. **Downtown West** runs from the lake north to College Street; the eastern boundary is Yonge Street. **Downtown East** goes from the lake north to Carlton Street (once College St. reaches Yonge, it becomes Carlton St.); the western boundary is Yonge Street.

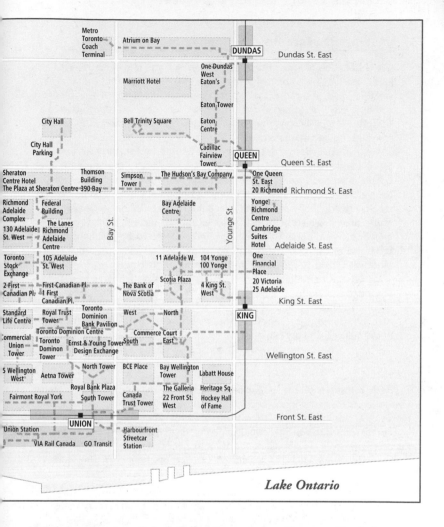

Metro Toronto Coach Terminal

Atrium on Bay

DUNDAS Dundas St. East

One Dundas West Eaton's

Marriott Hotel

Eaton Tower

City Hall

Bell Trinity Square

Eaton Centre

City Hall Parking

Cadillac Fairview Tower

QUEEN Queen St. East

Sheraton Centre Hotel
The Plaza at Sheraton Centre

Thomson Building
390 Bay

Simpson Tower

The Hudson's Bay Company

One Queen St. East
20 Richmond Richmond St. East

Richmond Adelaide Complex
130 Adelaide St. West

Federal Building

The Lanes
Richmond Adelaide Centre

Bay St.

Bay Adelaide Centre

Yonge St.

Yonge Richmond Centre

Cambridge Suites Hotel Adelaide St. East

Toronto Stock Exchange

105 Adelaide St. West

11 Adelaide W.

104 Yonge
100 Yonge

One Financial Place

2-First Canadian Pl.

First Canadian Pl.
1 First Canadian Pl.

Scotia Plaza

The Bank of Nova Scotia

4 King St. West

20 Victoria
25 Adelaide

King St. East

Standard Life Centre

Royal Trust Tower

Toronto Dominion Bank Pavilion

West

North

KING

Commercial Union Tower

Toronto Dominion Centre
Toronto Dominion Tower

Ernst & Young Tower
Design Exchange

Commerce Court South East

Wellington St. East

5 Wellington West

Aetna Tower

North Tower

BCE Place

Bay Wellington Tower

Labatt House

Royal Bank Plaza
South Tower

Canada Trust Tower

The Galleria
22 Front St. West

Heritage Sq.

Fairmont Royal York

Hockey Hall of Fame

Front St. East

UNION

Union Station

Harbourfront Streetcar Station

VIA Rail Canada GO Transit

Lake Ontario

Midtown West extends from College Street north to Davenport Road; the eastern boundary is Yonge Street. **Midtown East/The East End** runs from Carlton Street north to Davenport and farther east along Danforth Avenue; the western boundary is Yonge Street. **Uptown** is the area north of Davenport Road.

In Downtown West, you'll find many of the lakeshore attractions—Harbourfront, Ontario Place, Fort York, Exhibition Place, and the Toronto Islands. It also boasts the CN Tower, City Hall, SkyDome, Chinatown, the Art Gallery, and the Eaton Centre. Downtown East includes the St. Lawrence Market, the Hummingbird Centre, the St. Lawrence Centre for the Arts, and St. James Cathedral. Midtown West contains the Royal Ontario Museum, the Gardiner Museum, the University of Toronto, Markham Village, and chic Yorkville, a prime area for browsing and dining alfresco. Midtown East/The East End features Riverdale Farm, the historic Necropolis cemetery, and Greektown. Uptown has traditionally been a residential area, but it's now a fast-growing entertainment area, too. Its attractions include the Sunnybrook park system and the Ontario Science Centre.

Underground Toronto

It is not enough to know the streets of Toronto; you also need to navigate the labyrinth of walkways beneath the pavement. If the weather's bad, you can eat, sleep, dance, shop, and go to the theater without even donning a coat. Consult our map, "Underground Toronto," on p. 42, or look for the large, clear underground PATH maps throughout the concourse.

You can walk from the Dundas subway station south through the Eaton Centre until you hit Queen Street, turn west to the Sheraton Centre, then head south. You'll pass through the Richmond-Adelaide Centre, First Canadian Place, and Toronto Dominion Centre, and go all the way (through the dramatic Royal Bank Plaza) to Union Station. En route, branches lead off to the stock exchange, Sun Life Centre, and Metro Hall. Additional walkways link Simcoe Plaza to 200 Wellington West and to the CBC Broadcast Centre. Other walkways run around Bloor Street and Yonge Street and elsewhere in the city.

While its wide-ranging network makes this an excellent way to get around the downtown core when the weather is grim, the underground city has its own attractions, too. First Canadian Place in particular is known for free lunch-hour lectures, opera and dance performances, and art exhibits.

North Toronto is another burgeoning area, with theaters, such as the Toronto Centre for the Arts, galleries, and some excellent dining. It's not yet a prime tourist destination, but it gets a few mentions throughout this guide.

Toronto sprawls so widely that quite a few of its primary attractions lie outside the downtown core. They include the Toronto Zoo, Paramount Canada's Wonderland, and the McMichael Canadian Art Collection. Be prepared to journey somewhat.

FINDING AN ADDRESS   This isn't as easy as it should be. Your best bet is to call ahead and ask for directions, including landmarks and subway stations. Even the locals need to do this.

THE NEIGHBORHOODS IN BRIEF

Downtown West

The Toronto Islands These three islands in Lake Ontario—Ward's, Algonquin, and Centre—are home to a handful of residents and no cars. They're a spring and summer haven where Torontonians go to in-line skate, bicycle, boat, and picnic. Centre Island, the most visited, holds the children's theme park Centreville. Catch the ferry at the foot of Bay Street by Queens Quay.

Harbourfront/Lakefront The landfill where the railroad yards and dock facilities once stood is now a glorious playground opening onto the lake. This is home to the Harbourfront Centre, one of the most important literary, artistic, and cultural venues in Canada.

Financial District Toronto's major banks and insurance companies have their headquarters here, from Front Street north to Queen Street, between Yonge and York streets. Toronto's first skyscrapers rose here; fortunately, some of the older structures have been preserved. Ultramodern BCE Place incorporated the facade of a historic bank building into its design.

Theater District An area of dense cultural development, this neighborhood stretches from Front Street north to Queen Street, and from Bay Street west to Bathurst Street. King Street West is home to most of the important sights, including the Royal Alexandra Theatre, the Princess of Wales Theatre, Roy Thomson Hall, and Metro Hall. Farther south are the Convention Centre and the CN Tower.

Chinatown Dundas Street West from University Avenue to Spadina Avenue, and north to College Street are the boundaries of Chinatown. As the Chinese community has grown, it has extended along Dundas Street and north along Spadina Avenue. Here you'll see a fascinating mixture of old and new. Hole-in-the-wall restaurants share the sidewalks with glitzy shopping centers built with Hong Kong money.

Queen Street West This stretch from University Avenue to Bathurst Street offers an eclectic mix—popular mainstream shops, funky boutiques, secondhand bookshops, and vintage clothing emporiums. It's also home to Toronto's gourmet ghetto, with bistro after trattoria after cafe lining the street. There's excellent food along this strip, but it's too frequently served with heaps of attitude. Despite the intrusion of mega-retailers, many independently owned boutiques flourish.

West Queen West In the past, Queen Street West was considered edgy. Now, that appellation is applied to West Queen West, which starts at Bathurst Avenue and runs west past Ossington Avenue. The neighborhood is now known as one of the coolest places in the city. It's full of interesting boutiques for clothing, housewares, and antiques, excellent small art galleries, and up-and-coming restaurants.

Little Italy This thriving, lively area, filled with open-air cafes, trattorias, and shops, serves the Italian community along College Street between Euclid and Shaw. The trendies can't seem to stay away, which has driven up prices in this once-inexpensive neighborhood.

Downtown East

Old Town/St. Lawrence Market During the 19th century, this area, east of Yonge Street between the Esplanade and Adelaide Street, was the focal point of the community. Today the market's still going strong, and attractions like the glorious St. James Cathedral draw visitors.

The Beaches Communal, youthful, safe, and comfortable—these adjectives best describe the Beaches, just 15 minutes from downtown at the end of the Queen Street East streetcar line. It was a summer resort in the mid-1800s, and its boardwalk and beach continue to make it a casual, family-oriented neighborhood.

Midtown West

Queen's Park and the University Home to the Ontario Legislature and many of the colleges and buildings that make up the University of Toronto, this neighborhood extends from College Street to Bloor Street between Spadina Avenue and Bay Street.

Yorkville Originally a village outside the city, this area north and west of Bloor and Yonge streets became Toronto's Haight-Ashbury in the 1960s. Now, it's a *haute* district filled with designer boutiques, galleries, cafes, and restaurants.

The Annex This area fell into neglect for many years, but since the early 1980s much of it has been lovingly restored. It stretches from Bedford Road to Bathurst Street, and from Harbord Street to Dupont Avenue. Many of the tremendous turn-of-the-20th-century homes are still single-family dwellings, though as you walk west it segues into the U of T student ghetto. Revered urban-planning guru Jane Jacobs has long called this area home.

Koreatown The bustling blocks along Bloor Street West between Bathurst and Christie streets are filled with Korean restaurants, alternative-medicine practitioners such as herbalists and acupuncturists, and shops filled with made-in-Korea merchandise. One of the first Korean settlements in Toronto, it is now primarily a business district.

Midtown East/The East End

Rosedale Meandering tree-lined streets with elegant homes and manicured lawns are the hallmarks of this residential community, from Yonge and Bloor streets northeast to Castle Frank and the Moore Park Ravine. Named after Sheriff Jarvis's residence, its name is synonymous with Toronto's wealthy elite.

Church Street Between Gerrard Street and Bloor Street East along Church Street lies the heart of Toronto's gay and lesbian community. Restaurants, cafes, and bars fill this relaxed, casual neighborhood. Church Street is where 19th-century Toronto's grandest cathedrals stood.

Cabbagetown Once described by writer Hugh Garner as the largest Anglo-Saxon slum in North America, this gentrified neighborhood of Victorian and Edwardian homes stretches east of Parliament Street to the Don Valley between Gerrard Street and Bloor Street. The sought-after residential district got its name because the front lawns of the homes, occupied by Irish immigrants (who settled here in the late 1800s), were, it is said, covered with row upon row of cabbages. Riverdale, Toronto's only inner-city farm, is at the southeastern end of this district.

Greektown Across the Don Valley Viaduct, Bloor Street becomes the Danforth, which marks the beginning of Greektown. It's lined with old-style Greek tavernas and hip Mediterranean bars and restaurants that are crowded from early evening until early morning. The densest wining-and-dining area starts at Broadview Avenue and runs 6 blocks east.

Uptown

Forest Hill Second to Rosedale as the city's prime residential area, Forest Hill is home to Upper Canada College and Bishop Strachan School for girls. It stretches west of Avenue Road between St. Clair Avenue and Eglinton Avenue.

Eglinton Avenue The neighborhood surrounding the intersection of Yonge Street and Eglinton Avenue is jokingly known as "Young and Eligible." It's a bustling area filled with restaurants—including some of the town's top-rated—and nightclubs. To the east, it intersects with the 243-hectare (600-acre) Sunnybrook park system and with the Ontario Science Centre.

2 Getting Around

BY PUBLIC TRANSPORTATION

The **Toronto Transit Commission,** or TTC (© **416/393-4636** for 24-hr. information; recordings available in 18 languages; www.city.toronto.on.ca/ttc), operates the subway, bus, streetcar, and light rapid transit (LRT) system.

The TTC Subway Sy

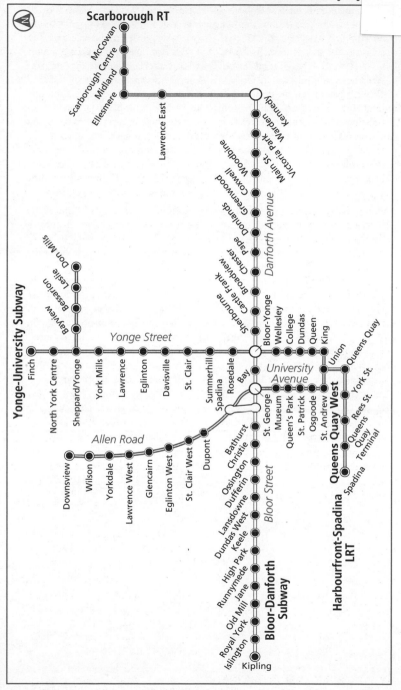

Fares, including transfers to buses or streetcars, are C$2.25 (US$1.60) or 10 tickets for C$19 (US$13) for adults. Students under 20 and seniors pay C$1.50 (US$1.05) or 10 tickets for C$13 (US$8.75), and children under 12 pay C50¢ (US35¢) or 10 tickets for C$4.25 (US$3). You can buy a special day pass for C$7.75 (US$5.40) that's good for unlimited travel for one person after 9:30am on weekdays, and all day on weekends. There's also a group pass for C$7.75 (US$5.40) that's good for up to six people (a maximum of two adults) anytime on Sunday and statutory holidays only. There are no multiple-day deals.

For surface transportation, you need a ticket, a token, or exact change. You can buy tickets and tokens at subway entrances and at authorized stores that display the sign TTC TICKETS MAY BE PURCHASED HERE. Bus drivers do not sell tickets, nor will they make change. Always obtain a free transfer *where you board the train or bus,* in case you need it. In the subways, use the push-button machine just inside the entrance. On streetcars and buses, ask the driver for a transfer.

THE SUBWAY   It's fast (especially when you compare it to snarled surface traffic), clean, and very simple to use. There are two major lines—Bloor-Danforth and Yonge-University-Spadina—and one smaller line, Sheppard, in the northern part of the city. The Bloor Street east-west line runs from Kipling Avenue in the west to Kennedy Road in the east (where it connects with Scarborough Rapid Transit to Scarborough Centre and McCowan Rd.). The Yonge Street north-south line runs from Finch Avenue in the north to Union Station (Front St.) in the south. From there, it loops north along University Avenue and connects with the Bloor line at the St. George station. A Spadina extension runs north from St. George to Downsview station at Sheppard Avenue. The Sheppard line connects only with the Yonge line at Sheppard Station, and runs east through north Toronto for just 6km (4 miles).

The light rapid transit (LRT) system connects downtown to Harbourfront. The fare is one ticket or token. It runs from Union Station along Queens Quay to Spadina, with stops at Queens Quay ferry docks, York Street, Simcoe Street, and Rees Street, then continues up Spadina to the Spadina subway station. The transfer from the subway to the LRT (and vice versa) at Union Station is free.

The subway operates Monday to Saturday from 6am to 1:30am, and Sunday from 9am to 1:30am. From 1am to 5:30am, the Blue Night Network operates on basic surface routes. It runs about every 30 minutes. For route information, pick up a "Ride Guide" at subway entrances or call ✆ 416/393-4636. Multilingual information is available. You can also use the automated information service at ✆ 416/393-8663.

Smart commuters park their cars at subway terminal stations at Kipling, Islington, Finch, Wilson, Warden, Kennedy, York Mills, Victoria Park, and Keele. Certain conditions apply. Call ✆ 416/393-8663 for details. You'll have to get there very early.

BUSES & STREETCARS   Where the subway leaves off, buses and streetcars take over. They run east-west and north-south along the city's arteries. When you pay your fare (on bus, streetcar, or subway), always pick up a transfer so that you won't have to pay again if you want to transfer to another mode of transportation. For complete TTC information, call ✆ 416/393-4636.

BY TAXI

As usual, this is an expensive mode of transportation. It's C$2.50 (US$1.75) the minute you step in, and C25¢ (US15¢) for each additional 0.2km (about

¼ mile). Fares can quickly mount up, especially during rush hours. You can hail a cab on the street, find one in line in front of a big hotel, or call one of the major companies—**Diamond** (© **416/366-6868**), **Royal** (© **416/777-9222**), or **Metro** (© **416/504-8294**). If you experience problems with cab service, call the **Metro Licensing Commission** (© **416/392-3082**).

BY CAR

Toronto is a rambling city, but that doesn't mean that a car is the best way to get around. Toronto has the dubious distinction of being recognized as the worst city in Canada in which to drive. It has gotten so bad that the government has started monitoring certain intersections with cameras. Driving can be a frustrating experience because of the high volume of traffic, drivers' disregard for red lights, and meager but pricey parking options. This is particularly true downtown, where traffic inches along and parking lots are scarce. I strongly recommend that you avoid driving in the city.

RENTAL CARS   If you decide to rent a car, try to make arrangements in advance. Companies with outlets at Pearson International Airport include **Thrifty** (© 800/367-2277), **Budget** (© 800/527-0700), **Avis** (© 800/331-1084), **Hertz** (© 800/654-3001), **National** (© 800/227-7368), and **Enterprise** (© 800/736-8222). Keep in mind that there's usually a steep fee when you rent a vehicle in one city and drop it off in another. The rental fee depends on the type of car you want, but the starting point is around C$45 (US$30) a day—not including the 15% in sales taxes. This also does not include insurance; if you pay with a particular credit card, you might get automatic coverage (check with your credit-card issuer before you go). Be sure to read the fine print of the rental agreement—some companies add conditions that will boost your bill if you don't fulfill certain obligations, like filling the gas tank before returning the car. *Note:* If you're under 25, check with the company—many will rent on a cash-only basis, some only with a credit card, and others will not rent to you at all.

Car rental insurance probably does not cover liability if you cause an accident. Check your own auto insurance policy, the rental company policy, and your credit-card coverage for the extent of coverage: Is your destination covered? Are other drivers covered? How much liability is covered if a passenger is injured? (If you rely on your credit card for coverage, you may want to bring a second credit card with you, as damages may be charged to your card and you may find yourself stranded with no money.)

PARKING   Parking lots downtown run about C$4 to $6 (US$2.80–$4.20) per half hour, with a C$16 to $20 (US$11–$14) maximum between 7am and 6pm. After 6pm and on Sunday, rates drop to around C$8 (US$5). Generally, the city-owned lots, marked with a big green "P," are slightly cheaper than private facilities. Observe the parking restrictions—otherwise the city will tow your car away, and it'll cost more than C$100 (US$70) to get it back.

DRIVING RULES   A right turn at a red light is permitted after coming to a full stop, unless posted otherwise. The driver and front-seat passengers must wear seat belts; if you're caught not wearing one, you'll incur a substantial fine. The speed limit in the city is 50kmph (30 mph). You must stop at pedestrian crosswalks. If you are following a streetcar and it stops, you must stop well back from the rear doors so passengers can exit easily and safely. (Where there are concrete safety islands in the middle of the street for streetcar stops, this rule does not apply, but exercise care nonetheless.) Radar detectors are illegal.

BY FERRY

Toronto Parks and Recreation operates ferries that travel to the Toronto Islands. Call 📞 416/392-8193 for schedules and information. Round-trip fares are C$5 (US$3.50) for adults, C$3 (US$2.10) for seniors and students 15 to 19 (with valid ID), and C$2 (US$1.40) for children 14 and under.

FAST FACTS: Toronto

Area Code Toronto's area codes are **416** and **647;** outside the city, the code is **905** or **289.** You must dial all 10 digits for all local phone numbers.

Babysitting Hotel concierges can suggest reliable sitters if there aren't child-care facilities on site. In a pinch, call **Care-on-Call (📞 416/975-1313),** a 24-hour service.

Business Hours Banks are generally open Monday through Thursday from 10am to 3pm, Friday 10am to 6pm. Most stores are open Monday through Wednesday from 10am to 6pm and Saturday and Sunday from 10am to 5pm, with extended hours (until 8–9:30pm) on Thursday and usually Friday.

Currency Exchange Generally, the best place to exchange your currency is at an ATM or bank. You can also change money at the airport, but at a less favorable rate.

Dentists For emergency services from 8am till midnight, call the **Dental Emergency Service (📞 416/485-7121).** After midnight, your best bet is the **Toronto Hospital,** 200 Elizabeth St. (📞 416/340-3948). Otherwise, ask the front-desk staff or concierge at your hotel.

Doctors The staff or concierge at your hotel should be able to help you locate a doctor. You can also call the **College of Physicians and Surgeons,** 80 College St. (📞 416/967-2600, ext. 626), for a referral between 9am to 5pm. See also "Emergencies," below.

Electricity It's the same as in the United States—110 volts, 50 cycles, AC.

Embassies/Consulates All embassies are in Ottawa, the national capital. They include the **Australian High Commission,** 50 O'Connor St., Suite 710, Ottawa, ON K1P 6L2 (📞 613/236-0841); the **British High Commission,** 80 Elgin St., Ottawa, ON K1P 5K7 (📞 613/237-1530); the **Irish Embassy,** 130 Albert St., Ottawa, ON K1P 5G4 (📞 613/233-6281); the **New Zealand High Commission,** 727–99 Bank St., Ottawa, ON K1P 6G3 (📞 613/238-5991); the **South African High Commission,** 15 Sussex Dr., Ottawa, ON K1M 1M8 (📞 613/744-0330); and the **U.S. Embassy,** 100 Wellington St., Ottawa, ON K1P 5T1 (📞 613/238-4470). Consulates in Toronto include **Australian Consulate-General,** 175 Bloor St. E., Suite 314, at Church Street (📞 416/323-1155); **British Consulate-General,** 777 Bay St., Suite 2800, at College (📞 416/593-1290); and the **U.S. Consulate,** 360 University Ave. (📞 416/595-1700).

Emergencies Call 📞 911 for fire, police, or ambulance. The **Toronto General Hospital,** 200 Elizabeth St., provides 24-hour emergency service (📞 416/340-3946 for emergency or 416/340-4611 for information). Also see "Hospitals," below.

Hospitals In the downtown core, go to **Toronto General,** 200 Elizabeth St. (📞 416/340-4611, or 416/340-3946 for emergency); **St. Michael's,** 30 Bond St. (📞 416/360-4000, or 416/864-5094 for emergency); or **Mount Sinai,** 600

University Ave. ((C) **416/596-4200,** or 416/586-5054 for emergency). Also downtown is the **Hospital for Sick Children,** 555 University Ave. ((C) **416/ 813-1500).** Uptown, there's **Sunnybrook Hospital,** 2075 Bayview Ave., north of Eglinton ((C) **416/480-6100,** or 416/480-4207 for emergency). In the eastern part of the city, go to **Toronto East General Hospital,** 825 Coxwell Ave. ((C) **416/461-8272,** or 416/469-6435 for emergency).

Hot Lines **Poison Information Centre** ((C) 416/813-5900); **Distress Centre** suicide prevention line ((C) 416/598-1121); **Rape Crisis Line** ((C) 416/597-8808); **Assaulted Women's Help Line** ((C) 416/863-0511); **AIDS & Sexual Health InfoLine** ((C) 800/668-2437); **Toronto Prayer Line** ((C) 416/929-1500). For kids or teens in distress, there's **Kids Help Phone** ((C) 800/668-6868).

Internet Access As in most other North American cities, the Web is a social magnet in Toronto. **Insomnia,** 563 Bloor St. W. ((C) **416/588-3907),** is more social than your average Net cafe—maybe it's the sign over the door that reads THE INTERNET IS A STRANGE PLACE. DON'T SURF ALONE. There are several curtained computer terminals (C$10/US$7 per hr.), as well as comfortable couches and a big-screen TV. The pizza and panini are usually pretty good. Open daily from noon to 1am.

If you just want to surf fast and not hang out, look for a **Kinko's.** There are several in the city, but one sure bet is the location at 505 University Ave. at Dundas ((C) **416/970-8447).**

Laundry/Dry Cleaning **Bloor Laundromat,** 598 Bloor St. W., at Bathurst Street ((C) **416/588-6600),** is conveniently located. At the **Laundry Lounge,** 531 Yonge St., at Wellesley Street ((C) **416/975-4747),** you can do your wash while sipping a cappuccino and watching TV in the lounge. It's open daily from 7am to 11pm. **Careful Hand Laundry & Dry Cleaners Ltd.** has outlets at 195 Davenport Rd. ((C) **416/923-1200),** 1415 Bathurst St. ((C) **416/530-1116),** and 1844 Avenue Rd. ((C) **416/787-6006);** for pickup and delivery, call (C) **416/ 787-6006.**

Liquor Laws The minimum drinking age is 19. Drinking hours are daily from 11am to 2am. The government is the only retail vendor. **Liquor Control Board of Ontario** (LCBO) stores sell liquor, wine, and some beers. They're open Monday through Saturday. Most are open from 10am to 6pm; some stay open evenings, and a few are open Sunday from noon to 5pm. One of the very best is at the **Manulife Centre,** 55 Bloor St. W. ((C) **416/ 925-5266),** which has longer hours than most, opening at 9:30am and closing at 9pm Monday through Saturday, and noon to 5pm on Sunday.

The **Wine Rack** has several locations, including 77 Wellesley St. E., at Church ((C) **416/923-9393),** and sells only Ontario wines. Most branches of the **Beer Store** (also part of the LCBO) are open Monday through Saturday from 10am to 8pm; there's a downtown location at 614 Queen St. W. ((C) **416/504-4665),** near Bathurst.

Lost Property If you leave something on a bus, a streetcar, or the subway, call the **TTC Lost Articles Office** ((C) **416/393-4100)** at the Bay Street subway station. It's open Monday through Friday from 8am to 5pm.

Luggage Storage/Lockers Lockers are available at Union Station and at the Eaton Centre.

Mail Postage for letters and postcards to the United States costs C65¢ (US45¢); overseas, C$1.05 (US75¢). Mailing letters and postcards within Canada costs C48¢ (US35¢).

Postal services are available at convenience and drug stores. Almost all sell stamps, and many have a separate counter where you can ship packages from 8:30am to 5pm. Look for the sign in the window indicating such services. There are also post-office windows in **Atrium on Bay** (✆ 416/506-0911), in **Commerce Court** (✆ 416/956-7452), and at the **TD Centre** (✆ 416/ 360-7105).

Maps Free maps of Toronto are available in every terminal at **Pearson International Airport** (look for the Transport Canada Information Centre signs), the Metropolitan Toronto Convention & Visitors Association at **Harbourfront,** and the Visitor Information Centre in the **Eaton Centre,** on Yonge Street at Dundas Street. Convenience stores and bookstores sell a greater variety of maps. Or try **Canada Map Company,** 63 Adelaide E., between Yonge and Church streets (✆ 416/362-9297), or **Open Air Books and Maps,** 25 Toronto St., near Yonge and Adelaide streets (✆ 416/363-0719).

Newspapers & Magazines The four daily newspapers are the *Globe and Mail,* the *National Post,* the *Toronto Star,* and the *Toronto Sun. Eye* and *Now* are free arts-and-entertainment weeklies. *Xtra!* is a free weekly targeted at the gay and lesbian community. In addition, many English-language ethnic newspapers serve Toronto's Portuguese, Hungarian, Italian, East Indian, Korean, Chinese, and Caribbean communities. *Toronto Life* is the major monthly city magazine; its sister publication is *Toronto Life Fashion. Where Toronto* is usually free at hotels and some Theater District restaurants.

Pharmacies One big chain is **Pharma Plus,** which has a store at 63 Wellesley St., at Church Street (✆ 416/924-7760). It's open daily from 8am to midnight. Other Pharma Plus branches are in College Park, Manulife Centre, Commerce Court, and First Canadian Place. The only 24-hour drugstore near downtown is **Shopper's Drug Mart** at 700 Bay St., at Gerrard Street West (✆ 416/979-2424).

Police In a life-threatening emergency, call ✆ 911. For all other matters, contact the **Metro police,** 40 College St. (✆ 416/808-2222).

Post Office See "Mail," above.

Radio The Canadian Broadcasting Corporation offers a great mix of intelligent discussion and commentary as well as drama and music. In Toronto, the **CBC** broadcasts on 740AM and 94.1FM. **CHIN** (1540AM and 100.7FM) will get you in touch with the ethnic and multicultural scene in the city; it broadcasts in more than 30 languages.

Restrooms Finding a public restroom is usually not difficult. Most tourist attractions have them, as do hotels, department stores, and public buildings. There are restrooms at major subway stations such as Yonge/Bloor, but they are best avoided.

Safety As large cities go, Toronto is generally safe, but be alert and use common sense, particularly at night. The Yonge/Bloor, Dundas, and Union subway stations are favorites with pickpockets. In the downtown area, Moss Park is considered one of the toughest areas to police. Avoid Allan Gardens and other parks at night.

Taxes The provincial retail sales tax is 8%; on accommodations it's 5%. There is an additional 7% national goods-and-services tax (GST).

In general, nonresidents may apply for a tax refund. They can recover the accommodations tax, the sales tax, and the GST for nondisposable merchandise that will be exported for use, provided it is removed from Canada within 60 days of purchase. The following do not qualify for rebate: meals and restaurant charges, alcohol, tobacco, gas, car rentals, and such services as dry cleaning and shoe repair.

The quickest and easiest way to secure the refund is to stop at a duty-free shop at the border. You must have proper receipts with GST registration numbers. Or you can apply through the mail, but it will take about 4 weeks to receive your refund. For an application form and information, you can contact **Visitor Rebate Program, Canada Customs and Revenue Agency,** Ottawa, ON K1A 0L8 (fax 613/954-3577; www.ccra-adrc.gc.ca); forms are also available at tourism kiosks around town. You can also contact **Ontario Travel,** Queen's Park, Toronto, ON M7A 2R9 (© **800/668-2746** or 416/314-0944).

Taxis See "Getting Around," earlier in this chapter.

Telephone A local call from a telephone booth costs C25¢ (US15¢). Watch out for hotel surcharges on local and long-distance calls; often a local call will cost at least C$1 (US70¢) from a hotel room. The United States and Canada are on the same long-distance system. To make a long-distance call between the United States and Canada, use the area codes as you would at home. Canada's international prefix is **1.**

Time Toronto is on Eastern Standard Time. Daylight savings time is in effect from April to October.

Tipping Basically it's the same as in major U.S. cities: 15% in restaurants (up to 20% in the finer spots), 10% to 15% for taxis, C$1 (US70¢) per bag for porters, C$1 to C$2 (US70¢–$1.40) per day for hotel housekeepers (more if you're traveling with messy kids and/or pets).

Transit Information For information on the subway, bus, streetcar, and light rapid transit (LRT) system, call the TTC at © **416/393-4636** or check www.city.toronto.on.ca/ttc.

Weather Call the **talking yellow pages** (© **416/292-1010**) for a current weather report and lots of other information. Or check the *Toronto Star*'s website, **www.thestar.com.**

4

Where to Stay

Toronto has no shortage of hotels. Whether you're seeking old-world elegance in a historic building or looking for all the conveniences of the office in your home away from home, you'll find it here. Similarly you'll find a range that spans intimate boutique inns to monolithic hotels.

Wherever you stay though, make sure to get the best deal you can. Proximity to major attractions, such as the Harbourfront Centre, SkyDome, and the Eaton Centre, can cost a bundle. Even budget hotels may charge more than C$100 (US$70) a night in the high season, which runs from April to October. And remember to factor in the 5% accommodations tax and the 7% GST into what you spend (note that if you're not a Canadian resident, you can get a tax refund on the GST; see "Fast Facts: Toronto" in chapter 3 for details).

There are some guidelines to keep in mind when booking your accommodations. First, always ask for a discount when you book your accommodations. Even the most expensive luxury hotel will reduce its rates during the low season and on weekends, and sometimes simply because the hotel isn't full. This discount can be anywhere from 20% to 50%—after all, having a guest pay a reduced rate is preferable to having an empty room that generates no revenue.

Do not be shy—always ask for a deal. If you belong to a group (such as the military, seniors, students, or an auto club), so much the better. You'll qualify for an instant discount as long as you have appropriate ID. Members of frequent flyer clubs may qualify for discounts, room upgrades, or other perks—if they ask for them. A hotel may offer special packages, which might include theater tickets, meals, or museum passes with the cost of your accommodations. At the risk of sounding like a broken record, I will say it again: Always ask for a deal.

When you make your reservations, it's important to keep in mind what you're planning to see and do. Toronto is a vast metropolis, with attractions, dining districts, and ethnic communities scattered throughout. Keep in mind that you want to be as close as possible to the sights that interest you most.

I have grouped accommodations by price and location. Most are in the neighborhoods defined in chapter 3 as Downtown West, Downtown East, Midtown West, the East End, and Uptown. I've also included a few hotels to the east of the city and close to Pearson International Airport.

TWO IMPORTANT NOTES ON PRICES The prices quoted in this chapter are rack rates; discounts can knock the price down as much as 50%. The 5% accommodations tax and the 7% GST are refunded to nonresidents upon application (see "Taxes" under "Fast Facts: Toronto," in chapter 3).

A NOTE TO NONSMOKERS Hotels that reserve floors for nonsmokers are now commonplace, so we don't single them out in this guide. However, people who want a smoke-free room should make that clear when making a reservation. Rooms for smokers are concentrated on particular floors, and the rooms and even the hallways in those areas tend to smell strongly of smoke, even in the cleanest hotels. Never assume that you'll get a smoke-free room if you don't specifically request one.

BED-AND-BREAKFASTS   A B&B can be an excellent—and relatively inexpensive—alternative to standard hotel accommodations. **Toronto Bed & Breakfast,** 253 College St., P.O. Box 269, Toronto, ON M5T 1R5 (© **877/ 922-6522** or 416/588-8800; www. torontobandb.com), has a list of 12 accommodations in the city. Doubles cost roughly C$75 to $125 (US$52–$88). The organization will make your reservation and send you a confirmation. The **Downtown Association of Bed-and-Breakfast Guest Houses,** P.O. Box 190, Station B, Toronto, ON

M5T 2W1 (© **416/368-1420;** www. bnbinfo.com), lists only nonsmoking B&Bs. Doubles range from C$70 to $130 (US$49–$91). **Bed and Breakfast Canada,** P.O. Box 46093, College Park Post Office, 44 Yonge St., Toronto, ON M5B 2L8 (© **416/363-6362;** www.bbcanada.com), has a very long list of independent B&B operators. Doubles run from about C$65 to $130 (US$45–$91).

ACCOMMODATIONS SERVICES If you're having trouble finding a hotel, call **Tourism Toronto** (© **800/ 363-1990** or 416/203-2600), for advice and special deals.

FOR TRAVELERS IN NEED If you run into trouble in Toronto and you need a place to stay, call the **Travellers Aid Society of Toronto** (© **416/ 366-7788**). The organization provides shelter for people in crisis situations.

1 Downtown West

VERY EXPENSIVE

Hilton Toronto ⨁⨁   The Hilton Toronto isn't what it used to be: With a gorgeous C$25 million (US$18 million) renovation completed in the spring of 2000, it became one of the most attractive hotels in the city. On the western edge of the Financial District, the 32-story Hilton boasts generously sized rooms decorated with streamlined luxury in mind. Because of the hotel's excellent location overlooking the wide boulevard of University Avenue, many rooms (and the glass elevators) have superb vistas. Because of its proximity to the Financial District, the Hilton is a favorite among business travelers. Executive rooms include perks such as an ultraplush terry bathrobe, a trouser press, and access to a private lounge that serves complimentary breakfast and evening snacks.

The Hilton is more cutting-edge than you'd expect from a business hotel, making it a sophisticated choice. The design of the grand foyer is dramatic, with an illuminated canopy, floor lights and backlights, and copious use of glass. There are photographic art exhibits on the public floors. Last but not least, as part of its renovation, the Hilton unveiled the magnificent Tundra, which serves top-notch Canadian cuisine (review on p. 86).

145 Richmond St. W., Toronto, ON M5H 2L2. © **800/445-8667** or 416/869-3456. Fax 416/869-1478. www. hilton.com. 601 units. C$269–$449 (US$188–$314) double. Extra person C$22 (US$15). Children 18 and under stay free in parent's room. Weekend packages available. AE, DC, MC, V. Parking C$22 (US$15). Subway: Osgoode. **Amenities:** 3 restaurants; bar; indoor and outdoor lap pools; health club; Jacuzzi; sauna; children's programs; concierge; business center; 24-hr. room service; massage; babysitting; same-day laundry service/dry cleaning. *In room:* A/C, TV, dataport, minibar, coffeemaker, hair dryer, iron.

Hôtel Le Germain ⨁⨁⨁   The Groupe Germain has become something of a legend in Québec for its excellent boutique hotels. Their first Toronto venture has been eagerly anticipated, and in spring 2003 it opened to instant accolades. Located in Toronto's Entertainment District, the Hôtel Le Germain has an elegant but slightly offbeat sensibility. Its design is edgier than what you'll find in other Toronto hotels. The public spaces are magnificent: The vast lobby manages the amazing trick of being at once intimate and grand. The library lounge area boasts a fireplace, an espresso maker, a wall of objets d'art, and cozy white couches. The breakfast "room" on the second floor is like an expansive landing (there's a staircase that leads down from here to the lobby), and the tables are all communal. Attention is paid to the smallest details, which explains why the elevators are "wrapped" in words of English and French poetry, and why the corridors are so broad (the Groupe Germain built this hotel from scratch, so they could do exactly as they pleased).

The guest rooms are just as precise: The ceilings are high, the desk can be moved around to your liking (it's attached to the wall on one side), and the linens and robes are by Frette. My favorite feature, though, is the glass wall in every bathroom, which allows light in from the main room and makes everything feel more spacious (there are blinds for those who want their privacy). All guests have access to the exercise room on the 11th floor, which has floor-to-ceiling windows and an open-air terrace. The hotel will also pair you up with a personal trainer or arrange for an in-room massage for you (there are extra fees for these services).

30 Mercer St., Toronto, ON M. © 866/345-9501 or 416/345-9500. Fax 416/345-9501. www.germaintoronto.com. 122 units. From C$225 (US$158) double. AE, DC, MC, V. Parking C$25 (US$17.50). Subway: St. Andrew. **Amenities:** Restaurant; bar; health club; concierge; business center; 24-hr. room service; laundry service; dry cleaning. *In room:* A/C, TV, dataport, minibar, coffeemaker, hair dryer, iron, safe.

SoHo Metropolitan Hotel ★★★ I'm a huge fan of the Metropolitan Hotel (below), and so I've been anxiously awaiting the latest Toronto venture by this small hotel group. This new boutique hotel—opened in April 2003—does not disappoint. This is grown-up elegance at its most refined.

The guest rooms are beautiful: A serene palette of neutral tones and blond wood make for a soothing setting. But more importantly, the SoHo Met's rooms make the best use of technology I've found in any Toronto hotel. It's as if the designers compiled a list of all of the most frustrating aspects about staying in a hotel room and resolved to fix them. Hate hopping into bed and then discovering you have to jump out again to turn out a light? All of the lights in the room can be controlled by switches right next to the headboard. Hate opening and closing curtains and drapes? All it takes here is the flick of another switch. Even better, another control will lower a privacy screen that lets light in but shields you from view. The marble bathroom floor heats up at your command. The in-room safe is big enough for a laptop and has an outlet inside so you can charge your computer battery. There are no tatty DO NOT DISTURB signs; instead, another control panel lets you indicate your desire to be left alone or request housekeeping as need be. And of course the telephones are cordless (it's a small thing but one I wish that other hotels would understand is important).

The SoHo Met is also home to one of Toronto's best restaurants, Senses (p. 90). It's appropriately named, because all of your senses will be charmed by this property. This is an excellent choice for business and leisure travelers; the only people I wouldn't recommend this property for are those with kids in tow, as it's a very glamorous spot for grown-ups.

318 Wellington St. W., Toronto, ON M5V 3T4. © 800/668-6600 or 416/599-8800. Fax 416/599-8801. www.metropolitan.com/soho. 86 units. From C$295 (US$207) double. AE, DC, MC, V. Valet parking C$15 (US$10.50), self-parking C$10 (US$7). Subway: St. Andrew. **Amenities:** Restaurant; bar; health club; concierge; business center; 24-hr. room service; laundry service; dry cleaning. *In room:* A/C, TV, dataport, minibar, coffeemaker, hair dryer, iron, safe.

Where to Stay in Downtown West

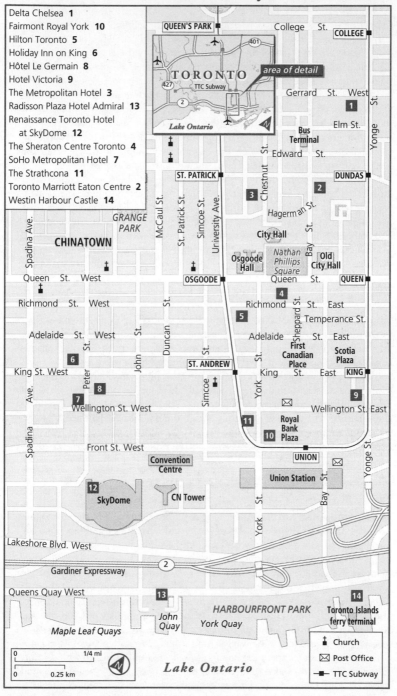

Delta Chelsea **1**
Fairmont Royal York **10**
Hilton Toronto **5**
Holiday Inn on King **6**
Hôtel Le Germain **8**
Hotel Victoria **9**
The Metropolitan Hotel **3**
Radisson Plaza Hotel Admiral **13**
Renaissance Toronto Hotel
  at SkyDome **12**
The Sheraton Centre Toronto **4**
SoHo Metropolitan Hotel **7**
The Strathcona **11**
Toronto Marriott Eaton Centre **2**
Westin Harbour Castle **14**

QUEEN'S PARK

College   St.

COLLEGE

TORONTO
TTC Subway
Lake Ontario
area of detail

401
427
2

Gerrard   St.   West

Elm   St.

Bus
Terminal

Edward   St.

DUNDAS

ST. PATRICK

Chestnut   St.

Hagerman   St.

GRANGE
PARK

McCaul St.

St. Patrick St.

Simcoe St.

University Ave.

City Hall

Nathan
Phillips
Square

Old
City Hall

CHINATOWN

Osgoode
Hall

Spadina Ave.

Queen   St.   West

OSGOODE

Queen   St.

QUEEN

Richmond   St.   West

St.

Richmond   St.   East

Sheppard St.

Temperance St.

Adelaide   St.   West

St.

Duncan   St.

John   St.

Adelaide   St.   East

First
Canadian
Place

Scotia
Plaza

King St. West

Peter   Ave.

Simcoe   St.

ST. ANDREW

York   St.

King   St.   East

KING

Spadina

Wellington St. West

Wellington St. East

Royal
Bank
Plaza

Front St. West

UNION

Convention
Centre

Union Station   St.

Bay   St.

SkyDome

CN Tower

York   St.

Lakeshore Blvd. West

Gardiner Expressway

2

Queens Quay West

HARBOURFRONT PARK

Toronto Islands
ferry terminal

Maple Leaf Quays

John
Quay

York Quay

✝ Church
✉ Post Office
▬■ TTC Subway

0   1/4 mi
0   0.25 km

Lake Ontario

Yonge   St.

57

EXPENSIVE

Fairmont Royal York ⭐⭐   Looming across from Union Station, Toronto's hub for rail travel, is the Fairmont Royal York, a historic hotel built by the Canadian-Pacific Railroad in 1929. Fairmont hotels across the country tend to the gigantic, and this one is no exception, with 1,365 guest rooms and suites, and 35 meeting and banquet rooms.

The old-fashioned lobby is magnificent, and just sitting on a plush couch and watching the crowd is an event. Still, you have to decide whether you want to stay under the same roof with more than 1,000 others—business travelers, shoppers, tour groups, and particularly conventioneers. Service is remarkably efficient but necessarily impersonal; the downtown location, just steps from the Entertainment District and the Hummingbird Centre, is excellent.

Guest rooms, though furnished with charming antique reproductions, are a mixed bag. Some are reasonably airy, but there's generally not much spare space. If you're willing to spring for a Fairmont Gold room, you'll stay on a private floor with superior, spacious rooms, separate check-in and concierge, a private lounge, and complimentary breakfast (the extra cost is well worth it, in my opinion).

If you're interested in pampering yourself, ask about special spa packages—the Elizabeth Milan Day Spa, in the shopping arcade, is one of the best in the city. Among the multitude of dining and drinking spots in the hotel, the don't-miss ones are Epic (p. 88) and the Library Bar, which serves the best martinis in the city.

In summer 2002, the Fairmont launched its ongoing VIP (Very Important Pets) program: For an extra C$30 (US$21) per night, guests and their furry friends can stay in a special "dog friendly" room that comes with toys, treats, and other amenities. (Part of the extra fee is donated to the Toronto Humane Society.)

The hotel pays particular attention to accessibility, making adaptations to some guest rooms, so that they are specially designed for wheelchair users, the hearing impaired, and the visually impaired. And Fairmont completed renovations in 2003 that made every public area in the hotel wheelchair-accessible.

100 Front St. W., Toronto, ON M5J 1E3. ℂ 800/441-1414. Fax 416/368-9040. www.fairmont.com. 1,365 units. C$175–$370 (US$123–$259) double. Packages available. AE, DC, DISC, MC, V. Parking C$26 (US$18). Subway: Union. Pets accepted. **Amenities:** 5 restaurants; 4 bars/lounges; skylit indoor pool; health club; spa (with special packages for guests); Jacuzzi; sauna; concierge; car-rental desk; business center; shopping arcade; salon; 24-hr. room service; babysitting; same-day laundry service/dry cleaning. *In room:* A/C, TV, dataport, minibar, coffeemaker, hair dryer, iron.

The Metropolitan Hotel ⭐⭐⭐   One of the few major hotels in Toronto that isn't part of a large chain, the Metropolitan prides itself on offering a boutique atmosphere (for the group's new and genuine boutique hotel, see the SoHo Met review above). The hotel caters to a business-oriented clientele, and it offers many of the same features and amenities as its competitors at a comparatively lower cost (which is not to say it's inexpensive, just very competitive). Just off Dundas Street West, the hotel is a 5-minute stroll north of the business district and about 2 minutes west of the Eaton Centre. But why walk when you can take advantage of the complimentary limo service to any downtown core address?

That perk is just one of the ways in which the Metropolitan attempts to compete with its pricier competitors. Rooms are well sized and furnished with comfort in mind. The luxury and executive suites boast Jacuzzis, Dolby Surround Sound televisions, and CD players. Many rooms also feature two-line cordless phones.

The two restaurants are huge draws. Lai Wah Heen (p. 89), which serves classic Cantonese cuisine, is a top choice for business entertaining with natives as

Where to Stay in Downtown East

College St.

COLLEGE 1

area of detail

TORONTO

TTC Subway

Lake Ontario

Carlton St.

2

ALLAN GARDENS

3

Gerrard St. East

Bus Terminal

Elm St.

Edward St.

Yonge St.

DUNDAS

Church St.

Jarvis St.

Sherbourne St.

Hagerman St.

Dundas St. East

4

City Hall

Nathan Phillips Square

Bay St.

Old City Hall

Victoria St.

Shuter St.

MOSS PARK

Queen St.

QUEEN

Queen St. East

Sheppard St.

Richmond St. East

Temperance St.

5

Lombard St.

6

Adelaide St. East

First Canadian Place

Scotia Plaza

OLD TOWN

Church St.

Jarvis St.

Sherbourne St.

King St. East

KING

7

Market St.

Wellington St. East

Royal Bank Plaza

Scott St.

Front St. East

The Esplanade

UNION

Yonge St.

Union Station

Bay St.

0   1/4 mi
0   0.25 km

Bond Place Hotel **4**
Cambridge Suites Hotel **5**
Courtyard Toronto Downtown **1**
Days Inn & Conference Centre **2**
Le Royal Meridien King Edward **7**
Neill-Wycik College Hotel **3**
Quality Hotel Downtown **6**

2

Lakeshore Blvd. East

Queens Quay East

✝ Church
✉ Post Office
■– TTC Subway

Where to Stay in Midtown & Uptown

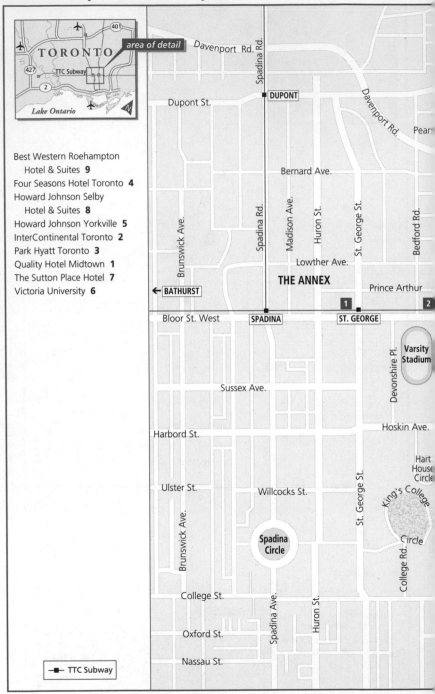

Best Western Roehampton
  Hotel & Suites **9**
Four Seasons Hotel Toronto **4**
Howard Johnson Selby
  Hotel & Suites **8**
Howard Johnson Yorkville **5**
InterContinental Toronto **2**
Park Hyatt Toronto **3**
Quality Hotel Midtown **1**
The Sutton Place Hotel **7**
Victoria University **6**

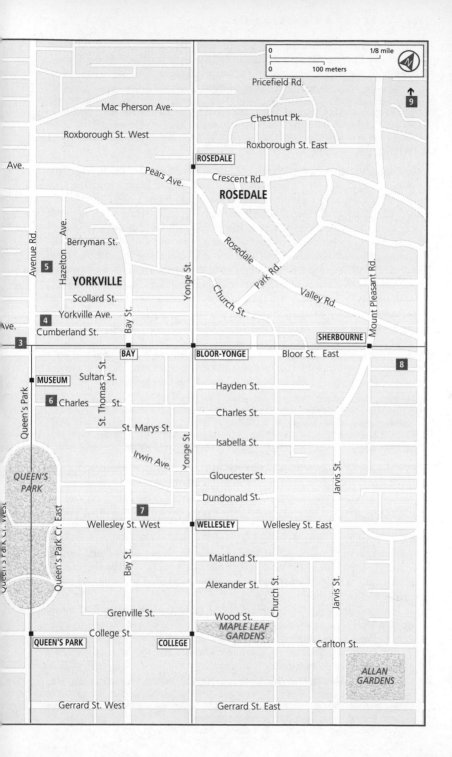

Pricefield Rd.

Mac Pherson Ave.

Roxborough St. West

Chestnut Pk.

Roxborough St. East

Ave.

Pears Ave.

ROSEDALE

Crescent Rd.

ROSEDALE

Avenue Rd.

Hazelton Ave.

Berryman St.

5

Rosedale

Yonge St.

Park Rd.

Valley Rd.

Mount Pleasant Rd.

YORKVILLE

Scollard St.

Church St.

Yorkville Ave.

Bay St.

4

Cumberland St.

Ave.

3

BAY

BLOOR-YONGE

Bloor St. East

SHERBOURNE

MUSEUM

Sultan St.

St. Thomas St.

Hayden St.

8

6 Charles St.

Charles St.

Queen's Park

St. Marys St.

Isabella St.

Yonge St.

Irwin Ave.

Gloucester St.

QUEEN'S PARK

Dundonald St.

Queen's Park Cr. East

7

Wellesley St. West

WELLESLEY

Wellesley St. East

Jarvis St.

Bay St.

Maitland St.

Alexander St.

Church St.

Jarvis St.

Grenville St.

Wood St.

Queen's Park Cr. West

College St.

MAPLE LEAF GARDENS

Carlton St.

QUEEN'S PARK

COLLEGE

ALLAN GARDENS

Gerrard St. West

Gerrard St. East

0   1/8 mile
0   100 meters

9

61

well as visitors. The modern-style ground-floor Hemispheres restaurant offers a Continental menu. Also, the Metropolitan has a partnership with the Toronto Symphony Orchestra, which offers guests special packages.

108 Chestnut St., Toronto, ON M5G 1R3. © **416/977-5000.** Fax 416/977-9513. www.metropolitan.com. 425 units. C$280–$310 (US$196–$217) double. Children 17 and under stay free in parent's room. AE, DC, DISC, MC, V. Valet parking C$24 (US$17), self-parking C$19 (US$13). Subway: St. Patrick. **Amenities:** 2 restaurants; bar; indoor pool; health club; sauna; Jacuzzi; concierge; courtesy limo; 24-hr. business center (w/PCs and Macs); limited room service; massage; babysitting; same-day laundry service/dry cleaning. *In room:* A/C, TV, dataport, minibar, coffeemaker, hair dryer, iron, safe.

Radisson Plaza Hotel Admiral

While not exactly small, the Radisson has an intimate, clubby feel. It overlooks Lake Ontario and is steps from the Harbourfront Centre. Its location can be seen as a big plus or a big minus. On the one hand, guests have beautiful lakefront vistas, as well as close access to one of Canada's premier arts centers and to the Toronto Islands. But this area of town can feel completely desolate at night. Toronto's waterfront, south of the hideous Gardiner Expressway, is woefully underdeveloped, making it a must to travel northward to seek good food, shopping, and entertainment. If your primary concern is location, this probably isn't the hotel for you.

What the Radisson does well is exploit its location for those who want to feel that they're getting away from the city without actually leaving it. This works especially well in summer. Its nautical-theme decor includes lacquered wood and gleaming brass in the lobby, with oil paintings of marine scenes littering the walls. The rooms are generally not large, but they are nicely appointed and boast floor-to-ceiling windows. Lakefront rooms offer superb views, and all guests can enjoy the sights (and a dip in the outdoor pool) on the roof deck.

249 Queens Quay W., Toronto, ON M5J 2N5. © **800/333-3333** or 416/203-3333. Fax 416/203-3100. www. radisson.com/torontoca_admiral. 157 units. C$189–$299 (US$132–$209) double. Extra person C$20 (US$14). Weekend packages available. AE, DC, DISC, MC, V. Parking C$18 (US$12). Subway: Union, then LRT to Rees St. **Amenities:** Restaurant; bar; outdoor pool; health club; Jacuzzi; concierge; business center; 24-hr. room service; laundry service. *In room:* A/C, TV, dataport, coffeemaker, hair dryer, iron.

Renaissance Toronto Hotel at SkyDome

A while ago, I was traveling and met a woman who had just visited Toronto. I asked where she'd stayed, and she told me that it was at "that hotel where they filmed people having sex and put it on a big screen." This is *that* hotel. It's a dream come true for diehard baseball fans—70 rooms overlook the diamond's verdant Astroturf. Unfortunately, those who enjoy the view should remember that it goes both ways: Just after it opened, the hotel became notorious when the amorous antics of a pair of guests ended up on the JumboTron (the giant screen that's supposed to be showing the on-field action). The incident is now a minor local legend. The lesson: All rooms have shades—remember to use them.

The hotel finished a C$10 million (US$7 million) renovation and refurbishment in 2001. The guest rooms are pretty much all a good size, but there's a definite pecking order: Rooms that face the city are the least expensive, with uninspiring views. Still, this is a strong contender as a tourist hotel—it's in a great location for theater, dining, and sights.

1 Blue Jays Way, Toronto, ON M5V 1J4. © **800/237-1512** or 416/341-7100. Fax 416/341-5091. www. renaissancehotels.com/yyzbr. 348 units. City view from C$189 (US$132) double; field side from C$305 (US$214) double. AE, DC, DISC, MC, V. Parking C$18 (US$12). Subway: Union. **Amenities:** Restaurant; bar; indoor pool; squash courts; health club; sauna; concierge; business center; 24-hr. room service; same-day laundry service/dry cleaning. *In room:* A/C, TV, dataport, coffeemaker, hair dryer, iron.

The Sheraton Centre Toronto 🏨🏨 *Kids*   A convention favorite, the Sheraton is across the street from New City Hall, a block from the Eaton Centre, and
a short stroll from the trendy restaurant and boutique area of Queen Street West.
It's entirely possible to stay here and never venture outside—the Sheraton complex includes restaurants, bars, and a cinema, and the building connects to
Toronto's fabled underground city. If you long for a patch of green, the hotel
provides that, too: The south side of the lobby contains a manicured garden with
a waterfall. Am I making the place sound like a monolith? Well, it is. But it's an
excellent home base for families because of its location and extensive list of
child-friendly features, including a children's center and huge pool.

Most of the guest rooms in this skyscraper-heavy neighborhood lack a serious
view, though as you near the top of the 46-story complex, the sights are inspiring indeed. Designed for business travelers, Club Level rooms were renovated in
2001; they contain mini business centers with a fax/printer/copier and two-line
speakerphone.

123 Queen St. W., Toronto, ON M5H 2M9. ℂ 800/325-3535 or 416/361-1000. Fax 416/947-4854. www.
sheratoncentretoronto.com. 1,377 units. C$260–$295 (US$182–$207) double. Extra person C$20 (US$14).
2 children 17 and under stay free in parent's room. Packages available. AE, DC, MC, V. Parking C$28 (US$20).
Subway: Osgoode. **Amenities:** 2 restaurants; bar; gigantic heated indoor/outdoor pool; health club; sauna;
spa; Jacuzzi; children's center; concierge; activities desk; business center; shopping arcade; 24-hr. room service; babysitting; laundry service; dry cleaning. *In room:* A/C, TV, dataport, coffeemaker, hair dryer, iron.

Toronto Marriott Eaton Centre   Attention, shoppers: Those who want
proximity to Toronto's central shrine to commerce should seriously consider
checking in here. Connected to the Eaton Centre, the Marriott is just a few
minutes' walk from the financial and theater districts, Chinatown, and Sky-
Dome. This hotel caters to the tourist crowd: While a good concierge at any
hotel can point you in the direction of, say, a hot restaurant, the Marriott has
desks set up to facilitate day-trip planning and other activities. Because of its
unmatched location, this is an excellent choice for determined sightseers. One
caveat is that the area immediately surrounding the Eaton Centre veers toward
the grungy and depressing; it isn't dangerous, but it is pickpocket heaven.

Most of the Marriott's guest rooms are well sized—all the better to store your
loot. The views from many of the rooms aren't the best, because you'll find office
towers in all directions. A pleasant surprise is the view of the beautiful 19th-century
Holy Trinity Church from the Parkside restaurant.

525 Bay St. (at Dundas St.), Toronto, ON M5G 2L2. ℂ 800/905-0667 or 416/597-9200. Fax 416/597-9211. www.
marriotteatoncentre.com. 459 units. C$189–$239 (US$132–$167) double. AE, DC, DISC, MC, V. Parking C$16
(US$11). Subway: Dundas. **Amenities:** 2 restaurants; 2 bars; indoor rooftop pool; health club; Jacuzzi; sauna;
concierge; activities desk; car-rental desk; business center; 24-hr. room service; massage; same-day laundry service and dry cleaning. *In room:* A/C, TV, dataport, coffeemaker, hair dryer, iron.

Westin Harbour Castle 🏨   A popular spot for conventions, the Westin is on
the lakefront, just across from the Toronto Islands ferry docks and down the
road from the Harbourfront Centre and Queens Quay. Not surprisingly, the
views are among the best in the city. The trade-off is that, like the nearby Radisson Plaza Hotel Admiral, this hotel is somewhat out of the way. It's a 5-minute
walk to Union Station, but to get there you have to cross under the Gardiner
Expressway, one of the ugliest and most desolate patches of the city. The hotel
tries to get around this difficulty with shuttle bus service; there's also a public-
transit stop and a queue of cabs at the hotel. But it's unlikely you'll want to go
for an evening stroll around here.

Perhaps recognizing the lack of things to do in the vicinity, management has populated the hotel with attractions. The dining options are extremely fine: The excellent restaurant, Toula, attracts Toronto residents as well as visitors in droves. There are also terrific sports facilities, giving this monolithic hotel the feel of a resort. Who needs to go outside anyway?

1 Harbour Sq., Toronto, ON M5J 1A6. ℭ 800/WESTIN-1 or 416/869-1600. Fax 416/361-7448. www.westin. com/harbourcastle. 977 units. C$180–$360 (US$126–$252) double; from C$335 (US$235) suite. Extra person C$30 (US$21). Children stay free in parent's room. Weekend packages available. AE, DC, MC, V. Parking C$25 (US$18). Subway: Union, then LRT to Queens Quay. **Amenities:** 2 restaurants; bar; indoor pool; 2 tennis courts; 2 squash courts; excellent health club; spa; Jacuzzi; sauna; children's center; concierge; business center; salon; 24-hr. room service; laundry service; dry cleaning. *In room:* A/C, TV, dataport, minibar, coffeemaker, hair dryer, iron.

MODERATE

Delta Chelsea (Kids) (Value)   While not a budget hotel, the Delta Chelsea offers bang for the buck. Its downtown location draws heaps of tour groups and a smattering of business travelers, its family-friendly facilities lure those with tykes, and its weekend packages capture the cost-conscious. It's impossible for a hotel to be all things to all people, but the Delta Chelsea comes pretty close. Luxury seekers should look elsewhere, and backpackers won't be able to afford it, but the Delta Chelsea is talented at meeting the needs of everyone in between.

The Delta Chelsea celebrated its 25th anniversary in 2000, when it opened Bb33 Bistro and Brasserie, a two-in-one restaurant with a formal dining room and a fuss-free buffet room. The guest rooms, many of which were renovated in 2001, are as bright and cheery as ever; a few have kitchenettes. On the Signature Club floor for business travelers, rooms have cordless speakerphones, faxes, well-stocked desks, and ergonomic chairs.

One special feature of the Delta Chelsea is its entertainment department. The hotel has partnerships with CanStage, Soupepper Theatre, the CN Tower, and the Canadian National Exhibition, to mention a few. Guests enjoy access to tickets for everything from blockbuster shows to special events.

33 Gerrard St. W., Toronto, ON M5G 1Z4. ℭ 800/243-5732 or 416/595-1975. Fax 416/585-4362. www.delta hotels.com. 1,590 units. C$129–$340 (US$90–$238) double; C$149–$360 (US$104–$252) deluxe double; C$195–$380 (US$137–$266) Signature Club double (business floor); from C$475 (US$333) suite. Extra person C$20 (US$14). Children 17 and under stay free in parent's room. Weekend packages available. AE, DC, DISC, MC, V. Valet parking C$26 (US$18); self-parking C$21 (US$15; parking available only to 575 cars). Subway: College. **Amenities:** 3 restaurants; 3 bars; 2 pools (1 for adults only); health club; Jacuzzi; sauna; children's center; billiards room; concierge; activities desk; business center; salon; babysitting; laundry service; dry cleaning. *In room:* A/C, TV, coffeemaker, hair dryer, iron.

Holiday Inn on King   The blinding-white facade of this building suggests that some architect mistook Toronto for the tropics. No matter—its location is hot, with the Theater District, gourmet ghetto, Chinatown, and SkyDome nearby (in fact, its location is better than that of any other hotel in this price category except the Delta Chelsea). It's also close to the Financial District, which explains the mix of business travelers and vacationers. Half the floors are office space; guest rooms start at the 9th floor and go up to the 20th. The good-sized, pastel-colored rooms are vintage Holiday Inn.

370 King St. W. (at Peter St.), Toronto, ON M5V 1J9. ℭ 800/263-6364 or 416/599-4000. Fax 416/599-7394. www.hiok.com. 431 units. C$179–$319 (US$125–$223) double. Extra person C$15 (US$11). AE, DISC, MC, V. Parking C$18 (US$12). Subway: St. Andrew. Pets accepted. **Amenities:** Restaurant; bar; small outdoor pool; health club; Jacuzzi; sauna; limited room service; massage. *In room:* A/C, TV, coffeemaker, hair dryer.

INEXPENSIVE

Hotel Victoria   In a landmark downtown building near the Hummingbird Centre and the Hockey Hall of Fame, the Victoria boasts the glamorous touches of an earlier age, such as crown moldings and marble columns in the lobby. It's Toronto's second-oldest hotel (built in 1909), but all of the guest rooms underwent a complete renovation in 2000, and the facilities are upgraded yearly. Because of its small size, the 48-room hotel offers an unusually high level of personal service and attention, which you normally wouldn't expect in a budget accommodation; the staff is fluent in several languages. Standard rooms are on the small side but are nicely put together; deluxe rooms are larger and have coffeemakers and minifridges.

56 Yonge St. (at Wellington St.), Toronto, ON M5E 1G5. © 800/363-8228 or 416/363-1666. Fax 416/363-7327. www.hotelvictoria-toronto.com. 48 units. C$129–$169 (US$90–$118) double. Extra person C$15 (US$11). Rates include continental breakfast. AE, DC, MC, V. Parking C$20 (US$14). Subway: King. **Amenities:** Restaurant; access to nearby health club; babysitting; laundry service; dry cleaning. *In room:* A/C, TV, dataport, hair dryer, iron.

The Strathcona *Value*   The Strathcona has a unique status: It's pretty much the only budget hotel in the Financial District, and for years it has been one of the best buys in the city. It sits in the shadow of the Royal York, making this hotel a short walk from all major downtown attractions. If you want to be in this neighborhood but don't want to pay a bundle, this is your best option. The trade-offs aren't as extensive as you might think. The Strathcona's rooms may be on the small side, but they are designed with efficiency in mind. The hotel doesn't have a health club, but guests have access to the nearby Wellington Club for a C$10 (US$7) fee.

60 York St., Toronto, ON M5J 1S8. © 800/268-8304 or 416/363-3321. Fax 416/363-4679. www.thestrathcona hotel.com. 193 units. May–Oct C$129–$179 (US$90–$125) double; Nov–Apr C$109–$139 (US$76–$97) double. AE, DC, MC, V. Parking nearby C$20 (US$14). Subway: Union. **Amenities:** Cafe; bar; access to nearby health club; bike rental; children's center; concierge; tour desk; car-rental desk; babysitting; limited room service; laundry service; dry cleaning. *In room:* A/C, TV, hair dryer, iron.

2 Downtown East

VERY EXPENSIVE

Cambridge Suites Hotel   This hotel has three main selling points: location, location, and location. Sitting on the edge of the Financial District, it caters to a corporate crowd that never wants to be more than a few steps from the office. Of course there are other drawing cards, such as the fact that all units are suites. The emphasis is on luxury, and the Cambridge succeeds in making its point.

The suites start at a generous 550 square feet and move up to deluxe duplexes. (In fact, the Jacuzzi-outfitted penthouse suites have come to the attention of celebrities tired of Toronto's tried-and-true star-catering hotels; the views are breathtaking.) The amenities for business travelers are solid. If you can drag yourself away from the comfy desk area, which has two two-line telephones and a fax, you can enjoy some of the comforts of home: refrigerator, microwave, and dining ware, plus coffee, tea, and snacks. And if you hand over your shopping list, the staff will stock the fridge, too.

15 Richmond St. E. (near Yonge St.), Toronto, ON M5C 1N2. © 800/463-1990 or 416/368-1990. Fax 416/601-3751. www.cambridgesuiteshotel.com. 231 units. From C$219 (US$153). Rates include continental breakfast. AE, DC, DISC, MC, V. Parking C$20 (US$14). Subway: Queen. **Amenities:** Restaurant; bar; small health club (and access to much larger health club nearby); Jacuzzi; sauna; spa; concierge; business center; limited room service; babysitting; laundry service; dry cleaning. *In room:* A/C, TV, fax, dataport, minibar, fridge, coffeemaker, hair dryer, iron.

Le Royal Meridien King Edward Hotel 🌟🌟 At one time, the King Eddy was the only place in Toronto that Hollywood royalty like Liz Taylor and Richard Burton would consider staying. In the 1980s, after many years of neglect, a group of local investors spent C$40 million (US$28 million) to rescue it. The result recalls its former glory, with rosy marble columns and a glass-domed rotunda dominating the lobby. The sense of grandeur carries into the accommodations. Not every room is spacious in terms of square footage, but their uniformly high ceilings give them a sweeping grandeur that is rare to find. The rooms are also charmingly appointed; unlike those at many competitors, where you'd be hard-pressed to tell the difference between one room and the next, these guest rooms have been decorated with a personal touch. The bathrooms are particularly nice, with generously proportioned marble tubs.

The formal dining room, Café Victoria, wins solid reviews for its cooking. This is one of the most glamorous settings in the city, and its astonishing Edwardian beauty is the reason the hotel wasn't torn down in the 1970s. Just off the lobby is a mirrored lounge that serves a traditional English afternoon tea; I highly recommend partaking in this delicious pastime whether or not you're a guest in the hotel (if you do, try the Lady Grey tea—it's irresistible). The wood-paneled Consort Bar is wonderfully clubby, and its 2.5m-high (8-ft.) windows afford fun people-watching while you sip a champagne cocktail. It's got a surprising long menu, which includes everything from crispy calamari to thin-crust pizzas.

37 King St. E., Toronto, ON M5C 2E9. © **800/543-4300** or 416/863-3131. Fax 416/367-5515. www.lemeridien-kingedward.com. 294 units. C$375–$450 (US$263–$315) double; from C$800 (US$560) suite. Children 12 and

---

Kids Family-Friendly Hotels

Delta Chelsea (p. 64) This is a perennial family favorite—with good cause. In March 2003, the hotel opened the Family Fun Zone, a multi-room play area with live bunnies and fish, a video arcade, and the only waterslide in downtown Toronto. You can play together in the family pool here or drop off the tyke for babysitting. Kids will enjoy the in-room family movies, Super Nintendo, cookie jar (replenished daily), and nightly turndown gift. Further reducing the strain on the family purse, kids have a half-price menu at some of the Delta Chelsea's restaurants.

Four Seasons Hotel Toronto (p. 68) A hop and a skip from the Royal Ontario Museum, this hotel has its own attractions. There are free bicycles and video games for borrowing, and an indoor-outdoor pool. Upon arrival, room service brings the kids complimentary cookies and milk. The concierge and housekeeping staff work magic, including conjuring up excellent babysitting services.

The Sheraton Centre Toronto (p. 63) The endless attractions of this complex—including restaurants with special menus for tykes, and a cinema—mean there's a lot to keep the kiddies entertained. There's a supervised play center as well as on-call babysitting services. Kids also enjoy in-room video games and a welcome gift. There are a limited number of Family Guest Rooms, which boast a toy chest, some kiddie-size furniture, a fridge and a microwave.

under stay free in parent's room. AE, DC, MC, V. Parking C$26 (US$18). Subway: King. Pets accepted. **Amenities:** 2 restaurants; bar; health club; Jacuzzi; sauna; concierge; 24-hr. room service, babysitting; laundry service; dry cleaning. *In room:* A/C, TV, fax, dataport, minibar, hair dryer, iron.

MODERATE

Bond Place Hotel   The location is right—a block from the Eaton Centre, around the corner from the Pantages and Elgin theaters—and so is the price. Perhaps that's why this hotel tends to be popular with tour groups. (The fact that the staff speaks several European and Asian languages doesn't hurt, either.) The rooms are on the small side, but all were freshened up in a 2002 renovation and refurbishment.

65 Dundas St. E., Toronto, ON M5B 2G8. ℂ 800/268-9390 or 416/362-6061. Fax 416/360-6406. www.bond placehoteltoronto.com. 287 units. High season C$140 (US$98) single or double; low season C$79 (US$55) single or double. Extra person C$15 (US$11). Weekend packages available. AE, DC, DISC, MC, V. Parking C$12 (US$8.40). Subway: Dundas. **Amenities:** Restaurant; bar; concierge; tour desk; car-rental desk; limited room service; laundry service; dry cleaning. *In room:* A/C, TV, hair dryer, iron.

Courtyard Toronto Downtown ☞   Anyone who knows the Marriott chain of hotels knows that their Courtyard hotels are usually out of the city center, not smack-dab in the middle of things. Here's one exception: Marriott has taken on an over-the-hill property near Yonge & College (the former Westbury Hotel), stripped it down to its skeleton, and built it back up as a bright and shiny Courtyard by Marriott in 1999. The result is exactly what this neighborhood needed. The location is equally convenient to the Financial District downtown and the chic cafes and shops of Midtown—a claim few other hotels in the city can make.

The lobby with its double-sided fireplace has a surprisingly intimate feel given the size of the hotel (truth be told, there's actually a separate reception area for tour groups, and that's why). The guest rooms don't tend to be big, but they do have a lot of comforts, including windows that open, high-speed Internet access ports, and a second sink outside of the bathroom. Like all Marriott hotels, there is an ongoing refurbishment program here, so the guest rooms tend to look fresh rather than lived-in. While Courtyards are generally regarded as business hotels, this one has family-friendly facilities such as a children's wading pool.

475 College St., Toronto, ON M4Y 1X7. ℂ 800/847-5075 or 416/924-0611. Fax 416/924-8692. www.courtyard. com/yyzcy. 575 units. C$149 (US$104) double. AE, DC, MC, V. Valet parking C$20 (US$14), self-parking C$15 (US$10.50). Subway: College. **Amenities:** 2 restaurants; bar; health club; tour desk; business center; limited room service; laundry service; dry cleaning. *In room:* A/C, TV, dataport, minibar, coffeemaker, hair dryer, iron, safe.

Days Inn & Conference Centre Toronto Downtown   Now that Maple Leaf Gardens is semi-retired (hockey has moved to the Air Canada Centre), the Days Inn's location isn't what it used to be. Still, this hotel isn't far from the downtown core, and its reasonable rates continue to draw business, particularly with those traveling for leisure (and on a budget). Also, extensive renovations in 2000 and ongoing improvements through 2002 have really spruced up both the public areas and the guest rooms.

30 Carlton St., Toronto, ON M5B 2E9. ℂ 800/329-7466 or 416/977-6655. Fax 416/977-0502. www.daysinn. com. 536 units. C$99–$169 (US$69–$118) double. Extra person C$15 (US$11). Children 17 and under stay free in parent's room. Summer discounts available. AE, DISC, MC, V. Parking C$15 (US$11). Subway: College. **Amenities:** Restaurant; bar; indoor pool; sauna; concierge; tour desk; car-rental desk; laundry service; dry cleaning. *In room:* A/C, TV, dataport, fridge, coffeemaker, hair dryer, iron.

INEXPENSIVE

Neill-Wycik College Hotel   During the school year, this is a residence for nearby Ryerson Polytechnic University. Some students work here in the summer, when the Neill-Wycik morphs into a guesthouse. Travelers on tight budgets won't mind the minimalist approach—rooms have beds, chairs, desks, and phones, but no air-conditioning or TVs (although there is a TV lounge). Groups of five bedrooms share two bathrooms and one kitchen with a refrigerator and stove. The hotel has two roof decks, on the 5th and 23rd floors. It's less than a 5-minute walk to the Eaton Centre. The neighborhood is not as appealing as that around Victoria University at the University of Toronto, which offers a similar arrangement (p. 71).

96 Gerrard St. E. (between Church and Jarvis sts.), Toronto, ON M5B 1G7. © 800/268-4358 or 416/977-2320. Fax 416/977-2809. www.neill-wycik.com. 300 units (none w/private bathroom). C$61 (US$42) double; C$70 (US$49) family (2 adults plus children). MC, V. Closed Sept–early May. Limited parking nearby C$10 (US$7). Subway: College. **Amenities:** Cafe; sauna; 24-hr. coin-op laundry.

Quality Hotel Downtown   Close to the Financial District and the Eaton Centre, this hotel always seems to be running a special promotion, so be sure to ask for a deal. Rooms tend to be small, though they do have all the standard amenities. This is basically a no-frills hotel whose main selling point is its location.

111 Lombard St. (between Adelaide and Richmond sts.), Toronto, ON M5C 2T9. © 800/4-CHOICE or 416/367-5555. Fax 416/367-3470. www.choicehotels.ca/cn311. 196 units. C$109–$209 (US$76–$146) double. Rates include continental breakfast buffet. Children 18 and under stay free in parent's room. AE, DC, DISC, MC, V. Parking C$16 (US$11). Subway: King or Queen. **Amenities:** Health club; laundry service; dry cleaning. *In room:* A/C, TV, coffeemaker, hair dryer, iron.

3 Midtown West

VERY EXPENSIVE

Four Seasons Hotel Toronto 𝒜𝒜 *Kids*   The Four Seasons is famous as the favored haunt of many visiting celebrities. The Rolling Stones call it home in Toronto, and during the Toronto International Film Festival every September you can't get in here for love or money. The hotel, in the ritzy Yorkville district, has earned a reputation for offering fine service and complete comfort. While not even close to being the largest hotel in the city, the building—with its myriad ballrooms, meeting rooms, and restaurants—is monolithic. It's easy to get lost inside (I've done it myself).

Even if you do get lost, it's an interesting place. The public areas are decorated like a French parlor, with marble floors and dramatic floral arrangements. Once you make it to your room, you'll find that while it may tend to be on the small side (a standard model is only about 325 sq. ft.), it's well designed and easy on the eye. Corner rooms have charming balconies—all the better to appreciate street scenes. The formal dining room, Truffles, is a Toronto institution (p. 101). The second-floor Studio Cafe is a favorite with the business crowd; its menu features many health-conscious, low-fat dishes. The Avenue bar is a perfect perch for people-watching—it overlooks Yorkville Avenue.

21 Avenue Rd., Toronto, ON M5R 2G1. © 800/268-6282 or 416/964-0411. Fax 416/964-2301. www.fourseasons.com. 380 units. C$305–$440 (US$214–$308) double; from C$485 (US$340) suite. Weekend discounts and packages available. AE, DC, DISC, MC, V. Parking C$25 (US$18). Subway: Bay. **Amenities:** 2 restaurants; 2 bars/lounges; indoor/outdoor pool; health club; Jacuzzi; bike rental; concierge; weekday courtesy limo to downtown; business center; 24-hr. room service; in-room massage; babysitting; same-day laundry service/dry cleaning. *In room:* A/C, TV, dataport, minibar, hair dryer, iron, safe.

InterContinental Toronto 𝒜   Just a little west of its higher-profile competitors the Park Hyatt and the Four Seasons, the InterContinental is less than a 5-minute walk from the Royal Ontario Museum, the Bata Shoe Museum, and

Yorkville, one of the best shopping districts in the city. It's a favorite with travelers, who appreciate its attentive, personalized service. The atmosphere exclusive but low-key. It doesn't get the starry crowd that its rivals draw, either, and that can be a blessing (anyone who has witnessed some of the weird behavior of the stars will know exactly what I mean). The building looks nondescript from the street, but inside, abundant European and Art Deco details give it character. The spacious guest rooms contain stylish love seats and roomy desks. The focus throughout the hotel is on business, from room design to the extensive business center to the Signatures restaurant, which is perfect for entertaining.

220 Bloor St. W., Toronto, ON M5S 1T8. © **800/267-0010** or 416/960-5200. Fax 416/960-8269. www. toronto.intercontinental.com. 210 units. C$275–$400 (US$193–$280) double. AE, DC, MC, V. Parking C$27 (US$19). Subway: St. George. **Amenities:** Restaurant; bar; indoor pool; health club; sauna; concierge; tour desk; business center; 24-hr. room service; in-room massage; babysitting; same-day laundry service/dry cleaning. *In room:* A/C, TV/VCR, fax, dataport, minibar, fridge, coffeemaker, hair dryer, iron, safe.

Park Hyatt Toronto 𝓡𝓡𝓡   With its ongoing C$60 million (US$42 million) renovations, the Park Hyatt has cemented its reputation for being the last word in luxe. It is, in my opinion, the very best hotel in Toronto at the moment, and it's where I'd choose to stay if price were no object (though both of the new boutique accommodations—the Hôtel Le Germain and the SoHo Metropolitan— are very tempting, too).

The location of the Park Hyatt is prime: It's in the posh Yorkville district, steps from the Royal Ontario Museum and the Bata Shoe Museum. Chicago-based Hyatt has renovated nearly every corner of the 71-year-old Art Deco building. The biggest change was the building of the North Tower, which is entirely new but designed to match the original structure (which is now known as the South Tower). The guest rooms in the North Tower are among the most generously proportioned in town—the *smallest* is 500 square feet. An extensive renovation and refurbishment of the South Tower was completed in 2003; here, the guest rooms are smaller, but they are more individual—there are 90 rooms and 40 different room layouts. All rooms in both towers have free high-speed Internet access.

A glamorous lobby dotted with Eastern-inspired objets d'art links the North and South towers. The ground-floor restaurant Annona (p. 101) is a treat for gourmets. While the Park Hyatt's neighbor, the Four Seasons, has for years been luring the glitterati, while the Park Hyatt prides itself on luring the literati. The 18th-floor Roof Lounge is famous for attracting writers (Mordecai Richler famously called the lounge the only civilized place in Toronto). In winter you will appreciate the couches in front of the fireplace, but in any other season, the lounge's open-air terrace is the place to be for a perfect view of the city (and an impressive daiquiri).

Another major development for the hotel was the 2001 unveiling of the Stillwater Spa, which is unique in both its design and some of its treatments. One signature therapy is a "watsu"-style massage, in which you float in a water-filled room while a therapist applies shiatsu moves—it's very soothing. See "Spas & the City" on p. 149 for a complete review.

4 Avenue Rd., Toronto, ON M5R 2E8. © **800/233-1234** or 416/925-1234. Fax 416/924-6693. www.park toronto.hyatt.com. 346 units. C$225–$499 (US$158–$349) double; from C$299 (US$209) suite. Weekend packages available. AE, DC, DISC, MC, V. Parking C$25 (US$18). Subway: Museum or Bay. Pets accepted. **Amenities:** Restaurant; 2 bars; health club; sauna; Jacuzzi; spa; concierge; business center; 24-hr. room service; babysitting; laundry service; dry cleaning. *In room:* A/C, TV, fax, dataport, minibar, coffeemaker, hair dryer, iron, safe.

EXPENSIVE
The Sutton Place Hotel ⋆⋆   Although it towers over the intersection of
Bay and Wellesley, The Sutton Place boasts the advantages of a small hotel—
particularly detail-oriented, personalized service. In addition to hosting a galaxy
of stars and celebrities, the hotel draws sophisticated business and leisure travelers in search of serious pampering. The emphasis is on sophistication—famous
guests expect to be left alone, and management protects their privacy. In other
words, no autograph seekers.

The hotel aims for European panache, littering the public spaces with antiques
and tapestries. The spacious guest rooms are decorated in a similar, though scaled-
down, style, and all were refurbished in 2001. A few suites have full kitchens.
Not that you'd want to cook while you're here—the lovely ground-floor Accents
restaurant serves continental fare, and across the street the star-studded Bistro 990
produces perfect French cuisine. One downside is that The Sutton Place stands
alone in its neighborhood. It's about a 10- to 15-minute walk to attractions such
as the Royal Ontario Museum and the Yorkville shopping district.

955 Bay St., Toronto, ON M5S 2A2. © **800/268-3790** or 416/924-9221. Fax 416/924-1778. www.suttonplace.
com. 294 units. C$235–$325 (US$165–$228) double; from C$400 (US$280) suite. Extra person C$20 (US$14).
Children 17 and under stay free in parent's room. Weekend discounts available. AE, DC, MC, V. Valet parking
C$28 (US$20); self-parking C$20 (US$14). Subway: Wellesley. Pets accepted. **Amenities:** Restaurant; bar;
indoor pool; health club; sauna; concierge; business center; salon; 24-hr. room service; massage; babysitting;
laundry service; dry cleaning. *In room:* A/C, TV, dataport, minibar, coffeemaker, hair dryer, iron, safe.

MODERATE
Howard Johnson Yorkville   Formerly the Venture Inn, this hotel is a bargain
in a very expensive neighborhood. It's a little more expensive than it used to be,
but it also has a few more amenities now. The Yorkville location is excellent,
which is the trade-off for small rooms. As with many value-priced hotels, you're
not going to want to spend much time in your room.

89 Avenue Rd., Toronto, ON M5R 2G3. © **800/446-4656** or 416/964-1220. Fax 416/964-8692. www.hojo-
canada.com. 71 units. C$89–$229 (US$62–$160) double. Rates include continental breakfast. AE, DC, MC, V.
Parking C$10 (US$7). Subway: Bay or Museum. Pets accepted. **Amenities:** Concierge; laundry service; dry
cleaning. *In room:* A/C, TV, dataport, hair dryer, iron.

Quality Hotel Midtown *Value*   Considering this hotel's tony location—steps
from Yorkville and several museums, including the Royal Ontario Museum—
the price is hard to beat. The rooms are small but comfortable, and outfitted
with well-lit worktables. Choice Club members have access to in-house secre-
tarial services; executive rooms have fax-modem hookups. However, there aren't
many other amenities or services. This is a good home base for a leisure traveler
who prizes location over other considerations. If you're not planning on hang-
ing out a lot in your hotel room, it's a small tradeoff to make for the price.

280 Bloor St. W. (at St. George St.), Toronto, ON M5S 1V8. © **416/968-0010.** www.choicehotels.ca. 210
units. C$139–$209 (US$97–$146) double. Weekend and other packages available. AE, DC, DISC, MC, V. Parking C$12 (US$8.40). Subway: St. George. **Amenities:** Restaurant; coffee shop; access to nearby health club;
limited room service; laundry service; dry cleaning. *In room:* A/C, TV, coffeemaker, hair dryer, iron.

INEXPENSIVE
Howard Johnson Selby Hotel & Suites ⋆ *Finds*   This hotel is one of Toronto's
better-kept secrets. Ornate chandeliers, stucco moldings, and high ceilings make
the 1890s Victorian building an absolute stunner. In a predominantly gay neighborhood, the Selby attracts gay and straight couples, as well as seniors (the latter

group gets special discounts). All of the rooms now have private bathrooms, but only a few have an old-fashioned claw-foot tub. The staff is very friendly, and while there's no concierge, there's no shortage of advice and recommendations for what to see and do.

592 Sherbourne St., Toronto, ON M4X 1L4. ⓒ **800/387-4788** or 416/921-3142. Fax 416/923-3177. www.hojo-canada.com. 82 units. C$79–$119 (US$55–$83) double; C$125–$165 (US$88–$116) suite. Rates include continental breakfast. AE, DISC, MC, V. Parking C$10 (US$7). Subway: Sherbourne. **Amenities:** Access to nearby health club; laundry room. *In room:* A/C, TV, coffeemaker.

Victoria University *Value*   This is a summer steal: You could not find a better deal in this part of town. From early May to late August, Victoria University (which is federated with the University of Toronto) makes its student accommodations available to travelers. Furnishings are simple—a bed, desk, and chair are standard—but the surroundings are splendid. Many of the rooms are in Burwash Hall, a 19th-century building that overlooks a peaceful, leafy quad. All rooms are down the street from the Royal Ontario Museum, and up the street from Queen's Park. Guests are provided with linens, towels, and soap.

140 Charles St. W., Toronto, ON M5S 1K9. ⓒ **416/585-4524.** Fax 416/585-4530. accom.victoria@utoronto.ca. 700 units (none w/private bathroom). C$66 (US$46) double. Rates include breakfast. MC, V. Closed Sept–April. Nearby parking C$12 (US$8.40). Subway: Museum. **Amenities:** Access to health club with Olympic-size pool; tennis courts; laundry room. *In room:* No phone.

4 Uptown
MODERATE

Best Western Roehampton Hotel & Suites   The Roehampton is removed from downtown attractions, but still well located—for some people. It is a short walk from one of the best dining districts in the city, and a short bus ride from the Ontario Science Centre and 243 hectares (600 acres) of parkland (including hiking and cross-country skiing trails, and the Sunnybrook stables). The large, nicely furnished rooms boast big windows and peaceful views. With the wealth of hotels downtown, there's no reason to come this far north unless you need to—but if you do, this is a nice, relatively inexpensive place to stay.

808 Mount Pleasant Rd., Toronto, ON M4P 2L2. ⓒ **800/387-8899** or 416/487-5101. Fax 416/487-5390. www.bestwestern.com. 112 units. C$145–$175 (US$102–$123) double. Packages available. Children 17 and under stay free in parent's room. AE, DC, DISC, MC, V. Parking C$8 (US$5.60). Subway: Eglinton. **Amenities:** Restaurant; outdoor rooftop pool; health club; concierge; limited room service; babysitting; laundry service; dry cleaning. *In room:* A/C, TV, dataport, minibar, coffeemaker, hair dryer, iron.

5 The East End

Although it's not close to the downtown attractions, this area has many sights that are worth noting. They include the Ontario Science Centre, the Toronto Zoo, the Scarborough Bluffs (which homesick English settlers compared to the white cliffs of Dover), and the Scarborough Town Centre, a vast shopping complex.

There are a number of moderately priced chain hotels in this area. They include **Embassy Suites,** 8500 Warden Ave., Markham, ON L6G 1A5 (ⓒ 905/470-8500); **Howard Johnson,** 940 Progress Ave., Scarborough, ON M1G 3T5 (ⓒ 800/446-4656); **Radisson,** 1250 Eglinton Ave. E., Don Mills, ON M3C 1J3 (ⓒ 416/449-4111); **Ramada,** 185 Yorkland Blvd., Don Mills, ON M2J 4R2 (ⓒ 800/2-RAMADA); and **Sheraton,** 2035 Kennedy Rd., Scarborough, ON M1T 3G2 (ⓒ 416/299-1500).

EXPENSIVE

Westin Prince Hotel Ⓞ   This hotel is less than half an hour from downtown, but its location and 6 hectares (15 acres) of parkland make it feel like a secluded resort. The generously proportioned rooms are designed for comfort. Many have a bay window or balcony, and the view makes Toronto look like one big forest. Standard features include a refrigerator, two phones, and a marble bathroom.

900 York Mills Rd., Don Mills, ON M3B 3H2. Ⓞ 800/WESTIN-1 or 416/444-2511. Fax 416/444-9597. www. westin.com. 384 units. C$150–$320 (US$105–$224) double. Extra person C$20 (US$14). Children 17 and under stay free in parent's room. Weekend packages available. AE, DC, MC, V. Free parking. Subway: York Mills. **Amenities:** 3 restaurants; bar; outdoor heated pool; 9-hole putting green; tennis courts; health club; sauna; children's center; concierge; business center; 24-hr. room service; laundry service; dry cleaning. *In room:* A/C, TV, fridge, coffeemaker, hair dryer, iron.

INEXPENSIVE

University of Toronto at Scarborough   Like the downtown U of T campus, this student residence opens to travelers from mid-May to late August. The greenery-surrounded student village consists of town houses that sleep a maximum of six. Each has a complete kitchen, but none has air-conditioning, a telephone, or a TV.

Student Village. Scarborough Campus, University of Toronto, 1265 Military Trail, Scarborough, ON M1C 1A4. Ⓞ 416/287-7356. Fax 416/287-7323. C$180 (US$126) double with 2-night minimum; each additional night C$90 (US$63). Family rates available. MC. V. Closed Sept to mid-May. Free parking. Subway: Kennedy, then Scarborough Rapid Transit to Ellesmere, then bus no. 95 or 95B to college entrance. By car: Take exit 387 north from Hwy. 401. **Amenities:** Cafeteria; pub; access to health club with squash and tennis courts. *In room:* No phone.

6 At the Airport

Don't be fooled by anyone who tells you that the airport isn't far from the city. It's at least a 30-minute drive to downtown, depending on traffic. A taxi downtown costs roughly C$36 (US$25); the cheap public-transit options from the airport take an hour. Many of the hotels along the airport strip cater to business travelers. Others may wish to stay in this area if they're planning to divide their time between Toronto and its outlying areas, such as the Niagara region. Serious golfers come here for the area's many golf courses, including the 18-hole championship layout at the Royal Woodbine Golf Club.

EXPENSIVE

Hilton Toronto Airport Ⓞ   I'm not enthusiastic about staying out by Pearson International Airport, but one of the luxuries of doing so is that you can expect a spacious room. The Hilton certainly makes good on this opportunity. In fact, one of its main attractions is its 152 minisuites—all of which have a king-size bed in the bedroom, a sofa bed in the living room, a color TV in both rooms, and three phones. Another lure is the chain's well-regarded array of business-oriented amenities. The building underwent a C$9 million (US$6.3 million) face-lift in 1999, and a smaller renovation in the fall of 2001.

5875 Airport Rd., Mississauga, ON L4V 1N1. Ⓞ 800/567-9999 or 905/677-9900. Fax 905/677-7782. www. hilton.com. 413 units. From C$219 (US$153) double; from C$244 (US$171) minisuite. Extra person C$25 (US$18). Children stay free in parent's room. Weekend packages available. AE, DC, DISC, MC, V. Parking C$12 (US$8.40). **Amenities:** Restaurant; bar; indoor pool; nearby golf course; health club; sauna; spa; children's center; concierge; car-rental desk; business center; 24-hr. room service; same-day laundry service/dry cleaning. *In room:* A/C, TV, fax, dataport, minibar, coffeemaker, hair dryer, iron.

Sheraton Gateway Hotel in Toronto International Airport Ⓞ   Talk about convenience: You don't even need to go outdoors to get here—just take the skywalk from Terminal 3 (or a free shuttle from the other terminals). If you're planning a very short trip that requires flying out of the city almost as soon as you fly in, this hotel makes an awful lot of sense. Rooms are comfortable, spacious, and, more to the point, fully soundproofed (remember, you're still at the airport!). Club rooms have extra inducements, such as ergonomic chairs, a fax/printer/copier, and access to a private lounge that serves complimentary breakfast and snacks.

Toronto AMF, Box 3000, Toronto, ON L5P 1C4. ℂ 800/325-3535 or 905/672-7000. Fax 905/672-7100. www.sheraton.com. 474 units. C$190–$280 (US$133–$196) double. AE, DC, DISC, MC, V. Parking C$19 (US$13). Pets accepted. **Amenities:** Restaurant; bar; indoor pool; health club; Jacuzzi; sauna; concierge; business center; 24-hr. room service; in-room massage; babysitting; laundry service; dry cleaning. *In room:* A/C, TV, dataport, minibar, coffeemaker, hair dryer, iron, safe.

Wyndham Bristol Place 🕊🕊   For a hotel by the airport, the Wyndham has a lot to offer. I'd never recommend staying near the airport unless you absolutely have to, but if you do, the Wyndham is an excellent choice. This is undoubtedly the most glamorous hotel for miles around—and the only one with a waterfall in its lobby. The decor throughout the building is sophisticated, but the hotel's real claim to fame is its personalized service. (You'll need to register for the Wyndham by Request program, which you can do online at www.wyndham.com; it's free, and filling out the questionnaire about everything from your dining to bedding preferences will improve your stay immeasurably.)

Guest rooms are well lit and spacious. Because it's a 30-minute journey to downtown Toronto, the good news is that the Wyndham boasts lots of amenities to keep you in the vicinity. The main dining room, Zachary's, aims high, with a seasonal menu and glamorously appointed dining room.

950 Dixon Rd., Toronto, ON M9W 5N4. ℂ 800/WYNDHAM or 416/675-9444. Fax 416/675-4426. www. wyndham.com. 287 units. C$175–$295 (US$123–$207) double; from C$400 (US$280) suite. Extra person C$20 (US$14). Children 17 and under stay free in parent's room. Packages available. AE, DC, DISC, MC, V. Parking C$12 (US$8.40). **Amenities:** 2 restaurants; bar; large skylit indoor pool; health club; sauna; concierge; business center; 24-hr. room service; babysitting; laundry service; dry cleaning. *In room:* A/C, TV, dataport, minibar, coffeemaker, hair dryer, iron.

MODERATE

Regal Constellation Hotel 🕊   This hotel has steadily grown into one of the best bets in the airport region. Its excellent meeting space makes it a favorite for trade shows and conventions. Because the hotel was constructed piece by piece, the rooms vary greatly from floor to floor. Every unit is a minisuite with a king or two double beds, a sturdy desk, and an L-shaped sofa. Not surprisingly, given the location, the hotel is a self-contained entertainment complex. There are two restaurants: the Royal Chinese, for formal dining, and the more casual Atrium. The Banyan Bar offers live entertainment on Friday and Saturday evenings.

900 Dixon Rd., Toronto, ON M9W 1J7. ℂ 800/222-8888 or 416/675-1500. Fax 416/675-4611. 710 units. C$115–$195 (US$81–$137). Extra person C$15 (US$11). Children 17 and under stay free in parent's room. Weekend and honeymoon packages available. AE, DC, MC, V. Parking C$8 (US$5.60). **Amenities:** 2 restaurants; bar; indoor/outdoor pool; exercise room; sauna; concierge; car-rental desk; business center; salon; 24-hr. room service; laundry service; dry cleaning. *In room:* A/C, TV, dataport, coffeemaker, hair dryer, iron.

Toronto Airport Marriott Hotel   One of the newest airport hotels, the Marriott is popular with business travelers. Of course, everything out here is really for business travelers. However, the Marriott is trying to attract leisure travelers, too, so expect a weekend discount of up to 50%. Rooms are comfortable and spacious. The amenities are in keeping with the Marriott name—no surprises here. There are two restaurants off the lobby: Take note of the Mikado, a Japanese restaurant where your meal can be cooked right at your table (think food as performance art).

901 Dixon Rd, Toronto, ON M9W 1J5. ✆ **800/905-2811** or 416/674-9400. Fax 416/674-8292. www.marriott. com. 424 units. C$120–$245 (US$84–$172) double. Extra person C$15 (US$11). Weekend packages available. AE, DC, DISC, MC, V. Parking C$8 (US$5.60). **Amenities:** 2 restaurants; bar; skylit indoor pool; nearby golf course; health club; Jacuzzi; sauna; concierge; car-rental desk; business center; 24-hr. room service; babysitting; same-day laundry service/dry cleaning. *In room:* A/C, TV, dataport, minibar, coffeemaker, hair dryer, iron.

INEXPENSIVE

Belaire Hotel Toronto Airport   Formerly a Comfort Inn, this hotel offers simple rooms at reasonable rates. Rooms are decorated in pine, and just big enough to hold a queen-size bed, dresser, desk and chair, and plush armchair or loveseat.

240 Belfield Rd., Rexdale, ON M9W 1H3. ✆ **416/241-8513.** Fax 416/249-4203. 114 units. C$90–$140 (US$63– $98) double. Extra person C$10 (US$7). Children 17 and under stay free in parent's room. Rates include continental breakfast. AE, DC, DISC, MC, V. Free parking. **Amenities:** Restaurant; lounge; limited room service; laundry service; dry cleaning. *In room:* A/C, TV, hair dryer.

Days Hotel—Toronto Airport   For the price, this is a very good bet on the airport strip; the facilities are similar to those at pricier hotels. The guest rooms are bright and cheery, and 20 of them were recently renovated to become Corporate Plus rooms geared towards business travelers. Upgraded units have bathrobes (unusual at a hotel in this price range), irons and ironing boards, and fax-modem hookups. The Garden Café Restaurant is open all day.

6257 Airport Rd., Mississauga, ON L4V 1N1. ✆ **800/387-6891** or 905/678-1400. Fax 905/678-9130. www. daysinn.com. 201 units. C$90–$169 (US$63–$118) double. Extra person C$10 (US$7). Children 16 and under stay free in parent's room. Weekend packages available. AE, DC, DISC, MC, V. Parking C$6 (US$4.20) per day, C$18 (US$13) per week. **Amenities:** Restaurant; outdoor pool; exercise room; sauna; limited room service; coin-op laundry. *In room:* A/C, TV, coffeemaker, hair dryer.

Delta Meadowvale Resort & Conference Centre   Set on 9 hectares (23 acres) of greenery, the Delta has all the attributes of a restful resort. There are hiking and biking trails, tennis and squash courts, and indoor and outdoor swimming pools. The cozy rooms have modern wooden furniture, and each boasts a small balcony, a refrigerator, and two phones. The Regatta Bar & Grille serves a variety of dishes throughout the day; there are also two lounges for evening drinks (one only in summer, as it's out of doors).

6750 Mississauga Rd. (at Hwy. 401), Mississauga, ON L5N 2L3. ✆ **800/422-8238** or 905/821-1981. Fax 905/542-4036. www.deltahotels.com. 374 units. C$110–$240 (US$77–$168) double. Weekend discounts available. AE, DC, DISC, MC, V. Free parking. Downtown shuttle C$11 (US$7.70) one-way. **Amenities:** 2 restaurants; 2 bars; children's center; business center; salon; 24-hr. room service; babysitting; laundry service; dry cleaning. *In room:* A/C, TV, coffeemaker, hair dryer.

Four Points Sheraton Toronto Airport   Talk about getting away from it all: on a 2.5-hectare (6-acre) woodland site, the Four Points Sheraton offers a relaxing—dare I say pastoral?—setting. Guest rooms were last renovated in 2002, with bathrooms, carpets, and draperies singled out for attention. The lobby, business center and meeting rooms were also renovated in 2002.

5444 Dixie Rd. (at Hwy. 401), Mississauga, ON L4W 2L2. ✆ **800/737-3211** or 905/624-1144. Fax 416/ 624-9477. www.fourpoints.com/torontoairport. 296 units. C$119–$265 (US$83–$186) double. Extra person C$15 (US$11). Weekend discounts available. AE, DC, DISC, MC, V. Free parking. **Amenities:** Restaurant; indoor pool; health club; Jacuzzi; sauna; children's center; business center; 24-hr. room service; babysitting; same-day laundry service/dry cleaning. *In room:* A/C, TV, dataport, fridge, coffeemaker, hair dryer, iron.

Where to Dine

Dining out is nothing short of a passion in Toronto. It's not that we're too lazy to cook, but we are spoiled by the embarrassment of edible riches in all parts of the city. Many restaurants are just as busy on a Wednesday as they are on a weekend, because dining out is a hallmark of the local culture.

The city is a restaurant-goer's nirvana for a wealth of reasons. For starters, there are more than 5,000 eateries. They represent cooking styles from any country or nationality you can name, making Toronto's culinary scene both eclectic and palate teasing. Eating out is also remarkably affordable: While the most expensive restaurants have some entrees priced above C$40 (US$28), many more boast top-notch cooking for bargain-basement prices—it's a very competitive market. (Keep in mind, too, that for American visitors, even the most expensive Toronto restaurants aren't so pricey given the weak Canadian dollar.)

Mediterranean and Asian cuisines dominate the scene—and often appear on the same plate. Fusion cooking caught on big here and has never lost its steam. Many restaurants that started out as, say, Italian, have incorporated ingredients and cooking styles from Southeast Asia and North Africa, among other *haute* spots. Each wave of immigration has carried new ideas and flavors.

While restaurants of all descriptions are found across the city, certain neighborhoods are renowned for their specialties: Little Italy for its trattorias,

Chinatown for its Chinese and Vietnamese eateries, and the Danforth for its Greek tavernas. In recent months, King Street West has unexpectedly become the new hot spot for in-the-know gourmets, offering a bevy of new bistros and *boîtes*.

DINING NOTES Dining out does not have to be an expensive venture, but the tax level is high. Meals are subject to the 8% provincial sales tax and to the 7% GST. In other words, tax and tip together can add 30% to your bill. Restaurants normally leave tipping to the diners' discretion, unless there are six or more people at the table. The usual amount for good service is 15%, jumping to 20% at the pricier establishments. The price of a bottle of wine is generally quite high because of the tax on imports; get around it by ordering an Ontario vintage—local wines enjoy a rising international reputation. Remember that there is a 10% tax on alcohol, whatever you're sipping.

NOTES ON THE REVIEWS Restaurants are grouped by neighborhood and listed alphabetically under the following main-course price ranges (not counting tax and tip): very expensive, C$30 (US$21) and up; expensive, C$20 to $29 (US$14–$20); and moderate, C$10 to $19 (US$7–$13). At inexpensive restaurants, it's possible to eat an entire meal for C$15 (US$11) or less. Many restaurants' offerings veer into higher and lower categories, so the ranges are general guidelines. Keep in mind that many

Where to Dine in Downtown

Agora **6**
Avalon **25**
Barberian's **38**
Biff's **50**
Blowfish Restaurant & Sake Bar **19**
Brassaii **23**
Bymark **45**
Canoe Restaurant & Bar **44**
Cities **16**
Citron **17**
Courthouse Market Grille **42**
Crush **22**
Eau **20**
Ecco La **1**
Epic **46**
Far Niente **47**
The Fifth **33**
Fortune Cookie **28**
Fressen **14**
Happy Seven **3**
Hiro Sushi **53**
HotHouse Cafe **52**
Juice for Life **12**
Jump Cafe & Bar **48**
La Bodega **5**
La Palette **2**
Lai Wah Heen **36**
Le Papillon **51**
Le Select **9**
Left Bank **13**
Lee Garden **4**
Monsoon **32**
Montréal Bistro & Jazz Club **54**
Oro **37**
Penelope **31**
Peter Pan **8**
Queen Mother Cafe **35**
Rain **29**
The Rivoli **11**
Rodney's Oyster House **26**
Rosewater Supper Club **41**
Sang Ho **7**
Senses **27**
Shopsy's **49**
Susur **21**
Swan **18**
Taro Grill **15**
360 Revolving Restaurant **30**
Torch Bistro **39**
Tortilla Flats **10**
Tundra **34**
Young Thailand **40**
YYZ **24**
ZooM Caffe & Bar **43**

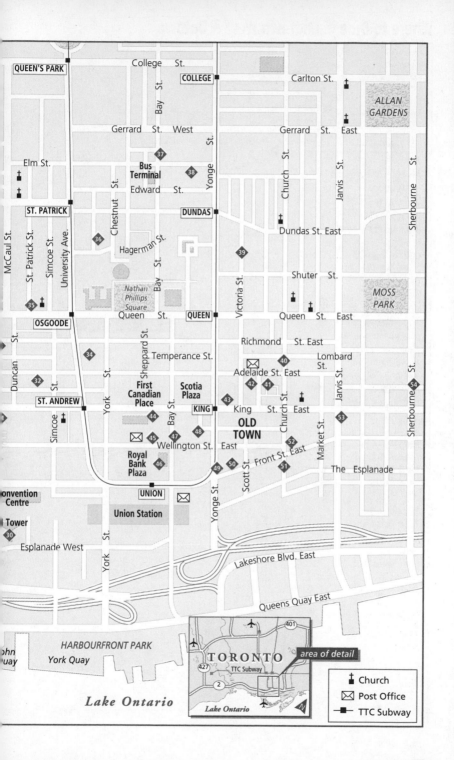

77

Where to Dine in Midtown West & Uptown

Annapurna Vegetarian
  Restaurant **1**
Annona **14**
Bistro 990 **32**
Bloor Street Diner **26**
Boba **15**
Café Nervosa **24**
Colony Kitchen **11**
Goldfish **4**
Gus **31**
Il Posto Nuovo **22**
Indian Rice Factory **2**
Jacques Bistro du Parc **23**
Japan Deli **27**
Joso's **17**
Kensington Kitchen **6**
Lakes **19**
Lox, Stock & Bagel **21**
Matignon **30**
Messis **7**
Mistura **3**
Nataraj **4**
Opus **9**
Pangaea **25**
Patriot **12**
Pho Hung **10**
Rebel House **20**
Rouge **5**
Serra **4**
Sotto Sotto **16**
Splendido Bar and Grill **8**
SpringRolls **28**
Thai Magic **18**
Truffles **13**
Wish **29**

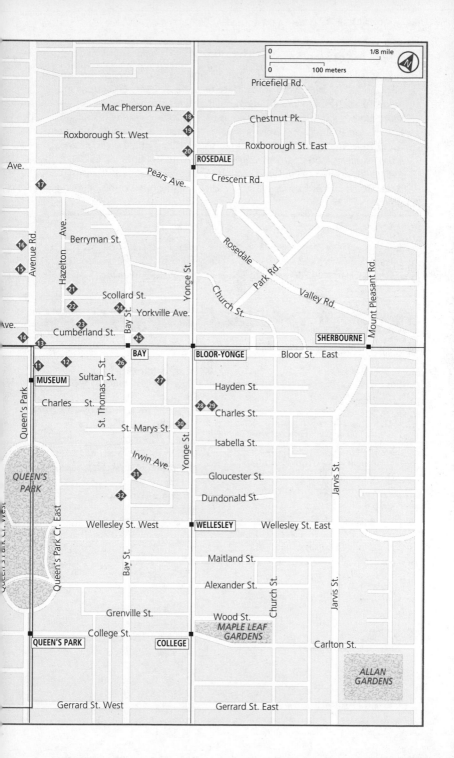

MAP KEY

- Mac Pherson Ave.
- Roxborough St. West
- **ROSEDALE**
- Pears Ave.
- Ave.
- Berryman St.
- Hazelton Ave.
- Scollard St.
- Yorkville Ave.
- Cumberland St.
- Ave.
- **BAY**
- **MUSEUM**
- Sultan St.
- Charles St.
- St. Thomas St.
- St. Marys St.
- Irwin Ave.
- **QUEEN'S PARK**
- Wellesley St. West
- Queen's Park Cr. East
- Grenville St.
- College St.
- **QUEEN'S PARK**
- **COLLEGE**
- Gerrard St. West
- Bay St.

Pricefield Rd.
Chestnut Pk.
Roxborough St. East
Crescent Rd.
Rosedale
Park Rd.
Valley Rd.
Church St.
Mount Pleasant Rd.
SHERBOURNE
BLOOR-YONGE
Bloor St. East
Hayden St.
Charles St.
Isabella St.
Gloucester St.
Dundonald St.
Jarvis St.
WELLESLEY
Wellesley St. East
Maitland St.
Alexander St.
Church St.
Jarvis St.
Wood St.
MAPLE LEAF GARDENS
Carlton St.
ALLAN GARDENS
Gerrard St. East

Yonge St.

0   1/8 mile
0   100 meters

Tips A Note on Smoking

Almost all Toronto restaurants are nonsmoking, the result of an anti-smoking bylaw that went into effect on June 1, 2001. Exceptions are made for patios and separately ventilated dining rooms. Some restaurants chose to designate themselves as bars to get around the restriction, but this led to another problem; they had to ban people under the age of 19 from the premises. Restaurateurs vowed to fight the regulation, which subjects both patrons and establishments to fines of C$200 to C$5,000 (US$140–$3,500) for infractions, but they've been unsuccessful to date. When making a reservation, ask about the restaurant's smoking policy.

restaurants change their menus and policies at a moment's notice. If a listing says a restaurant doesn't accept reservations, but you have your heart set on eating there, it doesn't hurt to call and ask if a reservation (or an exception) could be made.

1 Restaurants by Cuisine

AMERICAN
Far Niente 🏵🏵 (Downtown West, $$$, p. 88)
Jump Cafe & Bar 🏵🏵 (Downtown West, $$$, p. 89)

ASIAN
Fortune Cookie 🏵 (Downtown West, $$, p. 92)
Monsoon 🏵 (Downtown West, $$$$, p. 86)
Queen Mother Cafe (Downtown West, $, p. 95)
Rain 🏵 (Downtown West, $$$, p. 89)
SpringRolls (Midtown West, $, p. 107)

BELGIAN
Café Brussel (The East End, $$$, p. 108)

BISTRO
Biff's 🏵🏵 (Downtown East, $$$, p. 96)
Brassaii 🏵🏵🏵 (Downtown West, $$, p. 90)
Cities (Downtown West, $$, p. 91)

Crush 🏵 (Downtown West, $$, p. 91)
Lakes 🏵 (Uptown, $$$, p. 112)
La Palette 🏵 (Downtown West, $$, p. 92)
Le Sélect Bistro (Downtown West, $$, p. 92)
Lolo 🏵🏵 (Uptown, $$, p. 113)
Pony (Downtown West, $$, p. 94)
Stork on the Roof 🏵 (Uptown, $$, p. 113)
Torch Bistro (Downtown East, $$$, p. 97)
Wish 🏵 (Downtown East, $$, p. 99)

CAJUN
Southern Accent (Midtown West, $$, p. 105)

CANADIAN
Canoe Restaurant & Bar 🏵 (Downtown West, $$$$, p. 85)
Patriot 🏵🏵 (Midtown West, $$$, p. 102)
Splendido Bar and Grill (Midtown West, $$$, p. 102)
Tundra 🏵🏵 (Downtown West, $$$$, p. 86)

Key to Abbreviations: $$$$ = Very Expensive $$$ = Expensive $$ = Moderate $ = Inexpensive

Where to Dine from Chinatown to Bloor Street

Annapurna Vegetarian
  Restaurant 9
Annona 15
Boba 16
Chiado 1
Ecco La 21
Goldfish 11
Happy Seven 22
Kalendar 5
Kensington Kitchen 18
La Bodega 25
Lalibela 7
Lee Garden 24
Messis 20

Nataraj 10
Opus 13
Pho Hung 14
Pony 3
Rouge 12
Sang Ho 23
Serra 11
Sottovoce 4
Southern Accent 8
Splendido Bar & Grill 19
Truffles 17
Veni Vidi Vici 2
Xacutti 6

CHINESE

Grand Yatt ☆ (North of the City,
  $$, p. 116)
Happy Seven (Downtown West, $,
  p. 95)
Lai Wah Heen ☆☆☆ (Downtown
  West, $$$, p. 89)
Lee Garden (Downtown West, $,
  p. 95)
Sang Ho ☆ (Downtown West, $$,
  p. 94)

CONTINENTAL

Café Societa ☆ (Downtown West,
  $$, p. 91)

Centro ☆☆ (Uptown, $$$$,
  p. 110)
HotHouse Cafe (Downtown East,
  $$, p. 98)
Opus (Midtown West, $$$$,
  p. 100)
Oro (Downtown West, $$$, p. 89)
360 Revolving Restaurant (Down-
  town West, $$$$, p. 86)
Truffles ☆ (Midtown West, $$$$,
  p. 101)

DELI

Lox, Stock & Bagel (Midtown West, $, p. 106)

Shopsy's (Downtown East, $, p. 100)

ECLECTIC

Avalon 𝆏/𝆏 (Downtown West, $$$$, p. 84)

Citron (Downtown West, $$, p. 91)

The Fifth 𝆏/𝆏 (Downtown West, $$$$, p. 85)

Goldfish 𝆏𝆏 (Midtown West, $$, p. 103)

Messis 𝆏 (Midtown West, $$, p. 104)

Mildred Pierce 𝆏𝆏 (Downtown West, $$, p. 93)

Octavia (The East End, $$, p. 108)

Rouge 𝆏𝆏 (Midtown West, $$, p. 104)

Swan (Downtown West, $$, p. 94)

Taro Grill 𝆏 (Downtown West, $$, p. 94)

ETHIOPIAN

Lalibela (Midtown West, $, p. 106)

FRENCH

Auberge du Pommier 𝆏 (Uptown, $$$$, p. 110)

Bistro 990 𝆏𝆏𝆏 (Midtown West, $$$$, p. 100)

Jacques Bistro du Parc (Midtown West, $$, p. 104)

La Bodega (Downtown West, $$, p. 92)

Matignon (Midtown West, $$, p. 104)

Quartier 𝆏 (Uptown, $$$, p. 112)

FUSION

Boba 𝆏 (Midtown West, $$$, p. 101)

Colony Kitchen 𝆏𝆏 (Midtown West, $$, p. 103)

Eau (Downtown West, $$$$, p. 85)

Pangaea 𝆏 (Midtown West, $$$, p. 102)

The Rivoli 𝆏𝆏 (Downtown West, $, p. 96)

Susur 𝆏𝆏𝆏 (Downtown West, $$$$, p. 86)

Veni Vidi Vici 𝆏𝆏 (Downtown West, $$, p. 94)

GREEK

Astoria (The East End, $, p. 109)

Avli 𝆏 (The East End, $, p. 109)

Christina's (The East End, $$, p. 108)

Gus 𝆏 (Midtown West, $$, p. 103)

Mezes (The East End, $, p. 110)

Myth 𝆏𝆏 (The East End, $$, p. 108)

Octavia (The East End, $$, p. 108)

Ouzeri (The East End, $, p. 110)

Pan on the Danforth 𝆏 (The East End, $$, p. 108)

Penelope (Downtown West, $, p. 95)

INDIAN

Indian Rice Factory 𝆏 (Midtown West, $, p. 105)

Nataraj (Midtown West, $, p. 106)

Xacutti 𝆏𝆏 (Downtown West, $$$, p. 90)

INTERNATIONAL

Annona 𝆏 (Midtown West, $$$, p. 101)

Brassaii 𝆏𝆏𝆏 (Downtown West, $$, p. 90)

Bymark (Downtown West, $$$$, p. 85)

Courthouse Market Grille (Downtown East, $$$, p. 97)

Epic 𝆏𝆏 (Downtown West, $$$, p. 88)

North 44 𝆏𝆏𝆏 (Uptown, $$$$, p. 111)

Rosewater Supper Club 𝆏 (Downtown East, $$$, p. 97)

Scaramouche 𝆏 (Uptown, $$$$, p. 111)

Senses 🦊🦊 (Downtown West, $$$, p. 90)

Terra 🦊🦊 (North of the City, $$$, p. 116)

YYZ 🦊🦊 (Downtown West, $$$$, p. 87)

ZooM Caffe & Bar 🦊 (Downtown East, $$$, p. 98)

ITALIAN

Amore Trattoria 🦊🦊 (Uptown, $$, p. 113)

Café Nervosa (Midtown West, $$, p. 103)

Dante's 🦊🦊 (North of the City, $, p. 116)

Ecco La (Downtown West, $$, p. 92)

Grano 🦊 (Uptown, $$, p. 113)

Il Posto Nuovo (Midtown West, $$$, p. 101)

La Bruschetta 🦊 (Uptown, $$$, p. 111)

Mistura 🦊 (Midtown West, $$$, p. 102)

Serra (Midtown West, $, p. 107)

Sotto Sotto 🦊🦊 (Midtown West, $$, p. 105)

Terroni (Downtown East, $$, p. 99)

Veni Vidi Vici 🦊🦊 (Downtown West, $$, p. 94)

JAPANESE/SUSHI

Blowfish Restaurant & Sake Bar 🦊🦊 (Downtown West, $$$, p. 87)

Hiro Sushi 🦊 (Downtown East, $$$, p. 97)

Japan Deli (Midtown West, $, p. 106)

LAOTIAN

Vanipha Lanna 🦊🦊 (Uptown, $$, p. 114)

LIGHT FARE

Bloor Street Diner (Midtown West, $, p. 105)

Hannah's Kitchen (Uptown, $, p. 114)

Hello Toast (Downtown East, $, p. 99)

HotHouse Cafe (Downtown East, $$, p. 98)

Kalendar 🦊🦊 (Downtown West, $, p. 95)

Peter Pan (Downtown West, $$, p. 93)

Rebel House (Uptown, $, p. 115)

Sottovoce (Downtown West, $, p. 96)

Terroni (Downtown East, $$, p. 99)

MEDITERRANEAN

Agora 🦊 (Downtown West, $$$, p. 87)

Kensington Kitchen 🦊🦊 (Midtown West, $, p. 106)

Millie's Bistro 🦊🦊 (Uptown, $$$, p. 112)

Myth 🦊🦊 (The East End, $$, p. 108)

Octavia (The East End, $$, p. 108)

MIDDLE EASTERN

Mezzetta (Uptown, $$, p. 113)

PORTUGUESE

Chiado (Downtown West, $$$, p. 88)

QUEBECOIS

Le Papillon (Downtown East, $, p. 99)

Montréal Bistro & Jazz Club (Downtown East, $$, p. 99)

SEAFOOD

Joso's (Midtown West, $$, p. 104)

Rodney's Oyster House (Downtown West, $$, p. 94)

Sang Ho 🦊 (Downtown West, $$, p. 94)

STEAK

Barberian's 🦊 (Downtown West, $$$$, p. 84)

TEX-MEX

Tortilla Flats (Downtown West, $, p. 96)

THAI

Thai Magic *ᴿ* (Uptown, $$$, p. 112)

Vanipha Lanna *ᴿᴿ* (Uptown, $$, p. 114)

Young Thailand *ᴿᴿ* (Downtown East, $, p. 100)

VEGETARIAN

Annapurna Vegetarian Restaurant (Midtown West, $, p. 114)

Fressen (Downtown West, $$, p. 114)

Juice for Life (Downtown West, $, p. 114)

VIETNAMESE

Pho Hung (Midtown West, $, p. 106)

2 Downtown West

This is where you will find Toronto's greatest concentration of great restaurants. **Little Italy,** which runs along **College Street,** and **Chinatown,** which radiates from **Spadina Avenue,** has more restaurants than any other parts of the city.

You'll see a lot of high-price, low-quality eateries in the area, too. There also tends to be more attitude from wait staffs, particularly along the gourmet ghetto of **Queen Street West.** I'm a firm believer that even the best food can't make up for shoddy service, so the restaurants I've selected generally get high marks in both categories. Because service is so important to me, you won't find reviews of restaurants where it's totally substandard. A case in point is Little Italy's **Trattoria Giancarlo,** which has gained renown for its very good cooking and its celeb sightings. Unfortunately, you pretty much have to be a star to get even a glass of water brought to your table. Personally, no matter how charming a meal is, I find that lousy service leaves a bad taste in my mouth.

VERY EXPENSIVE

Avalon *ᴿᴿ* ECLECTIC   Follow the slim marble staircase into the elegant, compact dining room. Careful attention to detail is clear, whether in the spray of fresh flowers on each table or the daily chef's menu. (The regular menu changes with the seasons.) Avalon has one of the most inventive kitchens in the city, and it demonstrates its creativity through pairings of flavors rather than a showy multiplicity of ingredients. Main courses favor fish and fowl, such as steamed Boston fluke and Alaskan king crab with a sweet-pea sauce, or lightly smoked Moulard duck breast with pommes Anna and a blackcurrant coulis. Desserts include treats like pear-and-elderflower sorbet and a wide selection of cheeses. The globetrotting wine list represents New World and Old.

270 Adelaide St. W. (at John St.). ℭ **416/979-9918.** Reservations required. Main courses C$29–$40 (US$20–$28). AE, DC, MC, V. Thurs noon–2pm; Mon–Sat 5:30–10pm. Subway: St. Andrew.

Barberian's *ᴿ* STEAK   Not getting enough protein? Get thee to Harry Barberian's upscale steakhouse, which has been going strong since 1959 (his son, Arron, has since taken over). The room is cozy in a clubby way, with dark woods, framed newspapers, and pre-Confederation doodads. The menu rarely changes, but you won't hear any grousing—the crowd is too busy slurping martinis. The highlights are the eight steaks, from 9-ounce sirloin to 23-ounce porterhouse, all served with rice and spuds. The less traditional can partake of dishes like cheese or beef fondue for two, which is on the late-night menu (10pm–midnight). For all intents and purposes, there is only one dessert: Grand Marnier soufflé for two. The wine list is about 1,000 strong, so bring your reading specs. Celebrity sightings aren't uncommon, but autograph seeking is frowned upon.

7 Elm St. © **416/597-0335**. Reservations required. Main courses C$22–$37 (US$15–$26). AE, DC, MC, V. Mon–Fri noon–2:30pm; daily 5pm–midnight. Subway: Dundas.

Bymark *(Overrated* INTERNATIONAL   I feel terrible: For years I've hoped that Mark McEwan, the excellent chef behind North 44—one of my favorite restaurants in any city (p. 111)—would open a restaurant in downtown Toronto. Now that he has, I can hardly believe my disappointment. While the food here is very good and the design is subtly beautiful, the service is lacking and the atmosphere is abominable. If you don't mind your very expensive meal being disrupted repeatedly by drunken louts in suits at the neighboring tables, you've found your restaurant! This is one of the hot see-and-be-seen spots of the moment, and, if you're determined to stop in, take my advice and bypass Bymark's dining room for its bar.

66 Wellington St. W. © **416/777-1144**. Reservations required. Main courses C$30–$48 (US$21–$34). AE, DC, MC, V. Mon–Fri 11:30am–2:30pm; Mon–Sat 5–10pm. Subway: King.

Canoe Restaurant & Bar *ℛ* CANADIAN   The inspiring view makes this the place to see Toronto lit up at night. The interior isn't so shabby, either, with polished wooden floors and furnishings. Corporate types predominate, not only because Canoe is in the Financial District, but also because the prices best suit expense accounts. The meat-heavy menu showcases modern Canadian cuisine. Grilled veal tenderloin served with acorn squash and warm sage-infused goat cheese vies for attention with Maritime sea scallops served with a tartlet of caramelized potatoes and double-smokes bacon. A few "spa inspired" dishes are lower in fat. The wine list only scratches the surface—roughly two-thirds of the bottles in stock aren't included—so if you're craving a certain vintage, be sure to ask.

54th floor, Toronto Dominion Tower, 66 Wellington St. W. © **416/364-0054**. www.canoerestaurant.com. Reservations required. Main courses C$24–$40 (US$17–$28). AE, DC, MC, V. Mon–Fri 11:45am–2:30pm and 5–10:30pm. Subway: King.

Eau FUSION   There's a certain segment of the Toronto population that likes to think that their city is the New York of the North. That type would surely gravitate to Eau, one of the new restaurants that's enlivening the formerly sedate King Street West area. It's cool, it's stylish, and it's way overpriced. The cocktail menu is funny without meaning to be: With martinis like the "bubble-eau-seven" (peach and pineapple juices with vodka) and "the-big-eau" (vodka, champagne and ice wine) costing C$13 to $18 (US$9.10–$13) apiece, there must be some kind of joke afoot. But there is good news here: The kitchen does a fine job with appetizers like blue-crab-and-avocado salad and entrees like roasted duck breast drizzled with a glaze of sour cherry and bourbon. Furthermore, while the gorgeous staff do pose a bit, they are actually very sweet and helpful.

609 King St. W. © **416/203-9399**. Reservations strongly recommended. Main courses C$27–$39 (US$19–$27). AE, DC, MC, V. Wed–Sat 5:30–10:30pm. Subway: St Andrew.

The Fifth *ℛℛ* ECLECTIC   *Je pense que Le Cinquième n'est pas comme des autres.* Ah, *pardon,* was I just speaking French? I must have been confused by the menu at The Fifth, which insists on listing all its plates *en français* and *en anglais. Crème Arlequin* is translated as—get ready for this—crème Arlequin (no, I'm not joking). *Ça va?* In fairness, though, the kitchen does serve stellar fare, like fluke stuffed with scallop mousse. The delectable food and first-rate service attract an upscale, chic crowd. Now if they could just fire the translator . . .

225 Richmond St. W. © **416/979-3005**. www.easyandthefifth.com. Reservations required. 3-course prix-fixe menu C$80 (US$56). Thurs–Sat 6pm–midnight. Subway: Osgoode.

Monsoon ⚜ ASIAN   Monsoon is more famous for its award-winning interior design than for its food. That's a pity, because, while the brown-on-black Zen-like setting and the fabulously flattering lighting are easy on the eye, the cooking is subtly sensual. Sophisticated palates are familiar with Thai, Chinese, Japanese, and Indian flavors, but it's unusual to find them so seductively intertwined with North American staples—take for example the exquisite beef tenderloin in a Cabernet-teriyaki reduction that is teamed up with wasabi mashed potatoes. The wine list runs the gamut from French Bordeaux to Australian shiraz.

100 Simcoe St. © **416/979-7172**. www.monsoonrestaurant.ca. Reservations required. Main courses C$21–$37 (US$15–$26). AE, DC, MC, V. Mon–Fri noon–2:30pm; Mon–Sat 5:30pm–midnight. Subway: St. Andrew.

Susur ⚜⚜⚜ FUSION   If you visited Toronto a few years ago, you might have had the good fortune to dine at an exquisite restaurant called Lotus. The eatery's chef and owner, Susur Lee, broke the hearts of the city's foodies when he decided to close it and travel abroad. After some stints in foreign kitchens—he got as far away as Singapore—Lee is back and better than ever. Susur is a delight. For such a high-end establishment, its decor is refreshingly low-key, with stark white walls and oyster-pale upholstery warmed with colored lights. There is no pretension here, in either the ambience or the fine service.

But the biggest draw is what's on the plate. Lee serves stellar cuisine in the true fusion spirit, blending Asian and Western ingredients, cooking methods, and presentation. The menu changes frequently, with bold, savory offerings like rare venison loin with Gorgonzola–haw berry–red wine sauce. The cooking is complex, and the wine list, while pricey, has been put together with extreme care. When in doubt, ask the well-informed serving staff for recommendations.

601 King St. W. © **416/603-2205**. Reservations required. Main courses C$29–$43 (US$20–$30). AE, MC, V. Mon–Sat 6–10pm. Subway: St. Andrew, then streetcar west to Bathurst St. and walk 1 block west to Portland St.

360 Revolving Restaurant *Overrated* CONTINENTAL   Let's be frank: Most people do not come here for the food. The view's the thing, a breathtaking, awe-inspiring panorama that will make you see the city in a new light. Unfortunately, the kitchen doesn't keep pace—it offers uninspiring fare like cold crab and shrimp salad on Bibb lettuce. The highlight of the dessert list is a chocolate rendition of the CN Tower. The wine list makes for interesting viewing, with its collection of three-figure vintages, though there are a few choices by the glass.

CN Tower, 301 Front St. W. © **416/362-5411**. Reservations required. Main courses C$25–$40 (US$18–$28). AE, DC, MC, V. May–Sept daily 10:30am–2:30pm; year-round daily 4:30–10:30pm. Subway: Union.

Tundra ⚜⚜ CANADIAN   A key element of the Hilton's recent C$25 million (US$18 million) renovation was the creation of this luxurious restaurant just off its foyer. Sophisticated and opulent, the restaurant is designed to evoke elements of the Canadian landscape. How does one suggest the majesty of, say, a giant redwood? With columns wrapped in semi-transparent fabric and lit from within, of course! (The stunning result is like a gargantuan Naguchi lamp.) Every detail, from the one-armed wing chairs to the Frette linens, is beautifully executed.

The sense of theater doesn't stop with the design—the cuisine is just as artful. Arctic char (a fish that's often called a hybrid of salmon and trout) is paired with Malapeque oysters and fried leeks; Nova Scotia lobster mates with tomato-avocado-bean salad and Yukon Gold potatoes. The results are elegantly complex. While the wine list is exhaustive, don't hesitate to ask for recommendations— service is well informed and helpful.

Hilton Toronto, 145 Richmond St. W. ⓒ **416/860-6800.** Reservations strongly recommended. Main courses C$28–$40 (US$20–$28). AE, DC, MC, V. Daily 6:30–10:30am; Mon–Fri 11:30am–2pm; daily 5:30–11pm. Subway: Osgoode.

YYZ ⋒⋒ INTERNATIONAL   If you visited Toronto in 2001 or earlier, you might have had the good fortune to dine at the Mercer Street Grill. While that restaurant is no more, its owner, Simon Bower, has created a striking new spot in YYZ. Named after the call letters of Toronto's airport, the setting brings to mind a futuristic lounge—all chrome, steel, and glass. While the palette veers to the cool (unlike the city's other modernist spaces, there's not so much as a hint of greenery to temper its android appeal), this is now home to some of the hottest cooking in town. For starters, rare duck breast is paired with both spicy ginger and sweet pineapple. The substantial mains, like the rack of lamb with a celery-root-and-potato mash and mint purée, are artfully done. Do try to save space for dessert: The warm pumpkin tart is a great way to finish.

345 Adelaide St. W. ⓒ **416/599-3399.** Reservations required. Main courses C$26–$34 (US$18–$24). AE, MC, V. Mon–Sat 5–10:30pm. Subway: Osgoode.

EXPENSIVE

Agora ⋒ MEDITERRANEAN   I'm biased—restaurants attached to larger institutions usually scare me off. Agora at the Art Gallery of Ontario is an exception. Located in the beautiful Tannenbaum sculpture gallery, and open only for lunch and brunch, Agora serves food that's inventive without being artsy. It's worth a trip even if you're not visiting the gallery. The menu does have its precious moments, like "Still life with aubergine," but the food is uniformly delightful. Some dishes play it straight with a Continental flair, like grilled niçoise-style tuna with French green beans. The weekend brunch glams up scrambled eggs with fresh truffle shavings and chives; the cinnamon crepes with an almond-ricotta filling and apricot coulis are a treat.

At the Art Gallery of Ontario, 317 Dundas St. W. ⓒ **416/977-0414.** Reservations recommended for lunch. Main courses C$12–$20 (US$8.40–$14). AE, DC, MC, V. Tues–Fri noon–2:30pm; Sat–Sun 11am–3pm. Subway: St. Patrick.

Blowfish Restaurant & Sake Bar ⋒⋒ JAPANESE/SUSHI   Taking its name from a high-risk Japanese delicacy, this new hot spot only adds to the glamour of King Street West. Tucked inside a former bank building whose soaring ceilings lend the room true grandeur, this restaurant is a rare pleasure—just like the blowfish. Eateries in trendy areas come and go, but Blowfish's impressive attention to detail makes me hope that this one will be around for a while.

The menu features the expected sushi and sashimi, and the quality and presentation is uniformly excellent. But there are lots of other options, from the starters (barbecued salmon skin and green salad make a stellar pair in peppery dressing) to the mains (sea bass or black cod in a sweet miso marinade). Even the free bowls of warm and salty edamame are delicious, and the service is friendly and helpful. My one caveat to diners is to dine here on the early side, since the restaurant transforms into a lounge at 11pm.

668 King St. W. ℂ **416/860-0606.** www.blowfishrestaurant.com. Reservations strongly recommended. Main courses C$14–$24 (US$9.80–$17). AE, MC, V. Mon–Sat 5pm–2am. Subway: St Andrew, then streetcar west to Bathurst.

Chiado PORTUGUESE   Alone in this Mediterranean-obsessed part of town, Chiado serves modern Portuguese cuisine. Designed to evoke opulence, with marble floors, oil paintings, and fresh orchids, it draws a sophisticated crowd. Servers are models of Euro professionalism, attentive without hovering. The menu favors seafood, from starters—such as grilled squid with roasted peppers—to entrees, such as poached or grilled salted cod. Fresh fish is flown in daily. The fowl and game dishes include a choice of braised rabbit or capon. Don't skimp on the lovingly prepared sweets. The wine list is a treat. It includes many unfamiliar but rich and complex wines, most priced in the bargain range.

484 College St. (at Concorde Ave.). ℂ **416/538-1910.** Reservations required. Main courses C$17–$30 (US$12–$21). AE, DC, MC, V. Mon–Sat noon–3pm; Mon–Thurs 5–10pm; Fri–Sat 5pm–midnight. Subway: Queen's Park, then any streetcar west to Bathurst St.

Epic ☆☆ INTERNATIONAL   Not that I would ever counsel a visitor to stay within the confines of his or her hotel, but this stunning restaurant at the Fairmont Royal York is definitely worth a visit. The scene here is one of unabashed luxury, with velvety banquettes and Murano glass chandeliers. The attentive service is in keeping with the elegant atmosphere—don't come here if you don't want to be pampered.

The menu holds up its end of the deal, with luxurious ingredients that are cleverly matched up. The starters set the tone—think Dungeness crab salad with Segruva caviar, or a seafood tower that is built with the freshest lobster, scallops, and oysters. Mains are equally well turned out, varying from truffle and polenta–stuffed pheasant with asparagus and shallots, to the morel-crusted venison loin with seared Quebec foie gras. One of my favorite dishes—the tempura-fried halibut and hand-cut fries (an upscale version of fish 'n' chips)—is available only at lunch.

Fairmont Royal York, 100 Front St. W. ℂ **416/860-6949.** Reservations recommended. Main courses C$22–$34 (US$15–$24). AE, DC, MC, V. Mon–Fri 7–10am, noon–2pm, 5:30–10pm (till 11pm on Fri); Sat 7–11am and 5:30–11pm; Sun 7am–2pm and 5:30–10pm. Subway: Union.

Far Niente ☆☆ AMERICAN   A hangout favored by the suited set, this restaurant offers fine cuisine in a casual setting. The room recalls California, with an earthy palette, mounds of greenery, wine racks, and simple wooden tables and chairs. The kitchen uses garden-fresh ingredients and a light touch. The menu designates many staples—including tuna steak, grilled salmon, and even a Caesar salad—as "living well" dishes, which have reduced fat, cholesterol, and calories. You might try Sonoma spinach salad with cherry tomatoes, button mushrooms, and bean sprouts; the pumpkin ravioli with cranberries and pecans in apple cider butter sauce; or the skillet-seared sea bass in a saffron-vanilla sauce with ginger-scented veggies and mashed Yukon Gold potatoes. Steaks are a specialty, with filet mignon and New York strip loin available in 6- to 14-ounce cuts.

Downstairs is **Soul of the Vine,** a wine bar that has its own menu, mainly appetizers and pasta. The room can get loud and smoky, so serious eaters should stay upstairs.

187 Bay St. (at Wellington St.). ℂ **416/214-9922.** Reservations recommended. Main courses C$18–$36 (US$13–$25). AE, DC, MC, V. Mon–Fri 11:30am–11pm; Sat–Sun 5–11pm. Subway: King.

Jump Cafe & Bar 🎝🎝 AMERICAN   Jump is, appropriately enough, always hopping. A sprawling space in Commerce Court, it can be tricky to find. Just follow the buzz—as the decibel level rises (above romantic, but not uncomfortable), you'll know you're on the right track. Power brokers drop by for lunch or after-work drinks. The dinner scene is a mix of celebratory couples and suits in deal-making mode. The restaurant is such a see-and-be-seen spot that you might suspect it's all show and no substance. Actually, the food is anything but an afterthought. To start, consider steamed mussels in ginger-and-coconut-milk broth, or grilled tiger shrimps on Thai mango-peanut salad. The menu features "suitable" dishes like grilled 10-ounce New York Black Angus steak with Yukon Gold fries, salsa, and mushroom gravy. The more adventurous have other choices, such as roasted sea bass with fragrant coconut basmati rice and green curry, or osso buco with spinach-and-lemon risotto. The wine list favors the New World, and there are a fair number of selections by the glass. Luxe desserts will set your diet back by about a month. Service is smooth, and the only complaint I could possibly make is that Jump never seems to settle down.

1 Wellington St. W. © 416/363-3400. Reservations required. Main courses C$19–$32 (US$13–$22). AE, DC, MC, V. Mon–Fri 11:30am–11pm; Sat 4:30–11pm. Subway: King.

Lai Wah Heen 🎝🎝🎝 CHINESE   This is one hotel dining room where you'll find more locals than visitors. The interior is vintage Art Deco; spare pictograms dominate the walls of the two-level space. A suited-up crowd dominates at lunch; at dinner, a few dolled-up couples manage to sneak in. The massive menu is mainly Cantonese, with some Szechwan specialties. It offers more than a dozen shark's fin soups, from thick broth with bamboo fungi to Alaska king crab bisque. Abalone gets similar attention, shredded and stir-fried with bean sprouts or braised with fresh vegetables and oyster sauce. Those with tamer tastes (or restricted budgets) can choose from meat or noodle dishes; the dim sum list alone goes on for several pages. There are several lunch and dinner prix-fixe specials, which offer five or six dishes for C$38 (US$27) and up.

In the Metropolitan Hotel, 110 Chestnut St. © 416/977-9899. Reservations recommended. Main courses C$16–$30 (US$11–$21). AE, DC, MC, V. Daily 11:30am–3pm; Sun–Thurs 5:30–10:30pm; Fri–Sat 5:30–11pm. Subway: St. Patrick.

Oro CONTINENTAL   The trappings of modern luxury set the scene, with blond wood, a tile floor, and a substantial fireplace that warms that room (figuratively if not always literally). In its Eaton Centre neighborhood, Oro is uniquely sophisticated. Softly lit tables sit far apart—this is the perfect spot for a romantic rendezvous. The menu ventures further and further from its Italianate roots, with showstoppers like West-meets-East hoisin-tamarind glazed pork tenderloin accompanied by cumin-scented red onion purée. Desserts like the white chocolate cheesecake bombe are equally delightful. The lengthy wine list leans toward Italy and America, with only a select few by the glass. The oft-praised service is relaxed but attentive.

45 Elm St. © 416/597-0155. www.ororestaurant.com. Reservations recommended. Main courses C$18–$40 (US$13–$28). AE, DC, MC, V. Mon–Fri noon–2:30pm; Mon–Sat 5:30–10:30pm. Subway: Dundas.

Rain 🎝 ASIAN   One of Toronto's newest hot spots, Rain has gained a certain notoriety for employing a bouncer at the door; word has it that the bouncer determines who's chic enough to make it into this den of cool, reservations be damned. The *Toronto Star*'s restaurant critic was turned away, despite having a reservation; most famously, pop star Nelly Furtado was refused entry to her own private party (the restaurant's owners refuse to discuss the incident). You either love it or you hate it—Rain evokes strong emotions. Everyone agrees that the decor is a seductive hit, with its waterfall walls, backlit frosted-glass bars and screens, and sophisticated low black banquettes. The menu is equally sleek, albeit a tad confusing: Instead of dividing appetizers from entrees, it jumbles dishes together, with only their price tags indicating their relative size. The cooking is lovely, with some standouts like five-spice Peking duck roll, and miso black cod atop tatsoi greens. While the service is adequate, it's a little clunky for such a swank place.

19 Mercer St. ℂ **416/599-7246.** Reservations required. Main courses C$10–$30 (US$7–$21). AE, MC, V. Tues–Sat 5:30–11pm. Subway: St. Andrew.

Senses *ℝℝ* INTERNATIONAL   Harry Wu, who already has two excellent restaurants—Lai Wah Heen (p. 89) and Hemispheres—at the Metropolitan Hotel, is the man behind this venture, which is located at his new SoHo Metropolitan Hotel (p. 56). Senses encompasses a bakery, and a gourmet food emporium (see p. 186 in chapter 8). Dining here is an experience for—what else?—all the senses. The serene sandy tones are serious eye candy, the background music soothes, and velvety banquettes rub you the right way. Smell and taste get revved up for starters like the Spanish goat cheese empanada with olives and beet-root salad. The main-dish squab breasts with prawn sausage and wild rice pancake is beautifully executed. Service is extremely well informed and professional.

At the SoHo Metropolitan, 318 Wellington St. W. ℂ **416/961-0055.** www.senses.ca. Reservations strongly recommended. Main courses C$19–$46 (US$13–$32). AE, DC, MC, V. Mon–Fri 11:30am–2:30pm; Sat 11:30am–3pm; Mon–Sat 5–10pm. Subway: St. Andrew.

Xacutti *ℝℝ* INDIAN   There are a lot of reasons to love Xacutti (pronounced sha-koo-tee). One is that it brings a new and exotic flavor to the well-traveled Little Italy restaurant strip. Another is that the Indian-inspired cuisine is just so beautifully executed. Starters include galangal prawns in a lime-mint curry or baby greens in a kumquat vinaigrette; mains range from cardamom-smoked lamb with mango chutney and ginger frites to pan-fried cod with new potatoes, spinach and coconut-tomato curry. The weekend brunch menu is just as excellent, though it veers away from Indian food, serving up treats like blueberry pancakes with maple syrup and Devonshire cream or a wild-mushroom-and-goat-cheese omelet. The thoughtful service matches the cuisine.

503 College St. ℂ **416/323-3957.** Reservations strongly recommended. Main courses C$17–$34 (US$12–$24). AE, DC, MC, V. Mon–Fri 6:30pm–1am; Sat 10:30am–2pm; Sun 10:30am–3pm. Subway: Queen's Park, then streetcar west to Palmerston.

MODERATE

Brassaii *ℝℝℝ* *Value* BISTRO/INTERNATIONAL   This is my favorite among the Toronto restaurants that opened in 2003. Named for a 1920s French photographer—his black-and-white prints adorn the walls—Brassaii offers a picture-perfect setting. The long, cavernous dining room is decorated in dusky grey and black, and tall vases stand in the windows, each holding a single long-stemmed calla lily. The effect feels much like being inside a photograph, and the flattering lighting from the halogen spotlights that hang from the ceiling only enhance this image. Still, on King Street West these days, everyone looks cool (Eau, Blowfish, and others). But Brassaii still manages to stand out by offering both excellent cooking and brilliant service—and doing so for prices that are lower than most of its competition in the area. The kitchen really knows its stuff.

While the menu frequently changes, it might include entrees such as braised duck atop lentils and spinach, or shoulder of lamb with chickpeas and tomato. The desserts are not to be missed, particularly the elegant apple crumble with berries and caramel ice cream. The wine list is substantial, and there are some very good vintages available by the glass. Still, my favorite drink here is the Brassaii martini, which blends a couple of types of fruit juice with 7-Up and vodka. I know it sounds bizarre, but it's a deliciously sweet drink.

One more thing: Also unlike its competition, Brassaii is open for breakfast, lunch and dinner. Bon appétit, indeed.

461 King St. W. ℂ **416/598-4730.** Reservations recommended. Main courses C$14–$22 (US$9.80–$15). AE, MC, V. Mon–Sat 7am–11pm; Sun 11am–10pm. Subway: St. Andrew, then streetcar west to Spadina Ave.

Café Societa ✿ CONTINENTAL   The Lilliputian dining room is cramped, the menu is the shortest in the city, and yet the crowds can't stay away. Why? Simply because the food is seductive. The trick is in the unusual marriages of fruits and vegetables flavoring many of the dishes. Rosti and rhubarb compote enliven a veal chop, and it turns out that grilled calamari tastes better with citrus fruit. Who knew? The highlight of the triad of desserts is chocolate mousse with heavy cream and paper-thin pear shavings.

796 College St. ℂ **416/588-7490.** Reservations recommended. Main courses C$12–$21 (US$8.40–$15). MC, V. Sat–Sun 11am–3pm; daily 6–11pm. Subway: Queen's Park, then any streetcar west to Ossington Ave.

Cities BISTRO   This charming bistro, where a rococo Elvis presides over the bar, personifies the pleasures and problems of metropolitan life. It's overcrowded—19 tables for two cram the narrow room, forcing neighbors to rub elbows. The food, however, makes it all worthwhile. The menu is deliberately short, allowing the kitchen to focus hothouse-flower care on its featured selections: rack of lamb, Atlantic salmon, veal tenderloin. Starters, like three-mushroom salad, get equal attention.

859 Queen St. W. ℂ **416/599-7720.** Main courses C$12–$20 (US$8.40–$14). AE, MC, V. Daily noon–2:30pm and 5–10:30pm. Subway: Osgoode, then any streetcar west to Bathurst St.

Citron ECLECTIC   At once chic and attitude-free, Citron draws casual but hip 20-somethings. The menu borrows heavily from every corner of the globe, favoring seafood and vegetarian offerings. North African couscous stew, Tex-Mex lasagna, and Thai-spiced salmon compete for attention. For dessert, my sweet-tooth side recommends the divine white chocolate cheesecake.

813 Queen St. W. ℂ **416/504-2647.** Reservations not accepted. Main courses C$12–$20 (US$8.40–$14). AE, MC, V. Mon–Thurs 5–10:30pm; Fri–Sat 5–11pm. Subway: Osgoode, then any streetcar west to Bathurst St.

Crush ✿ BISTRO   This lively new spot is another reason that King Street West is now a major foodie destination. Crush is part bistro and part wine bar, and its atmosphere is appropriately convivial. The high-ceilinged, warehouse-like space has a huge open kitchen, so you can be entertained by the goings-on that are usually kept behind the scenes. Better still, you can be impressed by the results: The goat-cheese-and-tomato napoleon or the mussels on the half-shell topped with escargot butter make great opening acts. The juicy pork chop in Madeira sauce is a star is its own right. The wine list is diverse, with many varieties available by the glass (you can even choose whether to have a 3-ounce or 5-ounce serving, a boon for oenophiles who want to try new things). Service is smooth and obliging, making this a great place to go if you're planning on catching a show at one of the nearby theaters. The only potential problem with Crush is the decibel level: This is a lively spot, and warehouse spaces aren't known for great acoustics.

455 King St. W. ☎ **416/977-1234.** Reservations recommended. Main courses C$14–$25 (US$9.80–$18). AE, MC, V. Mon–Fri noon–10:30pm; Sat 5–10:30pm; Sun 5–10pm. Subway: St. Andrew, then streetcar west to Spadina Ave.

Ecco La ITALIAN   Tiny trattorias litter Little Italy, but Ecco La stands out. The rustic dining room is all red brick and ochre walls, with a wood-burning pizza oven as the centerpiece. Arugula and smoked salmon make a good match for robust tomatoes and Parmesan. There's also pasta (rigatoni goes nicely with wild mushrooms, sage cream, and truffle essence), and tender, meaty main dishes, which include capon and salmon. The menu always offers a vegetarian risotto, too. Desserts are strictly for chocolate lovers.

356 College St. ☎ **416/926-9899.** Reservations recommended. Main courses C$10–$21 (US$7–$15). AE, MC, V. Mon–Fri 11am–1am; Sat–Sun 4pm–1am. Subway: Queen's Park, then any streetcar west to Brunswick Ave.

Fortune Cookie 🌟 *Kids* ASIAN   Gourmet it isn't, but I really do like Fortune Cookie. Why? For starters, it's one of the best deals in the Entertainment District: For C$23 (US$16) per person (or C$10/US$7 for children 9 and under), you can order whatever you want from a 39-item tasting menu. You can also order as much as you like, so while the portions do tend to be small, you can get more of the General Tao chicken or the deep-fried spring rolls if you want. It's also a great way of getting around the problem of trying new things: If you always get the orange beef, here's your chance to try it *and* a slew of other dishes, too. The wait staff are friendly and helpful, even when you keep sending them back for more . . . and more . . . and more . . .

291 King St. W. ☎ **416/599-9995.** Reservations recommended. Tasting menu C$23 (US$16) per person (C$10/US$7 for children 9 and under). AE, DC, MC, V. Sun–Thurs 11:30am–10pm; Fri 11:30am–11pm; Sat noon–11pm. Subway: St. Andrew.

La Bodega FRENCH   This is a quiet spot infused with Gallic charm. In a turn-of-the-20th-century town house, La Bodega is a short walk from the Art Gallery of Ontario. The two dining rooms have fireplaces, and tapestries and gilt-framed mirrors line the walls. The menu is traditional French, with a focus on meats. Grilled beef tenderloin soaks up cognac sauce, and duck breast mixes well with wild blueberries. The wine list boasts some Bordeaux *grandes dames,* and there's a nice mix of Ontario vintages, too.

30 Baldwin St. ☎ **416/977-1287.** Reservations recommended. Main courses C$15–$27 (US$11–$19). AE, DC, MC, V. Mon–Fri 11:30am–2:30pm; Mon–Sat 5–11pm. Subway: St. Patrick.

La Palette 🌟 BISTRO   This is a terrific, offbeat addition to the Kensington Market neighborhood. It's so good, in fact, that you almost wonder why no one else ever thought of locating a classic French bistro on the edge of Chinatown. A quartet of Gallic flags announces its presence; inside, the 30-seat dining room is cozy and informal, with considerate, low-key service. The menu is classic, from ballantine of chicken stuffed with peppers and rice to lamb chops with a crusty coating of mustard and rosemary. If you're as much as a dessert fiend as I am, save room for irresistible citron tart and dark chocolate cake.

256 Augusta Ave. ☎ **416/929-4900.** Reservations recommended. Main courses C$10–$18 (US$7–$13). AE, MC, V. Sun–Thurs 5:30–11pm; Fri–Sat noon–midnight. Subway: St. Patrick, then streetcar west to Augusta Ave.

Le Sélect Bistro BISTRO   What says Paris bistro to you? Le Sélect sets the tone with posters, decorative objects straight from *grand-mère's* attic, and sultry jazz in the background. Breadbaskets hang from the ceiling above each table,

Kids Family-Friendly Restaurants

Fortune Cookie (p. 92)   The food offerings in the Entertainment District grow ever more sophisticated—a great thing, unless you're looking for a place to take the small fry. The all-you-can-order 39-item tasting menu is a mere C$9.95 (US$7) for children 9 and under.

Grano (p. 113)   Don't worry that a noisy babe-in-arms might disrupt diners—this lively, slightly chaotic eatery welcomes families. The owners have four kids, and they love to fuss over the *bambini.*

Kensington Kitchen (p. 106)   Whimsically decorated, with colorful toys and model airplanes. It seems to be easier to get kids to eat their greens when veggies are tucked into pita sandwiches, like the ones here.

Millie's Bistro (p. 112)   This is a perennially popular spot with families. There's a special menu for tykes, and most of the Mediterranean food can be eaten without cutlery.

Shopsy's (p. 100)   When the kids are sick of eating out and craving comfort food, this is where to take them. Home-style chili and macaroni and cheese hit the spot, and ice cream dominates a whole section of the menu.

and require gentle coaxing to reach the diners. The menu emphasizes traditional rib-sticking fare such as steak frites and cassoulet, all nicely done. The service can be a trifle slow, but the casually dressed professionals don't seem to mind.

328 Queen St. W. ✆ **416/596-6405.** www.leselect.com. Reservations recommended. Main courses C$13–$33 (US$9.10–$23). AE, DC, MC, V. Daily 11:30am–11:30pm. Subway: Osgoode.

Mildred Pierce ☆☆ ECLECTIC   Named after a Joan Crawford film, this restaurant is appropriately theatrical. Murals of a Roman feast cover the walls (a local in-joke, they depict characters including the restaurant's owner). The menu fits right in, rich in inspiration and dramatic flourishes borrowed from different countries. Grilled salmon accompanies saffron risotto and a ragout of fennel, baby beets, and bok choy, while a Thai hot pot boasts tiger shrimp, scallops, mussels, and clams brewing in a coconut-lime cilantro sauce. The short wine list includes options from Italy, Spain, South Africa, and California. Lush desserts include maple crème brûlée, and a rustic cranberry and walnut tart.

99 Sudbury St. ✆ **416/588-5695.** Reservations recommended; not accepted for Sun brunch. Main courses C$17–$26 (US$12–$18). AE, DC, MC, V. Mon–Fri noon–2pm; Sun 10am–3pm; Sun–Thurs 5:30–10pm; Fri–Sat 5:30–11pm. Subway: Osgoode, then any streetcar west to Dovercourt; walk south on Dovercourt and turn right at Sudbury.

Peter Pan LIGHT FARE   When I was in high school, Peter Pan was the classy restaurant you went to for pre-prom dinner or a big date. The crowd at this fun, relaxed place is forever young, easily impressed by the old-fashioned bar, ever-changing art exhibits, and friendly service. The menu is awash in Eurasian foodspeak; simpler dishes are best. The Peter Pan burger is always a top choice. Desserts are strictly for sweet tooths.

373 Queen St. W. ✆ **416/593-0917.** Reservations recommended. Main courses C$10–$18 (US$7–$13). AE, MC, V. Mon–Wed noon–midnight; Thurs–Sat noon–1am; Sun noon–11pm. Subway: Osgoode.

Pony BISTRO   On the periphery of hyper-trendy Little Italy, Pony is never-theless the kind of place where you can relax. The candlelit dining room is charming, the upholstered chairs are comfy, and the service is smooth. The menu sticks mainly to bistro classics, such as roasted chicken stuffed with pro-sciutto, smoked mozzarella, and apple slices. The Caesar salad has the creamiest dressing in town—even a devoted calorie-counter won't be able to resist.

488 College St. ⓒ 416/923-7665. Reservations recommended. Main courses C$16–$25 (US$11–$18). AE, MC, V. Mon–Sat 5–11pm. Subway: Queen's Park, then any streetcar west to Bathurst.

Rodney's Oyster House SEAFOOD   A favorite with the Financial District set, Rodney's is rowdy at all times of day. The setting is as unpretentious as you could find: Think lobster traps dangling from the ceiling and fishing nets hang-ing across the walls. The main draw is the incredibly fresh oysters, and the lobster and salmon dishes are worth more than a look.

469 King St. W. ⓒ 416/363-8105. Reservations recommended. Main courses C$16–$40 (US$11–$28). AE, DC, MC, V. Mon–Sat 11:30am–midnight. Subway: St. Andrew.

 Sang Ho ⚮ CHINESE/SEAFOOD   There's no end of eateries in the eastern end of Chinatown, but Sang Ho will be the one with the longest queue out front. The restaurant boasts not only a top-notch kitchen, but also a lovely dining room filled with several teeming aquariums. The regular menu of 100-plus dishes never changes; wall-mounted boards list many specials of the day. Seafood—shrimp, clams, or red snapper—is the obvious choice. Service is speedy and responsive. Try to go on a weeknight, when there's no more than a short wait for a table.

536 Dundas St. W. ⓒ 416/596-1685. Reservations not accepted. Main courses C$8–$18 (US$5.60–$13). MC, V. Sun–Thurs noon–10pm; Fri–Sat noon–11pm. Subway: St. Patrick.

Swan ECLECTIC   The room brings to mind a retro soda fountain, with a counter and swirly stools on one side, and booths with Formica tables on the other. Just don't expect to find a strawberry-banana float on the menu. The youngish hipsters who congregate here slurp up martinis and oysters. Happily, the menu avoids the trendy trap, managing both roasted capon with bourbon gravy and corn fritters, and braised beef short ribs marinated in beer and mar-malade. There's a nice selection of wines, almost all available by the glass. The popular weekend brunch features the usual eggy plates as well as some surprises: spicy Moroccan olives or smoked arctic char salad, anyone?

892 Queen St. W. ⓒ 416/532-0452. Reservations recommended. Main courses C$15–$20 (US$11–$14). AE, DC, MC, V. Mon–Fri noon–4:30pm; Sun–Fri 5–10:30pm; Sat 5–11pm; Sat–Sun 11:30am–2:30pm. Subway: Osgoode, then any streetcar west to Euclid Ave.

Taro Grill ⚮ ECLECTIC   Pass through the curtain hanging at the door, and enter a hip new world. Actually, it's not that new, but the Taro Grill has some-thing that most hot spots of the moment can't claim—staying power. Its secret? A mix of clever cooking, helpful service, and a glamorous high-ceilinged space. The menu refuses to be easily characterized. Just when you think you've pegged the Cal-Ital pizza-pasta-salad triad, out of the blue comes tempura veggies or Asian-influenced New Zealand lamb. Affordable bottles, mainly from Australia and South Africa, fill the wine list.

492 Queen St. W. ⓒ 416/504-1320. Reservations recommended. Main courses C$13–$20 (US$9.10–$14). AE, MC, V. Daily noon–4pm and 6–10pm. Subway: Osgoode, then any streetcar west to Bathurst St.

Veni Vidi Vici ⚮⚮ ITALIAN/FUSION   This is Little Italy's brightest new addition, a little gem that serves delicious food in a swanky setting—but, unlike many of its neighborhood cousins, it does so without attitude. I like it even better than established neighborhood favorite Ecco La. There's no sign outside, just a gilt-covered fresco of a mustachioed deity looming over the doorway. Inside, the staff is quick to usher diners to high-backed velvet banquettes.

The menu can be divided into two parts. On the Italian side, there are pasta dishes such as linguine with mixed seafood, or risotto with portobello, cremini, and porcini mushrooms. But the Asian-inspired fusion plates are the showstoppers: Think cashew-studded sea bass with fennel, or phyllo-wrapped salmon with basmati rice. Desserts return to the classics, like crème brûlée with fresh berries. The wine list is particularly strong in Italian reds.

650 College St. (at Grace St.). ℭ 416/536-8550. Reservations recommended. Main courses C$13–$25 (US$9.10–$18). AE, MC, V. Tues–Sun 11am–3pm and 5pm–midnight. Subway: Queen's Park, then streetcar west to Grace St.

INEXPENSIVE

Happy Seven CHINESE   This eatery boasts kitschy touches like plastic Buddhas and a tank full of fish and crawly critters. They may not be everybody's cup of (green) tea, but the kitchen is widely acknowledged as one of the best in Chinatown. The menu is classic Cantonese, with a few Szechwan choices. Seafood dishes are a favorite, though there are many plates for vegetarians; portions are extremely generous.

358 Spadina Ave. ℭ 416/971-9820. Reservations not accepted. Main courses C$7–$15 (US$4.90–$11). MC, V. Daily 4pm–5am. Subway: Spadina, then LRT south to Baldwin St.

Kalendar ☞☞ LIGHT FARE   I can't go to this restaurant without snickering at the menu, but the food inspires satisfied sighs. There are sandwiches stuffed with portobello mushrooms, havarti, and roasted red peppers, and five "scrolls"—phyllo pastries filled with delights like artichoke hearts, eggplant, and hummus. The "nannettes" (pizzas) are baked nan breads topped with ingredients like smoked salmon, capers, and red onions. The ambience recalls a French bistro. In summer the sidewalk patio is just the place to sit and watch the world.

546 College St. (just west of Bathurst St.). ℭ 416/923-4138. Main courses C$10–$13 (US$7–$9.10). MC, V. Mon–Fri 11am–4pm. Subway: Queen's Park, then any streetcar west to Bathurst St.

Lee Garden CHINESE   If lines are a measure of the success of a restaurant, then Lee Garden is, deservedly, the hands-down Toronto champ. The draw is a Cantonese menu weighted heavily toward seafood. Although there's no shark fin, there's no shortage of shrimp, lobster, and cod. The signature dish is fork-tender grandfather smoked chicken with honey and sesame seeds. The kitchen works wonders with tofu, too.

331 Spadina Ave. ℭ 416/593-9524. Reservations not accepted. Main courses C$10–$22 (US$7–$15). AE, MC, V. Daily 4pm–midnight. Subway: Spadina, then LRT south to Baldwin St.

Penelope GREEK   If you're in a rush to see a show at the Royal Alex or Roy Thomson Hall, this is one of your best bets. Give the friendly staff an hour or less, and they will stuff you with spanakopita, moussaka, or souvlaki. This is the home of hearty food in a hurry.

225 King St. W. ℭ 416/351-9393. Reservations recommended for pre-theater dinner. Main courses C$13–$22 (US$9.10–$15). AE, DC, MC, V. Mon–Wed 11:30am–10pm, Thurs–Fri 11:30am–11:30pm, Sat 4:30–11:30pm. Subway: St. Andrew.

Queen Mother Cafe ASIAN   Fussy dowager this is not. Beloved by vegetarians, trend-hoppers, and reformed hippies, the Queen Mum is a Queen Street West institution with old-fashioned wooden furnishings and an underlit interior. The menu's lengthy descriptions are required reading. "Ping Gai" turns out to be chicken breast marinated in garlic, coriander, and peppercorns, served with lime sauce atop steamed rice. "Salmon Sottha" is served with hotter-than-hot Cambodian chile sauce and black rice. The menu is anything but pricey, so the wine list is a surprise, with few bargains in sight.

208 Queen St. W. ℂ 416/598-4719. Reservations accepted only for groups of 6 or more. Main courses C$11–$18 (US$7.70–$13). AE, MC, V. Daily noon–1am. Subway: Osgoode.

The Rivoli 🎯🎯 FUSION   The Riv is better known as a club than as a restaurant—the 125-seat back room plays host to live music, stand-up comics, and poetry readings. What most people don't know is that the kitchen is just as creative. Chicken marinated in jerk spices comes with sautéed spinach and plantain chips; mussels are steamed in green curry jazzed up with coconut and lime. The less adventurous can partake of the spinach-and-pear salad or the house burger (beef on a challah bun with caramelized onions). The low prices draw a mixed crowd of starving artists, budget-conscious boomers, and Gen-Xers. *One caveat:* If you're planning to talk over dinner, get there before the back room starts filling up.

332 Queen St. W. ℂ 416/597-0794. www.rivoli.ca. Reservations accepted only for groups of 6 or more. Main courses C$9–$19 (US$6.30–$13). AE, MC, V. Daily noon–2am. Subway: Osgoode.

Sottovoce LIGHT FARE   The name of this tiny eatery is more than a little misleading. *Sotto* (soft) it isn't. Forget trying to have a conversation and instead try to score one of the window seats, which afford a full view of College Street. The youngish crowd that mills in after 7pm enjoys the pumped-up music that refuses to stay in the background. In the middle of this frenetic scene you will find the most lovingly prepared, and least expensive, salads and focaccia sandwiches in town. There are daily pasta specials, and many wines by the glass.

595 College St. ℂ 416/536-4564. Reservations not accepted. Main courses C$6–$12 (US$4.20–$8.40). AE, MC, V. Mon–Sat 5:30–11pm. Subway: Queen's Park, then any streetcar west to Clinton St.

Tortilla Flats TEX-MEX   Park your fear of sour cream and oil at the door, because it will spoil the fun. The dining room is all riotous color and Southwestern knickknacks; think Georgia O'Keeffe meets Salvador Dalí. The crowd is mainly 20- to 30-somethings, and a number of boomers come for the weekend brunch and the best frozen margaritas in town. The menu never changes, though there are some daily specials. Potato skins piled high with bacon and sharp cheddar are at the top of my list; the enchilada and chimichurri platters, which include rice, salad, and refried beans, are pretty satisfying, too.

429 Queen St. W. ℂ 416/593-9870. Reservations accepted only for groups of 5 or more. Main courses C$8–$20 (US$5.60–$14). MC, V. Sun–Wed noon–10pm; Thurs–Sat noon–11pm. Subway: Osgoode, then any streetcar west to Spadina Ave.

3 Downtown East

EXPENSIVE

Biff's 🎯🎯 BISTRO   The same team that created a trio of excellent eateries with Jump, Canoe, and Auberge du Pommier have been hard at work again. The intent this time was to create a classic bistro, with dishes priced somewhat lower than at the other establishments (in keeping with true bistro tradition, *naturellement*). The setting hits all the right notes, with wood paneling and potted palms among the cozy-but-chic touches. The menu is equally fine, with pan-fried halibut covered with a second skin of thinly sliced potatoes, and traditional roast leg of lamb. The prime downtown location is a boon for Financial District types at lunch and theatergoers in the evening (the St. Lawrence and the Hummingbird centers are a stone's throw away).

4 Front St. E. (at Yonge St.). ✆ **416/860-0086.** Reservations strongly recommended. Main courses C$18–$28 (US$13–$20). AE, DC, MC, V. Mon–Fri 11:30am–2:30pm; Mon–Sat 5:30–11pm. Subway: Union or King.

Courthouse Market Grille INTERNATIONAL   This hangout for the suited set boasts gargantuan fluted columns, sky-high ceilings, swinging chandeliers, and miles of marble. Pretty good for an 1850 building that used to be a jail. Financial District types lap it up, along with generous martinis. The menu features grilled and rotisserie meats of excellent quality, though timid seasoning will not please daring palates. Appetizers are uniformly fine, with simple but well-executed numbers like steamed Prince Edward Island mussels in creamy white wine sauce. The wine list includes some impressive vintages—and prices.

57 Adelaide St. E. ✆ **416/214-9379.** Reservations required. Main courses C$15–$32 (US$11–$22). AE, DC, MC, V. Mon–Wed 11:30am–10pm; Thurs–Fri 11:30am–midnight; Sat 5:30pm–midnight. Subway: King.

Hiro Sushi ✿ JAPANESE/SUSHI   Widely regarded as the best sushi chef in the city, Hiro Yoshida draws a horde of Financial District types at lunch and mainly couples at dinner. The monochromatic setting is comfortably minimalist, and diners are encouraged to relax and leave their meal in Hiro's capable hands. The sushi varieties range from the expected to the inventive; you can also choose sashimi, tempura, and bento box combinations. Service can be rather slow. Forget the few wines listed in favor of sake or beer.

171 King St. E. ✆ **416/304-0550.** Reservations recommended. Main courses C$20–$30 (US$14–$21). AE, DC, MC, V. Mon–Fri noon–2:30pm; Mon–Sat 6–10:30pm. Subway: King.

Rosewater Supper Club ✿ INTERNATIONAL   This triple-decked pleasure dome is packed almost every night with dressed-up diners who pass the time checking each other out. Personally, I'm still caught on the scenery: Marble, moldings, and a waterfall make quite the impression. So does the menu, which casually tours the globe. First up are delectables like carpaccio of seared caribou with a citrus-gin relish. Main courses include roast sirloin of lamb with parsnip gratin and hazelnut sauce, and coq au vin with butternut squash. The can't-miss desserts include rhubarb apple crisp with a vanilla-plum sorbet. The serious wine list focuses mainly on France and California, with some excellent Ontario vintages.

19 Toronto St. (at Adelaide). ✆ **416/214-5888.** Reservations required. Main courses C$20–$32 (US$14–$22). AE, DC, MC, V. Mon–Fri 11:30am–2:30pm and 5:30–10:30pm; Sat 5:30–11:30pm. Subway: King.

Torch Bistro BISTRO   The Senator Restaurant brought back the days when red meat, rich food, and cigar smoking weren't considered a threat to one's health. It closed in 2000 to make way for the Torch Bistro, a paean to the classic French bistro. The decor is much the same, with etched-glass doors and heavy wood paneling, but the menu is entirely new: Dishes include smoked duck breast with shiitake mushroom risotto, or grilled provimi calves liver with braised red cabbage and crispy pancetta. Upstairs, things haven't changed at all: There's jazz at the glamorous Top O' the Senator (p. 208), and the Victory Lounge for cigar aficionados.

249 Victoria St. ✆ **416/364-7517.** Reservations required. Main courses C$16–$36 (US$11–$25). AE, DC, MC, V. Tues–Thurs 5–11pm; Fri–Sat 5pm–midnight; Sun 5–10pm. Subway: Dundas.

Tips **Savory Surfing**

Trying to decide between two equally tantalizing restaurants? Why not sneak a peek at their menus online? The websites listed here will give you different perspectives on the city's eateries.

- **TorDine** (www.tordine.com): This award-winning site purports to be the best Toronto dining guide. You'll find restaurant reviews penned by average food-loving folks, as well as coupons and special deals. You can search the directory by name, food type, or price, and you can make reservations online. Each entry gives descriptive details, from dress codes to wheelchair access.

- **Toronto.com** (www.toronto.com): This site boasts a lot of features, but its restaurant reviews are the biggest draw for me. A photo or two usually accompanies the reviews, to give you a sense of what that space is like.

- **Toronto Life Online** (www.torontolife.com): Look to this magazine's "Best of T.O." section to learn where to find the city's best bets for gelato, falafel, or panini. The site also offers a section filled with reviews of just about every restaurant around town. There's a C$25 (US$18) Gourmet Guide for those who want to dine well without breaking the bank.

ZooM Caffe & Bar ✗ INTERNATIONAL   Perhaps because its design is so striking, ZooM has had some trouble being taken seriously as a restaurant. Located in the space of a long-gone bank, it has a vaulted ceiling, velvet lounges, and halogen lighting—a lovely setting for the Beautiful People. Its oft-over-looked menu is short but to the point. It features creations like taro root–encrusted foie gras as a starter, and a main course of "wonder spiced" lamb loin with smoked corn polenta and plantains. Desserts are less esoteric, though no less satisfying (I can't resist the chocolate mud pie). On the wine list, bargains are in short supply. And this is *the* spot for private parties, so be sure to call ahead.

18 King St. E. ☎ 416/861-9872. www.zoomrestaurant.com. Reservations recommended. Main courses C$18–$36 (US$13–$25). AE, DC, MC, V. Mon–Fri noon–3pm; Mon–Tues 5–11pm; Wed–Sat 5pm–midnight. Subway: King.

MODERATE

HotHouse Cafe CONTINENTAL/LIGHT FARE   When restaurants make the claim of having "something for everyone," I usually run the other way. But the HotHouse Café is an exception. The exhaustive menu ranges from salads to pizzas, omelets to pastas, and burgers to vegetarian mains, and they do a nice job with it all. (Don't expect complicated fare here—the HotHouse keeps things simple, which is a very wise move when offering so much.) The restaurant is famous for its Sunday buffet brunch, which at C$16 (US$11) per person is a good value if you're in the mood to indulge: there are made-to-order omelet stations, lots of options, and live jazz music.

35 Church St. ☎ 416/366-7800. Reservations strongly recommended, particularly for Sunday brunch. Main courses C$10–$20 (US$7–$14). AE, DC, MC, V. Mon–Tue 11am–10:30pm; Wed–Thurs 11am–midnight. Subway: King or Union.

Montréal Bistro & Jazz Club QUEBECOIS   Ontario and Quebec share a border, but it's no mean feat to find top-notch *tourtière* (traditional beef, veal, and pork pie) in Toronto. Anyone who craves Quebecois staples like pea soup and smoked-meat sandwiches can return their train ticket and stop at this bistro. Besides being a restaurant, this is one of the city's premier jazz clubs, so you can *écouter* while you *manger.*

65 Sherbourne St. (at Adelaide). (𝐶 **416/363-0179.** www.montrealbistro.com. Reservations recommended. Main courses C$10–$22 (US$7–$15). AE, DC, MC, V. Mon–Fri 11:30am–3pm; Mon–Thurs 6–11pm; Fri–Sat 6pm–midnight. Subway: King, then any streetcar east to Sherbourne St.

Terroni ITALIAN/LIGHT FARE   From its humble beginnings on Queen Street West, Terroni has grown into a local mini-chain with three locations. The setting is informal, with kitchen-style tables and chairs and a wall-mounted chalkboard that heralds the daily specials. The antipasti, salads, and pizzas, essentially the same at all three locations, are uniformly delightful. They range from the simplest margherita pizza (tomato, mozzarella, basil) to a gourmet salad of cooked oyster mushrooms drizzled with balsamic vinegar and served atop a bed of arugula. The two other locations are at 720 Queen St. W. and 1 Balmoral Ave.

106 Victoria St. (𝐶 **416/955-0258.** Main courses C$10–$18 (US$7–$13). MC, V. Mon–Sat 9am–10pm. Subway: Queen.

Wish ⚘ *Finds* BISTRO   This is a dream-come-true: Hidden behind a simple whitewashed facade, Wish is a charmer that offers cozy ambience, excellent cooking and friendly service (a rare combination in this neighborhood). In summer, the vibrant patio might draw you to it, but during the rest of the year you have to wait till you're through the front door before you're seduced by the setting, which is dominated by white-slipcovered couches, plush cushions and baroque details—very shabby chic. The menu is just as elegant, with starters such as Pernod-glazed calamari. Mains run the gamut from meat and fish to pasta and risotto. Note that the dessert selection is very limited, as is the wine list.

3 Charles St. E. (𝐶 **416/935-0240.** Reservations recommended. Main courses C$14–$25 (US$9.80–$18). AE, MC, V. Daily 11am–2am. Subway: Yonge/Bloor.

INEXPENSIVE

Hello Toast LIGHT FARE   Humorist Fran Lebowitz once asked why there were places called Bonjour Croissant but not Hello Toast. Well, now there is. Gleaming toasters and retro furniture bedeck the kitschy dining room. The menu is a mix of pizza and pasta specials, with a few salads, soups, and rich desserts mixed in. If you're springing for toast, choose the inspired challah.

993 Queen St. E. (𝐶 **416/778-7299.** Main courses C$7–$15 (US$4.90–$11). MC, V. Tues–Sun noon–10pm. Subway: Queen, then any streetcar east to Pape Ave.

Le Papillon QUEBECOIS   If you thought crepes were simply for breakfast, stop by Le Papillon for re-education. While there are many fruit-filled numbers, the best are savory crepes, which combine, for example, bacon, apples, and cheddar. Created from a mixture of white and buckwheat flour, the crepes make a satisfying lunch. For dinner, add some onion soup and a green salad, or go for *tourtière,* a traditional Quebecois pie that includes beef, veal, *and* pork.

16 Church St. (between Front St. E. and Esplanade). (𝐶 **416/363-0838.** www.lepapillon.ca. Reservations recommended. Crepes C$6–$10 (US$4.20–$7). AE, DC, MC, V. Tues–Fri noon–2:30pm; Tues–Wed 5–10pm; Thurs 5–11pm; Fri 5pm–midnight; Sat 11am–midnight; Sun 11am–10pm. Subway: Union.

Shopsy's (Kids) DELI   This Toronto institution has been in business for more than three-quarters of a century. Its large patio, festooned with giant yellow umbrellas, draws crowds for breakfast, lunch, and dinner and in between. This is where you go for heaping corned beef or smoked-meat sandwiches served on fresh rye. There's also a slew of comfort foods, like macaroni and cheese and chicken potpie. Shopsy's also boasts one of the largest walk-in humidors in the city (which is not subject to the new smoking crackdown).

33 Yonge St. ℂ 416/365-3333. Reservations accepted only for groups of 6 or more. Main courses C$7–$14 (US$4.90–$9.80). AE, MC, V. Mon–Wed 6:30am–11pm; Thurs–Fri 6:30am–midnight; Sat 8am–midnight; Sun 8am–10pm. Subway: Union or King.

Young Thailand ᏋᏋ THAI   Wandee Young was one of the first chefs to awake Toronto's taste buds to the joys of Thai cuisine. That was more than 2 decades ago, and Young Thailand is still going strong, with several locations around the city. The large dining room contains a few Southeast Asian decorative elements, but it's the low-priced, high-quality cuisine that attracts the hip-but-broke and boomers alike. The bargain buffet at lunch is always a mob scene. The dinner menu is a la carte, with popular picks like spiced chicken and bamboo shoots in coconut milk, satays with fiery peanut sauce, and the ever-present pad Thai. Soups tend to be sinus-clearing, and mango salads offer a sweet antidote.

81 Church St. (south of Lombard St.). ℂ 416/368-1368. Reservations recommended. Lunch buffet C$9.95 (US$7); main courses C$8–$16 (US$5.60–$11). AE, DC, MC, V. Mon–Fri 11:30am–2pm; daily 4:30–11pm. Subway: Queen or King.

4 Midtown West

VERY EXPENSIVE

Bistro 990 ᏋᏋᏋ FRENCH   Because Hollywood types frequent Toronto, it's no surprise to see the stars out for a night on the town. Bistro 990 is just across the street from the tony Sutton Place Hotel, so it drags in more than its fair share of big names. (One friend has had a couple of Whoopi Goldberg sightings here. Why do these things never happen when I'm around?) In any case, the Gallic dining room is charming, and the service is all-around attentive. The menu offers updated hors d'oeuvres, such as octopus and veggies in citrus marinade. Main dishes stick to *grand-mère's* recipes, like the satisfying roasted half chicken with garlicky mashed potatoes, and calf's liver in white-wine sauce. Sweets, such as the pineapple tarte tatin with kiwi coulis and blueberry ice cream, are made daily. The three-course prix fixe menus are an excellent value, at C$20 (US$14) for lunch and C$25 (US$17) for dinner.

990 Bay St. (at St. Joseph). ℂ 416/921-9990. Reservations required. Main courses C$19–$40 (US$13–$28). AE, DC, MC, V. Mon–Fri noon–3pm; Mon–Sat 5–11pm. Subway: Wellesley.

Opus CONTINENTAL   Popular with the price-is-no-object set, Opus is nonetheless low-key. Smooth, personable servers make you feel at home in the elegant renovated town house, which contains several small dining areas. The look is casually chic, and there's no shortage of suits. The menu changes every other month, and always features classic French as well as lightened-up dishes. Tuna tartare meets its match with black sesame seeds and lotus chips, and beef tenderloin with dauphinoise potatoes and rosemary-shallot *jus* is memorable. Desserts are easy on the eye and the palate. The wine list runs to volumes, with highlights of New and Old worlds; the knowledgeable staff can set you straight.

37 Prince Arthur Ave. © **416/921-3105.** Reservations recommended. Main courses C$25–$39 (US$18–$
AE, DC, MC, V. Daily 5:30–11:30pm; bar until 2am. Subway: St. George.

Truffles ⊛ CONTINENTAL On the second floor of the Four Seasons Hotel, this formal dining room is a study in elegance. Every last detail has been attended to, from the exotic sculptures to the stunning marquetry floor. The clientele is a mix of hotel guests and local businesspeople—it's a bit of an older crowd. Appetizers boast exquisite ingredients, with results such as pan-seared foie gras atop pineapple and mango chutney. Main courses, such as bacon-wrapped veal tenderloin served side-by-side with morel mushroom ravioli, are more down-to-earth. Desserts like peach Napoleon and lemon soufflé are uniformly delightful. The mile-long wine list frequently veers into the stratosphere.

In the Four Seasons Hotel, 21 Avenue Rd. © **416/928-7331.** Reservations required. Main courses C$34–$46 (US$24–$32). AE, DC, MC, V. Mon–Fri 6–11pm; Sat 5:30–10:30pm. Subway: Bay.

EXPENSIVE

Annona ⊛ INTERNATIONAL Why are so many of the city's fascinating restaurants in hotels? Annona, at the Park Hyatt, is the latest case in point. This street-level dining room is an exercise in elegance, with dusky blue draperies and banquettes, gold accents, and floor-to-ceiling windows (all the better to people-watch, my dears). It draws a business crowd, Yorkville shoppers, and hotel guests, serving scrambled eggs with smoked salmon and capers for breakfast, seafood risotto with morel mushrooms and asparagus at lunch, and pan-seared Black Angus medallions in red wine sauce for dinner. The desserts are to die for, especially the caramelized pineapple tart with rum ice cream.

Park Hyatt Toronto, 4 Avenue Rd. © **416/924-5471.** Reservations recommended for dinner. Main courses C$16–$30 (US$11–$21). AE, DC, MC, V. Mon–Fri 6:30am–11pm; Sat–Sun 7am–11pm. Subway: Museum or Bay.

Boba ⊛ FUSION There is no shortage of stunning turn-of-the-20th-century houses in this part of town, and Boba happens to be in one of the most charming. Set back from the street, it has a front patio for summer dining. Inside, the pastel-hued walls and tasseled lampshades exude warmth, Provençal style. Boba is a scene every night, with a mix of dressed-up and dressed-down professionals table-hopping with abandon. What draws them is the inventive cuisine, which has turned co-chefs Barbara Gordon and Bob Bermann into local celebrities. One highlight is Gordon's wonderful Muscovy duck two ways, with the breast cooked rare and the leg braised. Grilled salmon is also just so, nicely mated with curried vegetable risotto. Desserts are overwhelming, particularly the Valrhona chocolate triangle with crème fraîche ice cream, raspberries, and berry coulis.

90 Avenue Rd. © **416/961-2622.** Reservations recommended. Main courses C$20–$34 (US$14–$24). AE, DC, MC, V. Mon–Sat 5:45–10pm. Subway: Bay.

Il Posto Nuovo ITALIAN All of those ladies who lunch can't be wrong. Now celebrating its 20th year, Il Posto Nuovo (formerly known simply as Il Posto) has new management and a new direction—and business is booming. Still, some things don't change: White-linened tables sit cheek-by-jowl, making this an eavesdropper's Eden. The service is among the best in the city, considerate, efficient, and well versed in the intricacies of the menu. And what a menu it is, rich with classic dishes like bresaola salad (thinly sliced air-cured beef and Asiago cheese atop a bed of arugula), and ravioli stuffed with veal and spinach. The wine cellar favors Italy, France, and California; it's constantly updated, so do ask for recommendations.

148 Yorkville Ave. (at Avenue Rd.). ℭ **416/968-0469.** Reservations required. Main courses C$14–$25 (US$9.80–$18). AE, DC, MC, V. Mon–Sat noon–2:30pm and 6–11pm. Subway: Bay or Museum.

Mistura ✵ ITALIAN   While the curvy bar up front is a favorite place to meet, the modern Italian menu is the real draw for the well-dressed 20- and 30-somethings who dine at Mistura. The food is satisfying without being overly heavy—think spinach and ricotta gnocchi with light but creamy Gorgonzola sauce and toasted walnuts. The meaty entrees might include a tender veal chop with rosemary roasted potatoes and portobello mushrooms, or sweetbreads with chickpea polenta and caramelized root veggies. The well-organized wine list is heavy with Italian and California vintages.

265 Davenport Rd. ℭ **416/515-0009.** Reservations recommended. Main courses C$20–$28 (US$14–$20). AE, DC, MC, V. Mon–Sat 5–11pm. Subway: Bay.

Pangaea ✵ FUSION   I used to think this location was cursed. For years, I watched restaurants open with a bang and fold with a whimper. Well, Pangaea seems to have broken that losing streak—and deservedly so. The massive dining room is as dramatic as ever, complete with an undulating aluminum ceiling and coral walls. Perhaps to compete with the surroundings, the chic crowd likes to dress up. The menu changes every month. Appetizers such as white asparagus soup with roasted shallots and morel mushrooms are classically French. Main dishes strike boldly in different directions: glazed salmon with bok choy, water chestnuts, and ginger, for example, or rack of lamb roasted in sunflower seeds and honey and served with whiskey sauce. The professional staff knows its way around the wide-ranging wine list, which favors the Western Hemisphere.

1221 Bay St. ℭ **416/920-2323.** Reservations recommended. Main courses C$22–$28 (US$15–$20). AE, DC, MC, V. Mon–Sat 11:30am–11:30pm. Subway: Bay.

Patriot ✵✵ CANADIAN   Canadians are often accused of lacking patriotism; perhaps this elegant eatery was designed to arouse some national pride? Most of the menu staples, from veal to lobster to cheeses to mushrooms, are proudly sourced in Canada. But what really counts is what the kitchen makes of its bounty. The results are compelling, like the pairing of artichoke and oka cheese atop rich carrot soup, or slightly seared lamb carpaccio served with beet juice, basil oil, and balsamic vinegar. Because Canadians hail from all parts of the globe, it's only fair to throw in a few foreign elements, as the excellent pineapple tarte Tatin demonstrates. Canadian vintages dominate the wine list.

131 Bloor St. W. ℭ **416/922-0025.** Reservations recommended. Main courses C$17–$27 (US$12–$19). AE, MC, V. Mon–Sat 11am–11pm. Subway: Museum or Bay.

Splendido Bar and Grill CANADIAN   This longstanding favorite is under new ownership, and the resulting renovation has made it look even more like a private club than before: The dining room pairs brown with beige (much more attractive than it sounds), dark wood and leather chairs. The menu has also taken a new direction; with the Northern Italian standards taking a backseat to modern innovations that highlight Canadian produce. Mains run the gamut from a seared B.C. halibut filet in leek-and-champagne vinaigrette to Ontario butternut squash ravioli. For dessert, the lemon pudding cake with caramelized mango is hard to beat. The international wine list is pricey, but some nice vintages are available by the glass.

88 Harbord St. ℭ **416/929-7788.** Reservations required. Main courses C$20–$30 (US$14–$21). AE, DC, MC, V. Mon–Sat 5–11pm. Subway: Spadina, then LRT south to Harbord St.

MODERATE

Café Nervosa ITALIAN   There are reed-thin models playing with their food at the next table, leopard skin decking the room, and limos parked out front. Where are you? One possible answer is Café Nervosa, a casually hip Yorkville hangout. The name is borrowed from the coffee shop on TV's *Frasier*, with a wacky ambience all its own. The menu boasts nicely constructed panini, pizzas, and salads, and the portions tend to be generous (curious, given the you-can-never-be-too-rich-or-too-thin crowd).

75 Yorkville Ave. © **416/961-4642**. www.cafenervosa.ca. Reservations only for groups of 6 or more. Main courses C$10–$25 (US$7–$18). AE, DC, MC, V. Mon–Wed 11am–11pm; Thurs–Sat 11am–midnight; Sun 10:30am–3pm. Subway: Bay.

Colony Kitchen ★★ *(Finds)* FUSION   Please promise not to laugh when I tell you that one of Toronto's hottest new restaurants is located in the basement of Club Monaco. I can't explain it, but it's true. The flagship store at the corner of Bloor Street West and Avenue Road—just across the street from the ROM and a hop and a skip from Yorkville—now houses the Colony Kitchen. Not that Club Monaco staff is running the show here; this new restaurant is the work of Leslie Ng, the man who created the excellent Kubo (which, sadly, folded in late 2002 because of ongoing construction on its street). The new menu is hard to resist: Panko fish 'n' chips with a wasabi-ginger dipping sauce is excellent, but so is the five-spice lamb stew or the roast tenderloin of pork in a cumin-tamarind sauce. The desserts are fine but not divine, though in this neighborhood, sweet-tooths won't have a problem finding other sources. By the way, the patio seating area is one of my favorites.

157 Bloor St. W. © **416/591-9997**. www.thecolony.ca. Reservations recommended. Main courses C$12–$25 (US$8.05–$17). AE, MC, V. Tues–Sat 6–11pm. Subway: Museum or Bay.

Goldfish ★★ *(Value)* ECLECTIC   Behind the floor-to-ceiling front window, dining at this new hot spot is rather like being in a fishbowl. The cool, crisp lines of Scandinavian design mix with miniature Japanese plants for an upscale Zen ambience. While the look may be trendier-than-thou, the staff's attitude is consistently considerate. The menu is far less austere than the surroundings. Main dishes run the gamut from ostrich tenderloin with lobster orzo and cran-berry coulis to orange-poppy-seed-crusted salmon in an apple cider reduction. Even the simplest green salad benefits from dollops of pumpkin seeds and a light dressing that contains a hint of lavender emulsion. The short dessert list includes some inventive pairings, such as delicious apple tart with rosemary ice cream. The wine list is short but contains 10 selections by the glass.

372 Bloor St. W. © **416/513-0077**. Reservations strongly recommended. Main courses C$13–$27 (US$9.10–$19). AE, DISC, MC, V. Wed–Fri 11:30am–3:30pm; Sat–Sun 10am–3pm; daily 5:30–10:30pm. Subway: Spadina.

Gus ★ GREEK   This restaurant is out of its element so far as locale is concerned—Toronto's Greek restaurants tend to congregate along the Danforth (see "The East End" on p. 108). But this midtown newcomer is a welcome addi-tion to the neighborhood. Gus injects some creative cookery—and a pleasantly relaxed vibe—into an area that could benefit from cutting loose a little. Main courses run the gamut from rack of lamb in a sour-cherry reduction to seared tuna steak with a classic avgolemono sauce. Side plates, including the delicious feta-scalloped potatoes, are ordered separately. Portions are on the generous side, but do try to save space for the light but luscious Pavlova. The wine list has some well-chosen bottles, but the cocktail list is more of a draw: The lychee martini is a house specialty.

1033 Bay St. ℂ 416/923-8159. Reservations recommended. Main courses C$16–$25 (US$11–$18). AE, MC, V. Mon–Fri 5pm–midnight; Sat 6pm–2am. Subway: Wellesley.

Jacques Bistro du Parc FRENCH There are about three ladies who lunch for every lad who happens by Jacques Bistro du Parc around noontime. In the evening, the ratio evens out. The menu is that of a genuine French brasserie, with omelets, quiches, and niçoise salads galore. There are meatier main courses, too, like green peppercorn steak and Dijon-coated rack of lamb. Many wines are available by the glass, and bottles tend to be reasonably priced. Service can be considered relaxed or slow, depending on your mood.

126A Cumberland St. ℂ 416/961-1893. Reservations recommended on weekends. Main courses C$12–$30 (US$8.40–$21). AE, MC, V. Mon–Sat 11:30am–3pm and 5–10:30pm. Subway: Bay.

Joso's SEAFOOD This Annex mainstay keeps packing 'em in, drawing a crowd of regulars and a sprinkling of celebrities. The Spralja family has a show-biz history (chef Joso was half of the folk-singing duo of Malka and Joso, who appeared on *The Tonight Show*), which may explain the theatricality of the sur-roundings. The two-story house is crammed with art depicting the female form in all its naked glory. Tables are inches apart, foiling intimate conversation but letting you get to know your neighbors. Fresh seafood is carted to your table for inspection, then returned to the kitchen for cooking. There is also a selection of pastas, such as delightful spaghettini al Leonardo, which combines shrimp, octo-pus, and capers. Desserts range from jam-filled crepes to sorbets.

202 Davenport Rd. (just east of Avenue Rd.). ℂ 416/925-1903. Reservations recommended. Main courses C$14–$44 (US$9.80–$31); pasta dishes C$10–$16 (US$7–$11). AE, MC, V. Mon–Fri 11:30am–2:30pm; Mon–Sat 5:30–11pm. Subway: Bay.

Matignon *Finds* FRENCH A bit off the beaten track, this small restaurant offers the thrill of discovery. Spread over two floors, the intimate rooms are fes-tooned with all things French. The crowd includes many regulars, and the ambi-ence is that of a low-key bistro. The short menu is filled with classics from the old country, including Angus steak rolled in crushed pepper and flambéed with cognac, and rack of lamb with mustard and herbs of Provence. Desserts, like vanilla ice cream under hot chocolate sauce, stay on the same track.

51 St. Nicholas St. ℂ 416/921-9226. Reservations recommended. Main courses C$14–$18 (US$9.80–$13). AE, MC, V. Mon–Fri 11:30am–2:30pm; Mon–Thurs 5–10pm, Fri–Sat 5–11pm. Subway: Wellesley.

Messis *Value* ECLECTIC This is one of Toronto's prime training grounds for up-and-coming young chefs. The food is for gourmets, though the prices are com-paratively low. That explains the presence of earnest artsy types and casual boomers in the small, saffron-walled dining room. The menu changes frequently, keeping as its mainstays Italian pastas and Mediterranean meat dishes, and ranging into Asia, too. For a starter, the herbed goat cheese and cumin phyllo pastry is a deli-cious choice. Main courses include oven-roasted Atlantic salmon with jasmine rice and sun-dried fruit. Service is well intentioned though occasionally clunky. The California-dominated wine list is as reasonably priced as the food.

97 Harbord St. ℂ 416/920-2186. Main courses C$11–$21 (US$7.70–$15). AE, MC, V. Sun–Thurs 5:30–10pm; Fri–Sat 5:30–11pm. Subway: Spadina, then LRT south to Harbord St.

Rouge *Finds* ECLECTIC Oh, make me blush—not another minimalist, mod-ernist eatery along Bloor Street West. All right, that's exactly what it is—but it has nothing to be ashamed of. This skinny little room with its crimson walls and Japanese-inspired flower boxes is serving up some stellar fare. Appetizers go from sweet—tomato salad with roasted baby onions in balsamic vinaigrette—to sophisticated, like the seared foie gras with brioche and roasted pears. There are several impressive pastas, such as the gnocchi with double-smoked bacon and savory, as well as strong mains (the duo of Quebec leg of lamb and Australian lamb rack with gratin dauphinois offers a fascinating taste test for gourmets).

467 Bloor St. W. ✆ **416/413-0713.** Reservations recommended. Main courses C$12–$24 (US$8.40–$17). AE, MC, V. Daily 6–11pm. Subway: Spadina.

Sotto Sotto 🕭🕭 ITALIAN   Imagine the Bat Cave decorated by a Florentine, with aged frescoes, wall-mounted stonework, and wax-dripping candelabra. A few steps down from street level, this restaurant transports diners a world away. Tables are cheek-by-jowl, but the jovial suits and couples don't seem to mind. Efficient service lacks warmth, though the kitchen makes up for it. The menu leans to the lightweight, with a few irresistible creamy-sauced pastas. Main courses of meat or fish, like Cornish hen and swordfish, are nicely grilled. The risotto is fine—though, annoyingly, at least two people at the table must order it. There's a nice wine list, with many selections available by the glass.

116A Avenue Rd. (north of Bloor St.). ✆ **416/962-0011.** Reservations required. Main courses C$14–$24 (US$9.80–$17). AE, DC, MC, V. Daily 5:30–midnight. Subway: Bay or Museum.

Southern Accent CAJUN   Cajun food isn't Toronto's claim to fame, so this down-home Annex eatery is a find. Background blues and zydeco set the tone, and the menu attracts casual neighborhood boomers. Anyone who has admired the work of New Orleans celebrity chef Paul Prudhomme will cotton to the blackened entrees—chicken, steak, lamb, and fish all get the treatment. Gumbo and crawfish make occasional appearances, too. *Warning:* The corn bread is a mite addictive.

595 Markham St. ✆ **416/536-3211.** Reservations recommended on weekends. Main courses C$13–$26 (US$9.10–$18). AE, DC, DISC, MC, V. Tues–Sun 5:30pm–1am. Subway: Bathurst.

INEXPENSIVE

Bloor Street Diner LIGHT FARE   If you've shopped until you've dropped along Bloor Street West, this is just the place to grab a bite to eat and let your feet and your credit card recover. It's two restaurants in one: Le Café/Terrasse is an informal bistro that serves decent soups, salads, and sandwiches all day; La Rotisserie is a slightly more upscale dining room with heartier Provençal-style fare. The basics are what they do best. Try to snag a seat on the umbrella-covered patio overlooking Bay Street (all the better for people-watching).

In the Manulife Centre, 55 Bloor St. W. ✆ **416/928-3105.** Main courses C$10–$18 (US$7–$13). AE, DC, MC, V. Daily 7am–1am. Subway: Bay or Yonge/Bloor.

Indian Rice Factory 🕭 INDIAN   A Toronto institution since it opened in the late 1970s, the Indian Rice Factory is in a league of its own. The corduroy banquettes and macramé wall hangings still draw boomers who started coming here 20 years ago. The Punjabi-influenced menu features heaping helpings of beef *dhansak* (braised with lentil-eggplant-tomato curry) and chicken *khashabad,* stuffed with almonds, cashews, and raisins in coconut-milk cream. There are many beers from local microbreweries, and a small but well-chosen wine list.

414 Dupont St. ✆ **416/961-3472.** Reservations recommended. Main courses C$8–$16 (US$5.60–$11). AE, DC, MC, V. Mon–Sat noon–11pm; Sun 5–10pm. Subway: Dupont.

Japan Deli JAPANESE/SUSHI   Tucked into a cubbyhole on a side street just off Bloor Street West, Japan Deli succeeds at bringing tempura and teriyaki to the masses. Fine Japanese cuisine takes hours to prepare, but this is more like what time-pressed Tokyo residents are used to—a friend who used to live in Japan swears that this is as close as you can get to the experience without boarding a plane. Complete dinners include miso soup, salad, a meat dish, side vegetables, and fresh fruit for dessert—all nicely prepared, and all for under C$10 (US$7).

11 Balmuto St. © **416/920-2051**. Reservations not accepted. Main courses C$7–$9 (US$4.90–$6.30). MC, V. Mon–Sat noon–9pm. Subway: Yonge/Bloor.

Kensington Kitchen *Kids* MEDITERRANEAN   Drawing a crowd of regulars—students and profs—from the nearby University of Toronto, Kensington Kitchen is a perennial gem. The decor hasn't changed in years, with Oriental carpets covering the walls, a painted wood floor, and decorative objects scattered about. The tradition of big portions at small cost stays constant, too. The menu ventures between the ports of the Mediterranean. There's angel-hair pasta with heaps of shrimp, scallops, and mussels in tomato-coriander sauce; saffron paella with chicken and sausage; and Turkish-style braised lamb stuffed with raisins, eggplant, apricots, and figs. In clement weather, head to the rooftop patio, in the shade of a mighty Manitoba maple.

124 Harbord St. © **416/961-3404**. Reservations recommended. Main courses C$10–$14 (US$7–$9.80). AE, DC, MC, V. Mon–Sat 11:30am–11pm; Sun 11:30am–10pm. Subway: Spadina, then LRT south to Harbord St.

Lalibela ETHIOPIAN   Perhaps it's the fact that you don't need cutlery to dine in Ethiopian style that makes it so much fun. A flatbread called *injera* takes the place of flatware as you scoop up spicy hot meats and thick lentil stews. Lalibela has numerous choices for vegetarians and meat-lovers, and the helpful staff will arrange mixed plates with three different dishes for tasting.

869 Bloor St. W. © **416/535-6615**. Main courses C$5–$9 (US$3.50–$6.30). MC, V. Mon–Thurs 6–10pm; Fri–Sat 6–11pm. Subway: Christie.

Lox, Stock & Bagel DELI   If you're tuckered out while shopping in Yorkville—and not feeling up to facing the chic scene at the neighborhood's many bistros—head to the sanctuary of Lox, Stock & Bagel. Located in a courtyard of the Hazelton Lanes shopping complex, this deli serves snacks, salads, and sandwiches. The menu isn't sophisticated, but it's hard to resist comfort foods like cheese blintzes, matzo ball soup, and a classic Reuben sandwich. There are a few hot dishes too, such as vegetarian lasagna. Of course, you could always just grab a bagel, too.

Hazelton Lanes, 55 Avenue Rd. © **416/968-8850**. Reservations only for groups. Main courses C$8–$12 (US$5.60–$8.40). AE, DC, MC, V. Daily 7:30am–9pm. Subway: Bay or Museum.

Nataraj INDIAN   There's usually a bit of a wait for a table—Nataraj's upscale cuisine is popular with Annex residents, and its downscale prices are affordable to U of T students. But the service is swift, so tables do open up rather quickly. The cooking is from the northern part of the subcontinent, so there are lots of fish and seafood dishes. A number of plates will appeal to vegetarians. The tandoor-baked breads are simply sublime.

394 Bloor St. W. © **416/928-2925**. Reservations not accepted. Main courses C$7–$12 (US$4.90–$8.40). MC, V. Mon–Sat 5:30–10:30pm. Subway: Spadina.

Pho Hung VIETNAMESE   Pho usually translates as "soup," but that's a bit of a misnomer—it's more like a meal in a bowl. There are 15 good choices here, and the lemongrass- or coriander-scented broths are chock-full of meat, noodles, and vegetables. There's also a range of chicken, pork, and seafood dishes, and a tangy beef fondue. The clientele includes both suits and students, and the wine list is longer and better than you might expect.

200 Bloor St. W. ✆ 416/963-5080. Reservations recommended for groups of 4 or more. Main courses C$7–$15 (US$4.90–$11). V. Mon–Sat 11am–10pm. Subway: St. George or Museum.

Serra ✿✿ ITALIAN   This diminutive eatery would fit in nicely in Little Italy. The diners are casually chic, and the look is sleek, with a wood-paneled bar in one corner and mahogany tables for two. The trattoria-worthy fare includes thin-crust pizza topped with olives, prosciutto, and goat cheese; light-sauced pasta dishes teeming with shrimp; and grilled focaccia sandwiches.

378 Bloor St. W. ✆ 416/922-6999. www.serrarestaurant.com. Main courses C$10–$18 (US$7–$13). AE, DC, MC, V. Daily noon–10:30pm. Subway: Spadina.

SpringRolls ASIAN   What to have for dinner tonight: Chinese, Vietnamese, Thai, Singaporean? If you can't decide, your best bet is SpringRolls. The name may make you think its offerings are meager, but the multi-page menu will set you straight. Tenderly executed barbecued pork and fried shrimp dishes abound. Vegetarians don't have as many choices as you might expect, though there are a few top-notch vermicelli-and-veggie plates.

693 Yonge St. ✆ 416/972-7655. Reservations recommended. Main courses C$6–$15 (US$4.20–$11). MC, V. Sun–Thurs 11am–11pm; Fri–Sat 11am–midnight. Subway: Yonge/Bloor.

Great Greasy Spoons

While I'm enchanted by Toronto's top-notch dining spots, I just can't resist the lure of the greasy spoon. You know the kind of place I mean: fluorescent lighting, a bottle of ketchup on every Formica tabletop, vinyl-upholstered booths, and aromas of strong coffee and frying bacon. Some suggestions:

Perhaps Toronto's best-known greasy spoon, **Mars,** 432 College St. at Bathurst St. (✆ 416/921-6332), sports a neon sign that claims the diner is "Just out of this world." In addition to the all-day breakfast menu, it boasts cheese blintzes, grilled burgers, and a great turkey club. There's another location at 2363 Yonge St., just north of Eglinton Ave. (✆ 416/322-7111), but its kitschy mock-diner decor doesn't hold a candle to the real McCoy.

Avenue Coffee Shop, 222 Davenport Rd. at Avenue Rd. (✆ 416/924-5191), is just up the street from the Park Hyatt and the Four Seasons hotels, which explains the frequent celebrity sightings (signed and framed photos stand as a permanent record of stars' visits). In business since 1946, the Avenue serves a steady supply of omelets, French toast, and hamburgers.

The Goof, 2379 Queen St. E. (✆ 416/694-3605), is officially named the Garden Gate Restaurant. But certain letters burned out of the neon "Good Food" sign, giving this Beaches neighborhood mainstay its name. In addition to the usual diner grub, this spot has star power, as evidenced by recent Jennifer Lopez sightings.

5 The East End

Just about everything *will* be Greek to you in the East End along Danforth Avenue. Known appropriately enough as Greektown, this is where to come for low-cost, delicious dining, or for a midnight meal—the tavernas generally stay open until the wee hours, even on weeknights.

EXPENSIVE

Café Brussel BELGIAN   Perhaps this was to be a challenge to the supremacy of Greek food in this neighborhood. The Café Brussel is defiantly . . . Belgian? The only such eatery in the city, it draws a neighborhood crowd. The menu could pass for French in most regards, with staples like onion soup and duck confit. This is food you could get drunk on—try *carbonnades flamandes* (beef simmered in dark ale), or *moules au bourbon* (seafood with shots of hard stuff). There's also a great selection of European lagers and wines.

124 Danforth Ave. ℂ 416/465-7363. Reservations recommended. Main courses C$15–$28 (US$11–$20). AE, MC, V. Mon–Sat 5:30–11pm; Sun 11:30am–11pm. Subway: Broadview.

MODERATE

Christina's GREEK   This restaurant takes itself a little more seriously than its nearby cousins. The walls are plastered with photographs of celebrities caught in the act of dining here. (There's one infamous old snapshot of *Friends* star Matt LeBlanc dining with Alanis Morissette.) The menu offers reliable souvlakia and eggplant pies, but it veers into pasta and burger territory, too. The hearty all-day breakfast of feta-spiked omelets and herbed taters is a popular choice.

492 Danforth Ave. ℂ 416/463-4418. Reservations recommended. Main courses C$10–$24 (US$7–$17). AE, DC, MC, V. Daily 11am–4am. Subway: Chester.

Myth 𝒦𝒦 GREEK/MEDITERRANEAN   Part trendy bar, part restaurant, this generous space is large enough to encompass both. The ambience is classical Greece meets MTV. Ornate oversized shields share space with a series of TVs running an endless loop of mythic movies. Who can pay attention to what's on the plate with so much going on? Fortunately, the food calls attention to itself. Starters, ranging from traditional spanakopita to tuna tartar with beet and taro-root chips, are impossible to ignore. Main courses, such as rabbit braised in port and cinnamon, or pizza topped with spiced lamb, zucchini and onion purée, are just as demanding. As the night goes on, the crowd gathers at the bar, where a DJ starts spinning music at 11pm.

417 Danforth Ave. (between Logan and Chester). ℂ 416/461-8383. Reservations recommended. Main courses C$14–$26 (US$9.80–$18). AE, MC, V. Mon–Wed 5pm–11pm, Thurs–Sun noon–11pm; bar open till 2am nightly. Subway: Chester.

Octavia ECLECTIC/GREEK/MEDITERRANEAN   Who brought Thai satays onto the Danforth? The name of this swanky new addition to the Greektown strip fits right in, but its sensibility is decidedly different. The look is polished, with velvety banquettes against one wall and French doors that open to the sidewalk. Most of the main courses, such as grilled seafood and squid- ink pastas, come from the Mediterranean, but there's room on the menu for   California salads and satays.

414 Danforth Ave. ℂ 416/461-3562. Reservations not accepted. Main courses C$14–$22 (US$9.80–$15). AE, MC, V. Sun–Thurs 5pm–midnight; Fri–Sat 5pm–2am. Subway: Chester.

Pan on the Danforth 𝒦 GREEK   To the best of my knowledge, Pan was a god of music, not of food. I must have mixed it up, because if he is the inspiration

Sleepless in Toronto: What to Do
When the Midnight Munchies Attack

There are cities that never sleep. Well, Toronto isn't one of them. The city starts to doze off around 11:30pm, even on weekends. Sure, there are 24-hour doughnut shops, but if you're looking for something more substantial, try one of the following late-night options:

- **Caribbean Roti Corner,** 607 Queen St. W. (© **416/504-9558**), provides takeout dishes of jerk chicken, rice and peas, and meaty stews until 4am on weekends. Subway: Osgoode, then streetcar west to Spadina Ave.
- **Happy Seven** (p. 95) serves reliable Chinese food in a kitschy setting until 5am.
- **7 West Café,** 7 Charles St. W. (© **416/928-9041**), is open 24 hours a day. Delish sandwiches and pasta platters hit the spot. Those with severe sugar cravings can indulge in cakes and pies from several of the city's best bakers. Subway: Yonge/Bloor.
- If you're on the Danforth, you're in luck: Many of the terrific Greek tavernas and restaurants there, like **Myth** (p. 108), **Octavia** (p. 108), and **Christina's** (p. 108), stay open until the wee hours even on weeknights.

for this restaurant, he certainly knows his way around a kitchen. This long-established eatery updates classic Greek dishes with panache. Salmon is stuffed with mushrooms and spinach and wrapped in phyllo pastry, and a smoked baked pork chop comes with feta scalloped potatoes and zucchini relish. The well-chosen wine list favors the New World. The crowd is fairly sophisticated, which may explain the cryptic message over the bar: YOU'VE DONE IT ALREADY.

516 Danforth Ave. © 416/466-8158. Reservations accepted only for parties of 3 or more. Main courses C$13–$19 (US$9.10–$13). AE, DC, MC, V. Sun–Thurs 5–11pm; Fri–Sat 5pm–midnight. Subway: Chester or Pape.

INEXPENSIVE

Astoria GREEK   The restaurant subtitles itself a shish-kebab house, but its offerings are much broader. And it's more upscale than the name would suggest, with a patio fountain and colorful decor. Whatever the protein, it seems to respond well to broiling—beef, lamb, chicken, and seafood all get similar treatment. There are several choices for vegetarians, including souvlakia and moussaka. Expect a wait if you arrive after 8:30 or so on weekends.

390 Danforth Ave. © 416/463-2838. Reservations recommended; accepted on weekdays only. Main courses C$9–$15 (US$6.30–$11). AE, MC, V. Mon–Wed and Fri–Sat 11am–1am; Thurs and Sun 11am–midnight. Subway: Chester.

Avli GREEK   A white stucco archway contributes to the cave-like feel of the narrow street-level room, though the recent expansion to the second floor has created an airier place to dine. Always noisy, occasionally raucous, this taverna serves up some of the best food on the Danforth—non-greasy, thoughtfully prepared, and carefully seasoned. Meze starters are standard: *kopanisti* (spicy feta with peppers) and hummus for those who want cold food, grilled octopus and steamed mussels for those who like it hot. Main courses are standouts. The half chicken stuffed with cashews, dates, apples, and rice is exquisite, and the meat moussaka is the best around.

401 Danforth Ave. ☎ **416/461-9577.** www.avlirestaurant.com. Reservations recommended. Main courses C$9–$19 (US$6.30–$13). AE, DC, MC, V. Daily noon–midnight. Subway: Chester.

Mezes GREEK   This sophisticated space doles out exactly what it promises. *Mezes* are the Greek equivalent of tapas—light snacks meant to keep you going until you have a real dinner in front of you. Still, it's worth spoiling your appetite to indulge in these appetizers. Choices range from grilled calamari and octopus to spicy eggplant dip and leek pie. Do try to save room for the honey-sweet baklava.

456 Danforth Ave. ☎ **416/778-5150.** Reservations not accepted. Appetizers C$4–$10 (US$2.80–$7). AE, MC, V. Mon–Thurs 11am–midnight; Fri–Sat 11am–1am; Sun noon–midnight. Subway: Chester.

Ouzeri GREEK   One of the longtime stars of the neighborhood, Ouzeri has been packing in the crowds for years and shows no sign of slowing down. Just inside the foyer, TV sets make it look like a sports bar. Farther inside, colorful ceramic tiles and wrought iron surround terrazzo tables and wicker chairs. Charming as the interior is, if you're lucky you'll be outside on the small patio. Portions of main dishes, such as lamb pies and pork kebabs, tend to be quite generous. As the evening goes on, the convivial atmosphere evolves into festival-like celebration; on Tuesday nights, there's live Greek music.

500A Danforth Ave. ☎ **416/778-0500.** Reservations recommended. Main courses C$8–$18 (US$5.60–$13). AE, DISC, MC, V. Sun–Mon and Wed–Thurs 11am–midnight; Tues and Fri–Sat 11am–2am. Subway: Chester.

6 Uptown

This area is too large to be considered a neighborhood, stretching as it does from north of Davenport Road to Steeles Avenue. While it doesn't have the concentration of restaurants that the downtown area enjoys, a number of stellar options make the trip north worthwhile.

VERY EXPENSIVE

Auberge du Pommier ✋ FRENCH   Don't have time to drop by your French country house this weekend? To the rescue comes Auberge du Pommier, a cozy chateau that exudes Provençal-style charm. Diners outfitted in business casual relax in the care of expert servers. The menu doesn't offer many surprises, but, what it does, it does well. Appetizers set a high standard, with dishes like creamy lobster and white-bean soup, and baked artichokes stuffed with French goat cheese. Entrees, like pan-seared scallops with braised oxtail in a Cabernet *jus,* keep up the pace.

4150 Yonge St. ☎ **416/222-2220.** Reservations recommended. Main courses C$33–$38 (US$23–$27). AE, DC, DISC, MC, V. Mon–Fri 11:30am–2:30pm; Mon–Sat 5–10pm. Subway: York Mills.

Centro ✋✋ CONTINENTAL   The palace-grand main room, with its oxblood walls, is always bustling. The dressed-up all-ages crowd often starts out schmoozing at the wine bar downstairs, moves up to the main floor for dinner, then migrates back downstairs for R&B music and a nightcap (the wine bar stays open until 2am). The seasonal menu pays tribute to the restaurant's Northern Italian origins, with pasta dishes like homemade egg tagliolini with smoked chicken in a truffle emulsion. Many choices lean to contemporary Canadiana, like the grain-fed Québec capon paired with a foie gras mousse and sun-dried cherries, or French modern, like the rack of lamb in a Provençal honey mustard crust. Delicious desserts run the gamut from traditional tiramisu to warm banana bread pudding. The stellar wine list is sure to thrill oenophiles.

2472 Yonge St. ℂ 416/483-2211. www.centro.ca. Reservations required. Main courses C$28–$42 (US$20–$29). AE, DC, MC, V. Mon–Sat 5–11:30pm. Subway: Eglinton.

North 44 🌟🌟🌟 INTERNATIONAL   This is the one restaurant that even people who've never set foot in Toronto have heard about. It's profiled extensively in food and travel magazines, but can it possibly live up to its reputation? In a word, yes. The spare Art Deco decor recently got a face-lift, and the results are stunning. The soft lighting and strategically situated mirrors wrap the dining room—and its occupants—in a gorgeous glow. The menu, which changes with the seasons, borrows from Mediterranean, American, and Asian sources. The results are inspiring to the palate and the eye. On the list of main courses you might find grilled veal tenderloin with orange peppercorns, toasted barley, and root veggies, or roasted Muscovy duck breast with orange-soy marinade and foie gras. There are always a few pasta and pizza choices, such as caramelized squash ravioli with black truffle essence. It's impossible to come here without being seduced into a three-course meal. The desserts, like lemon meringue mille-feuille, are among the best in the city, and there's a wide selection of accompanying ice wines. The wine list is comprehensive, though most of the prices veer off into the stratosphere. What really sets North 44 apart is its seamless service. Those who don't like to be pampered should stay away.

2537 Yonge St. ℂ 416/487-4897. Reservations required. Main courses C$27–$45 (US$19–$32). AE, DC, MC, V. Mon–Sat 5–11pm. Subway: Eglinton.

Scaramouche 🌟 INTERNATIONAL   This is a contender for those who don't mind spending top dollar on splendid food. Tucked into an upscale apartment building, it isn't easy to find. That enhances its snob appeal—and the crowd here is more old money than the patrons at either of its uptown competitors, Centro and North 44. Scaramouche is blessed with one of the most romantic settings in the city. Floor-to-ceiling windows afford a panoramic view of the downtown skyline. (Securing a window seat is no mean feat, but fortunately most tables have decent sightlines.) The unobtrusive servers pay attention to the details. The menu is laden with caviar, foie gras, truffles, and oysters; main dishes include the likes of venison loin wrapped in smoke bacon in a red wine glaze. The wine list has a broad reach, and there's a nice selection of cognacs.

1 Benvenuto Place (off Avenue Rd.). ℂ 416/961-8011. Reservations required. Main courses C$25–$40 (US$18–$28); pasta dishes C$16–$25 (US$11–$18). AE, DC, MC, V. Dining room Mon–Sat 5:30–10pm; pasta bar Mon–Fri 5:30–10:30pm, Sat 5:30–11pm. Subway: St. Clair, then streetcar west to Avenue Rd., walk 4 blocks south to Edmund Ave.; Benvenuto is the first street on the left.

EXPENSIVE

La Bruschetta 🌟 ITALIAN   Star sightings are common in Toronto, but at La Bruschetta they're almost an everyday event. The entryway is covered from floor to ceiling with plates decorated by celebs such as Kelsey Grammer and Bette Midler. It's a surprise, then, to find the homey, kitchen-like dining room. Owner Benito Piantoni, who charms patrons with tales of Italy and Hollywood gossip, provides local color. The menu lists a dozen pastas, with cream sauces ranging from brandy to Gorgonzola. Mouthwatering main courses include veal medallions simply presented in white-wine sauce with garlic and mushrooms. After a rich meal, you'll welcome the delicate lemon ice for dessert.

1317 St. Clair Ave. W. ℂ **416/656-8622.** Reservations recommended. Main courses C$14–$26 (US$9.80–$18). AE, DC, MC, V. Mon–Sat 5:30–11:30pm. Subway: St. Clair West, then any streetcar west to Dufferin St.

Lakes ℱ BISTRO   Plush banquettes and close-set tables heighten the sense of intimacy in the narrow dining room. A casually well-dressed crowd drops by during the week; on Saturday, couples spend candlelit quality time. The menu changes every few months, with jazzed-up bistro classics such as duck confit with cranberry-shallot glaze and garlic mashed potatoes, grilled provimi veal liver, and Gruyère-and-Emmenthal fondue for two making frequent appearances. The banana crème brûlée is a perennial favorite dessert.

1112 Yonge St. ℂ **416/966-0185.** Reservations strongly recommended. Main courses C$14–$26 (US$9.80–$18). AE, DC, MC, V. Mon–Fri noon–3pm and 5:30–11pm; Sat 6–11pm. Subway: Rosedale.

Millie's Bistro ℱℱ *Kids* MEDITERRANEAN   Subtle as its signage is, Millie's is hard to miss. The sole gastronomic draw in this neighborhood, it lures even jaded downtown dwellers. It attracts an unusual mix of young-to-middle-age courting couples, families with tiny tykes, and groups gearing up for a night on the town. The sprawling menu includes dishes from Spain, southern France, Italy, Turkey, and Morocco. There is a kids' menu, too. Start with tapas—perhaps Catalan-style goat cheese with basil and olive oil; Turkish flatbread with a topping of lamb, yogurt, and mint; or a *b'stilla* (aromatic chicken wrapped in herbed semolina). Better still, sample them all—the cheery staff will arrange them on ceramic platters for sharing. Main dishes include paella with saffron, shrimp, clams, quail and chorizo sausage. Sweets are seductive, though generous portions make saving room for dessert almost impossible. On the wide-ranging wine list, Spanish selections are a particularly good value.

1980 Avenue Rd. (south of York Mills). ℂ **416/481-1247.** Reservations recommended. Main courses C$10–$27 (US$7–$19). AE, DC, MC, V. Daily 11:30am–11pm. Subway: York Mills, then walk (10–15 min.) west or take a taxi (about C$5/US$3.50).

Quartier ℱ FRENCH   The old-world elegance is palpable as you step into this refined bistro. Is it the languid sound of Edith Piaf's voice? Perhaps the baroque mirrors and look-again prints on the walls? No matter. The French-born proprietor, Marcel Rethore, has created a romance-tinged atmosphere for a casually chic crowd. The menu boasts classic dishes such as duck confit with sautéed potatoes and garlic-dressed endive, and Breton bouillabaisse. Desserts, for those who have room, include a tender lemon-cream mille-feuille and a delicate crème brûlée. The short wine list is particularly well chosen—it's hard to go wrong.

2112 Yonge St. ℂ **416/545-0505.** Reservations recommended. Main courses C$17–$27 (US$12–$19). AE, MC, V. Mon–Fri 11:30am–2:30pm; Mon–Sat 5:30–10:30pm. Subway: Eglinton.

Thai Magic ℱ THAI   Arrangements of orchids, cascading vines, and Thai statuary grace the enchanting entry. The serene staff handles frenetic crowds with ease; this spot is filled with locals, especially on Thursday and Friday nights. The meal is served Western-style, rather than in the Thai fashion of bringing all courses to the table at once. Delicate appetizers like chicken-filled golden baskets vie for attention with not-too-spicy soups. Entrees range from chicken with cashews and whole dried chiles to a coriander-infused lobster in the shell.

1118 Yonge St. ℂ **416/968-7366.** Reservations recommended. Main courses C$12–$20 (US$8.40–$14). AE, MC, V. Mon–Sat 5–11pm. Subway: Summerhill.

MODERATE

Amore Trattoria ★★ ITALIAN   This double-decker restaurant is a neighborhood favorite with groups and families alike. Pandemonium reigns on the first floor; upstairs, the cognoscenti can gaze over a balcony at the tumult below. The cheerful staff takes it all in stride. Reading the menu takes much too long: With 22 pastas, 21 pizzas, 6 meat dishes, and daily specials, it can be an intimidating experience for the indecisive. Fortunately, the kitchen consistently produces top-notch dishes, from simple salads of mesclun and goat cheese to spaghetti in brandy-tomato sauce with sweet Bermuda onion. Wine is served in tumblers in classic rustic-Italian style.

2425 Yonge St. ✆ 416/322-6184. Reservations accepted only for groups of 6 or more. Main courses C$10–$18 (US$7–$13). AE, MC, V. Daily noon–3pm and 5:30–10:30pm. Subway: Eglinton.

Grano ★ *Kids* ITALIAN   While Toronto has no shortage of Italian eateries, few spots have as much ambience as Grano. The old-fashioned trattoria contains several dining areas, with wooden furnishings, distressed stucco, and piles of greenery. The small courtyard at the back is heaven on sunny days. This is a high-energy spot that attracts celebratory groups (one clever friend of mine had her wedding rehearsal dinner here); it's also welcoming to families accompanied by *bambini*. The cooking is hearty, from tender *osso buco* to ricotta gnocchi paired with shrimp in white-wine sauce. The desserts are a serious draw—I insist that everyone try the divine white chocolate and raspberry tart at least once.

2035 Yonge St. ✆ 416/440-1986. Reservations recommended. Main courses C$11–$20 (US$7.70–$14). AE, DC, MC, V. Mon–Fri 9:30am–11pm; Sat 9am–11pm. Subway: Davisville or Eglinton.

Lolo ★★ *Finds* BISTRO   Tiny and intimate, Lolo is a perfect little bistro. Its romantic ambience is heightened by the fact that it has barely 40 seats neatly fitted between its deep-red walls. The mirrors and gold-painted crown molding around the room add a special touch, as does the warm and unrushed service. But for all of its charming airs, the menu—and the prices—are refreshingly down-to-earth. The mains are bistro classics, from the roasted supreme of chicken stuffed with spinach and mushrooms, to the grilled rib-eye steak with green peppercorn sauce and crispy frites. In addition to the a la carte menu, there's a prix-fixe option that lets you have three courses for a mere C$23 (US$16). All of the desserts—including the divine lemon tart—are made on the premises.

619 Mount Pleasant Rd. ✆ 416/483-8933. Reservations recommended. Main courses C$13–$21 (US$9.10–$15). AE, DC, MC, V. Daily 5–11pm. Subway: Eglinton, then bus east to Mount Pleasant Rd.

Mezzetta MIDDLE EASTERN   Tapas bars are a dime a dozen in Madrid, but in Toronto they're few and far between. Mezzetta is one such gem. Everything on the menu is served in appetizer-sized portions, from cold salads of feta, olives, and tomatoes to steamy *kofta*, an Egyptian dish of beef, lamb, and potato in a spicy sauce. There are also pita sandwiches and barbecued items. Much of the menu will appeal to vegetarians. The wine list is short but priced for value, and there's a lengthy list of brews, too.

681 St. Clair Ave. W. ✆ 416/658-5687. Reservations recommended on weekends. Appetizers C$3 (US$2.10). MC, V. Tues–Fri noon–2:30pm; Tues–Sun 5–10:30pm. Subway: St. Clair.

Stork on the Roof ★ BISTRO   The stork in question is a Dutch sign of good fortune. And luck it is to discover this charming bistro. The menu abounds with pan-European classics warmed by exotic elements, such as grilled pork

Vegetarian Delights

It used to be that vegetarian dining in Toronto was often more of an exercise in virtue than in good taste. Crunchy granola might be healthful for the body, but it's hell on the palate. But now a new wave of vegetarian eateries are making meat-free meals a gourmet's delight. Several of the city's finest restaurants are also offering special vegetarian tasting menus. Here are some of the best bets:

- **Annapurna Vegetarian Restaurant,** 1085 Bathurst St. (© 416/537-8513; subway: Bathurst). Annapurna has been around for more than 20 years, and it's still serving Indian vegetable dishes, hearty tofu burgers, and a variety of fruit and vegetable juices to a crowd of students and boomers. In keeping with the aura of health, Annapurna hosts free meditation classes every week. Main courses C$8–$12 (US$5.60–$8.40); MC, V; Mon–Tues and Thurs–Sat 11:30am–9pm, Wed 11:30am–6:30pm.
- **Fressen,** 478 Queen St. W. (© 416/504-5127; subway: Osgoode). This is a vegetarian oasis for sophisticates. From the freshly baked beet-infused buns to tender tofu with both hot tomato and sweet teriyaki sauces, this new hot spot makes every mouthful a gourmet delight. It's a hit with vegetarians *and* their carnivorous friends. Main courses C$12–$14 (US$8.40–$9.80); MC, V; Mon–Thurs 5:30– 10pm, Fri 5:30–11pm, Sat 10:30am–3:30pm and 5:30–11pm, Sun 10:30am–3:30pm and 5:30–10pm.
- **Juice for Life,** 336 Queen St. W. (© 416/599-4442; subway: Osgoode). If there's such a thing as an elixir of life, one of the bartenders at this

tenderloin with lemon curry sauce. Asian inspirations are in evidence, particularly in seafood dishes, like sautéed squid served with satay-worthy peanut sauce and pickled vegetables. For dessert, Dutch spiced apple pie is the standout.

2009 Yonge St. © 416/483-3747. Reservations required. Main courses C$15–$17 (US$11–$12). AE, MC, V. Wed–Fri noon–2pm; Tues–Sat 6–10pm. Subway: Davisville.

Vanipha Lanna ⋒⋒ LAOTIAN/THAI There's no shortage of Thai eateries in Toronto, but only a few specialize in the cooking of Thailand's northwestern Lanna region. Many Laos natives have relocated to Lanna, and strong, spicy Laotian influences permeate the cooking. One of the house specialties is grilled chicken and garlic served with lime-chile sauce. The busy dining room attracts casually dressed diners of all ages, all of whom the thoughtful staff treats with care.

471 Eglinton Ave. W. © 416/484-0895. www.vanipha.ca. Reservations recommended. Main courses C$8–$15 (US$5.60–$11). AE, MC, V. Mon and Wed noon–10pm; Tues and Thurs 5–10pm; Fri noon–10:30pm; Sat 1–10:30pm. Subway: Eglinton.

INEXPENSIVE

Hannah's Kitchen LIGHT FARE National magazines and newspapers have published several of its recipes, but this cubbyhole-like eatery remains defiantly low-key. Diners seat themselves at wooden banquettes or tiny tables. The menu includes many pasta dishes, both cold (pesto radiatore salad with chicken and

Annex favorite is sure to find it one day. They've already developed a Bionic Brain Tonic (peach, strawberry, and orange juices with gotu kola and ginseng) and about 40 other blends intended to boost your immune system, sex drive, or mood. The noodle and rice dishes have equally esoteric names (Buddha, Green Goddess), though their contents are down-to-earth. The high- protein almond grain burgers and hemp-seed bread get top marks. Main courses C$8–$12 (US$5.60–$8.40); Mon–Fri 8:30am–6:30pm, Sat 9am–6:30pm, Sun 10am–6pm.

- **Kalendar** (p. 95) may be a small bistro, but its list of vegetarian offerings is substantial.
- **Mezzetta** (p. 113) offers a collection of Middle Eastern appetizers, few of which contain meat; ordering a selection of three of four makes for a substantial meal.
- **Millie's Bistro** (p. 112) has a vegetarian lasagna with portobello mushrooms, sweet roasted peppers, and leeks that will make you wonder why anyone would want to add beef. The Mediterranean menu has many meat-free plates.
- **Senses** (p. 90) offers a vegetarian tasting menu that changes frequently, but might include curried-squash ravioli or a salad of Jerusalem artichoke, olives, and beets. Yum!
- **Truffles** (p. 101) is another top-notch restaurant with a vegetarian tasting menu. Called the Menu Terroir, it might feature the likes of white bean and truffle soup, or a salad of frisee with Roquefort, walnuts, and apples; C$65 (US$46) for five courses.

pine nuts is the top pick) and hot (penne arrabiata has the spiciest sauce in town), with three or four daily specials. Occasional forays into the exotic include a few Indonesian rice dishes and the ever-popular pad Thai. Desserts are a must, so check out the selection behind the counter on your way in.

2221 Yonge St. (416/481-0185. Reservations not accepted. Main courses C$7–$12 (US$4.90–$8.40). MC, V. Mon–Fri 10am–10pm. Subway: Eglinton.

Rebel House LIGHT FARE   This casual spot is beloved by locals. Is the draw the warm welcome, the better-than-average pub grub, or the impressive selection of microbrews? The crowd is mainly 20- to 30-somethings decked out in designer casualwear, more intent on socializing than eating. The specialty of the house is hearty, simple fare; grilled Atlantic salmon and seared Angus strip loin are top picks. Pastas and salads are worth a taste, too.

1068 Yonge St. (416/927-0704. Reservations not accepted. Main courses C$8–$18 (US$5.60–$13). AE, MC, V. Mon–Sat 11:30am–11pm; Sun 11:30am–10pm (bar open till 1am Mon–Sat and 11pm Sun). Subway: Rosedale.

7 North of the City

Toronto is a sprawling city, and as it has expanded, new and inspiring restaurants have cropped up in formerly out-of-the-way regions. The area north of Steeles Avenue is experiencing a remarkable boom. These restaurants are beyond the reach of the Toronto subway system. If you've rented a car to go to the McMichael Canadian Art Collection in Kleinburg or to the Canada's Wonderland theme park, you might want to stop on the way back downtown. (For driving directions, see chapter 6.)

EXPENSIVE

Terra ⊀⊀ INTERNATIONAL   This restaurant feels as if it was airlifted out of the downtown core. Sleek and sophisticated, it is the sibling of uptown's North 44, and the cooking at Terra is appropriately splendid. The kitchen favors seafood, from appetizers like butter-poached lobster with shallots and honey mushrooms to entrees like pan-fried sea bream with baby bok choy, candied beets and fava beans. There are several steak plates, with everything from a 10-ounce filet of beef to a 16-ounce porterhouse. Believe it or not, there are also numerous vegetarian offerings. Desserts include classic crème brûlée and a more unusual pecan and blueberry cheesecake. The lengthy wine list hits all the international high notes, though most bottles are quite pricey.

8199 Yonge St. (just south of Hwy. 407), Thornhill. ⓒ 905/731-6161. www.terrarestaurant.ca. Reservations recommended. Main courses C$17–$49 (US$12–$34). AE, DC, MC, V. Tues–Sun 6–11pm.

MODERATE

Grand Yatt ⊀ CHINESE   There's a Grand Yatt restaurant at the Westin Harbour Castle hotel; this is the original. The large space is quite plain in comparison with its downtown offspring, but the cooking here is widely considered better. This is Cantonese cuisine at its finest. The seafood—black cod, geoduck (a large clam), or jumbo shrimp—is fresh as a daisy, and needs only light seasoning to bring out the intense natural flavors. Shark's fin soup is a perennial favorite. The swift servers are extremely helpful.

9019 Bayview Ave., Richmond Hill. ⓒ 905/882-9388. Main courses C$12–$18 (US$8.40–$13). AE, MC, V. Daily 9am–3pm and 6–10pm.

INEXPENSIVE

Dante's ⊀⊀ ITALIAN   Predating the current boom in the area, Dante's has been the favorite local spot for down-home cooking since 1976. It's not hard to figure out why. The menu has something for everyone, the food is consistently good, and the prices are reasonable. Don't expect to find exotic risottos—stick to heaping plates of pasta like rigatoni with black and green olives, or homemade cannelloni. One serving of chicken parmigiano can feed two adults.

267 Baythorn Dr. (just off Yonge St.), Thornhill. ⓒ 905/881-1070. Main courses C$7–$14 (US$4.90–$9.80). AE, MC, V. Mon–Thurs noon–10pm; Fri–Sat noon–midnight.

6

What to See & Do

First the good news: Toronto has amazing sights to see and places to be that appeal to travelers of all stripes. The bad news? No matter how long your stay, you won't be able to fit everything in. Toronto is a sprawling city, and while downtown and midtown boast a sizable collection of attractions, some wonderful sights are in less accessible areas. Travelers in 2004 should note that some of the city's great sites, such as the Royal Ontario Museum and the George R. Gardiner Museum of Ceramic Art, will be undergoing extensive renovations throughout the year, making substantial parts of their collections unavailable for viewing— or even shutting down entirely for months.

Keep in mind that many Toronto attractions could take up a whole day. Ontario Place, Harbourfront, the Ontario Science Centre, and Paramount Canada's Wonderland all come to mind. That's not even mentioning the parks, the arts scene, or the shopping possibilities. My best advice is to relax and bring a good pair of walking shoes. There's no better way to appreciate Toronto than on foot.

SUGGESTED ITINERARIES

If You Have 1 Day

Start out early in the morning in **Kensington Market,** and pick up breakfast from one of the Middle Eastern, Asian, or North African cafes. Kensington adjoins Toronto's main **Chinatown;** stroll down Spadina Avenue and head east along Dundas Street to enjoy it. Along Dundas you'll find the **Art Gallery of Ontario;** spend at least a couple of hours there, and be sure to take in the collection of sculptures by British artist Henry Moore.

For lunch, head to the gallery's marvelous restaurant, Agora, or to nearby Baldwin Street for Chinese food. It's a short walk from here to **Queen's Park,** where the Ontario Legislature meets; the surrounding greenery affords a respite from the asphalt jungle. Head up to trendy **Yorkville,** with its small galleries, boutiques, and cafes. If you have kids in tow, you might want to check out the dinosaur displays at the **Royal Ontario Museum** (much of the ROM is under renovation, but the dinosaurs, as well as the Bat Cave and hands-on earth sciences areas are still easily accessible).

Before dinner, try to buy sameday tickets to a show in the adjoining **Theater District.** Then dine out at one of the fine restaurants along **King Street West** (see chapter 5 for suggestions).

If You Have 2 Days

On the first day, follow the itinerary for 1 day. On day 2, start by wandering the grounds of **Exhibition Place,** and arrive at the gates of **Ontario Place** at 10am sharp; allow about half a day for Ontario Place. If it's a clear sunny day, go from there to the top of the **CN Tower** and drink in the matchless view. Glance over at **SkyDome** as you pass by. Head up to the architectural wonder that is **City Hall at Nathan Phillips Square,** then continue east to the **Eaton Centre.**

After you've shopped until you drop, ride a streetcar to **Little Italy,** along College Street. There's no end of dining options; try to score a patio seat if the weather's fine. This is another prime neighborhood for nightlife, so unless you've scored tickets to a game at the **Air Canada Centre,** you can hang out here.

If You Have 3 Days
This is when I'd recommend going a little farther afield. (You could also just allot more time to the previously mentioned sights.) Start your day at the highly interactive **Ontario Science Centre.** If the weather's good, you could spend the rest of the day reveling in the 600 acres of **Sunnybrook Park.** If the weather isn't so favorable, this could be your afternoon to explore **Casa Loma** or the **Hockey Hall of Fame.** If another museum isn't your thing, head to the **Harbourfront Centre,** which offers restaurants, live music, activities for kids, and varied events. At night, go to **Greektown** along the Danforth, where the many tavernas stay open late.

If You Have 4 Days or More
Now you can really start to explore Toronto. If you've followed the itinerary for the first 3 days, you might want to return to some sights. Otherwise, you could head north of Toronto to see the **McMichael Canadian Art Collection** in Kleinburg or, if the kids outvote you, to spend the day at **Paramount Canada's Wonderland.** There's no better way to spend a day than picnicking on the lush **Toronto Islands,** where you can rent bicycles, take the kids to **Centreville** amusement park, and get a whole new view of the city. A less traveled site is scenic **Cabbagetown,** with its Edwardian and Queen Anne–style architecture, **Riverdale Farm,** and Gothic **Necropolis.** With 4 days or more, you should also be able to sample the city's lively arts scene, taking in a **theater** or **dance performance.** Try to hit a **comedy club** while you're at it, and check out one of Toronto's **sports** teams, too.

1 The Top Attractions
ON THE LAKEFRONT
Harbourfront Centre ⭐⭐⭐ (Kids)   Back in 1972, the federal government took over a 96-acre strip of waterfront land to preserve the vista. It wasn't exactly prime real estate at the time, but that has changed in the decades since. The abandoned warehouses and crumbling factories have yielded to a stunning urban playground that now stretches over the old piers. Today, Harbourfront is one of the most popular destinations for locals and visitors alike: a great place to spend a day strolling, picnicking, gallery-hopping, biking, shopping, and sailing.

Queens Quay, at the foot of York Street, is the first stop you'll encounter on the LRT line from Union Station (you can also get there in 5 minutes on foot walking south from Front Street, but that requires walking under the Gardiner Expressway, which I personally hate). From here, boats depart for harbor tours, and ferries leave for the Toronto Islands. In this renovated warehouse you'll find the Premiere Dance Theatre and two floors of shops. To get something to eat, you can stay at Queen's Quay for the casual Boathouse Grill or walk west to **York Quay** for its new Lakeside Terrace restaurant. York Quay also boasts an art gallery and ever-changing art installations, and an information booth where you can pick up information on Harbourfront events.

Harbourfront has several venues devoted to the arts. There's the **Power Plant,** a contemporary art gallery, and behind it, the **Du Maurier Theatre Centre.** At the **Craft Studio** you can watch artisans blow glass, throw pots, and make silk-screen prints, and you if you've inspired you can buy their works at **Bounty Contemporary Canadian Craft Shop.** There are the **Artists' Gardens,** which currently include 23 diverse outdoor gardens created by landscape architects, designers and other artists. In summer, one don't-miss experience is a visit to the **Toronto Music Garden,** which was created by cellist Yo Yo Ma and landscape designer Julie Moir Messervy to invoke Bach's First Suite for Unaccompanied Cello. Does it succeed? That's a matter of opinion, but in mine the series of free musical performances that run from late June to early September make this a heavenly place to visit.

More than 4,000 events take place annually at Harbourfront, including the **Harbourfront Reading Series** in June and the **International Festival of Authors** in October (see "Toronto Calendar of Events" in chapter 2). Other happenings include films, dance, theater, music, children's events, multicultural festivals, and marine events. Harbourfront is at its best in the summer, but it is a great destination for the whole family year-round.

235 Queens Quay W. ℭ 416/973-3000 for information on special events, or 416/973-4000 (box office). www.harbourfront.on.ca. Subway: Union, then LRT to Queens Quay or York Quay.

Ontario Place 🦖 *(Kids)*   When this massive recreation complex on the shores of Lake Ontario opened in 1971, it seemed futuristic. Thirty-three years later, it still does. (The major face-lift in 1989 no doubt helped.) From a distance, you'll see five steel-and-glass pods suspended on columns 32m (105 ft.) above the lake, three artificial islands, and a huge geodesic dome. The five pods contain a multimedia theater, a children's theater, a high-technology exhibit, and displays that tell the story of Ontario in vivid kaleidoscopic detail. The dome houses Cinesphere, where an 18-by-24m (60-by-80-ft.) screen shows specially made IMAX movies year-round.

In 2003, Ontario Place introduced several new attractions targeted at kids. These include the **H2O Generation Station,** a gigantic "soft play" structure with twisting slides, towers, and walkways. There's also the new **Atom Blaster,** which claims to be Canada's largest foam-ball free-for-all—this is fun for the whole family. For the small fry, there's the new **MicroKids** play area with its ball pit, climbing platforms, and other tot-appropriate draws.

At night, the **Molson Amphitheatre** can accommodate 16,000 concert-goers: 9,000 can fit in the reserved seating area under the canopy, and 7,000 more can find seating on the surrounding grass. The venue features top-line entertainers such as Tori Amos, Peter Gabriel, James Taylor, and Bryan Adams. For concert information, call ℭ **416/260-5600;** for tickets, call **Ticketmaster** (ℭ **416/870-8000**).

955 Lakeshore Blvd. W. ℭ 416/314-9811, or 416/314-9900 for recorded info. www.ontarioplace.com. Admission to grounds and Children's Village only is C$11 (US$7.70) for ages 4 and over; free for children 3 and under; separate fees for rides and events. Play All Day pass C$28 (US$20) adults and children 6 and over, C$16 (US$11) seniors and children 4–5, free for children 3 and under. IMAX movies C$8 (US$5.60) adults, C$6 (US$4.20) seniors and children 13 and under. Mid-May–Labour Day, daily 10am–dusk; evening events end and dining spots close later. Closed (except Cinesphere) early Sept–early May. Subway: Bathurst or Dufferin, then Bathurst streetcar south.

The Toronto Islands 🦖 *(Kids)*   In only 7 minutes, an 800-passenger ferry takes you to 245 hectares (612 acres) of island parkland crisscrossed by shaded paths and quiet waterways—a glorious spot to walk, play tennis, bike, feed the ducks,

What to See & Do in Downtown

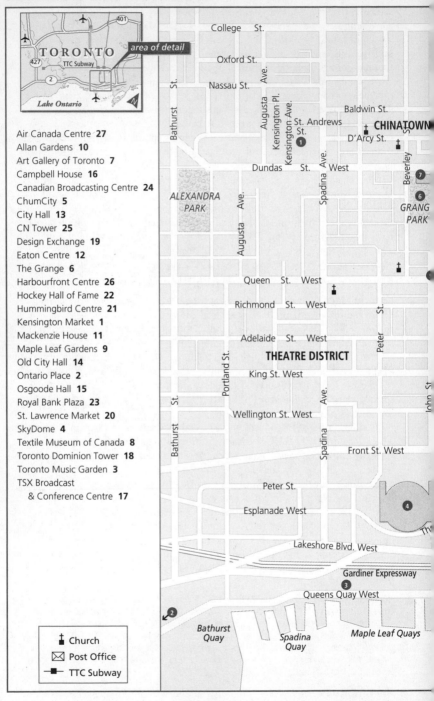

Air Canada Centre **27**
Allan Gardens **10**
Art Gallery of Toronto **7**
Campbell House **16**
Canadian Broadcasting Centre **24**
ChumCity **5**
City Hall **13**
CN Tower **25**
Design Exchange **19**
Eaton Centre **12**
The Grange **6**
Harbourfront Centre **26**
Hockey Hall of Fame **22**
Hummingbird Centre **21**
Kensington Market **1**
Mackenzie House **11**
Maple Leaf Gardens **9**
Old City Hall **14**
Ontario Place **2**
Osgoode Hall **15**
Royal Bank Plaza **23**
St. Lawrence Market **20**
SkyDome **4**
Textile Museum of Canada **8**
Toronto Dominion Tower **18**
Toronto Music Garden **3**
TSX Broadcast
& Conference Centre **17**

✝ Church
✉ Post Office
━■━ TTC Subway

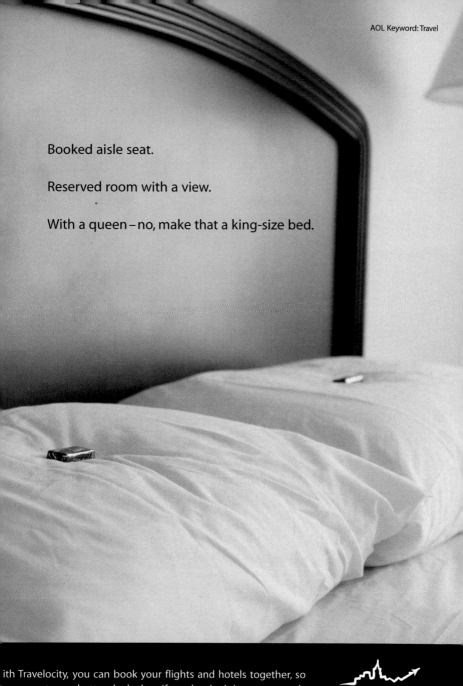

Booked aisle seat.

Reserved room with a view.

With a queen – no, make that a king-size bed.

ith Travelocity, you can book your flights and hotels together, so
u can get even better deals than if you booked them separately.
u'll save time and money without compromising the quality of
ur trip. Choose your airline seat, search for alternate airports, pick your
tel room type, even choose the neighborhood you'd like to stay in

Travelocity
**Visit www.travelocity.com
or call 1-888 TRAVELOCITY**

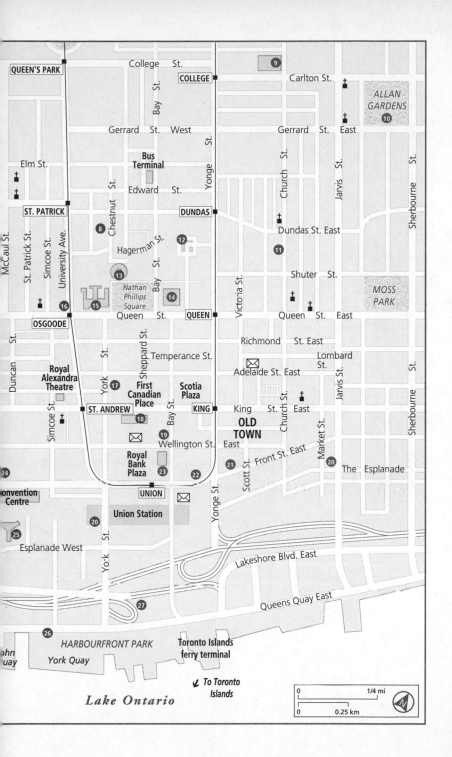

What to See & Do in Midtown

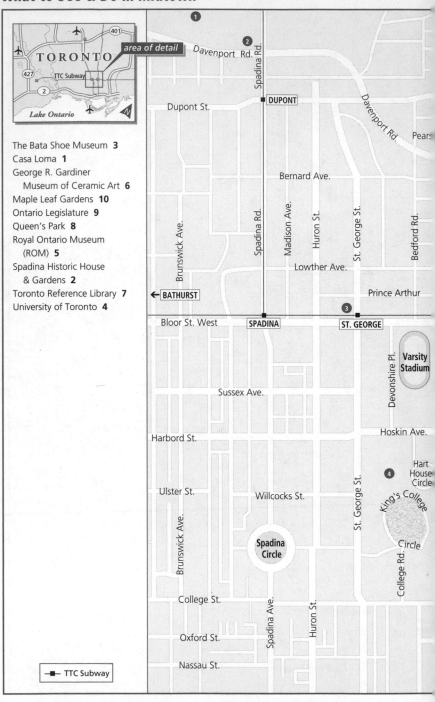

The Bata Shoe Museum **3**
Casa Loma **1**
George R. Gardiner
  Museum of Ceramic Art **6**
Maple Leaf Gardens **10**
Ontario Legislature **9**
Queen's Park **8**
Royal Ontario Museum
  (ROM) **5**
Spadina Historic House
  & Gardens **2**
Toronto Reference Library **7**
University of Toronto **4**

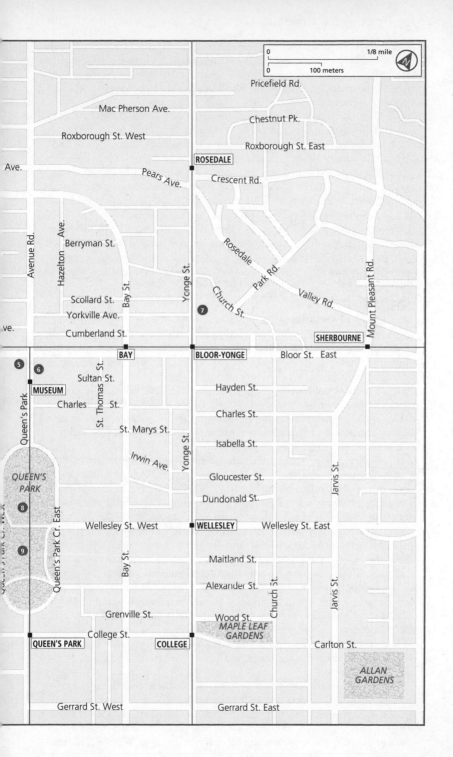

0   1/8 mile
0   100 meters

Pricefield Rd.

Mac Pherson Ave.

Chestnut Pk.

Roxborough St. West

Roxborough St. East

ROSEDALE

Ave.

Pears Ave.

Crescent Rd.

Avenue Rd.

Hazelton Ave.

Berryman St.

Rosedale Park Rd.

Yonge St.

Church St.

Valley Rd.

Mount Pleasant Rd.

Scollard St.

Bay St.

❼

Yorkville Ave.

ve.

Cumberland St.

SHERBOURNE

❺

BAY

BLOOR-YONGE

Bloor St. East

❻

Sultan St.

St. Thomas St.

MUSEUM

Hayden St.

Queen's Park

Charles St.

Charles St.

St. Marys St.

Isabella St.

Irwin Ave.

Yonge St.

Gloucester St.

QUEEN'S PARK

❽

Dundonald St.

Jarvis St.

Wellesley St. West

WELLESLEY

Wellesley St. East

❾

Queen's Park Cr. East

Bay St.

Maitland St.

Alexander St.

Church St.

Jarvis St.

Grenville St.

Wood St.

*MAPLE LEAF
GARDENS*

College St.

Carlton St.

QUEEN'S PARK

COLLEGE

*ALLAN
GARDENS*

Gerrard St. West

Gerrard St. East

putter around in boats, picnic, or lap up the sun. Of the 14 islands, the two major ones are **Centre Island** and **Ward's Island.** The first is the most popular with tourists; Ward's is more residential (about 600 people live in modest cottages on the islands). Originally, the land was a peninsula, but in the mid-1800s a series of storms shattered the finger of land into islands.

On Centre Island, families enjoy **Centreville** (© **416/203-0405**), an old-fashioned amusement park that's been in business since 1966. You won't see the usual neon signs, shrill hawkers, and greasy hot-dog stands. Instead you'll find a turn-of-the-century village complete with a Main Street, tiny shops, a firehouse, and the Far Enough Farm, where the kids can pet lambs, chicks and other barnyard animals. The kids will also love trying out the antique cars, fire engines, old-fashioned train, authentic 1890s carousel, flume ride, and aerial cars. An all-day ride pass costs C$16 (US$11) for those less than 124cm (49 in.) tall, C$22 (US$15) for those over 1.25m (4 ft.). Centreville is open from 10:30am to 6pm, daily from mid-May to Labour Day, and weekends in early May and September.

Lake Ontario. © 416/392-8193 for ferry schedules. Round-trip fare C$5 (US$3.50) adults, C$3 (US$2.10) seniors and children14–19, C$2 (US$1.40) children 13 and under, free for children 2 and under. Ferries leave from docks at the bottom of Bay St. Subway: Union Station, then LRT to Queens Quay.

DOWNTOWN

Art Gallery of Ontario ⓐ *Kids* The exterior gives no hint of the light and openness inside this beautifully designed gallery. The space is dramatic, and the paintings imaginatively displayed. Throughout, audiovisual presentations and interactive computer exhibits provide information on particular paintings or schools of painters.

The European collections are fine, but the Canadian galleries are the real treat. The paintings by the Group of Seven—which includes Tom Thomson, F. H. Varley, and Lawren Harris—are extraordinary. In addition, other galleries show the genesis of Canadian art from earlier to more modern artists. And don't miss the extensive collection of Inuit art.

The **Henry Moore Sculpture Centre,** with more than 800 pieces (original plasters, bronzes, maquettes, woodcuts, lithographs, etchings, and drawings), is the largest public collection of his works. The artist gave them to Toronto because he was so moved by the citizens' enthusiasm for his work—public donations bought his sculpture *The Archer* to decorate Nathan Phillips Square at City Hall after politicians refused to free up money for it. In one room, under a glass ceiling, 20 or so of his large works stand like silent prehistoric rock formations. Along the walls flanking a ramp are color photographs showing Moore's major sculptures in their natural locations, which reveal their magnificent dimensions.

The European collection ranges from the 14th century to the French Impressionists and beyond. Works by Pissarro, Monet, Boudin, Sisley, and Renoir fill an octagonal room. De Kooning's *Two Women on a Wharf* and Karel Appel's *Black Landscape* are just two of the modern pieces. There are several works of particular interest to admirers of the pre-Raphaelite painters, including one by Waterhouse. Among the sculptures, you'll find two beauties—Picasso's *Poupée* and Brancusi's *First Cry.*

Behind the gallery, connected by an arcade, stands **the Grange.** Dating back to 1817, it's Toronto's oldest surviving brick house, and it was the gallery's first permanent space. Originally the home of the Boulton family, it was a gathering place for many of the city's social and political leaders and for such eminent guests as Matthew Arnold, Prince Kropotkin, and Winston Churchill.

Meticulously restored and furnished to reflect the 1830s, it is a living museum of mid-19th-century Toronto life. Entrance is free with admission to the art gallery.

The gallery has an attractive restaurant, Agora (p. 87), which is open for lunch, as well as a cafeteria and a gallery shop. There's also a full program of films, concerts, and lectures.

317 Dundas St. W. (between McCaul and Beverley sts.). © 416/977-0414. www.ago.net. Admission C$12 (US$8.40) adults, C$9 (US$6.30) seniors and students, C$6 (US$4.20) children 6–15, free for children 5 and under. Free admission Wed 6–8:30pm. Tues and Thurs–Fri 11am–6pm; Wed 11am–8:30pm; Sat–Sun 10am–5:30pm. Grange House Tues–Sun noon–4pm; Wed noon–9pm. Closed Jan 1, Dec 25. Subway: St. Patrick.

CN Tower *Kids*   As you approach the city, whether by plane, train, or automobile, the first thing you notice is this slender structure. Glass-walled elevators glide up the 553m (1,815-ft.) tower, the tallest freestanding structure in the world. The elevators stop first at the 346m-high (1,136-ft.) Look Out level. (It takes just 58 seconds, so prepare for popping ears.) You can walk down one level to experience the Glass Floor, my favorite spot at the tower: Through it you can see all the way down to street level (even as your heart drops into your shoes). As a bonus, if you wait long enough, you'll undoubtedly see some alpha males daring each other to jump on the glass. (They do, and no, it doesn't break—the glass can withstand the weight of 14 adult hippos. Now *that's* a sight I'd like to see . . .)

The tower attractions are often revamped. Some perennial draws are the IMAX theater and two airplane simulators (one gentle and calm, the other a rugged ride through caves and over mountains). A series of interactive displays showcases the CN Tower along with such forerunners as the Eiffel Tower and the Empire State Building. The Look Out also contains broadcasting facilities, a nightclub, and the underwhelming **360 Revolving Restaurant** (p. 86).

Above the Look Out is the world's highest public observation gallery, the Skypod, 447m (1,465 ft.) above the ground (C$7/US$4.90 additional charge). From here, on a clear day you can't quite see forever, but the sweeping vista stretches to Niagara Falls, 161km (100 miles) south, and to Lake Simcoe, 193km (120 miles) north. Unless you're really taken with the tower, I wouldn't recommend it—the view from the Glass Floor is majestic enough for me (for other great—and less expensive—ways to view Toronto, see "Great Toronto Vistas"). Atop the tower sits a 102m (335-ft.) antenna mast erected over 31 weeks with the aid of a giant Sikorsky helicopter. It took 55 lifts (and no hippos) to complete the operation.

301 Front St. W. © 416/868-6937. www.cntower.ca. Basic admission (Look Out & Glass Floor) C$19 (US$13) adults, C$17 (US$12) seniors, C$14 (US$9.80) children 4–12; Observation Experience (Look Out, Glass Floor & Skypod) C$24 (US$17) adults, C$22 (US$15) seniors, C$19 (US$13) children 4–12; Total Tower Experience (includes Look Out, Glass Floor, Skypod, film, and 2 rides) C$32 (US$22) all ages. Motion simulator rides C$8 (US$5.60). Daily 9am–11pm. Closed Dec 25. Subway: Union, then walk west on Front St.

Fun Fact **Tough Enough**

The CN Tower is built of sturdy stuff to resist the elements—contoured reinforced concrete covered with thick glass-reinforced plastic—and designed to keep ice accumulation to a minimum. The structure can withstand high winds, snow, ice, lightning, and earth tremors.

Moments Great Toronto Vistas

I have a secret: While I know I should be impressed by the view from the CN Tower, I find it uninspiring. Don't get me wrong, it's great to see Niagara Falls on a clear day—but what I like is the view of Toronto itself, which looks more like a map and less like a metropolis from these dizzying heights. Here are some of my favorite viewing spots, where you'll get an altogether different picture of Toronto.

Bloor Street Viaduct   The viaduct over the Don Valley connects Bloor Street in midtown Toronto with the East End (where Bloor becomes the Danforth). The pedestrian walkway will afford you what is possibly the most enchanting view there is to be had. From here, Toronto doesn't even look like a city—it seems like a lush forest. There are trees as far as the eye can see, with skyscrapers and towers jutting out here and there. If you don't see it for yourself, you won't believe it. Subway: Castle Frank, and walk east along Bloor to the viaduct.

Canoe Restaurant   Yes, there's glorious food to be had here but the view's the thing. Located on the 54th floor of the imposing Toronto Dominion Tower, Canoe boasts an amazing view of the castles of commerce in the Financial District, and the city beyond. If you don't want to shell out for an expensive dinner here (see review on p. 85), stop by for a drink. Toronto Dominion Tower, 66 Wellington St. W. © 416/364-0054. Subway: King.

Casa Loma   Toronto's castle on a hill is one of the best perches from which to savor the city's beauty. Casa Loma has two towers, each with its own charms. The enclosed Scottish tower on its east side offers the highest viewing point, but the open-air Norman tower on the west side has my favorite vista. 1 Austin Terrace, © 416/923-1171. Subway: Dupont, then walk 2 blocks north.

The Roof Lounge at the Park Hyatt   It's only 18 stories up in Midtown, and yet this classic watering hole has one of the best views in town. If the weather's even halfway decent, try to score a table on the south-facing balcony. From here you can appreciate the sweeping grandeur of Queen's Park and of the historic University of Toronto grounds. Park Hyatt Toronto, 4 Avenue Rd. © 416/924-5471. Subway: Bay or Museum.

MIDTOWN

George R. Gardiner Museum of Ceramic Art   Across the street from the ROM, North America's only specialized ceramics museum houses a great collection of 15th- to 18th-century European pieces. Unfortunately, the Gardiner will be closed for most of 2004 and part of 2005; the good news is that when it reopens it will be grander than ever. Like its neighbor across the street, the museum will undergo a massive renovation. The C$15-million (US$11-million) All Fired Up plan will increase the Gardiner's floor space from 19,000 square feet to 29,000, and will allow far more of the vast—and growing—collection to be on display.

In case you manage to get to the Gardiner before the work begins, here's a taste of what you'll see. The pre-Columbian gallery contains fantastic Olmec and Maya figures, and objects from Ecuador, Colombia, and Peru. The majolica gallery displays spectacular 16th- and 17th-century salvers and other pieces from Florence, Faenza, and Venice, and a Delftware collection that includes fine 17th-century chargers. Upstairs, the galleries contain 18th-century Continental and English porcelain—Meissen, Sèvres, Worcester, Chelsea, Derby, and other great names. All are spectacular. Among the highlights are objects from the Swan Service—a 2,200-piece set that took 4 years (1737–41) to make—and an extraordinary collection of commedia dell'arte figures.

111 Queen's Park. ⓒ 416/586-8080. www.gardinermuseum.on.ca. Admission C$10 (US$7) adults, C$6 (US$4.20) seniors and students with ID. Free admission on the first Tues of every month. Mon, Wed, Fri 10am–6pm; Tues, Thurs 10am–8pm; Sat–Sun 10am–5pm. Closed Jan 1, Dec 25. Subway: Museum.

Royal Ontario Museum 🎭 *Kids*   This is one of my favorite museums anywhere. The ROM (rhymes with "tom"), as it's affectionately called, is Canada's largest museum, with more than 6 million objects in its collections. Unfortunately, in 2004, many of those pieces won't be on display because of the museum's ambitious renovation plan. Called Renaissance ROM, this C$200-million (US$142-million) project will add six new galleries overlooking Bloor Street West. The galleries will be encased inside an uber-modern palace of jutting crystal prisms designed by Daniel Libeskind. Personally, it brings to mind Superman's crystal palace at the North Pole, but I have to admit that the designs look spectacular (check out the ROM's website at www.rom.on.ca for details and a webcam that shows the work-in-progress).

While the results promise to be grand and will allow the ROM to display far more of its impressive collections, in the here and now the renovation makes the museum a less appealing place to visit, in my opinion. The breathtaking terrace galleries, which housed the world-renowned T. T. Tsui Galleries of Chinese Art, are one casualty of the reno, and the ROM has also lost its stellar restaurant, Jamie Kennedy at the Museum, which was one of the best in the city.

However, the ROM still deserves the two stars it gets this year. Intact exhibits include the **Ancient Egypt Gallery,** which features several mummies, and the **Roman Gallery,** which boasts the most extensive collection of its kind in Canada. There's also the **Gallery of Korean Art,** the largest exhibit of its kind in North America (it holds more than 200 works from the Bronze Age through

---

Finds **Serenity Now**

While I'm all for progress, my one complaint about the ROM's extensive renovation plan is that it has muddled up the **Bishop White Gallery,** which used to house a group of serene Southeast Asian Buddhas. (Last time I was in, there were still some Buddhas, but they were surrounded by construction equipment. That's not exactly the way to nirvana.) The Bishop White Gallery is worth remembering because it's supposed to be put back in place when the reno runs its course. In the meantime, serenity-seekers should head upstairs to the third-floor **History of Style** wing of the **Samuel European Galleries.** While the kiddies are busy with the dinosaurs on floor down, adults can rest in the roomy window seat–style nooks that dot the exhibit. Each one has an audio presentation that's well worth listening to; my favorite is the one about lighting, which includes several passages from *Madame Bovary.* Who knew that light at night used to be considered the ultimate luxury?

modern times). Another attraction is the new **Christopher Ondaatje South Asian Gallery** (in case you're curious, Christopher is the brother of Michael Ondaatje, author of *The English Patient*).

Many of the exhibits that kids love best are still here. One is the **Bat Cave,** a miniature replica of the St. Clair bat cave in Jamaica. It's complete with more than 3,000 lifelike bats roosting and flying through the air amid realistic spiders, crabs, a wildcat, and snakes. Kids also enjoy the spectacular **Dinosaur Gallery,** with its 13 skeletons on show. The hands-on Inco Limited Gallery of Earth Sciences in another drawing card, with plenty of interactive exhibits that teach kids how the world really works.

100 Queen's Park. ☎ **416/586-8000.** www.rom.on.ca. Admission C$10 (US$7) adults, C$7 (US$4.90) seniors and students with valid ID, C$6 (US$4.20) children 5–14, free for children 4 and under. Pay what you can Fri 4:30–9:30pm. Mon–Thurs 10am–6pm; Fri 10am–9:30pm; Sat 10am–6pm; Sun 11am–6pm. Closed Jan 1, Dec 25. Subway: Museum.

ON THE OUTSKIRTS
The McMichael Canadian Art Collection   In Kleinburg, 40km (25 miles) north of the city, the McMichael is worth a visit for the setting as well as the art. The collection occupies a log-and-stone gallery that sits amid quiet stands of trees on 40 hectares (100 acres) of conservation land. Specially designed for the landscape paintings it houses, the gallery is a work of art. The lobby has a pitched roof that soars 8m (27 ft.) on massive rafters of Douglas fir; throughout the gallery, panoramic windows look south over white pine, cedar, ash, and birch.

The collection includes the work of Canada's famous circle of landscape painters, the Group of Seven, as well as David Milne, Emily Carr, and their contemporaries. An impressive collection of Inuit and contemporary Native Canadian art and sculpture is also on display. In addition, four galleries contain changing exhibitions of works by contemporary artists.

Founded by Robert and Signe McMichael, the gallery began in 1965 when they donated their property, home, and collection to the province of Ontario. The collection has expanded to include more than 6,000 works. The museum has a good book and gift store, filled with reproductions as well as one-of-a-kind crafts, carvings and wall hangings by Canadian artisans.

10365 Islington Ave., Kleinburg. ☎ **888/213-1121** or 905/893-1121. www.mcmichael.com. Admission C$15 (US$11) adults, C$12 (US$8.40) seniors and students with ID, free for children 5 and under. May 1–Oct 31 daily 10am–5pm; Nov 1–Apr 30 daily 10am–4pm. Closed Dec 25. Parking C$5 (US$3.50). By car: From downtown, take Gardiner Expressway to Hwy. 427 north, follow it to Hwy. 7, and turn east. Turn left (north) at first light onto Hwy. 27. Turn right (east) at Major Mackenzie Dr. and left (north) at first set of lights to Islington Ave. and the village of Kleinburg. Or take Hwy. 401 to Hwy. 400 north. At Major Mackenzie Dr., go west to Islington Ave. and turn right. By bus: From Islington station, take bus no. 37 to Steeles Ave., then take the York Region bus no. 13 to the museum driveway (it's about a 10-min. walk up the driveway from the bus stop); note that separate fares are required for the 2 buses.

Ontario Science Centre 🛱🛱 ⟨Kids⟩   Described as everything from the world's most technical fun fair to a hands-on museum for the 21st century, the Science Centre holds a series of wonders for children—800 interactive exhibits in 10 cavernous exhibit halls. More than a million people visit every year, so it's best to arrive promptly at 10am to see everything.

Wherever you look, there are things to touch, push, pull, or crank. Test your reflexes, balance, heart rate, and grip strength; surf the Internet; watch frozen-solid liquid nitrogen shatter into thousands of icy shards; study slides of butterfly wings, bedbugs, fish scales, or feathers under a microscope; tease your brain with a variety of optical illusions; land a spaceship on the moon; watch bees making honey; see how many lights you can light or how high you can elevate a balloon with your own pedal power. The fun goes on and on through the 10 exhibit halls.

Throughout, small theaters show film and slide shows, and you can see regular 20-minute demonstrations of lasers, metal casting, and high-voltage electricity (which will literally make your hair stand on end). Another draw is the Omnimax Theatre, with a 24m (79-ft.) domed screen that creates spectacular effects. There are two eateries on-site: Galileo's Bistro, a buffet-style restaurant that serves alcohol, and Valley Marketplace, a cafeteria. The Mastermind shop has a vast collection of educational toys and games.

While most of the Ontario Science Centre's offerings are fun for the small fry, one area that adults will appreciate is the re-creation of a rainforest environment. On the bottom level of the building, it's large enough that you can wander a bit and forget the noise and blinking lights of the science arcade just beyond. One caveat: Roam in here for long and you'll feel as if you've hit a sauna.

770 Don Mills Rd. (at Eglinton Ave. E.). (✆) 416/696-3127, or 416/696-1000 for Omnimax tickets. www.ontariosciencecentre.ca. Admission C$14 (US$9.80) adults, C$10 (US$7) seniors and children 13–17, C$8 (US$5.60) children 5–12; free for children 4 and under. Omnimax admission C$11 (US$7.70) adults, C$8 (US$5.60) seniors and children 13–17, C$7 (US$4.90) children 5–12, free for children 4 and under. Combination discounts available. July 1–Sept 4 daily 10am–6pm; Sept 5–June 30 daily 10am–5pm. Closed Dec 25. Parking C$8 (US$5.60). Subway: Yonge St. line to Eglinton, then no. 34 Eglinton bus east to Don Mills Rd. By car: From downtown, take Don Valley Pkwy. to Don Mills Rd. exit and follow signs.

Paramount Canada's Wonderland ⟨ᖴ⟩ *(Kids)* Thirty minutes north of Toronto lies Canada's answer to Disney World. The 120-hectare (300-acre) park features more than 140 attractions, including 60 rides, a water park, a play area for tiny tots (KidZville), and live shows.

Adults and kids alike come for the thriller rides. Because the park relies on the local audience, it introduces new rides every year. In 2003, it opened Sledge Hammer, which it described as a "menacing mechanical giant"; true to its billing, the behemoth stands 80 feet tall and hurls riders through accelerated jumps and free-falls. Other top attractions include the Fly, a roller coaster designed to make every seat feel as if it's in the front car (the faint of heart can't hide at the back of this one!); Drop Zone, in which riders free-fall 70m (230 ft.) in an open cockpit; Cliffhanger, a "super swing" that executes 360-degree turns and makes riders feel immune to gravity; and the Xtreme Skyflyer, a hang-gliding and skydiving hybrid that plunges riders 46m (150 ft.) in a free fall. The roller coasters range from the looping, inverted Top Gun, to the track-free suspended Vortex.

Finds Retro Thrills

With the fanfare given to the new rides Paramount Canada's Wonderland introduces each summer, many park-goers overlook the older attractions. The Wilde Beaste is one of the original roller coasters, and it's still one of the best. The first few times you hurtle along the track you'll be convinced that the whole rickety structure is about to fall down at any moment. Guess what—it was designed to feel that way! (Wonderland's safety standards are top-notch, so have no worries on that front.) Other tried-and-true favorites include the Minebuster and the Dragon Fire. A bonus: shorter queues!

Where to Eat When You're Going to . . .

In my experience, one of the most difficult things about travel is coordinating where you want to go with where you want to eat. All too often you find yourself at a great museum, only to realize that the great restaurant you wanted to try out is on the other side of town. To make your planning easier, here are some of Toronto's top attractions, and the excellent restaurants that are nearby (note that all restaurants mentioned here are reviewed in chapter 5).

- **Art Gallery of Ontario:** The AGO has an excellent restaurant, **Agora,** but it's only open for lunch. Instead, head over to Chinatown for **Sang Ho** (536 Dundas St. W.), **Happy Seven** (358 Spadina Ave.) or **Lee Garden** (331 Spadina Ave.). Or, if you're in the mood for French cuisine, the best nearby is at **La Bodega** (30 Baldwin St.).

- **CN Tower** and **SkyDome:** The tower's main dining room, **360,** is popular with tourists, and while I can certainly recommend the view I'm less enthusiastic about the food. But it's a very short walk to **Senses** (at the SoHo Metropolitan Hotel, 318 Wellington St. W.), **Rain** (19 Mercer St.) and **Avalon** (270 Adelaide St. W.).

- **Hummingbird Centre** and **Hockey Hall of Fame:** You're in luck here, because the stellar **Biff's** (4 Front St. E.) is just across the street. You're also right by **Le Papillon** (16 Church St.), **HotHouse Cafe** (35 Church St.) and **Young Thailand** (81 Church St.)—three well-priced places that serve impressive food.

- **Ontario Science Centre:** While people who work at the OSC love to point out that it's in the geographic center of Toronto, it's Nowheresville as far as food is concerned. But if you head west to Yonge Street you'll be spoiled for choice. If you went to the OSC, presumably you have kids in tow, so **Grano** (2035 Yonge St.) would be an excellent choice. Other good bets include **Hannah's Kitchen** (2221 Yonge St.), which is open only on weekdays, or **Amore Trattoria** (2425 Yonge St.), which is open 7 days a week.

- **Royal Ontario Museum:** The ROM has lost its stellar restaurant to its ongoing renovations, but fortunately **The Colony Kitchen** (157 Bloor St. W.) has opened across the street. Nearby Yorkville is full of great spots, including **Jacques Bistro du Parc** (126A Cumberland St.). Head just a few blocks west past Spadina and you'll find a wide selection of moderately priced spots such as **Serra** (378 Bloor St. W.) and **Nataraj** (394 Bloor St. W.).

The Splash Works water park offers a huge wave pool and 16 water rides, from speed slides and tube rides to special scaled-down slides and a kids' play area. You'll also find Hanna-Barbera characters, including Scooby-Doo, strolling around the park (and ready to get their picture taken with the kids). Additional attractions include Wonder Mountain and its high divers (they take the 20m/66-ft. plunge down Victoria Falls to the mountain's base), restaurants, and shops. The Kingswood Theatre books top-name entertainers.

You'll definitely want to take a full day to see everything. If you picnic on the grounds and forgo souvenirs, a family of four can "do" the park for about C$200 (US$140), depending on the age of the kids. Watch out, though, for the extra attractions not included in the admission pass.

9580 Jane St., Vaughan. ⓒ **905/832-7000** or 905/832-8131. www.canadas-wonderland.com. Pay-One-Price Passport (includes unlimited rides and shows but not parking, special attractions, or Kingswood Music Theater) C$47 (US$33) adults and children 7 and over, C$23.50 (US$16) seniors and children 3–6, free for children 2 and under. Admission only (no rides) C$25 (US$18). June 1–25 Mon–Fri 10am–8pm, Fri–Sat 10am–10pm; June 26–Labour Day daily 10am–10pm; late May and early Sept–early Oct Sat–Sun 10am–8pm. Closed mid-Oct to mid-May. Parking C$7 (US$4.90). Subway: Yorkdale or York Mills, then GO Express Bus to Wonderland. By car: From downtown, take Yonge St. north to Hwy. 401 and go west to Hwy. 400. Go north on Hwy. 400 to Rutherford Rd. exit and follow signs. By car from the north, exit at Major Mackenzie.

The Toronto Zoo *Kids*   Covering 284 hectares (710 acres) of parkland, this unique zoological garden contains some 5,000 animals, plus an extensive botanical collection. Pavilions—including Africa, Indo-Malaya, Australasia, and the Americas—and outdoor paddocks house the plants and animals.

One popular zoo attraction is at the **African Savanna** project. It re-creates a market bazaar and safari through Kesho (Swahili for "tomorrow") National Park, past such special features as a bush camp, a rhino midden, elephant highway, and several watering holes. It also includes the **Gorilla Rainforest,** which opened in the spring of 2001; it's one of the most popular sights at the zoo—little wonder, as this is the largest indoor gorilla exhibit in North America. In the summer of 2002, the zoo opened Splash Island, a kids-only water park that includes a replica of a Canadian Coast Guard ship.

Ten kilometers (6 miles) of walkways offer access to all areas of the zoo. During the warmer months, the Zoomobile takes visitors around the major walkways to view the animals in the outdoor paddocks. The zoo has restaurants, a gift shop, first aid, and a family center. Visitors can rent strollers and wagons, and borrow wheelchairs. The African pavilion has an elevator for strollers and wheelchairs. There's ample parking and plenty of picnic areas with tables.

Meadowvale Rd. (north of Hwy. 401 and Sheppard Ave.), Scarborough. ⓒ **416/392-5900.** www.toronto zoo.com. Admission C$18 (US$13) adults, C$12 (US$8.40) seniors, C$10 (US$7) children 4–12, free for children 3 and under. Summer daily 9am–7:30pm; spring and fall 9am–6pm; winter 9:30am–4:30pm. Last admission 1 hour before closing. Closed Dec 25. Parking C$6 (US$4.20). Subway: Bloor–Danforth line to Kennedy, then bus no. 86A north. By car: From downtown, take Don Valley Pkwy. to Hwy. 401 east, exit on Meadowvale Rd., and follow signs.

2 More Museums

The Bata Shoe Museum *★*   Imelda Marcos—or anyone else obsessed with shoes—will love this museum, which houses the Bata family's 10,000-item collection. The building, designed by Raymond Moriyama, is spectacular. The main gallery, "All About Shoes," traces the history of footwear. It begins with a plaster cast of some of the earliest known human footprints (discovered in Africa by anthropologist Mary Leakey), which date to 4 million B.C.

You'll come across such specialty shoes as spiked clogs used to crush chestnuts in 17th-century France, Elton John's 12-inch-plus platforms, and Prime Minister Pierre Trudeau's well-worn sandals. One display focuses on Canadian footwear fashioned by the Inuit, while another highlights 19th-century ladies' footwear. The second-story galleries house changing exhibits.

327 Bloor St. W. (at St. George St.). © 416/979-7799. www.batashoemuseum.ca. Admission C$6 (US$4.20) adults, C$4 (US$2.80) seniors and students with ID, C$2 (US$1.40) children 5–14, C$12 (US$8.40) family (2 adults, 2 children). Free to all first Tues of the month. Tues–Wed and Fri–Sat 10am–5pm; Thurs 10am–8pm; Sun noon–5pm. Subway: St. George.

Black Creek Pioneer Village *Kids*   Life here moves at the gentle pace of rural Ontario as it was more than a century ago. The original pioneers on this land were Daniel and Elizabeth Strong, a newlywed couple in 1816 who cleared 100 acres of wilderness for farming and built a log house in their spare time. Eventually a village developed around this site, and many of the existing buildings date from the 1860s. You can watch the authentically dressed villagers going about their chores, spinning, sewing, rail splitting, sheep shearing, and threshing. Visitors can enjoy the villagers' cooking, wander through the cozily furnished homesteads, visit the working mill, shop at the general store, or rumble past the farm animals in a horse-drawn wagon. The beautifully landscaped village has more than 30 restored buildings to explore. Special events take place throughout the year, from a great Easter egg hunt to Christmas by lamplight.

The restaurant is open from 11am to 3pm and features a special children's menu. Light snacks and refreshments are on sale all day at the Visitor's Centre.

1000 Murray Ross Pkwy. (at Steeles Ave. and Jane St.), Downsview. © 416/736-1733. www.blackcreek.ca. Admission C$10 (US$7) adults, C$9 (US$6.30) seniors, C$6 (US$4.20) children 5–14, free for children 4 and under. May–June Mon–Fri 9:30am–4:30pm, Sat–Sun and holidays 10am–5pm; July–Sept daily 10am–5pm; Oct–Dec Mon–Fri 9:30am–4pm, Sat–Sun and holidays 10am–4:30pm. Closed Jan–Apr, Dec 25. Parking C$6 (US$4.20). Subway: Finch, then bus no. 60 west to Murray Ross Parkway.

Design Exchange   Located in the old Stock Exchange Building, the Design Exchange—or DX, as it prefers to be known—has become an important Canadian design museum. It showcases professionals' work, but its main purpose is to nurture designers of all types—graphic, industrial, interior, landscape, and urban. It also serves as a clearinghouse and resource center for the design community. One of its most popular programs is CONNECT, DX's national student design competition, which is intended to foster and promote young design talent. Note that Kubo DX, the on-site restaurant, is well worth a stop (see the review of its sibling, the Colony Kitchen, on p. 103).

Finds **Pssst . . . Want in on a Secret?**

Toronto has a unique museum that is one of the city's best-kept secrets. It's the **History of Contraception Museum**, at the Janssen-Ortho building, 19 Green Belt Dr. (© 416/449-9444). The collection occupies an airy atrium and contains more than 600 items, some of which will make your jaw drop. (Ever wonder what mule earwax, weasel testicles, and crocodile dung have in common? This is your chance to find out.) The museum is extremely well curated, and many of the prophylactics have fascinating stories behind them.

The only downside to the museum is that it's far off the beaten track—though the Ontario Science Centre is just a 5-minute drive away. If you've already made it that far, hop on a southbound Don Mills Road bus; there's a stop at Green Belt Drive, and the Janssen-Ortho building is a 2-minute walk up the street. It's open Monday through Friday from 9am to 5pm, and admission is free.

234 Bay St. © 416/363-6121. www.dx.org. Admission C$8 (US$5.60) adults, C$5 (US$3.50) seniors and students with ID, free for children 13 and under. Mon–Fri 10am–6pm; Sat–Sun noon–5pm. Closed Dec 25 and Jan 1. Subway: King.

Museum of Contemporary Canadian Art ✸ *Finds* This 9-year-old gallery's original mission was to collect and exhibit the best Canadian art created since 1985; however, it is now showing some works by international artists, too. Currently, the Canadian collection includes works by Stephen Andrews, Genevieve Cadieux, Ivan Eyre, Betty Goodwin, Micah Lexier, Arnaud Maggs, and Roland Poulin. MOCCA's mandate has been widening in recent years, and that has made this gallery increasingly interesting. Some of the temporary exhibits have been real eye-openers, in particular one about tattoo art entitled "Art for the Human Canvas." MOCCA is out of the way, geographically speaking, but it is on the subway line, so the museum is very accessible. Best of all, admission is free!

Toronto Centre for the Arts, 5040 Yonge St., Toronto. © 416/395-0067. www.mocca.toronto.on.ca. Free admission. Tues–Sun noon–5pm. Closed Dec 25 and Jan 1. Subway: North York Centre.

Textile Museum of Canada ✸ This fascinating museum is internationally recognized for its collection of more than 8,000 historic and ethnographic textiles and related artifacts. You'll find fine Oriental rugs, and cloth and tapestries from all over the world. One gallery presents the work of contemporary artists. The museum is small, so only a tiny portion of the collection is on display, but you'll always find a vibrant, interesting show.

55 Centre Ave. © 416/599-5321. www.museumfortextiles.on.ca. Admission C$8 (US$5.60) adults, C$6 (US$4.20) seniors, students, and children 5 and over, free for children 4 and under. Pay what you can ed 5–8pm. Tues and Thurs–Fri 11am–5pm; Wed 11am–8pm; Sat–Sun noon–5pm. Closed Dec 25 and Jan 1. Subway: St. Patrick.

3 Exploring the Neighborhoods

Toronto is a patchwork of neighborhoods, and the best way to discover its soul and flavor is to meander along its streets. On foot you can best appreciate the sights, sounds, and smells—those elements that lend a particular area its unique character. These are some of the most interesting neighborhoods.

DOWNTOWN WEST

CHINATOWN ✸ Stretching along Dundas Street west from Bay Street to Spadina Avenue and north and south along Spadina Avenue, Chinatown is home to some of Toronto's 350,000 Chinese-Canadian residents. Packed with fascinating shops and restaurants, it even has bilingual street signs.

In **Dragon City,** a large shopping mall at Spadina and Dundas, you'll find all kinds of stores. Some sell Chinese preserves (like cuttlefish, lemon ginger, whole mango, ginseng, and antler), and others specialize in Asian books, tapes, records, fashion, and food. Downstairs, a fast-food court features Korean, Indonesian, Chinese, and Japanese cuisine.

As you stroll through Chinatown, stop at the **Kim Moon Bakery,** 438 Dundas St. W. (© **416/977-1933**) for Chinese pastries and a pork bun, or go to one of the tea stores. A walk through Chinatown at night is especially exciting—the sidewalks fill with people, and neon lights shimmer everywhere. You'll pass windows where ducks hang, gleaming noodle houses, record stores selling the Top 10 in Chinese, and trading companies filled with Asian produce. Another stop might be the **New Asia Supermarket,** 299 Spadina Ave. (© **416/ 591-9314**), around the corner from Dundas Street.

To get to Chinatown, take the subway to St. Patrick and walk west. For more details, see "Walking Tour: Chinatown & Kensington Market," in chapter 7.

LITTLE ITALY   Along College Street between Euclid and Shaw, Little Italy competes with West Queen West for the hottest spot in the city. The area hums at night, as people crowd the coffee bars, pool lounges, nightclubs, and trattorias. Notable restaurants in the area include **Sottovoce** (p. 96), **Chiado** (p. 88), and **Veni Vidi Vici** (p. 94). There are also some great boutiques in the area, such as **Ewanika,** 490 College St. (© 416/927-9699), which features chic, tailored clothing for women who don't normally like suits, and **Mink,** 550 College St. (© 416/929-9214), a glittering oasis of faux gemstones. To get there, ride any College Street streetcar west to Euclid Avenue.

QUEEN STREET WEST   This street has over the years been known as the heart of Toronto's avant-garde scene. That would be a serious stretch today. Sure, it's home to several clubs—the **BamBoo** and the **Rivoli,** in particular—where major Canadian artists and singers have launched their careers (see chapter 9), but it's also where you'll find mainstream shops such as Club Monaco, Gap, and Le Chateau. Edgy? Queen Street West would love to be, but it just isn't anymore. (See West Queen West, below, if you want a walk on the—somewhat—wilder side.)

Queen Street West officially starts at Yonge Street, but it doesn't really pick up, style-wise, till you cross University Avenue; it ends at Bathurst Street. There are lots of great bistros in this neighborhood, such as **Le Sélect** (p. 92) and the **Taro Grill** (p. 94). This is also prime shopping territory, with one-of-a-kind clothing boutiques such as **Price Roman,** 267 Queen St. W. (© 416/979-7363), and **Peach Berserk,** 507 Queen St. W. (© 416/504-1711). You'll also find a number of fine antiquarian bookstores, antiques and/or junk shops, nostalgic record emporiums, kitchen supply stores, and discount fabric houses.

To start exploring, take the subway to Osgoode and walk west along Queen Street West.

WEST QUEEN WEST   Queen Street West beyond Bathurst Street used to be a no-man's land—not because it was dangerous, but because little of importance was believed to be that far from the downtown core. How times have changed: West Queen West, as the neighborhood is now known, is one of the liveliest 'hoods in the city (one magazine dubbed it the coolest in the country—not that a typically modest Torontonian would tell you that!).

West Queen West is all funky fun. It's got great shops for housewares and antiques, such as **Quasi Modo,** 789 Queen St. W. (© 416/703-8300), and excellent small art galleries, such as the **Stephen Bulger,** 700 Queen St. W. (© 416/504-0575). It's also got some fine-but-affordable dining, at spots like **Swan** (p. 94) and **Cities** (p. 91). To start exploring, take the subway to Osgoode and walk west along Queen Street West, or take the streetcar over to Bathurst.

DOWNTOWN EAST

THE BEACHES   This is one of the neighborhoods that makes Toronto a unique city. Here, near the terminus of the Queen Street East streetcar line, you can stroll or cycle along the lakefront boardwalk. Because of its natural assets, it has become a popular residential neighborhood for young boomers and their families, and there are plenty of browseable stores along Queen Street. Just beyond Waverley Road, you can turn down through Kew Gardens to the boardwalk and walk all the way past the Olympic Pool to Ashbridge's Bay Park. To get to the Beaches, take any Queen Street East streetcar to Woodbine Avenue.

MIDTOWN WEST

YORKVILLE   This area stretches north of Bloor Street, between Avenue Road and Bay Street. Since its founding in 1853 as a village outside the city proper, Yorkville has experienced many transformations. In the 1960s, it was Toronto's Haight-Ashbury, the countercultural mecca for young suburban runaways otherwise known as hippies. In the 1980s, it became the shopping ground of the chic, who dropped their money liberally at such boutiques as **Hermès, Chanel,** and **Cartier,** and at the neighborhood's many fine art galleries. In the early 1990s, the recession left its mark—a fact that became glaringly obvious when Creeds, a Toronto institution, shut its doors. The restored town houses began to look a little forlorn, but today the energy is back. Bloor Street and **Hazelton Lanes** continue to attract high-style stores, including a branch of **Tiffany's.**

Stroll around and browse—or sit out in the sun at one of the many cafes on Yorkville Avenue or Cumberland Avenue, and watch the parade go by. Make sure you wander through the labyrinths of Hazelton Lanes, between Avenue Road and Hazelton Avenue. You'll find a maze of shops and offices clustered around an outdoor court in the center of a building that is topped with apartments—one of the most sought-after addresses in the city. The courtyard plays host to outdoor dining in summer and skating in winter.

While you're in the neighborhood (especially if you're an architecture buff), take a look at the red-brick building on Bloor Street at the end of Yorkville Avenue that houses the **Toronto Reference Library.** Step inside and you'll find one of Toronto's most serene spots. To reach Yorkville, take the subway to Bay.

MIRVISH VILLAGE   One of the city's most illustrious characters is Honest Ed Mirvish, who started his career in the 1950s with a no-frills department store at the corner of Markham and Bloor streets (1 block west of Bathurst). Even from blocks away, neon signs race and advertisements touting bargains hit you from every direction. Among his other accomplishments, Mirvish saved the Royal Alexandra Theatre on King Street from demolition, established a row of adjacent restaurants for theater patrons, and developed this block-long area with art galleries, restaurants, and bookstores. He was responsible for saving and renovating London's Old Vic, too.

Stop by and browse, and don't forget to step into **Honest Ed's** (see "The Best Bargains" on p. 180). To start your visit, take the subway to Bathurst.

THE EAST END

THE DANFORTH/GREEKTOWN   This eclectic area along Danforth Street east of the Don River is hot, hot, hot. It swings until the early hours, when the restaurants and bars are still crowded and frenetic. During the day, visitors can browse the traditional Greek stores—like **Akropol,** a Greek bakery at no. 458 (© **416/465-1232**) that displays stunning multi-tiered wedding cakes in the window. The neighborhood is becoming more ethnically diverse, and its new character is reflected by stores like **Blue Moon,** no. 375 (© **416/778-6991**), which sells beautiful crafts from the developing world (the store supports only producers that provide healthy working conditions and fair pay); and **El Pipil,** no. 267 (© **416/465-9625**), which has colorful clothing, knapsacks, and jewelry. To get to the Danforth, ride the subway to Broadview and walk east.

4 Architectural Highlights

Toronto is a beautiful city in spite of itself—or rather, in spite of some of the city planners and developers who have torn down valuable parts of the city's architectural legacy in the name of progress. Toronto grew by leaps and bounds in the Victorian and Edwardian eras, which is why there are so many stunning buildings from those times (take a walk around the **University of Toronto campus** for a quick introduction to the different styles; also, the **Ontario Legislature** and the **old City Hall** stand out as particularly striking examples). However, much of the 20th century wasn't as kind: Clumsy planners plonked the Gardiner Expressway near the waterfront—making what should have been prime territory into a wasteland—and roughly 28,000 buildings were demolished between 1955 and 1975. A few of the buildings that went up during that era were stunners, such as Ludwig Mies van der Rohe's black-glass **Toronto-Dominion Centre** and Viljo Rewell's **new City Hall.** Still, there are a lot of forgettable buildings in town, but enough Gothic-inspired ones survived that Toronto makes a convincing stand-in for New York on-screen. If you're interested in exploring Toronto's architectural history, the Royal Ontario Museum's **ROMwalks** programs are an excellent way to go (see "Organized Tours" later in this chapter).

Casa Loma ★★★ *(Kids* Every city has its folly, and Toronto has an unusually charming one. It's complete with Elizabethan-style chimneys, Rhineland turrets, secret passageways, an underground tunnel, and a mellifluous name: Casa Loma.

Sir Henry Pellatt, who built it between 1911 and 1914, had a lifelong fascination with castles. He studied medieval palaces and gathered materials and furnishings from around the world, bringing marble, glass, and paneling from Europe, teak from Asia, and oak and walnut from North America. He imported Scottish stonemasons to build the massive walls that surround the 2.5-hectare (6-acre) site.

It's a fascinating place to explore. Wander through the majestic Great Hall, with its 18m-high (60-ft.) hammer-beam ceiling; the Oak Room, where three artisans took 3 years to fashion the paneling; and the Conservatory, with its elegant bronze doors, stained-glass dome, and pink-and-green marble. The castle encompasses battlements and a tower; Peacock Alley, designed after Windsor Castle; and a 1,800-bottle wine cellar. A 244m (800-ft.) tunnel runs to the stables, where the luxury of Spanish tile and mahogany surrounded the horses.

I find it amusing to compare the Pellatts' private suites. Lady Mary's is overwhelmingly extravagant—you could house a family of four in her bathroom, nevermind the bedroom, sitting area, sunroom, and so on. Sir Henry's suite is surprisingly modest: It's relatively tiny, with the greatest extravagance being the 18-inch-diameter showerhead in the bathroom. It does make you wonder which of them was the *real* driving force behind the building of the castle.

The tour is self-guided; pick up an audiocassette, available in eight languages, upon arrival. From May to October, the gardens are open, too. There's also a

---

⌒Finds Walk This Way

Several doors on the first story of Casa Loma open to a grand terrace that overlooks the gardens; most visitors step out, look at the gorgeous fountain and flowers below, and then proceed with the castle tour. Their mistake. From the terrace, it's almost impossible to see the entrances to several winding paths that lead around the extensive grounds and command amazing views. Follow the grand staircase down and enjoy a leisurely ramble.

Druxy's deli (part of a local chain) on-site, which is good to know, as there aren't many dining options nearby. Casa Loma hosts special events every March, July, and December.

1 Austin Terrace. © 416/923-1171. www.casaloma.org. Admission C$10 (US$7) adults, C$6.50 (US$4.55) seniors and children 14–17, C$6 (US$4.20) children 4–13, free for children 3 and under. Daily 9:30am–5pm (last entry at 4pm). Parking C$2.30 (US$1.60) per hour. Closed Jan 1, Dec 25. Subway: Dupont, then walk 2 blocks north.

City Hall ✪ An architectural spectacle, City Hall houses the mayor's office and the city's administrative offices. Daringly designed in the late 1950s by Finnish architect Viljo Revell, it consists of a low podium topped by the flying-saucer-shaped Council Chamber, enfolded between two curved towers. Its interior is as dramatic as its exterior.

In front stretches **Nathan Phillips Square** (named after the mayor who initiated the project). In summer you can sit and contemplate the flower gardens, fountains, and reflecting pool (which doubles as a skating rink in winter), as well as listen to concerts. Here you'll find Henry Moore's *The Archer* (formally, *Three-Way Piece No. 2*), purchased through a public subscription fund, and the Peace Garden, which commemorates Toronto's sesquicentennial in 1984. In contrast, to the east stands the **Old City Hall,** a green-copper-roofed Victorian Romanesque-style building.

100 Queen St. W. © 416/338-0338. www.city.toronto.on.ca. Free admission. Self-guided tours Mon–Fri 8:30am–4:30pm. Subway: Queen, then walk west to Bay.

Eaton Centre Buttressed at both ends by 30-story skyscrapers, this high-tech center, which cost over C$250 million (US$175 million) to build, stretches from Dundas Street south along Yonge Street to Queen Street, an area that encompasses 557,418 sq. m (6,000,000 sq. ft.). A **Sears** department store (which replaced the original Eaton's store) anchors the north sections, and more than 285 stores and restaurants and two garages fill the rest. Some 20 million people shop here annually.

Inside, the structure opens into the impressive **Galleria,** a 264m-long (866-ft.) glass-domed arcade dotted with benches, orchids, palm trees, and fountains; it's further adorned by Michael Snow's 60 soaring Canada geese, titled *Step Flight.* The birds are made from black-and-white photos mounted on cast fiberglass frames. Three tiers rise above, reached by escalator and glass elevators, which afford glorious views over this Crystal Palace and Milan–style masterpiece designed by Eb Zeidler (who also designed Ontario Place). Don't be surprised by the twittering of sparrows, some of which have decided that this environment is as pleasant as the outdoors.

Dundas and Yonge sts. © 416/598-8700. www.torontoeatoncentre.com. Mon–Fri 10am–9pm; Sat 9:30am–7pm; Sun noon–6pm. Subway: Dundas or Queen.

(Finds A Place in the Sun

While it's easy to get carried away in the shops of Eaton Centre, don't overlook Trinity Square, on the west side of the building near the Sears department store. The complex surrounds two of Toronto's oldest landmarks: **Trinity Church,** dating to 1847, and **Scadding House** (© 416/598-4521), home of Trinity's rector. Concerned citizens demanded that the developers not block sunlight from reaching the buildings. They got their way—the sun continues to shine on the church's twin towers.

Ontario Legislature ☆   At the northern end of University Avenue, with University of Toronto buildings to the east and west, lies Queen's Park. Embedded in its center is the rose-tinted sandstone-and-granite Ontario Legislature, with stately domes, arches, and porte-cochères. At any time of year other than summer, drop in around 2pm—when the legislature is in session—for some pithy comments during the question period, or take one of the regular tours. It's best to call ahead to check times.

111 Wellesley St. W. (at University Ave.). ✆ 416/325-7500. www.ontla.on.ca. Free admission. Year-round Mon–Fri; Victoria Day–Labour Day Sat–Sun. Weekend tours every half-hour 9–11:30am and 1–4pm; call ahead at other times. Subway: Queen's Park.

Royal Bank Plaza   Shimmering in the sun, Royal Bank Plaza looks like a pillar of gold, and with good reason. During its construction, 2,500 ounces of gold went into the building's 14,000 windows as a coloring agent. More important, the structure is a masterpiece of architectural design. Two triangular towers of bronze mirror glass flank a 40m-high (130-ft.) glass-walled banking hall. The external walls of the towers are built in a serrated configuration so that they reflect a phenomenal mosaic of color from the skies and surrounding buildings.

In the banking hall, hundreds of aluminum cylinders hang from the ceiling, the work of Venezuelan sculptor Jesús Raphael Soto. Two levels below, there's a waterfall and pine-tree setting that's naturally illuminated from the hall above.

Front and Bay sts. Free admission. Subway: Union.

Toronto Reference Library   Step inside—a pool and a waterfall gently screen out the street noise, and the space opens dramatically to the sky. Light and air flood every corner. This structure is another masterwork by Toronto architect Raymond Moriyama, who also designed the Bata Shoe Museum.

789 Yonge St. ✆ 416/395-5577. Free admission. Year-round Mon–Thurs 10am–8pm; Fri–Sat 10am–5pm; Thanksgiving–Apr Sun 1:30–5pm. Subway: Bloor.

5 Historic Buildings

Campbell House   Just across from Osgoode Hall (see below) sits the 1822 mansion of Sir William Campbell, a Loyalist and sixth chief justice of Upper Canada. In 1829, he retired to this mansion, where he lived until his death in 1834. It was moved several blocks from its original location in 1972. The beautifully restored building features a collection of period furniture. Guided tours take about half an hour and provide insight into Toronto's early history.

160 Queen St. W. (at University Ave.). ✆ 416/597-0227. Admission C$4.50 (US$3.15) adults; C$2.50 (US$1.75) seniors, C$3 (US$2.10) students with ID, C$2 (US$1.40) children ages 5–12, C$10 (US$7) family (2 adults, 2 children). Year-round Mon–Fri 9:30am–4:30pm; May–Oct also Sat–Sun noon–4:30pm. Subway: Osgoode.

Colborne Lodge   This charming, English-style Regency cottage with a three-sided verandah was built in 1836–37 to take advantage of the view of Lake Ontario and the Humber River. At the time, it was considered way out in the country, and a bother to travel to during the harsh winters. In 1873, the owner, a Toronto surveyor and architect named John Howard, donated the house and surrounding land to the city in return for an annual salary. That created High Park (see "Parks & Gardens," below), a great recreational area.

High Park. ✆ 416/392-6916. Admission C$3.50 (US$2.45) adults, C$2.75 (US$1.90) seniors and children 13–18, C$2.50 (US$1.75) children 12 and under. Tues–Sun 10am–4pm. Call ahead; hours vary. Subway: High Park.

Fort York (Kids   Established by Lieutenant Governor Simcoe in 1793 to defend "little muddy York," as Toronto was then known, Americans sacked Fort York in 1813. You can tour the soldiers' and officers' quarters, clamber over the ramparts, and view demonstrations. The fort really comes to life in summer, with daily demonstrations of drill, music, and cooking. The fort is a few blocks west of the CN Tower and 2 blocks east of Exhibition Place.

100 Garrison Rd., off Fleet St., between Bathurst St. and Strachan Ave. ☎ 416/392-6907. Admission C$5 (US$3.50) adults, C$3.25 (US$2.30) seniors and children 13–18, C$3 (US$2.10) children 6–12, free for children 5 and under. Free parking. Mid-May to Labour Day daily 10am–5pm; Sept to mid-May Mon–Fri 10am–4pm, Sat–Sun 10am–5pm. Subway: Bathurst, then streetcar no. 911 south.

Mackenzie House   This typical mid-19th-century brick row house, 2 blocks east of Yonge and south of Dundas, gives some idea of what Toronto must have looked like when the streets were lined with similar buildings. Concerned friends and fundraisers bought it for William Lyon Mackenzie, leader of the 1837 rebellion, and he lived here from 1859 to 1861. It's furnished in 1850s style, and in the back there's a print shop designed after Mackenzie's own.

82 Bond St. ☎ 416/392-6915. Admission C$3.50 (US$2.45) adults, C$2.75 (US$1.90) seniors and children 13–18, C$2.50 (US$1.75) children 5–12, free for children 4 and under. May–Sept 1 Tues–Sun noon–5pm, Sept 2–Dec Tues–Sun noon–4pm; Jan–Apr Sat–Sun noon–5pm. Subway: Dundas.

Osgoode Hall   West of City Hall, an impressive, elegant wrought-iron fence extends in front of an equally gracious public building, Osgoode Hall. Folklore has it that the fence was built to keep cows from trampling the flowerbeds. Tours of the interior reveal the splendor of the grand staircase, the rotunda, the Great Library, and the fine portrait and sculpture collection. Construction began in 1829, and troops were billeted here after the Rebellion of 1837. It's currently the home of the Law Society of Upper Canada, the headquarters of Ontario's legal profession. The Court of Appeal for Ontario has several magnificent courtrooms here. The courts are open to the public.

130 Queen St. W. ☎ 416/947-3300. Free admission. Mon–Fri 9am–6pm. Free tours July–Aug Mon–Fri 1:15pm. Subway: Osgoode.

Spadina Historic House & Gardens ✿   Here's a trick locals play on unsuspecting visitors: Get them to pronounce "Spadina." In the case of the avenue, it's spa-*dye*-na; for this lovely landmark, it's spa-*dee*-na. Why? Who knows! But if you want to see how the leading lights of the city lived in days gone by, visit the historic home of financier James Austin. The exterior is beautiful, the interior even more impressive. Spadina House contains a remarkable collection of art, furniture, and decorative objects. The Austin family occupied the house from 1866 to 1980, and successive generations modified and added to the house and its decor.

Tours (the only way to see the house) start on the quarter hour. Be warned that while the guides are excellent, the video that they force you to watch before the tour is laughable. (The narrator is the "spirit of the house," and his rambling

Finds **Park Yourself Here**

Spadina House is the next-door neighbor of Casa Loma (p. 136). Between the two is a small but lovely park that is almost hidden by the trees that shade it. Many visitors don't notice it, but locals love it. Grab a bench here if you want to take a breather.

comments—paired with a stagy Irish brogue—will make you wonder if the video is a joke. It isn't!). In summer, you can also tour the gorgeous gardens.

285 Spadina Rd. ℂ 416/392-6910. Guided tour C$5 (US$3.50) adults, C$3.50 (US$2.45) seniors and children over 12, C$3 (US$2.10) children 12 and under. Tues–Fri noon–4pm; Sat–Sun noon–5pm. Subway: Dupont.

6 For Sports Fans

Air Canada Centre   Toronto's newest sports and entertainment complex is home to the Maple Leafs (hockey) and the Raptors (basketball). Longtime fans were crushed when the Leafs moved here in 1999 from Maple Leaf Gardens— the arena that had housed the team since 1931—but the Air Canada Centre has quickly become a fan favorite. Seating 18,700 for hockey, 19,500 for basketball, and 20,000 for concerts, the center was designed with comfort in mind. Seating is on a steeper-than-usual grade so that even the "nosebleed" sections have decent sightlines, and the seats are wider . . . and upholstered.

40 Bay St. (at Lakeshore Blvd.). ℂ 416/815-5500. www.theaircanadacentre.com. Tours C$12 (US$8.40) adults, C$10 (US$7) seniors and students with ID, C$8 (US$5.60) children 12 and under. Tours on the hour daily 11am–3pm. Call ahead; no tours during events. Subway: Union, then LRT to Queens Quay.

Canada's Sports Hall of Fame   In the center of Exhibition Place, this three-floor space celebrates the country's greatest male and female athletes in all major sports. Complementing the displays are touch-screen computers that tell you everything you could want to know about particular sports personalities and Canada's athletic heritage.

Exhibition Place. ℂ 416/260-6789. Free admission. Mon–Fri 10am–4:30pm. Subway: Bathurst, then street-car no. 511 south to end of line.

Hockey Hall of Fame ⟨*Kids*⟩   Ice hockey fans will be thrilled by the artifacts collected here. They include the original Stanley Cup (donated in 1893 by Lord Stanley of Preston), a replica of the Montréal Canadiens' locker room, Terry Sawchuck's goalie gear, Newsy Lalonde's skates, and the stick Max Bentley used. You'll also see photographs of the personalities and great moments in hockey history. Most fun are the shooting and goalkeeping interactive displays, where you can take a whack at targets with a puck or don goalie gear and face down flying video pucks or sponge pucks.

In BCE Place, 30 Yonge St. (at Front St.). ℂ 416/360-7765. www.hhof.com. Admission C$12 (US$8.40) adults, C$8 (US$5.60) seniors and children 4–18, free for children 3 and under. Late June to Labour Day Mon–Sat 9:30am–6pm, Sun 10am–6pm; Sept to mid-June Mon–Fri 10am–5pm, Sat 9:30am–6pm, Sun 10:30am–5pm. Closed Jan 1, Dec 25. Subway: Union.

SkyDome   In 1989, the opening of 53,000-seat SkyDome, home to the Toronto Blue Jays baseball team and the Toronto Argonauts football team, was a gala event. In 1992, SkyDome became the first Canadian stadium to play host to the World Series, and the Blue Jays won the championship for the first of two consecutive years. The stadium represents an engineering feat, featuring the world's first fully retractable roof, which spans more than 3 hectares (8 acres), and a gigantic video scoreboard. It is so large that a 31-story building would fit inside the complex when the roof is closed.

1 Blue Jays Way. ℂ 416/341-2770. www.skydome.com. Tours C$12.50 (US$8.75) adults, C$8 (US$5.60) seniors and children 12–17, C$7 (US$4.90) children 4–11, free for children 3 and under. Tours on the hour daily 11am–3pm. Call ahead; no tours during events. Parking C$6.50 (US$4.55). Subway: Union.

7 Markets

Toronto's markets are an important part of its heritage—and not just because they bring regional produce into the city. The markets have traditionally been surrounded by neighborhoods that have absorbed wave after wave of immigrants into the city's fabric. Make like a local and dive into the fray.

Kensington Market ★★ This colorful, lively area should not be missed. You'll hear Caribbean, Portuguese, Italian, and other accents as merchants spread out their wares—squid and crabs in pails, chickens, pigeons, bread, cheese, apples, pears, peppers, ginger, and mangoes from the West Indies, salted fish from Portuguese dories, lace, fabrics, and other colorful remnants. There's no market on Sunday. Kensington Avenue itself is a treasure trove of vintage clothing stores. Admittedly there's a lot of junk here, but there are also amazing finds to be had at shops such as **Courage My Love** (14 Kensington Ave.; ℂ **416/ 979-1992**). Most of the shops display their wares out-of-doors in decent weather, adding to the color and charm of the area.

> **_Finds_ Say Cheese**
>
> One Kensington Market spot I can't resist is the **Global Cheese Shoppe,** 76 Kensington Ave. (ℂ **416/593-9251**). It stocks excellent offerings from around the world, and the staff is happy to let you try anything. One irresistible choice is the made-in-Ontario goat cheese. Mmm . . .

Bounded by Dundas St., Spadina Ave., Baldwin St., and Augusta Ave. No central phone. Most stores open Mon–Sat. Subway: St. Patrick, then Dundas St. streetcar west to Kensington.

St. Lawrence Market This handsome food market is in a vast building constructed around the facade of the second city hall, built in 1850. Vendors sell fresh meat, fish, fruit, vegetables, and dairy products as well as other foodstuffs. The best time to visit is early Saturday morning, shortly after the farmers arrive.

92 Front St. E. ℂ **416/392-7219**. Tues–Thurs 8am–6pm; Fri 8am–7pm; Sat 5am–5pm. Subway: Union.

8 Parks, Gardens & Cemeteries

DOWNTOWN

Allan Gardens George William Allan gave the city these gardens. He was born in 1822 into a wealthy merchant-banking family, and part of his vast estate was the land stretching from Carlton Street to Bloor Street between Jarvis and Sherbourne in downtown. A lawyer by training, he became a city councilor, mayor, senator, and philanthropist. The stunning glass-domed conservatory dates back to 1910 and contains six greenhouses that cover 1,486 sq. m (16,000 sq. ft.). They are filled with colorful flora from around the world. The outdoor park is rather seedy and should be avoided after sunset.

Between Jarvis, Sherbourne, Dundas, and Gerrard sts. ℂ **416/392-1111**. Free admission. Daily dawn–dusk. Subway: Dundas.

MIDTOWN

High Park This 160-hectare (400-acre) park in the far west of Midtown was surveyor and architect John G. Howard's gift to the city. He lived in Colborne Lodge, which still stands in the park. The grounds contain a large lake called

Grenadier Pond (great for ice-skating), a small zoo, a swimming pool, tennis courts, sports fields, bowling greens, and vast expanses of green for baseball, jogging, picnicking, bicycling, and more.

1873 Bloor St. W., stretching south to the Gardiner Expressway. No phone. Free admission. Daily dawn–dusk. Subway: High Park.

Necropolis   Located in Midtown East, this is one of the city's oldest cemeteries, dating to 1850. Many of the remains were originally buried in Potters Field, where Yorkville stands today.

Before strolling through the cemetery, pick up a History Tour at the office. You'll find the graves of William Lyon Mackenzie, leader of the 1837 rebellion, as well as those of his followers Samuel Lount and Peter Matthews, who were hanged for their part in the rebellion. Anderson Abbot, the first Canadian-born black surgeon; Joseph Tyrrell, who discovered dinosaurs in Alberta; world-champion oarsman Ned Hanlan; and many more notable Torontonians lie in the 15-acre cemetery. Henry Langley, who is also buried here, designed the porte-cochère and Gothic Revival chapel.

200 Winchester St. (at Sumach St.). ℂ **416/923-7911.** www.mountpleasantgroupofcemeteries.ca. Free admission. Daily 8am–dusk. Subway: Castle Frank, then bus no. 65 south on Parliament St. to Wellesley and walk 3 blocks east to Sumach.

UPTOWN

Edwards Gardens ⭐   This quiet, formal 14-hectare (35-acre) garden is part of a series of parks that stretch over 240 hectares (600 acres) along the Don Valley. Gracious bridges arch over a creek, rock gardens abound, and roses and other seasonal flowers add color and scent. The garden is famous for its rhododendrons. The Civic Garden Centre operates a gift shop and offers free walking tours on Tuesday and Thursday at 11am and 2pm. The Centre also boasts a fine horticultural library.

777 Lawrence Ave. E. (at Leslie St.). ℂ **416/397-8186.** Free admission. Daily dawn–dusk. Subway: Eglinton, then no. 51 (Leslie) or no. 54 (Lawrence) bus.

Mount Pleasant Cemetery ⭐   Home to one of the finest tree collections in North America, this cemetery is also the final resting place of many fascinating people. Of particular note are Glenn Gould, the celebrated classical pianist; Dr. Frederick Banting and Dr. Charles Best, the University of Toronto researchers who discovered insulin in 1922; golfer George Knudson; the Massey and Eaton families, whose mausoleums are impressive architectural monuments; Prime Minister William Lyon Mackenzie King; Canada's greatest war hero, Lieutenant Colonel William Barker; and writer and editor Jim Cormier.

375 Mount Pleasant Rd., north of St. Clair Ave. ℂ **416/485-9129.** www.mountpleasantgroupofcemeteries. ca. Free admission. Daily 8am–dusk. Subway: St. Clair.

9 Especially for Kids

The city puts on a fabulous array of special events for children at **Harbourfront.** In March, the **Children's Film Festival** screens 40 entries from 15 countries. In April, **Spring Fever** celebrates the season with egg decorating, puppet shows, and more; on Saturday mornings in April, the 5-to-12 set enjoys **cushion concerts.** In May, the **Milk International Children's Festival** brings 100 international performers to the city for a week of great entertainment. For additional information, call ℂ **416/973-3000.**

For 30 years, the **Young Peoples Theatre,** 165 Front St. E., at Sherbourne Street (℃ **416/862-2222** for box office or 416/363-5131 for administration), has been entertaining youngsters. Its season runs from August to May.

Help! We've Got Kids is an all-in-one directory for attractions, events, shops and services appropriate for kids under 13 in the Greater Toronto area. It doesn't provide a lot of detail about most of the entries, but the listings make a great starting point. A print copy costs C$12 (US$8.40); info is free at **www.help wevegotkids.com**.

Look in the sections above for the following Toronto-area attractions that have major appeal for kids of all ages. Tied for best venue (at least from a kid's point of view) are:

- **Harbourfront** (p. 118): Kaleidoscope is an ongoing program of creative crafts, active games, and special events on weekends and holidays. There's also a pond, winter ice-skating, and a crafts studio.
- **Ontario Place** (p. 119): The Children's Village, water slides, huge Cinesphere, futuristic pod, and other entertainment are the big hits at this recreational and cultural park. In the Children's Village, kids under 13 can scramble over rope bridges, bounce on an enormous trampoline, or drench one another in the water-play section.
- **Ontario Science Centre** (p. 128): Kids race to be the first at this paradise of hands-on games, experiments, and push-button demonstrations—800 of them.
- **Paramount Canada's Wonderland** (p. 129): The kids can't wait to get on the theme park's roller coasters and daredevil rides. And don't forget to budget for video games.
- **Toronto Zoo** (p. 131): One of the best in the world, modeled after San Diego's—the animals in this 284-hectare (710-acre) park really do live in a natural environment.

For more specialized interests:

- **Art Gallery of Ontario** (p. 124): For its hands-on kids' exhibit.
- **Black Creek Pioneer Village** (p. 132): For craft and other demonstrations.
- **Casa Loma** (p. 136): The stables, secret passageway, and fantasy rooms capture children's imaginations.
- **CN Tower** (p. 125): Especially for the interactive simulator games and the terror of the glass floor.
- **Fort York** (p. 139): For its reenactments of battle drills, musket and cannon firing, and musical marches with fife and drum.
- **Hockey Hall of Fame** (p. 140): Who wouldn't want the chance to tend goal against Mark Messier and Wayne Gretzky (with a sponge puck), and to practice with the fun and challenging video pucks?
- **Royal Ontario Museum** (p. 127): The top hits are the dinosaurs and the spooky bat cave, but the interactive earth sciences galleries are also a big draw.
- **Toronto Islands—Centreville** (p. 119): Riding a ferry to this turn-of-the-century amusement park is part of the fun.

Chudleigh's   A day here introduces kids to life on a farm. They'll enjoy hayrides, pony rides, and, in season, apple picking. There's a playground, a straw maze, and more. The store sells pies, cider, and other produce.

9528 Hwy. 25 (3km/1.8 miles north of Hwy. 401), Milton. ℂ **905/826-1252**. www.chudleighs.com. Orchard admission C$5 (US$3.50), free for children 3 and under, C$12 (US$8.40) family (2 adults, 2 children). July–Oct daily 10am–5pm. By car: From downtown, take Highway 401 west to Highway 25 (exit 320); follow Hwy. 25 north for about 3km (1.8 miles).

Cullen Gardens & Miniature Village

The half-scale village has great appeal. The 11 hectares (27 acres) of gardens, the playground (with two splash ponds), the shopping, and the live entertainment only add to the fun. There are special events year-round, including various flower festivals in summer, Halloween pumpkin carving in October, and fireworks at midnight on New Year's Eve.

Taunton Rd., Whitby. ℂ **905/686-1600**. www.cullengardens.com. Admission C$12.50 (US$8.75) adults, C$9 (US$6.30) seniors, C$5.50 (US$3.85) children 3–12, free for children 2 and under. Free parking. Summer daily 9am–8pm; spring and fall daily 10am–6pm. Closed early Jan to mid-Apr. By car: From downtown, take Hwy. 401 east to Hwy. 12 (exit 410); drive north on Hwy. 12 to Taunton Rd.; turn left (west) at Taunton Rd. and drive 1 km (½ mile).

Playdium

The Playdium is an interactive pleasure palace, with its 3,066-sq.-m (33,000-sq.-ft.) space filled with more than 200 games and simulators. It also has rock-climbing walls, a 1.2km (¾-mile) Go-Kart track, an IMAX theater, batting cages, mini golf, and a lounge and restaurant. Beyond the sliding steel door activated by an infrared sensor, you'll discover a surreal scene of huge TV screens, circuit boards, and neon and strobe-lit "alien squid mushrooms."

99 Rathburn Rd. W. ℂ **905/273-9000**. www.playdium.com. C$2–$23 (US$1.40–$16) per game or attraction. Mon–Thurs noon–midnight; Fri noon–2am; Sat 10am–2am; Sun 10am–midnight. By car: Take Hwy. 401 to Hwy. 10 (Hurontario St.), and go south to Rathburn Rd. W.

Riverdale Farm ⋆

Idyllically situated on the edge of the Don Valley Ravine, this working farm right in the city is a favorite with small tots. They enjoy watching the cows and pigs, and petting the other animals. There are farming demonstrations daily at 10:30am and 1:30pm.

201 Winchester St. (at Sumach St.). ℂ **416/392-6794**. Free admission. Daily 9am–5pm. Subway: Castle Frank, then bus no. 65 south on Parliament St. to Wellesley and walk 3 blocks east to Sumach.

Wild Water Kingdom

A huge water theme park, Wild Water Kingdom encompasses a 20,000-square-foot wave pool, tube slides, speed slides, giant hot tubs, and thrilling water rides (try the Midnight Express, which spirals through some very dark tunnels). There are bumper boats, pedal boats, canoes, batting cages, and mini golf, too. Note that the park may not be open in inclement weather, so call ahead if in doubt.

Finch Ave., 1.6km (1 mile) west of Hwy. 427, Brampton. ℂ **416/369-0123** or 905/794-0565. www.wild waterkingdom.com. Admission C$24.50 (US$17) adults and children 10 and over, C$18.50 (US$13) seniors and children 4–9, free for children 3 and under, flat rate of C$14.50 (US$10) per person after 4pm. June daily 10am–6pm; July to mid-Aug daily 10am–8pm; late Aug to Sept 2 daily 10am–6pm. By car: Take Hwy. 401 to Hwy. 427 north; exit at Finch Ave. and drive 1.6km (1 mile) west. Or from downtown, take Queen Elizabeth Way (QEW) to Hwy. 427 north; exit at Finch Ave. and drive 1.6km (1 mile) west.

10 Organized Tours

For summer weekends, it's always a good idea to make tour reservations in advance. At slower times, you can usually call the same day or simply show up.

BUS TOURS

If you enjoy bus tours, try the **Greater Toronto Double Decker Circle Tour** offered by **Gray Line,** 184 Front St. E. (ℂ **416/594-3310;** www.grayline.ca). It goes to such major sights as the Eaton Centre, City Hall, Casa Lom town, Harbourfront, SkyDome and the CN Tower, and a ticket allows hop on and hop off the bus over a 2-day period. These tours, which operate daily starting at 10am, cost C$32 (US$22) for adults, C$28 (US$20) for seniors, and C$17 (US$12) for children 4 to 11; free for children 3 and under.

HARBOR & ISLAND TOURS

Mariposa Cruise Line (© 800/976-2442 or 416/203-0178; www.mariposa cruises.com) operates 1-hour narrated tours of the harborfront and the Toronto Islands from mid-May to September. There are five cruises a day, departing between 11am and 4pm, and the cost is C$16.50 (US$12) for adults, C$15 (US$11) for seniors and students, and C$11.50 (US$8) for children 4 to 11. Tours leave from the Queen's Quay Terminal at 207 Queens Quay W.

For a real thrill, board the *Kajama,* a three-masted, 50m (164-ft.) schooner, for a 90-minute cruise. The schedule varies, but through July and August there are three tours a day on weekdays and weekends. Prices for the cruise are C$19 (US$13) for adults, C$17 (US$12) for seniors and students, and C$11 (US$8) for children. For more information, call the **Great Lakes Schooner Company,** 249 Queens Quay W., Suite 111 (© 800/267-3866 or 416/260-6355; www. greatlakesschooner.com).

INDUSTRIAL TOURS

Canadian Broadcasting Centre ☆☆ The headquarters for the CBC's English-language networks (including television and radio), this building was designed by Bregman + Hamann/Scott Associates, with John Burgee and Philip Johnson as consultants. It's one of the largest and most modern broadcasting facilities in North America. The tour, which includes a visit to the rooftop studios, is well worth the money, but you can also stop by to check out the **CBC Museum** (© 416/205-5574): It has a series of interactive exhibits and film clips showcasing the CBC's broadcast history; it's open weekdays from 9am to 5pm and Saturdays from noon to 4pm; and it's free!

250 Front St. W. © 416/205-8605. www.cbc.ca/aboutcbc. Tour C$7 (US$4.90) adults, C$5 (US$3.50) seniors, students, and children. Tours by appointment only. Subway: Union.

ChumCity This innovative television station contrasts dramatically with the CBC's formality. Housed in a beautifully restored early 20th-century building, it's a television factory where cameras are not hard-wired to studios or control rooms. Instead of formal shows confined to studios, programs can flow minute by minute from any working area in the building, including the hallways and rooftop. From this location, the cutting-edge company operates three channels: **Citytv,** a popular local news and "infotainment" station; **MuchMusic,** which is devoted to interviews with rock stars, videos, and live music; and **Bravo,** a 24-hour arts channel. ChumCity has 100 permanently fixed remote-control cameras, 25 mobile news cruisers, plus remote terminals at key locations such as City Hall, Metro Hall, the TTC, and police headquarters. The results air on "CityPulse" at noon, 6, and 11pm.

This futuristic, interactive TV station invites casual visitors to air their opinions and grievances. Simply enter **Speakers Corner,** a video booth at the corner of John and Queen streets, and bare your soul before the camera. If you're compelling or bizarre enough, you'll get your 15 seconds of fame on a weekly half-hour show, or in short blurbs on Citytv and MuchMusic.

299 Queen St. W. (at John St.). © 416/591-7400, ext 2770. www.citytv.com. Subway: Osgoode.

TSX Broadcast & Conference Centre   The Toronto Stock Exchange no longer has a trading floor—all of its transactions are electronic now—but this information center will be of interest to anyone who wants to learn more about buying low and selling high. Newly renovated and expanded in 2003, the centre is a popular site for private corporate events, so it's essential to call ahead to make sure it's open to the public on any given weekday.

Exchange Tower, 130 King St. W. (at York St.). ℂ 800/729-5556 or 416/947-4676. www.tse.com. Free admission. Mon–Fri 10am–5pm. Call ahead to ensure site is open the day of your visit. Subway: St. Andrew.

WALKING & BIKING TOURS

Toronto is a city made for walking, and there's no shortage of options for those willing to pound the pavement. The **Royal Ontario Museum** has a **ROMwalks** program (ℂ **416/586-5513**) throughout the summer that offers guided tours of neighborhoods from the Entertainment District to the Danforth. Tours start at 6pm Wednesday and 2pm Sunday come rain or shine. Many of the walks are free, though a few cost C$10 (US$7) per person. Also during the summer, the **Toronto Historical Board** (ℂ **416/392-6827**) offers free walking tours of several neighborhoods, including Cabbagetown and Rosedale. Call ahead for details.

Year-round, **A Taste of the World Neighbourhood Bicycle Tours and Walks** ☆ (ℂ 416/923-6813; www.torontowalksbikes.com) leads visitors through the nooks and crannies of places like Chinatown, Yorkville, and Rosedale. Walking tours cost C$15 (US$11) for adults, C$13 (US$9.10) for seniors and students, and C$9 (US$6.30) for children under 12. Bike tours cost C$45 (US$32), C$40 (US$28), and C$30 (US$21), respectively; the price includes bike and helmet rental.

11 Outdoor Activities

Toronto residents love the great outdoors, whatever the time of year. In summer, you'll see people cycling, boating, and hiking; in winter, there's skating, skiing, and snowboarding.

For additional information on facilities in the parks, golf courses, tennis courts, swimming pools, beaches, and picnic areas, call **Toronto Parks and Recreation** (ℂ **416/392-8186**; www.city.toronto.on.ca/parks). Also see "Parks, Gardens & Cemeteries," earlier in this chapter.

BEACHES

The Beaches is the neighborhood along Queen Street East from Coxwell Avenue to Victoria Park. It has a charming boardwalk that connects the beaches, starting at **Ashbridge's Bay Park,** which has a sizable marina. **Woodbine Beach** connects to **Kew Gardens Park** and is a favorite with sunbathers and volleyball players. Woodbine also boasts the **Donald D. Summerville Olympic Pool.** Snack bars and trinket sellers line the length of the boardwalk.

⸜Tips Don't Drink the Water!

Situated on Lake Ontario, Toronto boasts several beaches where you can lap up the sun. Just don't lap up the polluted H_2O, even though you'll see many Torontonians doing just that as they swim through the murky waters. Lake Ontario has high counts of *escherichia coli*, a very nasty bacteria that can cause ear, nose, and throat infections, skin rashes, and diarrhea—not exactly the kind of souvenir you were looking for.

The **Toronto Islands** are where you'll find the city's favorite beaches. The ones on **Centre Island,** always the busiest, are favorites with families because of nearby attractions like **Centreville.** The beaches on **Wards Island** are much more secluded. They're connected by the loveliest boardwalk in the city, with masses of fragrant flowers and raspberry bushes along its edges. **Hanlan's Point,** also in the Islands, is Toronto's only nude beach.

BOATING & CANOEING

At the **Harbourside Boating Centre,** 283 Queens Quay W. (© **416/203-3000**), you can rent sailboats or powerboats and take sailing lessons. Depending on the boat's size, a 3-hour sailboat rental costs at least C$60 (US$42). Power-boats cost C$95 (US$67) and up. The center also offers weeklong and weekend sailing courses.

The **Harbourfront Canoe and Kayak School,** 283A Queens Quay W. (© **416/203-2277**), rents kayaks for C$40 to $50 (US$28–$35) a day (higher rates apply on weekends). Canoes go for C$35 to $45 (US$25–$32). Open daily mid-June to Labour Day, weekdays only spring and fall, weather permitting.

You can also rent canoes, rowboats, and pedal boats on the **Toronto Islands** just south of Centreville.

CROSS-COUNTRY SKIING

Just about every park in Toronto becomes potential cross-country skiing terri-tory as soon as snow falls. Best bets are Sunnybrook Park and Ross Lord Park, both in North York. For more information, call **Toronto Parks and Recreation** (© **416/392-8186;** www.city.toronto.on.ca/parks). Serious skiers interested in day trips to excellent out-of-town sites like Horseshoe Valley can call **Trakkers Cross Country Ski Club** (© **416/763-0173**), which also rents equipment.

CYCLING

With biking trails through most of the city's parks and more than 29km (18 miles) of street bike routes, it's not surprising that Toronto has been acclaimed as one of the best cycling cities in North America. Favorite pathways include the **Martin Goodman Trail** (from the Beaches to the Humber River along the waterfront); the **Lower Don Valley** bike trail (from the east end of the city north to Riverdale Park); **High Park** (with winding trails over 160 hectares/400 acres); and the **Toronto Islands,** where bikers roam free without fear of cars. For advice, call the **Ontario Cycling Association** (© **416/426-7416**) or **Toronto Parks and Recreation** (© **416/392-8186**).

Bike lanes are marked on College/Carlton streets, the Bloor Street Viaduct leading to the Danforth, Beverly/St. George streets, and Davenport Road. The Convention and Visitors Association can supply more detailed information.

Finds   Walk/Jog/Cycle in Peace

One of the best places to walk, jog, or cycle in the city is the sprawling **Mount Pleasant Cemetery** (p. 142). No, I'm not joking! The wide paths of the cemetery are like roads, and there's lots of space for everyone, from athletic types to parents pushing strollers. Locals love this park-like space, which abounds with trees and antique statuary, not just tombstones. It's a lively scene, and it's anything but depressing.

Moments **Spas & the City**

Maybe you have a kink in your neck you just can't work out. Maybe you've got a nasty case of jet lag that won't quit. Or perhaps you're just in the mood for some pampering. In Toronto, you won't have to look too far: This city is spa heaven as far as I'm concerned. The standards are top-notch, the treatments range from the tried-and-true to the innovative, and the prices tend to be quite reasonable. All of the spas listed here cater to both women and men—so boys, don't be shy about trying them out.

Elizabeth Milan Hotel Day Spa   Located in the underground concourse beneath the Fairmont Royal York, this spa has 11 treatment rooms, including a luxuriously appointed bank vault that is now a VIP treatment room for those who *really* want privacy. This spa has a number of treatments designed for men, including the Balinese Coffee Scrub, a 60-minute treatment that exfoliates the skin and detoxes the body. For men and women, there's the Chocolate Body Indulgence, a 90-minute therapy that promises to soothe your body and mind. By the way, there really is an Elizabeth Milan, and you'll find her at work at her eponymous spa every day. Fairmont Royal York, 100 Front St. W. © 416/350-7500. www.elizabethmilanspa.com. Subway: Union.

Estée Lauder Spa   Located in one of Toronto's most luxurious stores is, appropriately enough, one of the city's most luxurious spas. Decorated in modern-chic blond wood and glass (and with a seemingly endless number of private treatment rooms), the spa provides a full range of services, from manicures to massage. One of the most interesting treatments is the Jet Lag facial, which rehydrates the skin; during the facial, "lymphatic leg therapy" reduces puffiness and swelling. My personal favorite is the new 90-minute Hot Lava Rock Body

---

There's no shortage of bike-rental options. Renting usually runs about C$12 to $24 (US$8.40–$17) a day. On Centre Island, try **Toronto Island Bicycle Rental** (© 416/203-0009). In the city, head for **Wheel Excitement,** 5 Rees St., near Harbourfront (© 416/260-9000); **McBride Cycle,** 180 Queens Quay W., at York Street, on the Harbourfront (© 416/203-5651); or **High Park Cycle and Sports,** 24 Ronson Dr. (© 416/614-6689). If you're interested in cycling with a group, call the **Toronto Bicycling Network** (© 416/766-1985) for information about daily excursions and weekend trips.

FITNESS CENTERS

The **Metro Central YMCA,** 20 Grosvenor St. (© **416/975-9622**), has excellent facilities, including a 25m (82 ft.) swimming pool, all kinds of cardiovascular machines, Nautilus equipment, an indoor track, squash and racquetball courts, and aerobics classes. A day pass costs C$20 (US$14). The **University of Toronto Athletic Centre,** 55 Harbord St., at Spadina Avenue (© **416/978-4680**), offers similar facilities for the same price.

For yoga aficionados, there's no better place to stretch than the **Yoga Studio,** 344 Bloor St. W. (© **416/923-9366;** www.yogastudio.net). A single class costs

Massage, which will leave you soothed and happy after a 90-minute deep-tissue massage. Just say aaaaaahhh . . . That *really* hit the spot. Holt Renfrew, 50 Bloor St. W. © 416/960-2909. www.holtrenfrew.com. Subway: Yonge/Bloor.

Stillwater Spa This is as serene a setting as you'll find anywhere in the city. Water is the theme here, and it undulates in streams under transparent floor panels and courses down walls in mini-waterfalls. Before you even get to the treatment rooms, you'll be dazzled by the changing areas, which include the expected whirlpool and sauna, but also have private cabana-like nooks where you can recline which watching TV with a headset (come in for a spa treatment and you can spend all day here—seriously). Venture into the main lounge area and you'll find an aquarium, a fireplace, and a generous supply of biscotti. Many of the treatments are hydro-centric too, like the delicious-smelling Mandarin Honey Body Glow, which uses a Vichy shower (you lie on the table while warm water cascades over you). Park Hyatt Toronto, 4 Avenue Rd. © 416/924-5471. www.stillwaterspa.com. Subway: Bay or Museum.

Victoria Spa I'm a longtime massage fan, and one of the best I've ever had was at the Victoria Spa, which is located on the third floor of the Crowne Plaza Hotel. Decorated in an elaborate style that veers from the classical to the baroque, this spa is wrapped around an indoor pool and lounge. The woman behind the spa is Victoria Sutherland, and like Elizabeth Milan, you'll find her daily at her pride and joy. The Victoria Spa is famous for its luxurious pedicures, which involve a hot milk foot bath, salt scrub, and massage—but in my opinion, all of the treatments, from facials to body therapies, meet the same standard of excellence. Crowne Plaza Hotel, 225 Front St. W. © 416/413-9100. www.victoriaspa.com. Subway: St. Andrew.

C$15 (US$11), or you can attend five classes for C$70 (US$49). Incidentally, the studio has been known to draw visiting celebrities to its classes.

GOLF

Toronto is obsessed with golf, as evidenced by its more than 75 public courses within an hour's drive of downtown. Here's information on some of the best.

- **Don Valley,** 4200 Yonge St. south of Highway 401 (© **416/392-2465**). Designed by Howard Watson, this is a scenic par-71 course with some challenging elevated tees. The par-3 13th hole is nicknamed the Hallelujah Corner (it takes a miracle to make par). It's a good place to start your kids. Greens fees are C$45 (US$32) from Monday to Thursday, and C$49 (US$34) Friday through Sunday.
- **Humber Valley,** 40 Beattie Ave. at Albion Road (© **416/392-2488**). The relatively flat par-70 course is easy to walk, and gets lots of shade from towering trees. The three final holes require major concentration (the 16th and 17th are both par-5s). Greens fees are C$27 to $42 (US$19–$29).

- The **Tam O'Shanter**, at 2481 Birchmount Ave., north of Sheppard Avenue East (✆ **416/392-2547**). The par-70 course features links holes and water hazards among its challenges. Greens fees are C$27 to $43 (US$19–$30).
- The **Glen Abbey Golf Club**, 1333 Dorval Dr., Oakville (✆ **905/844-1800;** www.glenabbey.com). The championship course is one of the most famous in Canada. Designed by Jack Nicklaus, the par-73 layout traditionally plays host to the Canadian Open. Greens fees are C$130 (US$91) in early spring and fall, C$235 (US$165) in summer.

Other championship courses of note include the **Lionhead Golf Club** in Brampton (✆ **905/455-8400**). It has two 18-hole par-72 courses; greens fees are C$135 (US$95) for the tougher course, C$125 (US$88) for the easier course. In Markham, the **Angus Glen Golf Club** (✆ **905/887-5157**) has a Doug Carrick–designed par-72 course. The greens fees range from C$120 to $175 (US$84–$123).

Travelers who are really into golf might want to consider a side trip to **Muskoka** (see chapter 10). This area just 90 minutes north has some of the best golfing in the country at courses such as **Taboo** and the **Deerhurst Highlands.**

ICE-SKATING & IN-LINE SKATING

Nathan Phillips Square in front of City Hall becomes a free ice rink in winter, as does an area at Harbourfront Centre. Rentals are available on-site. More than 25 parks contain artificial rinks (also free), including Grenadier Pond in High Park—a romantic spot, with a bonfire and vendors selling roasted chestnuts. They're open from November to March.

In summer, in-line skaters pack Toronto's streets (and sidewalks). Go with the flow and rent some blades from **Planet Skate,** 2144 Queen St. E. (✆ **416/690-7588**) or **Wheel Excitement** (see "Cycling," above). A 1-day rental runs C$18 to $22 (US$13–$15). Popular sites include the Beaches, Harbourfront, and the Toronto Islands.

> **Tips** **Skate Till You Drop?**
>
> Let's say you'd like to go skating while your traveling companion wants to hit the shops. If you head to **Hazelton Lanes,** you can both get what you want. A central courtyard doubles as a skating rink. Better yet, the shopping center's **Customer Service Centre** (✆ **416/968-8600**) offers complimentary skate rentals. It's hard to beat a deal like that.

JOGGING

Downtown routes might include **Harbourfront** and along the lakefront, or through **Queen's Park** and the University. The **Martin Goodman Trail** runs 20km (12 miles) along the waterfront from the Beaches in the east to the Humber River in the west. It's ideal for jogging, walking, or cycling. It links to the **Tommy Thompson Trail,** which travels the parks from the lakefront along the Humber River. Near the Ontario Science Centre in the Central Don Valley, **Ernest Thompson Seton Park** is also good for jogging. Parking is available at the Thorncliffe Drive and Wilket Creek entrances.

These areas are generally quite safe, but you should take the same precautions you would in any large city.

PARACHUTING

The **Parachute School of Toronto** (© 800/361-5867; www.parachuteschool. com), is based at the Baldwin Airport, about 40 minutes north of Toronto. Going for a dive costs C$220 (US$154) during the summer (the prices drops to C$150/US$105 in winter). After morning instruction, you jump in the afternoon. Reservations aren't required, but it's essential to call ahead to make sure the school's plane is sky-bound that day. Geronimo!

ROCK-CLIMBING

The dilemma: indoors or outdoors? Toronto has several climbing gyms, including **Joe Rockhead's,** 29 Fraser Ave. (© 416/538-7670), and the **Toronto Climbing Academy,** 100 Broadview Ave. (© 416/406-5900). You can pick up the finer points of knot tying and belaying. Both gyms also rent equipment.

For the real thing, you need to head out of town. Weekend excursions to the Elora Gorge are organized through **Humber College** (© 416/675-5097).

SNOWBOARDING & SKIING

The snowboard craze shows no sign of abating, at least from January to March (or anytime there's enough snow on the ground). One popular site is the **Earl Bales Park,** Bathurst Street (just south of Sheppard Ave.), which offers rentals. The park also has an alpine ski centre, which offers both equipment rentals and coaching. Call **Toronto Parks and Recreation** (© 416/392-8186) for more information.

SWIMMING

The municipal parks, including High and Rosedale parks, offer a dozen or so outdoor pools (open June–Sept). Several community recreation centers have indoor pools. For **pool information,** call © 416/392-7838.

Visitors may buy a day pass (C$20/US$14) and use the pools at the **YMCA,** 20 Grosvenor St. (© 416/975-9622), and the **University of Toronto Athletic Centre,** 55 Harbord St., at Spadina Avenue (© 416/978-4680).

TENNIS

More than 30 municipal parks have free tennis facilities. The most convenient are the courts in High, Rosedale, and Jonathan Ashridge parks. They are open in summer only. At Eglinton Flats Park, west of Keele Street at Eglinton Avenue, six of the courts can be used in winter. Call City Parks (© 416/392-8186) for additional information.

12 Spectator Sports

AUTO RACING   The Molson Indy (© 416/872-4639; www.molsonindy. com) runs at the Exhibition Place Street circuit, usually on the third weekend in July.

BASEBALL   SkyDome, 1 Blue Jays Way, on Front Street beside the CN Tower, is the home of the **Toronto Blue Jays.** For information, contact the Toronto Blue Jays, P.O. Box 7777, Adelaide St., Toronto, ON M5C 2K7 (© 416/341-1000; www.bluejays.ca). For tickets, which cost C$16 to C$60 (US$11–$42), call © 416/341-1234.

BASKETBALL   Toronto's basketball team, the Raptors, used to be the hottest ticket in town, but it's much easier to get one now. The team's home ground is the **Air Canada Centre,** 40 Bay St., at Lakeshore Boulevard. The NBA schedule runs from October to April. The arena seats 19,500 for basketball. For information, contact the **Raptors Basketball Club,** 40 Bay St. (ⓒ **416/815-5600;** www.nba.com/raptors). For tickets, which cost C$25 to $125 (US$18–$88), call **Ticketmaster** (ⓒ **416/870-8000).**

FOOTBALL   Remember Kramer on *Seinfeld?* He would only watch Canadian football. Here's your chance to catch a game. **SkyDome,** 1 Blue Jays Way, is home to the **Argonauts** of the Canadian Football League. They play between June and November. For information, contact the club at SkyDome, Gate 3, Suite 1300, Toronto, ON M5V 1J3 (ⓒ **416/341-5151;** www.argonauts.on.ca). Argos tickets cost C$13 to $48 (US$9.10–$34); call **Ticketmaster** (ⓒ **416/ 870-8000).**

GOLF TOURNAMENTS   Canada's national golf tournament, the **Bell Canadian Open,** usually takes place at the **Glen Abbey Golf Club** in Oakville, about 40 minutes from the city (ⓒ **905/844-1800).** Most years, it runs over the Labour Day weekend.

HOCKEY   While basketball is still in its honeymoon phase in Toronto, hockey is a longtime love. The **Air Canada Centre,** 40 Bay St., at Lakeshore Boulevard, is the home of the **Toronto Maple Leafs** (www.torontomapleleafs. com). Though the arena seats 18,700 for hockey, tickets are not easy to come by, because many are sold by subscription. The rest are available through **Ticketmaster** (ⓒ **416/870-8000);** prices are C$25 to $100 (US$18–$70).

HORSE RACING   Thoroughbred racing takes place at **Woodbine Racetrack,** Rexdale Boulevard and Highway 427, Etobicoke (ⓒ **416/675-6110** or 416/675-7223). It's famous for the Queen's Plate (usually contested on the third Sun in June); the Canadian International, a classic turf race (Sept or Oct); and the North America Cup (mid-June). Woodbine also hosts harness racing in spring and fall.

TENNIS TOURNAMENTS   Canada's international tennis championships, the **AT&T Rogers Cup** (for women) and the **Montréal/Toronto Tennis Masters Series** (for men), are important stops on the pro tours. They attract stars like Jennifer Capriati, the Williams sisters, and Andre Agassi to the National Tennis Centre at York University in August. The men's and women's championships alternate cities each year. In 2004, the women play in Montréal and the men in Toronto. For more information, call ⓒ **416/665-9777** or check www.tenniscanada.com.

City Strolls

7

Toronto is one of the best walking cities in the world. I know I'm boasting, but look at the evidence: the patchwork of dynamic, ethnic neighborhoods, the impressive architecture, and the many parks. Because the city is such a sprawling place, however, you'll need to pick your route carefully.

The walking tours in this chapter aren't designed to give you an overview. They offer a look at the most colorful, exciting neighborhoods in the city, as well as areas that are packed with sights on almost every corner.

WALKING TOUR 1	CHINATOWN & KENSINGTON MARKET

Start:	Osgoode subway station.
Finish:	Queen's Park subway station.
Time:	At least 2 hours. Depending on how long you want to linger at the Art Gallery of Ontario and at various stops, perhaps as long as 8 hours.
Best Times:	Tuesday through Saturday during the day.
Worst Times:	Sunday, when many of the stores in Kensington Market close, and Monday, when the Art Gallery is closed.

This walk takes you through the oldest of Toronto's several Chinatowns. The original Chinatown was on York Street between King and Queen streets, but skyscrapers replaced it long ago. Although today there are at least four Chinatowns and most Chinese live in the suburbs, the intersection of Dundas Street and Spadina Avenue is still a major shopping and dining area for the Asian community. As a new wave of immigrants has arrived from Southeast Asian countries—Thailand and Vietnam in particular—this old, original Chinatown has taken them in. Today, many businesses are Vietnamese or Thai.

Successive waves of immigration have also changed the face of the nearby Kensington Market. From the turn of the century until the 1950s, it was the heart of the Jewish community. In the 1950s, Portuguese immigrants arrived to work in the food-processing and meatpacking industries and made it their home. In the '60s, a Caribbean presence arrived. Today, traces of all these communities remain in the vibrant life of the market.

From the Osgoode subway station, exit on the northwest corner of Queen Street and University Avenue, and walk west on Queen Street. Turn right onto McCaul Street. If you're interested in crafts, you'll want to stop at 52 McCaul St., on the left side of the street, and visit the:

❶ Prime Gallery
It sells ceramics, jewelry, fabrics, and other art objects crafted by contemporary artisans.

On the right is:

❷ Village by the Grange

The apartment and shopping complex consists of a series of courtyards (one even contains a small ice-skating rink). Go into the complex at the southern end and stroll through, emerging from the food market. En route you'll come across some small fashion boutiques and **18 Karat** (✆ **416/593-1648**), where the proprietors design and create jewelry behind the counter.

TAKE A BREAK
Also in Village by the Grange is one of the city's oldest and most popular Chinese restaurants, **Sun Lok** (✆ **416/593-8808**). The **Food Market** contains stalls that sell everything—freshly brewed coffee, schnitzels, satay, Japanese noodles, salads, falafel, hot dogs, Chinese food, kabobs, pizza, and fried chicken.

Exit at McCaul Street and turn right to continue walking north. You'll pass the Ontario College of Art on the other side of the street. At Dundas Street, you'll encounter a Henry Moore sculpture, *Large Two Forms,* which describes precisely what it is. Turn left onto Dundas Street. On the left is the entrance to the:

❸ Art Gallery of Ontario

If you don't want to go in to see the collections, you can browse the gallery stores without paying admission. The wonderful restaurant, **Agora** (p. 87), is open for lunch.

Cross to the north side of Dundas Street, opposite the Art Gallery. A worthwhile stop is:

❹ Bau-Xi

This gallery, at 340 Dundas St. W. (✆ **416/977-0600**), represents modern Canadian artists. From here, continue west along Dundas Street.

At the northwest corner of Dundas and Beverley is the:

❺ Consulate General of Italy

It doesn't look like a government building: The rambling late 19th-century mansion, with its sandy brick, quasi-Gothic windows, and wrought-iron decoration, is a beauty. Too bad it doesn't offer tours.

You're now walking into the heart of Chinatown, with its grocery stores, bakeries, bookstalls, and emporiums selling foods, handcrafts, and other items from Asia.

What follows are some of my favorite stops along the stretch of Dundas Street between Beverley Street and Spadina Avenue. On the south or left side as you go west is:

❻ Tai Sun Co.

At nos. 407–09, the supermarket carries dozens of different mushrooms, all clearly labeled in English, as well as fresh Chinese vegetables, meats, fish, and canned goods. **Melewa Bakery,** no. 433, has a wide selection of pastries, like mung-bean and lotus-paste buns. Outside **Kiu Shun Trading,** no. 441, dried fish are on display; inside you'll find numerous varieties of ginseng and such miracle remedies as "Stop Smoking Tea."

On the north side of the street is:

❼ J & S Arts and Crafts

This shop, at no. 430, is a good place to pick up souvenirs, including kimonos and happy coats, kung-fu suits, address books, cushion covers, and all-cotton Chinatown T-shirts. **Kim Moon,** no. 438, is an Asian bakery that features almond cookies, deep-fried taro pastries, and dim sum pork buns.

At the northwest corner of Huron and Dundas streets, is:

❽ Ten Ren Tea

At no. 454, Ten Ren sells all kinds of tea—black, oolong, and so forth—stored in large canisters in the back of the store. Charming small ceramic teapots are priced from C$25 to $75 (US$18–$53). You will probably be asked to sample some tea in a tiny cup. The large variety of gnarled ginseng root on display is also for sale. Next door, **W Y Trading Co., Inc.,** has a great selection of records, CDs, and

Walking Tour 1: Chinatown & Kensington Market

1 Prime Gallery
2 Village by the Grange
3 Art Gallery of Ontario
4 Bau-Xi
5 Consulate General
   of Italy
6 Tai Sun Co.
7 J & S Arts and Crafts
8 Ten Ren Tea
9 Dragon City
10 Tai Kong Supermarket
11 Tap Phong Trading
   Company
12 Plaiter Place
13 Medeiro's Fish Market

14 My Market Bakery
15 Abyssinia
16 Mendels Creamery
17 Asylum
18 Courage My Love
19 Dancing Days
20 The Pineapple Room
21 Win's Flowers
22 Bellevue Park
23 Kiever Synagogue
24 Sasmart Smart Wear
25 Casa Acoreana
26 Perola Supermarket
27 Iberica Bakery

■ TTC Subway
☺ Take a Break

tapes—everything from Chinese folk songs and cantatas to current hit albums from Hong Kong and Taiwan. At no. 482A, **Po Chi Tong** is a fun store that sells exotic remedies, like deer-tail extract and liquid-gold ginseng or royal jelly. The best remedy of all time is the "slimming tea." Watch the staff weigh each item out and total the bill with a fast-clicking abacus.

At Spadina Avenue, cross over to the southwest corner to:

9 Dragon City

The three-level Asian shopping complex at 280 Spadina Ave. is complete with a food court. Here you'll find books, music, clothing, toys, and homeopathic remedies under one roof.

Spadina (pronounced spa-*dye*-na) Avenue is the widest street in the city because the wealthy Baldwin family had a 40m (132-ft.) swath cut through the forest from Queen Street to Bloor Street so that they could view the lake from their new home on top of Spadina Hill. Later, in the early 20th century, Spadina Avenue became Toronto's garment center and the focal point of the city's Jewish community. Although it's still the garment center, with wholesale and discount fashion houses, as well as the fur district (farther south around Adelaide), today it's more Asian than Jewish.

If you enjoy strolling through supermarkets filled with exotic Asian delights, including such fruits as durian in season, visit the:

10 Tai Kong Supermarket

Look at all the different provisions— chile and fish sauces, fresh meat and fish (including live tilapia in tanks), preserved plums, chrysanthemum tea and other infusions, moon cakes, and large sacks of rice.

TAKE A BREAK
For fine, reasonably priced food, a Chinatown favorite is **Happy Seven**, 358 Spadina Ave. (☎ 416/971-9820; see p. 95). If you don't mind lining up, head for the ever-popular **Lee Garden**, 331 Spadina Ave. (☎ 416/593-9524; see p. 95). For speedy service, check out **Co Yen**, 334 Spadina Ave. (☎ 416/597-1573), a Vietnamese takeout spot (there are no seats). Continuing north, cross St. Andrews Street.

11 Tap Phong Trading Company

This shop, at 360 Spadina Ave., stocks terrific wicker baskets of all shapes and sizes, as well as woks and ceramic cookware; attractive mortars and pestles; and other household items.

Cross Baldwin Street and you'll come to:

12 Plaiter Place

At 384 Spadina Ave., it has a huge selection of finely crafted wicker baskets, birdcages, woven blinds, bamboo steamers, hats, and other fun items. **Fortune Housewares,** no. 388, carries kitchen and household items— including brand names—for at least 20% off prices elsewhere in the city.

Now double back to Baldwin Street. You're heading into the heart of the **Kensington Market** area, which has always reflected the city's waves of immigration. Once it was primarily a Jewish market; later it became a Portuguese neighborhood. Today, it is largely Asian and Caribbean, but there are still many Jewish and Portuguese elements.

As you walk west, you'll find:

13 Medeiro's Fish Market, Seven Seas, and Coral Sea

At these and other fish stores on the north side of the street, folks buy their supplies of salt cod.

⓮ My Market Bakery

The merchandise at 172 Baldwin St. (℡ **416/593-6772**) will doubtless lure you in to buy some bread. Focaccia, sourdough—you name it, they have it.

When you reach Kensington Avenue, turn left and you'll find:

⓯ Abyssinia

It specializes in African and West Indian products. You'll also find **Patty King,** which stocks Jamaican breads and other West Indian goods, including roti, bread pudding, and tamarind balls. Several **seafood stores** display a variety of fresh fish and salted cod piled in boxes on the sidewalk; and the **Royal Food Centre** sells a variety of Jamaican specialties, including goat.

⓰ Mendels Creamery

This shop, at no. 72, sells smoked fish, herring, cheeses, and fine dill pickles. Another door down, **Global Cheese,** no. 76, offers an enormous selection at good prices.

As you stroll south along Kensington Avenue and pass Andrews Street, you will find a series of secondhand and vintage clothing stores.

⓱ Asylum

At no. 42 Kensington Ave., on the west side of the street, the store has good jeans, leather jackets, and assorted accessories. I once found a silk Anne Klein scarf for C50¢ (US35¢) in one of the bargain bins here.

⓲ Courage My Love

The best spot for cheap but chic vintage clothing is at no. 14. It stocks retro gowns and wedding dresses, suits, and accessories, as well as new jewelry and beads for do-it-yourself projects.

⓳ Dancing Days

At no. 17 (on the east side of the street), you'll find party-ready glad rags that will make you look like an extra in *Grease!*.

⓴ The Pineapple Room

This shop at no. 2 stocks classic cocktail shakers and other doodads among the clothes.

When you reach Dundas Street, turn right and walk one block to Augusta Avenue. Along the way you pass:

㉑ Win's Flowers

They have gorgeous greenery and blossoms. The jade plants in particular are extraordinarily beautiful.

Turn right on Augusta Avenue; as you walk north, in the center of Denison Square, you'll find:

㉒ Bellevue Park

The houses facing the south edge of the park have cherry trees in front of them; they are a colorful sight in season.

Stroll through the park; at the corner of Bellevue Avenue and Denison Square you'll find:

㉓ Kiever Synagogue

This building at 28 Denison Square was completed in 1927. Architect Benjamin Swartz designed it with Byzantine style in mind. The most striking features outside are the twin domes atop the building; inside, stained-glass windows, brass ornaments, and a gigantic Holy Ark dominate the space. (The Kiever Synagogue was the first specifically Jewish building designated a historic site by the province of Ontario.)

Turn back toward Augusta Avenue and you'll see:

㉔ Sasmart Smart Wear

This discount store has the strangest assortment of goods you'll find anywhere. OshKosh clothing for kids is on display near antique china; a little farther along is kitchen gear (new and used), luggage, and gadgets. It's a weird, cluttered space, but the prices are unbeatable.

Walk north on Augusta to:

㉕ Casa Acoreana

An old-fashioned store at no. 235, it stocks a full range of fresh coffees, as well as great pecans and filberts. Just up the block at no. 214 is the **Alvand Food Mart** (© 416/597-2252), which specializes in Middle Eastern foods and stocks imported goods from the region.

Just up the street is:

㉖ Perola Supermarket

This store at 247 Augusta Ave. displays cassava and strings of peppers—ancho, arbol, pasilla—hung up to dry and sitting in bins, plus more exotic fruits and herbs.

TAKE A BREAK
If you're in the neighborhood after 5:30pm, a perfect place to stop is **La Palette,** 256 Augusta Ave. (© 416/929-4900; p. 92). Enjoy a meal of classic French bistro staples—or tuck into one of the many divine desserts.

Cross Nassau Street to get to:

㉗ Iberica Bakery

The bakery, where you can enjoy coffee and pastries at a handful of tables, is on the east side of the street at 279 Augusta Ave. It represents one of the few remaining traces of the Portuguese presence in the Kensington Market area. Other vestiges are the Portuguese church on Nassau Street and the Portuguese radio station around the corner on Oxford Street. Now just walk up to College Street and hop on the streetcar that runs east to the Queen's Park subway station. The southbound train will take you back downtown.

WALKING TOUR 2 | **HARBOURFRONT**

Start:	Union Station.
Finish:	Toronto Music Garden.
Time:	At least 2 hours.
Best Times:	Weekdays in summer.
Worst Time:	Weekends in summer, when Harbourfront is packed from end-to-end. Weekends during the rest of the year are much better.

As you start your tour, pause to look at the beaux-arts interior of **Union Station,** which opened in 1927. The hall has a cathedral-like ceiling, and 22 pillars that weigh 70 tons each. From here, either take the LRT to York Quay or walk south along York Street (away from the Fairmont Royal York hotel) to Queens Quay West. On the way you'll pass the **Air Canada Centre,** home to the Toronto Maple Leafs hockey team and the Toronto Raptors basketball team. The Gardiner Expressway looms overhead, making this a noisy, dark spot.

When you reach the end of the street, you're at Queens Quay West. Look across to:

❶ Queen's Quay Terminal

This large complex houses more than 100 shops and restaurants. On the third floor is a theater designed for dance performances. Built in 1927 when lake and railroad trade flourished, this eight-story concrete warehouse has been attractively renovated. The light, airy two-story marketplace has garden courts, skylights, and waterfalls. Condos occupy the floors above.

Although you'll find few bargains here, there are some charming stores on the street level. They include **Oh Yes Toronto,** which specializes in souvenirs and Toronto-centric clothing.

On the upper level, options include the classic **Tilley Endurables,** founded by Torontonian Alex Tilley (who invented the world's most adaptable hat). **First Hand Canadian Crafts** represents more than 200 contemporary folk artists who make both decorative and functional pieces, and **Table of Contents** sells all kinds of kitchen gear.

TAKE A BREAK
If you want to sit out and watch the lakefront traffic—boat and human—go for a light meal or a drink at **Spinnakers** (℡ 416/203-0559), or the **Boathouse Cafe** (℡ 416/203-6300), on the ground floor of Queens Quay. **Pearl Harbourfront Chinese Cuisine** (℡ 416/203-1233) offers more formal dining. The Queens Quay complex also has a variety of cafes, and food vendors just outside.

From Queen's Quay Terminal, walk along the water to the:
❷ Power Plant Contemporary Art Gallery
This was indeed a power plant when it was built in 1927. Identifiable by its towering smokestack, the space has been converted to display modern art. The same building houses the Du Maurier Theatre Centre, which presents works in French.

Behind this building, adjacent to Queens Quay West, is the Tent in the Park, where events take place during the summer season.

Walk next door to the:
❸ York Quay Centre
A complex converted from a 1940 trucking warehouse, it contains a number of interesting restaurants and galleries. Spend some time in the Craft Studio watching the glassblowers, potters, jewelry makers, and other artisans at work, and browse in the store that sells their work.

On the waterfront side in front of York Quay, there's a pond where kids operate model boats in summer; in winter it turns into an ice-skating rink.

From York Quay, cross the Amsterdam Bridge above Marina 4, checking out the wealth that's bobbing down below. You'll arrive on:
❹ John Quay
The first building you'll come to contains four restaurants, beyond which are the towers of the:

❺ Radisson Plaza Hotel Admiral and Admiralty Point Condominiums
The complex sits across Queens Quay West from the HarbourPoint Condominiums. The ground level of the Admiralty Point Condos houses a few interesting stores. The **Nautical Mind** sells marine books, photographs, navigational charts, and boating videos; the **Dock Shoppe** overflows with all kinds of sailing gear and fashions.

TAKE A BREAK
Pop into the **Radisson Plaza Hotel Admiral** (℡ 416/203-3333), 249 Queens Quay W. It has a couple of dining options (the **Commodore's Dining Room** and the **Gallery Café**, which serves light fare), plus a pleasant terrace if it's a sunny day.

Continue west along Queens Quay West past:
❻ Maple Leaf Quay
You can stop at the Nautical Centre to sign up for sailing classes first. Continue west and you'll see the Maple Leaf Quay Apartments on your right and the Harbour Terrace Condominiums farther along on your left, on the waterfront.

Next door to the westernmost tower of the Maple Leaf Quay Apartments is the:
❼ Toronto Music Garden
A terrific destination for whiling away an afternoon, the Music Garden was designed by world-renowned cellist Yo Yo Ma and landscape architect Julie Moir Messervy to invoke Bach's First

Walking Tour 2: Harbourfront

1 Queen's Quay Terminal
2 Power Plant Contemporary Art Gallery
3 York Quay Centre
4 John Quay
5 Radisson Plaza Hotel Admiral and Admiralty Point Condominiums
6 Maple Leaf Quay
7 Toronto Music Garden

Take a break

Suite for Unaccompanied Cello. The venue is open 7 days a week and admission is free. Even better, there are special musical performances scheduled here throughout the summer, on both weekdays and weekends.

To return to downtown, board the LRT and head back to Union Station.

WALKING TOUR 3 THE FINANCIAL DISTRICT

Start:	The CN Tower, near the corner of John and Front streets.
Finish:	A Queen Street West watering hole.
Time:	2 to 4 hours.
Best Time:	Weekdays during business hours.
Worst Times:	Weekends, when the stock market is closed and the Financial District is dead.

This is the Wall Street of Toronto, the financial engine that has made Ontario the nation's strongest and wealthiest economy. For more information about some of the major sights mentioned below, see chapter 6.

Start by going up the:
① CN Tower
This is the tallest freestanding structure in the world. Although it has become a symbol of the city, the CN Tower drew a great deal of criticism when it was built in 1975. It has since been recognized as an important symbol of a city

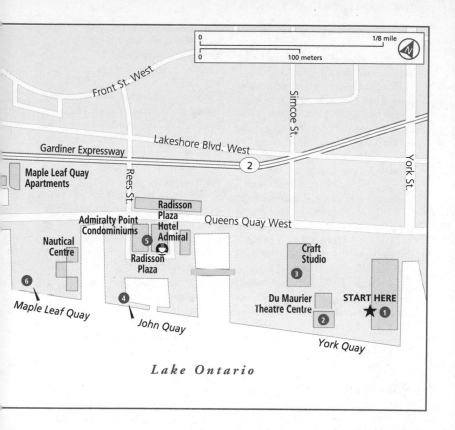

trying to forge a new identity. Robert Fulford writes about it in *Accidental City:* "In the 1970s [Toronto] was struggling to shake off the dowdy self-image that was part of its heritage as a colonial city . . . Torontonians were starting to consider, with shy pleasure, the novel idea that their city might be attractive, even enviable . . . At that happy moment, the tower reinforced local exuberance and asserted the city's claim to even more attention." However you view it, the most enjoyable thing is the view *from* it.

Once you're back down at the base, exit at the corner of John and Front streets. From here, look to the right along Front Street to see the glistening golden Royal Bank towers (part of the Royal Bank Centre). The CBC Centre stretches along the north side of Front Street for a whole long block. Inside,

you can peek at the lobby radio studios and take a nostalgic radio-TV trip in the free museum.

Walk north on John Street (with the CN Tower behind you), cross Wellington Street, and continue up to King Street. Turn right. On the northeast corner, sports fans will want to stop in at **Legends of the Game,** 322 King St. W. (© **416/971-8848**). Doors with baseball-shaped handles open onto an emporium that features the Wall of Fame and every conceivable sports collectible.

Continue walking along the north side of King Street 1 block to:

❷ The Princess of Wales Theatre

Princess Diana opened it in 1993. Constructed for a production of *Miss Saigon,* the theater was the brainchild of impresario Ed Mirvish and his son, David. Try to pop inside for a peek at the 929 sq. m (10,000 sq. ft.) of murals created by Frank Stella. There's one on the exterior back of the building that's worth walking around to see.

Exit the theater and continue along King Street past a cluster of restaurants owned by Ed Mirvish. (Drop in to one to check out the larger-than-life decor Ed has purchased at antiques closeouts.) You'll also pass a wall of newspaper clippings about this gutsy Torontonian. Booster and benefactor of the city, he started out in bleak circumstances as owner of a bankrupt store during the Depression. He paid off the debt and launched **Honest Ed's** (p. 180), a discount store at Bloor and Bathurst that brought him fame and fortune. He saved the Royal Alex (see below) from demolition, and he and his son have become theater impresarios in Toronto and in London, where Ed outbid Andrew Lloyd Webber in 1982 for the Old Vic.

Cross Duncan Street. Next you'll come to:

❸ The Royal Alexandra

John M. Lyle built this beloved theater in 1906 and 1907 at a cost of C$750,000 (US$525,000). In 1963, it was scheduled for demolition, but Ed Mirvish bought it for C$200,000 (US$140,000) and refurbished it. Named after Queen Alexandra, wife of Edward VII, the magnificent beaux-arts structure is Edwardian down to the last detail. It abounds with gilt and velvet, and green marble lines the entrance foyer.

Across the street from these two theaters stands the new **Metro Hall,** 55 John St., designed by Brisbin Brook Beynon. This building is pretty much a white elephant these days—it was constructed when Toronto had six separate municipal governments and a Metro Council for joint projects and concerns. If you go in, check out the art installations. Free tours (© 416/392-8000) of the first three floors are available, but they're not very interesting.

Also on the south side of the street, at the corner of King and Simcoe streets, is:

❹ Roy Thomson Hall

The hall bears the name of newspaper magnate Lord Thomson of Fleet (a Canadian press baron who wound up taking a seat in the British House of Lords). Built between 1972 and 1982 and designed by Arthur Erickson, the building's exterior looks very space age. Inside, the mirrored effects are dramatic.

Continue walking east on King Street. You'll pass through the heart of the Financial District, surrounded by many towers owned and operated by banks and brokerage, trust, and insurance companies.

On the northeast corner of King and Simcoe rises the first of the towers that make up the Sun Life Centre; on the southeast corner stands:

❺ St. Andrew's Presbyterian Church

The church (1874–75) is a quietly inviting retreat from the city's pace and noise. It was designed by the city's premier architect of the time, W. G. Storm, in an inspired picturesque Scottish Romanesque style. Sun Life paid C$4.3 million (US$3 million) for the church's air rights. Continue along King Street to University Avenue.

Opposite, on the northeast corner, is the:

❻ Sun Life Centre's second tower

A Sorel Etrog sculpture marks this tower. Farther along the block you'll find another sculpture, *Parent I,* by British sculptor Barbara Hepworth. It's in a courtyard setting, complete with a splashing fountain, at the northwest corner of York and King streets.

On the northeast corner stands:

❼ 2 First Canadian Place

The north corner of the structure is the **Toronto Exchange Tower,** at the corner of Adelaide and York streets. The Sculptor's Society Gallery, which always has an interesting free show, is

Walking Tour 3: The Financial District

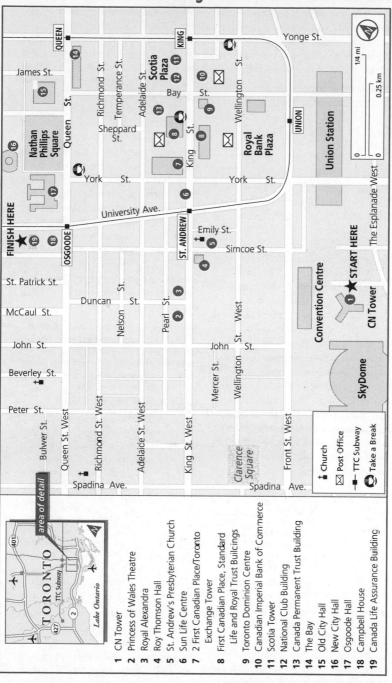

1 CN Tower
2 Princess of Wales Theatre
3 Royal Alexandra
4 Roy Thomson Hall
5 St. Andrew's Presbyterian Church
6 Sun Life Centre
7 2 First Canadian Place/Toronto
   Exchange Tower
8 First Canadian Place, Standard
   Life and Royal Trust Buildings
9 Toronto Dominion Centre
10 Canadian Imperial Bank of Commerce
11 Scotia Tower
12 National Club Building
13 Canada Permanent Trust Building
14 The Bay
15 Old City Hall
16 New City Hall
17 Osgoode Hall
18 Campbell House
19 Canada Life Assurance Building

Legend:
† Church
⊠ Post Office
■– TTC Subway
🔊 Take a Break

in 2 First Canadian Place. Also on the ground floor in the building, stop in to see the fabulous glass sculptures and other glass pieces in the **Sandra Ainsley** gallery (📞 **416/362-4480**).

Continue along King Street past:

❽ First Canadian Place

It sits on the north side, and the **Standard Life** and **Royal Trust buildings** (part of the Toronto Dominion Centre) are on the south. At the end of this block, you'll reach Bay Street. The Standard Life building is the work of New York architect Edward Durell Stone with Bregman & Hamann; the marble facing contrasts with the TD Centre, which is black. Again, there are views of the magnificent towers of the Royal Bank Centre from here.

The intersection of Bay and King streets was once considered the geographical center of Toronto's financial power. During the mining booms in the 1920s and 1950s, Bay Street was lined with offices that were filled with commission salesmen peddling stocks to the equivalent of the little old lady from Dubuque. This is the hub that gave Torontonians their reputation as a voracious band of money-grubbing folks. Today it's called Mint Corner because a major bank occupies each corner.

TAKE A BREAK
Your best bet for a leisurely lunch in this neighborhood is a block south and a block east at **Jump Café and Bar,** 1 Wellington St. W. (📞 **416/363-3400**; p. 89). For a quick snack, seek out one of the casual spots in the concourse of **First Canadian Place.**

If it's near lunchtime and your stomach is rumbling, this isn't a bad place to:

Our next stop, at King and Bay streets, is the:

❾ Toronto Dominion Centre

Built between 1963 and 1969, the center was designed by Mies van der Rohe in his sleek trademark style. The black steel and dark-bronze-tinted glass tower rises from a gray granite base. Go through the Royal Trust and Toronto Dominion Towers, stopping to browse in the **Toronto Dominion Gallery of Inuit Art,** 79 Wellington St. W. (📞 **416/982-8473**), on the ground floor and mezzanine of the Toronto Dominion Tower. Close to 100 marvelous soapstone sculptures are on display. Exit the TD Centre on Wellington Street and walk right; you'll come to a small staircase that leads to the courtyard behind the Toronto Dominion Bank Tower. Here you'll find a patch of grass that holds half a dozen lazing bronze cows. Artist Joe Fafard's *Pasture* reminds the bankers and stockbrokers that Toronto's wealth derived from other stock, too.

Walk through the Centre to the King Street exit. Exit onto King Street and turn right to continue east. Cross Bay Street. On the south side of King Street, you'll come to the entrance to Commerce Court. Architecture buffs will also want to go into the:

❿ Canadian Imperial Bank of Commerce

Visit this building (1929–31) if only to see the massive banking hall—44m (145 ft.) long, 26m (85 ft.) wide, and 20m (65 ft.) high—with its coffered ceiling, gilt moldings, and sculpted friezes. Squirrels, roosters, bees, bears, and figures representing industry, commerce, and Mercury decorate the main entrance. For years, this 34-story building dominated the Toronto skyline. New Yorkers York and Sawyer, with Darling and Pearson, designed it. Note the carved heads on the top of the building depicting courage, observation, foresight, and enterprise. In the early 1970s, I. M. Pei was asked to design a new complex while preserving the old building. He set the new mercury-laminated stainless-steel bank tower back from King Street, creating Commerce Court.

Opposite, on the north side of King Street, note the:

⓫ Scotia Tower

It's a red-granite building, designed by Webb Zerafa Menkes Housden between 1985 and 1988.

Walk back to Bay Street and turn right. You're now going north. At no. 303, on the east side, is the:

⓬ National Club Building

In 1874, the nationalist Canada First Movement, which had started in Ottawa in 1868, became centered in Toronto. It established a weekly, *The Nation,* entered politics (as the Canadian National Association), and founded the National Club, which moved here in 1907. Today, it's a prestigious private club.

Across the street on the west side, at the corner of Bay and Adelaide streets, stands the:

⓭ Canada Permanent Trust Building (1928)

Enter this structure, at 7 King St. E., to view the beautifully worked Art Deco brass and bronze, particularly the elevator doors, which are chased and engraved with foliage and flowers.

Cross Adelaide Street. As you walk up Bay Street, the magnificent Old City Hall is clearly in view. First, on the east side of Bay Street between Richmond and Queen streets, look at—or stop into:

⓮ The Bay

This is one of Canada's venerable retailers. The Bay, along with its archrival, Eaton's, has influenced the development of the downtown areas of most major Canadian cities.

Across Queen Street looms:

⓯ Old City Hall

Its reflection appears dramatically in the Cadillac Fairview Office Tower at the corner of James and Queen streets. This solid, impressive building, designed by Edward James Lennox, was built out of Credit River Valley sandstone. The magnificent Romanesque Revival style shows the obvious influence of H. H. Richardson. Begun in 1885, it opened in 1899, and for years its clock tower was a skyline landmark. Today, the building houses the provincial criminal courts. Go in to see the impressive staircase, columns with decorative capitals, and mosaic floor. The stained-glass window (1898) by Robert McCausland depicts the union of Commerce and Industry watched over by Britannia. Note the carved heads on the exterior entrance pillars—supposedly portraits of political figures and citizens of the period, including the architect.

Exit along Queen Street and turn right. Pause at the intersection of Queen and Bay streets. Bay, Toronto's equivalent of Wall Street, curves at this intersection, offering a good view north and south. Cross Bay Street and you'll find yourself in Nathan Phillips Square. Looming above you'll see the:

⓰ New City Hall

The city's fourth, it was built between 1958 and 1965 in modern sculptural style. It's the symbol of Toronto's postwar dynamism, although not everyone felt that way when it was built. According to Pierre Berton, Frank Lloyd Wright said of it, "You've got a headmarker for a grave and future generations will look at it and say: 'This marks the spot where Toronto fell.'" The truth is quite the opposite—this breathtaking building was the first architectural marker of an evolving metropolis. Finnish architect Viljo Revell won a design competition that drew entries by 510 architects from 42 countries, including I. M. Pei. The building has a great square in front with a fountain and pool; people flock here in summer to relax, and in winter to skate. The square's namesake, Nathan Phillips, was Toronto's first Jewish mayor.

City Hall also has some art worth viewing. Look just inside the entrance for *Metropolis,* which local artist David Partridge fashioned from more than 100,000 common nails. You'll need to stand well back to enjoy the effect. Henry Moore's sculpture *The Archer* stands in front of the building—thanks to Mayor Phil Givens, who raised the money to buy it through public subscription after city authorities refused. The gesture encouraged Moore to bestow a major collection of his works on the **Art Gallery of Ontario** (p. 124). Two curved concrete towers, which house the bureaucracy, flank the Council Chamber. From the air, the whole complex supposedly looks like an eye peering up at the heavens.

TAKE A BREAK
For some light refreshment, stop in at one of several dining spots in the **Sheraton Centre**, 123 Queen St. W. They include the pub **Good Queen Bess** (✆ 416/361-1000).

From City Hall, walk west along Queen Street. On your right, behind an ornate wrought-iron fence that once kept out the cows, you'll see:

⑰ Osgoode Hall

Since the 1830s, this has been the headquarters of the Law Society of Upper Canada, a professional association. Named after the first chief justice of Upper Canada, the building was constructed in stages. It started with the East Wing (1831–32), then the West Wing (1844–45), and the center block (1856–60). The last, designed by

W. G. Storm with a Palladian portico, is the most impressive. Inside is the **Great Library**—34m (112 ft.) long, 12m (40 ft.) wide, and 12m (40 ft.) high—with stucco decoration and a domed ceiling. The Ontario Supreme Court is across Queen Street.

Walk west 1 block to University Avenue. On the northwest corner, you can visit:

⑱ Campbell House

This elegant Georgian residence was home to Sir William Campbell, a Scot who moved to York in 1811 and rose to become chief justice of Upper Canada. A handsome piece of Georgian architecture, it was moved to this location from a few miles farther east.

Stretching northward behind Campbell House, on the northwest side of University Avenue, is the:

⑲ Canada Life Assurance Building

Atop the tower a neon sign provides weather reports—white flashes for snow, red flashes for rain, green beacon for clement weather, red beacon for cloudy weather. If the flashes move upward, the temperature is headed that way, and vice versa.

At University Avenue and Queen Street, you can end the tour by boarding the subway at Osgoode to your next destination. Or continue walking west along Queen Street to explore its many shops and cafes.

WALKING TOUR 4 ST. LAWRENCE & DOWNTOWN EAST

Start:	Union Station.
Finish:	King subway station.
Time:	2 to 3 hours.
Best Time:	Saturday, when the St. Lawrence Market is in full swing.
Worst Time:	Sunday, when it's closed.

At one time, this area was at the center of city life. Today it's a little off-center, and yet it has some historic and modern architectural treasures, and a wealth of history in and around the St. Lawrence Market.

Walking Tour 4: St. Lawrence & Downtown East

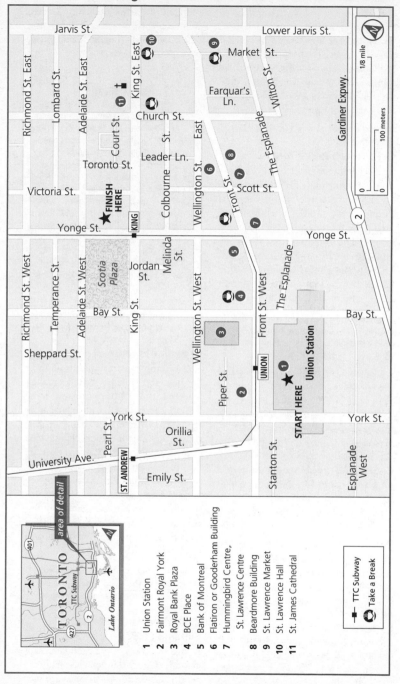

1/8 mile

100 meters

Jarvis St.
Lower Jarvis St.

Richmond St. East
Lombard St.
Adelaide St. East
King St. East
Market St.
Wilton St.

Richmond St. West
Temperance St.
Adelaide St. West
Scotia Plaza
Jordan St.
Melinda St.
King St.
Wellington St. West
The Esplanade
Bay St.
Victoria St.
Yonge St.
Yonge St.

Church St.
St.
Leader Ln.
Colbourne
Wellington St.
East
Scott St.
Front St.
Toronto St.
Court St.

FINISH HERE
KING

Farquar's Ln.

Sheppard St.
Piper St.
Front St. West
Union Station
The Esplanade
Bay St.

Pearl St.
York St.
Orillia St.
Stanton St.
START HERE
Union Station
York St.

University Ave.
ST. ANDREW
Emily St.
Esplanade West

UNION

Gardiner Expwy.

2

area of detail

TORONTO
401
427
TTC Subway
Lake Ontario
2

1 Union Station
2 Fairmont Royal York
3 Royal Bank Plaza
4 BCE Place
5 Bank of Montreal
6 Flatiron or Gooderham Building
7 Hummingbird Centre, St. Lawrence Centre
8 Beardmore Building
9 St. Lawrence Market
10 St. Lawrence Hall
11 St. James Cathedral

■— TTC Subway
🍴 Take a Break

Begin at:

① Union Station

Check out the interior of this classical revival beauty, which opened in 1927 as a temple to and for the railroad. The shimmering ceiling, faced with vitri-fied Guastavino tile, soars 27m (88 ft.) above the 79m-long (260-ft.) hall.

Across the street, at York and Front streets, stands the:

② Fairmont Royal York

The venerable railroad hotel is a long-time gathering place for Torontonians. It's the home of the famous Imperial Room cabaret and nightclub, which used to be one of Eartha Kitt's favorite venues. The hotel was once the tallest building in Toronto and the largest hotel in the British Commonwealth. Check out the lobby, with its coffered ceiling and opulent furnishings.

As you leave the hotel, turn left and walk east on Front Street. At the corner of Bay and Front streets, look up at the stunning:

③ Royal Bank Plaza

The two triangular gold-sheathed towers rise 41 floors and 26 floors. A 40m-high (130-ft.) atrium joins them, and 150 pounds of gold enhances the mirrored glass. Webb Zerafa Menkes Housden designed the project, which was built between 1973 and 1977.

Cross Bay Street and continue east on Front Street. On the south side of the street is the impressive sweep of **One Front Street,** the main post office building (okay, not an exciting-sounding sight, but an attractive one).

On the north side of the street is the city's latest financial palace and most impressive architectural triumph, Bell Canada Enter-prises':

④ BCE Place

Go inside to view the soaring galleria. Skidmore, Owings, and Merrill, with Bregman & Hamann, designed it in 1993. The twin office towers connect through a huge glass-covered galleria five stories high, spanning the block between Bay and Yonge streets.

Designed by artist-architect Santiago Calatrava with Bregman & Hamann, it links the old Midland Bank build-ing to the twin towers.

TAKE A BREAK
For an unusual dining experi-ence, stop in at **BCE Place's Movenpick Marché** (✆ 416/366-8986), which turns diners into hunter-gatherers. Rather than waiting for table service, you forage for salads, pas-tas, and meat dishes at various counters. If you can't bear the thought of chasing down your grub, head across the court-yard to **Acqua** (✆ 416/368-7171) for Italianate dishes. The downstairs food court offers a variety of fast food and casual dining choices. If you prefer a deli sandwich, head for **Shopsy's**, 33 Yonge St. (✆ 416/365-3333; p. 100).

Back out on Front Street, turn left and con-tinue to the northwest corner of Yonge and Front, stopping to admire the:

⑤ Bank of Montreal

The suitably ornate building (1885–86) held the most powerful Canadian bank of the 19th century, a force behind the colonial and federal gov-ernments. Inside, the banking hall rises to a beamed coffered ceiling with domed skylights of stained glass. It now houses the Stanley Cup and other hockey trophies, plus the **Hockey Hall of Fame** (p. 140), another exam-ple of the city's genius for architectural adaptation. The exterior, embellished with carvings, porthole windows, and a balustrade, is a sight.

From here, you can look ahead along Front Street and see the weird mural by Derek M. Besant that adorns the famous and highly photogenic:

⑥ Flatiron or Gooderham Building (1892)

It was built as the headquarters of George Gooderham, who had ex-panded his distilling business into rail-roads, insurance, and philanthropy. At one time his liquor business was the biggest in the British Empire, and he was also president of the Bank of Toronto. The five-story building occupies a triangular site, and the western tip (and the windows) is beautifully curved and topped with a semicircular tower. The design is by David Roberts.

At the southwest corner of Yonge and Front streets, you can stop in at:
❼ The Hummingbird Centre
It sits across Scott Street from the **St. Lawrence Centre.** The former is home to the National Ballet of Canada and, at the moment, to the Canadian Opera Company (plans for a new opera house are tentative).

Continue east along Front Street to the:
❽ Beardmore Building
It's at 35–39 Front St. E. This and the many other cast-iron buildings that line the street were the heart of the late-19th-century warehouse district, close to the lakefront and railheads. Now they hold stores like **Frida Crafts,** which sells imports from Guatemala, India, and Bangladesh, as well as jewelry, bags, candles, and other knick-knacks; and **Mountain Equipment Co-op,** stocked with durable outdoor adventure goods. At no. 41–43, note the **Perkins Building,** and at no. 45–49, look for the building with a totally cast-iron facade. The **Nicholas Hoare** bookstore, one of the coziest in the city, is at no. 45.

Continue browsing as you pass Church Street. **Wonderful & Whites,** 83 Front St., features delicate pieces—Victorian linens, lace, pillows, china, and glass. Some of the pieces even have beautiful, colorful patterns. Next door, **Ra** offers an array of Indian and other decorative accents—bedspreads and pillows, along with apparel and jewelry.

Now cross Market Street to the:
❾ St. Lawrence Market
The old market building on the right holds this great market hall, which was constructed around the city's second

city hall (1844–45). The elegant pedimented facade that you see as you stand in the center of the hall was originally the center block of the city hall. Today, the market abounds with vendors selling fresh eggs, Mennonite sausage, seafood, meats, cheeses, and baked goods. From Thursday to Saturday, in the north building across the street, a farmers' market starts at 5am.

> **TAKE A BREAK**
> The most fun place to stop is at one of the stands offering fresh produce in the market itself. Other choices include **Le Papillon,** 16 Church St. (☎ **416/363-0838;** p. 99), which features a raft of savory dessert crepes, and **HotHouse Cafe,** 35 Church St. (☎ **416/366-7800**).

Exit the market where you came in. Cross Wellington Street and cut through Market Lane Park and the shops at Market Square, past the north market building. Turn right onto King Street to:
❿ St. Lawrence Hall
This was the focal point of the community in the mid-19th century. This hall was the site of grand city occasions, political rallies, balls, and entertainment. Frederick Douglass delivered an antislavery lecture; Jenny Lind and Adelina Patti sang in 1851 and 1860, respectively; General Tom Thumb appeared in 1862; and George Brown campaigned for Confederation. William Thomas designed the elegant Palladian-style building, which boasts a domed cupola.

Cross King Street and enter the 19th-century garden. It has a cast-iron drinking fountain for people, horses, and dogs, and flowerbeds filled with seasonal blooms.

If you like, rest on a bench while you admire the handsome proportions of St. Lawrence Hall and listen to the chimes of:
⓫ St. James Cathedral
Adjacent to the garden on the north side of King Street, this is one of my

favorite places in Toronto. The beautiful building and its surrounding park make a serene setting to rest and gather one's thoughts—at least for now. A condo developer is hoping to build on the grounds of the park that surrounds St. James. Now *there* goes the neighborhood. Enjoy this beautiful oasis while you still can.

York's first church was built here from 1803 to 1807. Originally a frame building, it was enlarged in 1818 and 1819, and replaced in 1831. The second church burned in 1839. The first cathedral replaced it, only to be destroyed in the great fire of 1849. The present building was begun in 1850 and finished in 1874. It boasts the tallest steeple in Canada. Inside, at the northern end of the east aisle, there's a Tiffany window in memory of William Jarvis, one of Toronto's founding fathers.

St. James' first incumbent was the Rev. George O'Kill Stuart; his successor, John Strachan (pronounced Strawn), later became the first bishop of Toronto. Strachan wielded tremendous temporal as well as spiritual power. For 50 years, until his death in 1867, he was an indomitable spirit. He threatened the Americans with the vengeance of the British Navy after they occupied York (Toronto), defied the British prelates by keeping King's College open over their objections that the charter was too liberal, and dismissed Thomas Jefferson as "a mischief maker." He revered British institutions and abhorred anything Yankee.

From here, you can view one of the early retail buildings that was built when King Street was the main commercial street. **Nos. 129–35** were originally an Army and Navy Store; cast iron, plate glass, and arched windows allowed the shopper to see what was available in the store. Also note nos. 111 and 125. The **Toronto Sculpture Garden,** 115 King St. (© 416/485-9658), is a quiet corner for contemplation.

WINDING DOWN
From St. James, the venerable **Le Royal Meridien King Edward,** 37 King St. E. (© 416/863-9700), is only a block away. You can stop for afternoon tea in the lobby lounge, or light fare or lunch in the **Café Victoria.** Both **La Maquette,** 111 King St. E. (© 416/366-8191), and **Biagio,** 157 King St. E. (© 416/366-4040), have appealing courtyards.

From St. James, go south on Church Street for 1 block and turn right into Colbourne Street. From Colbourne, turn left down Leader Lane to Wellington, where you can enjoy a fine view of the mural on the Flatiron Building and of the rhythmic flow of mansard rooflines along the south side of Front Street.

Turn right and proceed to Yonge Street, then turn right and walk to King Street to catch the subway to your next destination.

8

Shopping

Shopping in Toronto can be a kaleidoscopic experience. The *haute*-est international retailers—like Prada, Chanel, and Gucci—compete for attention with discount emporiums like Honest Ed's. Megastores dominate the landscape, yet boutiques are blossoming. And while foreign chains stake their claim in shopping arcades and malls, they stand shoulder to shoulder with homegrown talent.

The result of this chaos is a cornucopia of shops that fit a wide range of budgets and tastes. The bad news: While window-shopping is a laudable pastime, don't fool yourself that it will stop there. Just don't break the bank.

1 The Shopping Scene

While you may want to check out the impressive array of international retailers, it would be a mistake to overlook the locals. If your passion is fashion, do check out Canadian labels such as Lida Baday, Ross Mayer, Misura by Joeffer Caoc, Linda Lundstrom, Crystal Siemens, Frette by Michelle Secours, Brian Bailey, Mimi Bizjak, Mercy, Wolves, and Comrags.

Toronto also has a bustling arts and crafts community, with many galleries, custom jewelers, and artisans. Some of the best buys are on native and Inuit art. Artwork can be imported into the United States duty-free.

Stores usually open at around 10am from Monday to Saturday. Closing hours change depending on the day. From Monday to Wednesday, most stores close at 6pm; on Thursday and Friday, hours run to 8pm or 9pm; on Saturday, closing is quite early, usually around 6pm. Most stores are open on Sunday, though the hours may be restricted—11am or noon to 5pm is not unusual.

Almost every establishment accepts MasterCard and Visa, and a growing number take American Express. Many retailers accept U.S. cash, and the exchange rate tends to be a favorable one, especially downtown in the Eaton Centre area.

2 Great Shopping Areas

DOWNTOWN

CHINATOWN It's crowded and noisy, but don't let that put you off. Sure, there's the usual touristy junk, like cheapo plastic toys and jewelry, but the real Chinatown has a lot more to offer, including fine rosewood furniture, exquisite ceramics, and homeopathic herbs. Just don't try driving here: This is traffic purgatory, and best navigated on foot.

THE EATON CENTRE Okay, you're short on time, but you still want to fit in all your shopping. Where else can you go but the Eaton Centre? With more than 300 shops, including Browns, Danier, Birks, Nine West, La Vie en Rose, Femme de Carriere, Eddie Bauer, Banana Republic, Mendocino, Laura Secord, and Indigo, you'll be sure to find something.

> ⌐*Tips* **Good to Know: Taxes & Rebates**
>
> The provincial sales tax (PST) is 8%, and the national goods-and-services tax (GST) is 7%. Visitors can apply for a rebate of both when they leave the country. For details, see "Taxes" under "Fast Facts: Toronto," in chapter 3.

QUEEN STREET WEST   Queen Street West between University Avenue and Bathurst Street is rich with boutiques for both fashion and housewares, though there are a lot of familiar names thrown in the mix. Locals complain that this neighborhood isn't what it was before the Gap moved in, but it's still a great stomping ground for fashionistas in need of a fix.

THE UNDERGROUND CITY   Subterranean Toronto is a hive of shopping activity. While you won't find too many shops down here that don't have an aboveground location, the Underground City is a popular place in winter, and with those whose schedules don't allow them out of the Financial District.

WEST QUEEN WEST   Playing down its grittier roots, this hot new neighborhood has got the reputation for cutting-edge fashion that Queen Street West used to enjoy. Starting at Bathurst Avenue and running west a few blocks past Ossington Avenue, this is where you'll find an incredible array of fashion talent, art galleries, and great new restaurants.

MIDTOWN

BLOOR STREET WEST   This strip of real estate, bordered by Yonge Street to the east and Avenue Road to the west, is where most of the top international names in fashion set up shop. If you're in the mood to see what Karl Lagerfeld is designing or to pick up a glittering bauble from Cartier or Tiffany, this is your hunting ground.

YORKVILLE   A far cry from its days as a hippie hangout and commune in the 1960s, this is now one of Toronto's best known—and most expensive—shopping neighborhoods. Little alleyways crisscross the streets, giving Yorkville a romantic, old-fashioned appeal. The shops here tend to be small boutiques that specialize, say, in beaded handbags or fine handmade papers. Bistros and cafes abound, giving rise to Yorkville's other pastime: people-watching.

3 Shopping A to Z

ANTIQUES

Toronto's antiques scene has exploded. Throw a stone in any direction and you're bound to hit an Edwardian console, or at least a classic Eames chair. For fine antiques, head north from Bloor Street along Avenue Road until you reach Davenport Avenue, or walk north on Yonge Street from the Rosedale subway station to St. Clair Avenue. Another top area is Mount Pleasant Road from St. Clair Avenue to Eglinton Avenue. For less pricey finds, head west on Queen Street to the Bathurst Street area. Merchandise at the Harbourfront Antique Market varies widely in quality and price.

At Home *Finds*   An inviting, airy room filled with an ever-changing collection of furniture and accessories, including French chairs (often in pairs), fine tables, vintage lamps, and decorative mirrors. 1156 Yonge St. © **416/924-6590.** Subway: Summerhill or Rosedale.

Midtown Shopping: Bloor/Yorkville

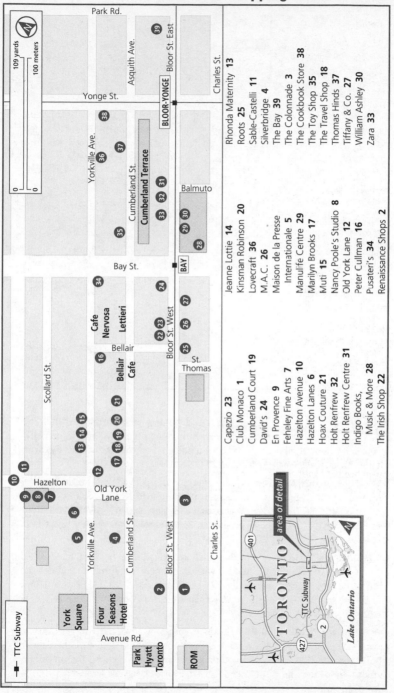

109 yards
100 meters

Park Rd.

Asquith Ave.

Yonge St.

BLOOR-YONGE

Bloor St. East

Charles St.

Yorkville Ave.

Cumberland St.

Cumberland Terrace

Balmuto

Bay St.

BAY

Cafe
Nervosa
Lettieri

Bloor St. West

Bellair

Scollard St.

Bellair
Cafe

St.
Thomas

Hazelton

Old York
Lane

Yorkville Ave.

Cumberland St.

Bloor St. West

Charles S..

York
Square

Four
Seasons
Hotel

Avenue Rd.

Park
Hyatt
Toronto

ROM

TTC Subway

TORONTO

area of detail

TTC Subway

Lake Ontario

Capezio **23**
Club Monaco **1**
Cumberland Court **19**
David's **24**
En Provence **9**
Feheley Fine Arts **7**
Hazelton Avenue **10**
Hazelton Lanes **6**
Hoax Couture **21**
Holt Renfrew **32**
Holt Renfrew Centre **31**
Indigo Books,
  Music & More **28**
The Irish Shop **22**

Jeanne Lottie **14**
Kinsman Robinson **20**
Lovecraft **36**
M.A.C. **26**
Maison de la Presse
  Internationale **5**
Manulife Centre **29**
Marilyn Brooks **17**
Muti **15**
Nancy Poole's Studio **8**
Old York Lane **12**
Peter Cullman **16**
Pusateri's **34**
Renaissance Shops **2**

Rhonda Maternity **13**
Roots **25**
Sable-Castelli **11**
Silverbridge **4**
The Bay **39**
The Colonnade **3**
The Cookbook Store **38**
The Toy Shop **35**
The Travel Shop **18**
Thomas Hinds **37**
Tiffany & Co. **27**
William Ashley **30**
Zara **33**

173

Downtown Shopping: Queen Street West & West Queen West

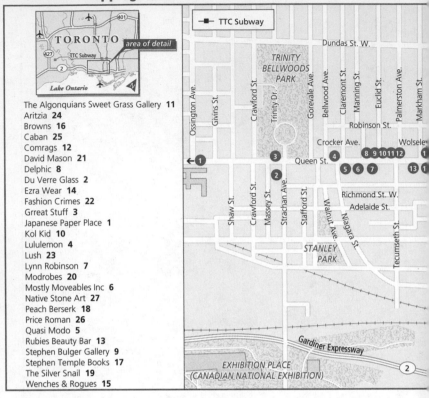

TTC Subway

The Algonquians Sweet Grass Gallery **11**
Aritzia **24**
Browns **16**
Caban **25**
Comrags **12**
David Mason **21**
Delphic **8**
Du Verre Glass **2**
Ezra Wear **14**
Fashion Crimes **22**
Grreat Stuff **3**
Japanese Paper Place **1**
Kol Kid **10**
Lululemon **4**
Lush **23**
Lynn Robinson **7**
Modrobes **20**
Mostly Moveables Inc **6**
Native Stone Art **27**
Peach Berserk **18**
Price Roman **26**
Quasi Modo **5**
Rubies Beauty Bar **13**
Stephen Bulger Gallery **9**
Stephen Temple Books **17**
The Silver Snail **19**
Wenches & Rogues **15**

Belle Epoque   If you're feeling pretty and looking for furniture to match, this attic-like shop is worth a look. The furnishings are luxurious, and some pieces would not be out of place at Versailles, gilt and all. Some reproductions mix with the real articles. 1066 Yonge St. ℂ 416/925-0066. Subway: Rosedale.

Bernardi's Antiques   The tiny showroom is jam-packed with furniture, silver flatware, paintings, bronzes, and carpets. Discontinued Royal Doulton figurines are a specialty. 699 Mount Pleasant Rd. (south of Eglinton Ave.). ℂ 416/483-6471. www.bernardisantiques.com. Subway: Eglinton, then no. 34 bus to Mount Pleasant, and walk 1 block south.

Constantine ✿   Every item in this newly renovated shop has been handpicked by its owner, Rita Tsantis. It's stocked with imposing wood furniture and delicate baubles. Be sure to check out the lighting selection—hand-painted Fortuny lamps are a house specialty—and gilt-trimmed glassware. 1110 Yonge St. ℂ 866/929-1177 or 416/929-1177. Subway: Rosedale.

Decorum Decorative Finds   If you're going on an ocean voyage, can you resist a C$2,200 (US$1,540) vintage Louis Vuitton trunk? The wares here range from tables and chaise lounges to oil paintings and old books. All are top priced, but also top of the line. 1210 Yonge St. ℂ 416/966-6829. Subway: Summerhill.

Horsefeathers!   If your taste runs to English and French country house styles, this emporium's for you. The 12,000-square-foot space boasts striking wooden pieces in walnut and mahogany that share the spotlight with tapestries and Persian carpets. A new, smaller outlet is at 1212 Yonge St. (✆ 416/934-1771), 630 Mount Pleasant Rd. ✆ 416/486-4555. Subway: Eglinton, then no. 34 bus to Mount Pleasant.

L'Atelier   This is about as glamorous as it gets. Napoleon III side tables share space with chrome bar stools and rococo Italian lamps. Many of the price tags hit four digits, but there are lovely accoutrements for as little as C$10 (US$6.80). 1224 Yonge St. ✆ 416/966-0200. Subway: Summerhill.

Mark McLaine Collection   This shop features styles as diverse as Art Deco and chinoiserie (a blend of Asian and French design). Many of the furnishings, carvings, and jewelry are the real McCoy, mixed with some fabulous fakes. Hazelton Lanes, 55 Avenue Rd. ✆ 416/927-7972. Subway: Bay.

Michel Taschereau Antiques   In business since 1955, this attic-like shop is filled with 18th-, 19th-, and early 20th-century pieces from England, France, and North America. There's also a collection of decorative glass objects, ceramics, and folk art. 176 Cumberland St. ✆ 416/923-3020. Subway: Bay.

Mostly Movables Inc   Turn-of-the-20th-century Canadiana and English Jazz Age furnishings fill this shop. The pieces are generally in fine form, and the prices are somewhat lower than those at many Yorkville and Rosedale competitors. 785 Queen St. W. (west of Bathurst St.). ✆ 416/504-4455. Subway: Osgoode, then any streetcar west to Euclid Ave.

Putti 𝕲   Two generously proportioned rooms hold grand (and grandly priced) European treasures old and new: dining sets, armoires, cushions, and china. A recent addition is the floral department, which features both fresh and dried flowers. *Victoria* magazine has repeatedly featured this shop. 1104 Yonge St. ℂ 416/972-7652. Subway: Rosedale.

Whim Antiques   The store is aptly named—whimsical it is. In business since 1973, it's filled with beautiful baubles, silverware, and decorative *objets*, and walking through it feels rather like being let loose in great-grandma's attic. 561 Mount Pleasant Rd. ℂ 416/481-4474. Subway: St. Clair, then Mount Pleasant bus to Belsize Ave.

Zig Zag   This shop carries a mélange of styles, but the specialty is early Modernist pieces. The names to watch out for are Eames, Saarinen, Arne Jacobsen, and Warren Platner. There are some bargains, with excellent pieces in the C$200 to $400 (US$140–$280) range, with a few stellar finds that run as high as C$3,500 (US$2,450). 1107 Queen St. E. ℂ 416/778-6495. Subway: Queen, then any streetcar east to Pape Ave.

ART

Bau-Xi   After viewing the masterworks at the Art Gallery of Ontario, you can head across the street and buy your own. Founded in 1965, Bau-Xi features contemporary works by artists from across the country. 340 Dundas St. W. ℂ 416/977-0600. Subway: St. Patrick.

Bay of Spirits Gallery   Here you'll find works by native Indians from across Canada. Most of the collection focuses on the art of the Pacific Northwest, including totem poles, masks, prints, and jewelry. 156 Front St. W. ℂ 416/971-5190. Subway: Union.

Eskimo Art Gallery   This award-winning gallery has the largest collection of Inuit sculpture in Toronto. At any given time, it shows more than 500 pieces, with prices ranging from C$16 to $22,000 (US$11–$15,400). 12 Queens Quay W. (opposite Westin Harbour Castle). ℂ 800/800-2008 or 416/366-3000. Subway: Union, then LRT to Queens Quay.

Feheley Fine Arts   The Feheleys have been personally selecting every piece in their gallery for over 40 years, making this one of the most individualized collections of early and contemporary Inuit art anywhere. 14 Hazelton Ave. ℂ 416/323-1373. Subway: Bay.

Gallery Moos   German native Walter Moos has been a fixture on the Toronto art scene for 30 years. His gallery features top Canadian artists as well as international figures. 622 Richmond St. W. ℂ 416/504-5445. Subway: Osgoode, then any streetcar west to Bathurst St., and walk 1 block south.

Jane Corkin Gallery 𝕲   Most items here are historical and contemporary photographs from around the world. They include works by Cylla von Tiedemann, Irving Penn, and Herb Ritts. There is also a small collection of modernist painting and sculpture. 179 John St. ℂ 416/979-1980. Subway: Osgoode.

Kinsman Robinson Galleries   The two stories of this Yorkville gallery display 20th-century figurative paintings, sculpture, and drawings. Artists represented include Stanley Cosgrove, Robert Katz, Esther Wertheimer, and Donald Liardi. Native Canadians Robert Davidson and Norval Morrisseau also exhibit their work here. There are a few paperworks by Zuniga, Braque, and Chagall, among others. 108 Cumberland St. ℂ 800/895-4278 or 416/964-2374. Subway: Bay.

Nancy Poole's Studio   This intimate gallery of painting and sculpture has been in business for 3 decades. Most of the art is contemporary, much of it Canadian in origin. The gallery launches solo exhibitions every 3 weeks. 16 Hazelton Ave. © 416/964-9050. Subway: Bay.

Olga Korper Gallery   Established in 1973, this gallery houses contemporary Canadian and international works. Artists represented include Averbuch, John Brown, Sankawa, and the estate of Louis Comtois. 17 Morrow Ave. (off Dundas St. W.). © 416/538-8220. Subway: Dundas West.

Ontario College of Art & Design Gallery *(Finds)*   If you're interested in the work of an emerging generation of artists, check out the ongoing exhibitions at the OCAD. Students display sculpture, photography, painting, and multimedia installations. 115 McCaul St., 3rd floor © 416/977-6000, ext. 262. Subway: St. Patrick.

Sable-Castelli   This highly regarded gallery has been in business for more than 25 years. It represents contemporary American and Canadian artists, including heavy hitters like Warhol and Oldenburg. 33 Hazelton Ave. © 416/961-0011. Subway: Bay.

Sandra Ainsley *(R)*   Specializing in glass sculpture, this renowned gallery represents more than 50 artists from across North America, including Dale Chihuly, Jon Kuhn, Peter Powning, Tom Scoon, Susan Edgerley, and David Bennett. The one-of-a-kind pieces have big price tags, but there are also some affordable items, such as paperweights, vases, and jewelry. Toronto Exchange Tower, 130 King St. W. © 416/362-4480. Subway: St. Andrew.

Stephen Bulger Gallery   This gallery displays contemporary Canadian and international photography; some of the artists represented include Diana Shearwood, Volker Seding, Lida Moser, and Vincenzo Pietropaolo. 700 Queen St. W. (west of Bathurst St.). © 416/504-0575. Subway: Osgoode, then any streetcar west to Palmerston Ave.

Susan Hobbs Gallery   This small gallery, in an unprepossessing warehouse far from the Yorkville crowd, is a major player in Canadian contemporary art. Hobbs represents 11 of Toronto's best artists, including Ian Carr-Harris, Shirley Wiitasalo, Robin Collyer, and Sandra Meigs. 137 Tecumseth St. (at Queen St.) © 416/504-3699. Subway: Osgoode, then any streetcar west to Tecumseth St.

Ydessa Hendeles Art Foundation   This is one of the most interesting contemporary art collections in the city. Hendeles features installations by international artists. Works on display include paintings, photography, and multimedia projects. 778 King St. W. © 416/603-2227. Subway: St. Andrew, then any streetcar west to Bathurst St.

AUDIO-VISUAL & ELECTRONIC GOODS

Bay-Bloor Radio   This 13,000-square-foot store carries all the latest and greatest audio equipment, from portable units to in-home theater systems. Manulife Centre, 55 Bloor St. W. © 416/967-1122. Subway: Bay.

Canadian Tire   This is handyman heaven. The endless aisles overflow with gadgets for home, yard, office, car, and any place in between. This is where I head as Father's Day approaches. 839 Yonge St. © 416/925-9592. www.canadiantire.com. Subway: Yonge/Bloor.

Henry's *(R)*   This bi-level shop deals in analog and digital photography. The first floor has electronic equipment, darkroom supplies, and a photo-processing lab. Upstairs, there's a wide selection of secondhand cameras and gear. 119 Church St. © 416/868-0872. Subway: Queen.

SpyTech James Bond wannabes, welcome. Entering Spy Tech is like having a free pass to Q's lab. Looking for a gadget to modify your telephone voice or a spook-worthy camera? You'll find it all here, though the price tags do get a little steep—all the way up to C$100,000 (US$70,000) for a bulletproof car. 2028 Yonge St. ℂ 416/482-8588. Subway: Davisville.

BOOKS

Another Man's Poison This shop boasts an international collection of books about graphic arts, interior design, and architecture. Anything you can't find on the shelves can be special ordered. There's also a substantial selection of out-of-print titles. 29 McCaul St. (just north of Queen St.). ℂ 416/593-6451. Subway: Osgoode.

Atticus Books Bookworms can while away hours in this crowded shop filled with secondhand scholarly tomes. It stocks many volumes of philosophy, psychology, and psychoanalysis. Antiquarian books and illuminated manuscripts are at the back of the store. 84 Harbord St. ℂ 416/922-6045. Subway: Spadina, then walk south.

Ballenford Books on Architecture Interior designers, whether amateur or pro, will love this well-arranged store. The books cover everything from antique furniture to architectural theory, from urban design to landscaping. The shop also displays sketches and drawings by local architects. 600 Markham St. (south of Bloor St. W.) ℂ 416/588-0800. Subway: Bathurst.

Bob Miller Book Room When I was a student at the University of Toronto, I would come into this academic bookstore looking for one text and end up browsing for ages. It stocks mainly literary fiction, humanities, and social sciences. Works in translation are carefully selected. 180 Bloor St. W., lower concourse. ℂ 416/922-3557. Subway: St. George.

Book City All the books here are new, and many are discounted by 10% to 30%. There is also a good assortment of international magazines. Book City also has branches at 1430 Yonge St. (ℂ 416/961-1228), 1950 Queen St. E. (ℂ 416/698-1444), and 348 Danforth Ave. (ℂ 416/469-9997). 501 Bloor St. W. ℂ 416/961-4496. Subway: Bathurst.

Chapters 🞳 While the Chapters bookstores are now owned and operated by Indigo (see below), they retain their own unique charm. Eminently browse-worthy and well-stocked, Chapters boasts comfy chairs, a Starbucks cafe, and a host of free special events. Celebrity authors Sophia Loren and Sarah, Duchess of York, had their Toronto engagements here. There's another Chapters store at 142 John St. (ℂ 416/595-7349). The stores are open late, usually until 10 or 11pm on weeknights and midnight on weekends. 110 Bloor St. W. ℂ 416/920-9299. Subway: Bay.

The Cookbook Store I call it food porn: lush, gooey close-ups of scallop ceviche and tiramisu. This store specializes in the kind of book that makes a gourmet's heart go pitter-patter. There are also tomes about wine, health, and restaurants. 850 Yonge St. ℂ 416/920-2665. Subway: Yonge/Bloor.

David Mason This charming used-book store is straight out of Dickens. It stocks many travel books, and a number of first editions of Canadian, American, and British works. The collections of 19th- and 20th-century literature are vast. 342 Queen St. W. ℂ 416/598-1015. Subway: Osgoode.

Glad Day Bookshop This was the first gay-oriented bookstore in Canada, and it remains one of the best. The shelves hold a sizable collection of gay and lesbian fiction, biography, and history books, and the offerings have expanded to include magazines, CDs, videos, calendars, posters, and cards. 598A Yonge St., 2nd floor. ℂ 877/783-3725 or 416/961-4161. Subway: Wellesley.

Indigo Books Music & More 🟊   This Canadian-owned chain boasts an excellent selection of books, magazines, and videotapes. It has tables and chairs to encourage browsing, a cafe, and helpful staff. Best of all, there are special events (author visits, live performances, even seminars) almost daily. There are also events for kids. The store is a favorite with night owls—it's open until 11pm or midnight every day. There are branches at the Eaton Centre (ℂ 416/591-3622) and at 2300 Yonge St., at Eglinton Avenue (ℂ 416/544-0049). Manulife Centre, 55 Bloor St. W. ℂ 416/925-3536. www.indigo.ca. Subway: Yonge/Bloor or Bay.

Mabel's Fables 🟊   This charming shop is stocked with every book a child could possibly want—and a lot more. Offerings are grouped by age, going up to early adolescence. On weekends there are author visits and other special events. 662 Mount Pleasant. ℂ 416/322-0438. Eglinton, then no. 34 bus to Mount Pleasant, and walk 2 blocks south.

Nicholas Hoare   This shop has the cozy feel of an English library, with hardwood floors, plush couches, and a fireplace. There's an extensive selection of Canadian and international fiction, as well as heavyweight art tomes and children's books. 45 Front St. E. ℂ 416/777-2665. Subway: Union.

Open Air Books & Maps   This shop caters to nature lovers and ecology buffs. It carries a vast assortment of travel guidebooks and maps. 25 Toronto St. ℂ 416/363-0719. Subway: King.

Seekers Books   New and old books about Eastern religion, mysticism, meditation, and the occult mix on the shelves. The focus is definitely New Age, but you'll find general-interest fiction and nonfiction, too. 509 Bloor St. W. ℂ 416/925-1982. Subway: Bathurst.

The Silver Snail 🟊   Remember those comic books you read as a kid? Well, they're all here, with adult-oriented comics like the *Sandman* series. You'll see a sizable section of imported editions, and posters and movie memorabilia, too. 367 Queen St. W. ℂ 416/593-0889. Subway: Osgoode.

Steven Temple Books   If you're looking for a rare first edition of a 19th- or 20th-century literary work in English, be sure to visit this shop, which is open by appointment only. It also carries secondhand books about a variety of subjects. 489 Queen St. W., 2nd floor. ℂ 416/703-9908. Subway: Osgoode, then any streetcar west.

The World's Biggest Bookstore   The debate about whether the World's Biggest is *really* the world's biggest rages on. Either way, the 27km (17 miles) of bookshelves do contain a good selection. Browsing is welcome, but the bright, bright lights are headache-inducing after a while. There are also software, video, and magazine departments. 20 Edward St. ℂ 416/977-7009. Subway: Dundas.

CHINA, SILVER & GLASS

Du Verre Glass   The store name is a bit of a misnomer. Gorgeous glassworks are on display, but they share this airy, open space with ceramics, wood and wrought-iron furniture, lamps, and candlesticks. 188 Strachan Ave. ℂ 416/593-0182. Subway: Osgoode, then any streetcar west.

Muti   Murano glass designs and cheery ceramics from Italy dominate this store. Look a little closer and you'll find a few French tapestries and tablecloths, too. 88 Yorkville Ave. ℂ 416/969-0253. Subway: Bay.

⌒ *Value* The Best Bargains

Maybe you can't get something for nothing . . . but you can score some pretty fab finds on the cheap in Toronto. It's a treasure hunt of sorts, and the spoils are anything but certain, but when you find that perfect piece marked down to next-to-nothing, well, that just makes it all worthwhile. Many Toronto retailers, including luxurious Holt Renfrew, have their own outlet shops. Here's my own little black book of favorite foraging grounds. Happy hunting!

Dixie Outlet Mall   Ten minutes from Pearson International Airport is the answer to bargain-shoppers' prayers. It's hard to beat the Dixie Outlet Mall for number of bargains per square foot. There are more than 120 outlet shops here, including Femme de Carriere and chocolatier Laura Secord, so you're bound to find something. 1250 S. Service Rd., Mississauga. ✆ **905/278-7492.** Gardiner Expressway/Queen Elizabeth Way (QEW) west to Dixie Rd. exit. Turn left, follow Dixie Rd. south to S. Service Rd.

Grreat Stuff   There's an awful lot of men's clothes packed into this small retail space, but if you're not troubled by claustrophobia, dig in for some amazing deals. Business casual is this shop's mainstay, though there are *grreat* prices on Italian silk ties and brand-name suits. 870 Queen St. W. ✆ **416/533-7680.** Subway: Osgoode, then streetcar west to Shaw St.

Holt Renfrew Last Call   It might not be the most organized store you've laid eyes on, but what it lacks in tidiness it makes up for in bargains. The racks are laden with brands such as Donna Karan, Prada, and Versace, marked down to one-half to one-fifth of what they would normally cost. There have been rumors of Kate Spade handbags on sale here, but I have yet to arrive in time. May you have better luck. 370 Steeles Ave. W. ✆ **905/886-7444.** Subway: Finch, then Steeles West bus.

Honest Ed's World Famous Shopping Centre ⌒*Finds*   Ed's is a Toronto institution, framed with flashing red and yellow lights both outdoors *and* indoors. "Don't just stand there, buy something!" blurts out one brazen sign. This idiosyncratic store has a deal on everything from housewares to carpets, from clothing to sundries. Crazy-making as shopping here can be, the bargains are unbeatable—but be warned, the queues are, too. 581 Bloor St. W. ✆ **416/537-2111.** Subway: Bathurst.

William Ashley ⌒   The last word in luxe, whether it be fine china, crystal, or silver. All of the top manufacturers are represented, including Waterford, Baccarat, Christofle, Wedgewood, and Lenox. Even if you're not in a buying mood, the detailed displays are fascinating. If you are in a buying mood, the prices are better than you'll find elsewhere. Manulife Centre, 55 Bloor St. W. ✆ **416/964-2900.** Subway: Bay.

CIGARS & TOBACCO
Thomas Hinds   This is Havana heaven for the stogie set. Thomas Hinds carries a wide range of Cuban cigars and cigarillos, as well as pipes and the other smoking accouterments. Upstairs there's a lounge and humidor. 8 Cumberland St. ✆ **416/927-7703.** Subway: Yonge/Bloor.

Marilyn's   Here's a rare thing: knockdown prices paired with attentive service. The specialty is Canadian fashions for women, from sportswear to glamorous gowns. There are also in-store seminars about fashion-forward topics like traveling with just one suitcase. 130 Spadina Ave. © 416/504-6777. Subway: Spadina, then LRT to Queen St. W.

Paris Samples   This store snaps up designers' samples and marks them down 20% to 75%. The clothes range from wool pants to velvet dresses to micro-miniskirts. *One caveat:* The sizes are all under 14, and many clothes come only in the smallest sizes. 101 Yorkville Ave. © 416/926-0656. Subway: Bay.

The Shoe Company   This is every foot fetishist's dream: great shoes for men and women from Unisa, Nine West, and others, marked down to unbeatable prices. There are lots of funky styles that won't be stylish for long, but it won't hurt your pocketbook to splurge. There are outlets around the city, including First Canadian Place. 711 Yonge St. © 416/923-8388. Subway: Yonge/Bloor.

Tom's Place   After more than 40 years in business, Tom's Place looks sharper than ever. While the shop devotes an entire floor to women's wear, the best buys are in the men's department: You'll find brand-name merchandise by the likes of Armani and Valentino. Suits that cost C$495 to $1,800 (US$347–$1,260) elsewhere ring up for C$299 to $850 (US$209–$595) here. Tom's Place stocks sizes from 36 short to 50 tall. 190 Baldwin St. © 416/596-0297. Subway: Spadina, then LRT to Baldwin St.

Winner's   This northern outpost of the U.S.-owned T.J. Maxx chain offers great deals on clothes for men and women (think Jones New York, Tommy Hilfiger, and Earl Jeans), and top-name togs for the kiddies. There's also an ever-changing selection of housewares, cookware, linens, toiletries, and toys. The new 40,000-square-foot outlet at College Park is always packed, but its large, airy space is filled with deals. College Park. © 416/598-8800; Subway: College. The smaller but long-standing location in the Fashion District is another good bet. 57 Spadina Ave. © 416/585-2052. Subway: Spadina, then LRT to King St. W.

CRAFTS

The Algonquians Sweet Grass Gallery ⚅   Ojibway-owned and -operated, this shop specializes in exquisite Native Canadian arts and crafts. The collection includes porcupine-quill jewelry, soapstone sculpture, Iroquois masks, prints, antique spearheads, and moccasins. 668 Queen St. W. © 416/703-1336. Subway: Osgoode, then any streetcar west.

Arctic Canada   Here you'll find a wide range of arts and crafts, from soapstone carvings to jewelry and clothing, all hailing from the Arctic Circle. There's another branch at Pearson International Airport, Terminal 2 (© 905/678-6064). 207 Queens Quay W. © 416/203-7889. Subway: Union, then LRT to Queens Quay.

on King This 10,000-square-foot complex consists of boutiques selling original art, folk crafts, and furniture. Connected to it is the Wagner Rosenbaum Gallery, which exhibits work by new and established Toronto artists every month. 169 King St. E. ℂ **416/777-9617.** Subway: King.

Art Zone Sisters Jane and Kathryn Irwin own and operate this gallerylike space. Their main medium is stained glass, and their style is colorful and modern. They also carry a limited number of glass gift items, including bowls, trays, and sculptural objects. 592 Markham St. (south of Bloor St. W.). ℂ **416/534-1892.** Subway: Bathurst.

Five Potters Studio Phone ahead for an appointment, and you're free to watch the ceramic artists—all women—at work. The pieces on display vary from functional to sculptural items. Prices range from C$15 to $300 (US$11–$210). 131A Pears Ave. ℂ **416/924-6992.** Subway: St. George.

Frida *(Finds)* Arts and crafts from Africa, Southeast Asia, and Latin America share space in this bi-level shop. It offers an assortment of colorful woven mats, clothes, carved statuettes, jewelry, and candelabras. 39 Front St. E. ℂ **416/366-3169.** Subway: Union.

Lynn Robinson Robinson herself creates many of the bronze and raku (Japanese earthenware) objects on display. In addition to the sculpture and glass, wood, and clay pieces, you'll see objects by five jewelers working with precious metals. Visitors are often treated to the sight of a potter working near the entrance. 709 Queen St. W. ℂ **416/703-2467.** Subway: Osgoode, then any streetcar west to Bathurst St.

Native Stone Art This shop houses the creations of native Indian artisans from across North America. There are Mohawk and Iroquois carvings, Cree moccasins, and Navajo, Zuni, and Hopi jewelry. The quality is very high. 2 McCaul St. (at Queen St. W.). ℂ **416/593-0924.** Subway: Osgoode.

DEPARTMENT STORES

Holt Renfrew Designers such as Donna Karan, Christian Lacroix, and Yves St. Laurent figure in Holt Renfrew's four levels of merchandise. The basement connects with an underground mall, and features a gourmet food department and a cafe. Holt Renfrew Centre, 50 Bloor St. W. ℂ **416/922-2333.** Subway: Yonge/Bloor.

The Hudson's Bay Company Started as a fur-trading business when the first French-speaking settlers came to Canada, the Bay boasts excellent mid-range selections of clothing and housewares. It schedules weekend sales almost every week, though shoppers should be warned that winning the staff's attention requires patience. There are several locations around the city; addresses for the two best ones are listed here. (1) 176 Yonge St. (at Queen St.). ℂ **416/861-9111.** Subway: Queen. (2) 2 Bloor St. E. (at Yonge St.). ℂ **416/972-3333.** Subway: Yonge/Bloor.

Sears If you visited Toronto before 2000, you'll remember the gorgeous Eaton's department store, which anchored the Eaton Centre complex. Owned and operated by the Toronto-based Eaton family for more than a century, it closed in 1999. Sears Canada bought the Eatons name (minus the apostrophe) and opened this department store in its place. Now branded as a Sears store, it's more upscale than your average Sears. Eaton Centre. ℂ **416/343-2111.** Subway: Dundas.

FASHION

Let's get this out of the way first: Toronto has all of the requisite big-name European boutiques along Bloor Street West between Yonge Street and Avenue Road. You'll find **Louis Vuitton** at no. 110, **Gucci** at no. 130, and **Chanel, Prada,** and

Hermès bundled together at The Colonnade shopping arcade at no. 131. The listings below focus primarily on shops that are unique to Toronto (with just a couple of exceptions). Also see the listings under "Shoes" and "Vintage Clothing," later in this chapter.

CHILDREN'S

Kids Cats & Dogs   Not just for kids—the shop carries its signature T-shirts, pajamas, and sweats in sizes from infant to adult. Everything, including knapsacks and comforters, sports a cat or dog motif. 508 Eglinton Ave. W. © 416/484-1844. Subway: Eglinton.

Kol Kid *(Finds*   West Queen West isn't just for grown-ups, you know. This charming boutique carries Canadian- and European-made clothing for kids, plus toys and furnishings. 670 Queen St. W. © 416/681-0368. Subway: Osgoode, then streetcar west to Palmerston Ave.

Lovechild   A favorite with tiny tots who are already developing fashion savvy, Lovechild offers a selection of groovy clothes in a rainbow of colors. 2523 Yonge St. © 416/486-4746. Subway: Eglinton.

Misdemeanors *(*   Located just across the street from Pat Chorley's shop for grown-ups, Fashion Crimes (p. 185), Misdemeanors stocks the stuff that little girls' dreams are made of. In addition to gossamer gowns, there's a selection of flower-power home accents. 322½ Queen St. W. © 416/351-8758. Subway: Osgoode.

MEN'S & WOMEN'S

Club Monaco   This is Club Monaco's flagship store in Toronto. It's an airy, high-ceilinged space filled with casual wear and sportswear, with a smattering of work-ready clothes. It also has its own accessories and makeup lines. There are 19 other outlets around the city, including 403 Queen St. W. (© 416/979-5633). 157 Bloor St. W. © 416/591-8837. www.clubmonaco.com. Subway: Museum.

Hoax Couture   The corset-topped dresses on display in the front window bring a Moulin Rouge cancan show to mind, but the shop's owners, Chris Tyrell and Jim Searle, design dramatic, playful clothes for men and women. 114 Cumberland St. © 416/929-4629. Subway: Bay.

The Irish Shop   If you're yearning for the Emerald Isle, you'll welcome the sight of lace shawls, linens, sweaters, and Celtic music, books, and giftware. There's also a selection of linen suits by Dublin designer Paul Costelloe. 150 Bloor St. W. © 416/922-9400. Subway: Bay.

Modrobes *(Value*   Renowned for its comfy, casual clothing, Canadian-owned Modrobes got its start when its founder, Steven Debus, was still attending the university. Debus designed "exam pants"—trousers so comfy you could spend a day writing exams in them without your bum going numb. Today, the store's offerings include T-shirts, jackets, and hats. 239 Queen St. W. © 416/597-9560. www.modrobes.com. Subway: Osgoode.

Old Navy *(Overrated*   The Gap's little brother hit Toronto like a hurricane when it opened in 2001. There are no longer queues to get into the store, but it remains incredibly popular—a fact that's an enduring mystery to me. Sure, the prices are reasonable, but the store is cramped and chaotic, and the product selection is much smaller than at its U.S. counterparts. Unless you've never been to an Old Navy outlet before, steer clear. Eaton Centre. © 416/593-2551. Subway: Dundas.

Roots   This is one Canadian retailer that seems to be universally loved. The clothes are casual, from hooded sweats to fleece jackets, and there's a good selection of leather footwear. Don't overlook the tykes' department, which has the same stuff in tiny sizes. Other locations include the Eaton Centre (📞 416/593-9640). 95A Bloor St. W. 📞 416/323-9512. www.roots.ca. Subway: Bay.

Sim & Jones   Shop owners Pui Sim and Alarice Jones design clothes that move easily between a "smart casual" office environment and the smart chic of the latest bistro. The women's clothes are available in sizes 6 to 16. 388 College Street. 📞 416/920-2573. Subway: Queen's Park, then streetcar to Borden St.

TNT Man/TNT Woman *Finds*   The acronym stands for "The New Trend," and this small chain offers just that, with fashions from Betsey Johnson and Plein Sud for les femmes, and Diesel and Iceberg Jean for les hommes. There are also locations uptown at 368 and 388 Eglinton Avenue. Hazelton Lanes, 55 Avenue Rd. 📞 416/975-1960 (men's shop) and 416/975-1810 (women's shop). Subway: Bay.

Wenches & Rogues 🌟   This upscale shop carries the latest and greatest in Canadian design for men and women. Featured labels include Misura by Joeffer Caoc, as well as up-and-coming talent from around the country. 610 Queen St. W. 📞 416/536-2172. Subway: Osgoode, then streetcar west to Bathurst.

Zara *Value*   This Spanish retailer is renowned for transferring the latest looks into affordable fashions less than a month after they appear on the runway. This bi-level shop has a women's department at street level; the equally stylish men's shop is on the lower concourse. 50 Bloor St. W. 📞 416/916-2401. www.zara.com. Subway: Bay.

MEN'S

Boomer 🌟   Ever wonder where the Barenaked Ladies or Moist get the glad rags they wear in their videos? Look no farther than Boomer, a hip shop that stocks staples like Hugo Boss and Cinque, and well as the latest from Swedish trendsetter J. Linderberg. 309 Queen St. W. 📞 416/598-0013. Subway: Osgoode.

Decibel   This trendy shop is a terrific spot to pick up the latest and greatest in casualwear. Labels range from well-known brands like Kenneth Cole to up-and-comers like Psycho Cowboy or Pusch (from Denmark and Calgary, respectively). 200 Queen St. W. 📞 416/506-9648. Subway: Osgoode.

Delphic   Don't like trendy? Then don't shop here. If you do, you'll be confronted by fashion favorites like Evisu Jeans, which are imported from Japan. 706 Queen St. W. 📞 416/603-3334. Subway: Osgoode, then streetcar west to Manning Ave.

Eza Wear *Finds*   West Queen West has more than its fair share of up-and-coming designers, and this is one example. Design duo Susanne Langlois and Erin Murphy make many of their cool clothes from hemp, which looks as elegant as linen. 695 Queen St. W. 📞 416/975-1388. Subway: Osgoode, then streetcar west to Markham St.

Harry Rosen 🌟   Designed like a mini department store, Harry Rosen carries the crème de la crème of menswear designers, including Hugo Boss, Brioni, and Versace. There's also a good selection of work-worthy footwear, and a famous "Great Wall of Shirts." 82 Bloor St. W. 📞 416/972-0556. www.harryrosen.com. Subway: Bay.

Moores   There's something for everyone at this spacious shop. Most of the suits, sport coats, and dress pants are Canadian-made, and international designers like Oscar de la Renta are represented, too. Sizes run from extra short to extra tall and oversize. The prices tend to be reasonable, and bargains abound. 100 Yonge St. 📞 416/363-5442. Subway: King.

WOMEN'S

Aritzia   This Vancouver retailer now has an outpost on Queen West (another one is set to open in the Eaton Centre). The clothes tend to be sporty and fun, though there are some sexy numbers by the hard-to-find French label Kookaï. 280 Queen St. W. ℭ **416/977-9919.** Subway: Osgoode.

Comrags   Designers Judy Cornish and Joyce Gunhouse create retro-inspired clothing that looks great on a variety of body types. 654 Queen St. W. ℭ **416/360-7249.** www.comrags.com. Subway: Osgoode, then streetcar west to Palmerston.

Ewanika *(Finds*   Little Italy is famous for its nightlife, but if you happen by during the day be sure to check out designer Trish Ewanika's boutique. Her tailored creations are perfect for women who don't like suits but want to look polished at work. 490 College St. ℭ **416/927-9699.** Subway: Queen's Park, then streetcar west to Palmerston Ave.

Fashion Crimes   If Misdemeanors (p. 183) is a playground for little princesses, then Fashion Crimes is the stomping ground for their fairy godmothers. The glamorous dresses, designed by shop owner Pam Chorley, are a tribute to playful femininity. 395 Queen St. W. ℭ **416/592-9001.** Subway: Osgoode.

Femme De Carriere   For a dose of Quebecois savoir-faire, look no further than this elegant emporium. While the name translates into "career woman," the offerings range from shapely suits to evening-appropriate dresses and chic separates. Eaton Centre. ℭ **416/595-0951.** Subway: Queen.

Fresh Baked Goods *(Finds*   No, this *isn't* a bakery. Owner Laura Jean "the knitting queen" features a line of flirty knitwear made of cotton, mohair, wool, or lace. This is a favorite haunt of the celebrity set—stars like Neve Campbell drop by when they're in town. The staff is friendly and incredibly helpful; if you like a sweater but not its buttons, they will sew on different ones from their sizeable collection free of charge. They also do custom orders. 274 Augusta Ave. ℭ **416/966-0123.** www.freshbakedgoods.com. Subway: Spadina, then LRT to Baldwin St., and walk 2 blocks west.

F/X   The significance of the name is clear from the start: This is dressing for dramatic effect. Funkier pieces from the prêt-à-porter collections of Vivienne Westwood and Anna Sui are at the back of the store. There are also cutting-edge shoes and boots, a makeup collection, and candy. 152 Spadina Ave. ℭ **416/703-5595.** Subway: Spadina, then LRT to Queen St. W.

Jeanne Lottie *✿*   Can you make a fashion statement with a handbag? Canadian designer Jane Ip thinks so. Purses for all occasions, from zebra-patterned boxy bags for day to glittering sequin-encrusted numbers for a night out, fill her boutique. Prices are surprisingly low, with most offerings in the C$50 to $80 (US$35–$56) range. 106 Yorkville Ave. ℭ **416/975-5115.** Subway: Bay.

Linda Lundstrom   Lundstrom has been designing women's clothing since the early 1970s. Her distinctive brand of sportswear incorporates native Canadian art and themes. The famous La Parka coat is still a bestseller. 136 Cumberland St. ℭ **416/927-9009.** Subway: Bay.

Lululemon *✿*   Yoga devotees will be delighted by this West Queen West shop. In addition to the house label's nicely designed workout wear you'll find Ayurvedic skin care products by Christy Turlington, yoga mats, and other accessories. 734 Queen St. West ℭ **416/703-1399.** Subway: Osgoode, then streetcar west to Claremont St.

Maxi Boutique   Homegrown talent takes center stage here, with designs from Lida Baday, Ross Mayer, and Misura by Joeffer Caoc. There's a full complement of suits, separates, and eveningwear. 575 Danforth Ave. ℭ **416/461-6686.** Subway: Pape.

Peach Berserk *✿*   Toronto designer (and local legend) Kingi Carpenter creates dramatically printed silk separates, dresses and coats. But don't look for demure florals—prints range from bold martini glasses to the ironic "Do I Look Fat in This?" logo. 507 Queen St. W. ℂ 416/504-1711. Subway: Osgoode, then streetcar west to Spadina.

Pink Cobra   I have to admit, the name alone would attract me. Shoppers here are mesmerized by the clothes: hard-to-get labels like Buddhist Punk, Rude, URCA, and Fake Genius. 758 Queen St. W. ℂ 416/504-7804. Subway: Osgoode, then streetcar west to Niagara St.

Price Roman ⭐   The husband-and-wife team of Derek Price and Tess Roman produces sleek, tailored clothes with a sultry edge. They are rightly famous for their special occasion dresses. 267 Queen St. W. ℂ 416/979-7363. Subway: Osgoode.

Rhonda Maternity   For the last of the red-hot mamas, there's this glamorous boutique. The stylish suits, sweater sets, and sportswear are this store's exclusive designs. 110 Cumberland St. ℂ 416/921-3116. Subway: Bay.

FOOD

The Big Carrot   Who says health food can't be fun? This large-scale emporium stocks everything from organic produce to vitamins to all-natural beauty potions. Stop in at the cafe for a vegetarian snack or light meal. 348 Danforth Ave. ℂ 416/466-2129. Subway: Chester.

The Bonnie Stern School   Crammed to the rafters with cooking accoutrements (such as stovetop grills) and exotic books, this store also features the raw ingredients you need to produce fine cuisine. It carries top-notch olive oil, balsamic vinegar, Asian sauces, and candied flower petals. If you take a course or seminar, you get a 10% discount on everything you buy. 6 Erskine Ave. ℂ 416/484-4810. Subway: Eglinton.

Global Cheese Shoppe ⭐ *(Value*   Cheese, glorious cheese. More than 150 varieties are available, from mild boccocini to the greenest of Gorgonzola, and the staff is generous with samples. 76 Kensington Ave. ℂ 416/593-9251. Subway: Spadina, then LRT to Baldwin Ave.

House of Tea   Visitors to this shop can drink in the heady scent of more than 150 loose teas. And the selection of cups, mugs, and tea caddies runs from chic to comical. 1017 Yonge St. ℂ 416/922-1226. Subway: Rosedale.

Pusateri's *(Finds*   The Pusateri's store up at Lawrence and Avenue Road is a Toronto institution—and a delight for gourmets—but because of its out-of-the-way location, I haven't recommended it for visitors. Now that problem has been solved: In 2003, Pusateri's opened a gorgeous new store on Yorkville Avenue at the corner of Bay Street. The quality is as high as ever, though some of the offerings differ from the uptown shop—for example, travelers will appreciate the excellent prepared meals that can be eaten on the go. 37 Yorkville Ave. Telephone number unavailable at press time. Subway: Bay.

Senses Bakery ⭐   Located in the new SoHo Metropolitan Hotel, the food here is delicate, exquisite, and priced accordingly. There are counters of terrines and pâtés, caviar, pastries, and chocolates, as well as shelves filled with bottled Hong Kong sauces and boxed Dean & Deluca spices. 318 Wellington St. W. ℂ 416/961-0055. www.senses.ca. Subway: St. Andrew.

Simone Marie Belgian Chocolate   All of the rich truffles, colorful almond dragées, and fruit jellies in this shop are flown in from Belgium. If you're going to splurge, you may as well do it in style. 126A Cumberland St. ℂ 416/968-7777. Subway: Bay.

Sugar Mountain Confectionery Remember Pez, candy necklaces, and lollipop rings? Sugar Mountain carries the tooth-aching sweets of youth, several of which have been elevated to cult status. Teens are drawn to this store, but the biggest customers are nostalgic boomers. 320 Richmond St. W. ✆ 416/204-9544. Subway: Osgoode.

GIFTS & MORE

Down East Gifts and Gallery If your travels won't take you any farther east than Toronto, drop in on this shop to check out the folk art of the Atlantic provinces. The carvings, prints, and knickknacks are whimsical and charming. 508 Bathurst St. ✆ 416/925-1642. Subway: Bathurst.

French Country ✪ Owner Viola Jull spent several years living in France, and she re-creates a Parisian atmosphere in her shop. Many items are unique, including painted lampshades, antique silver, and framed prints. There are also a few gourmet food products and hand-milled soaps. 6 Roxborough St. W. ✆ 416/944-2204. Subway: Rosedale.

Ice This small store is a big lure for visiting celebs. Do the Bliss Spa and Philosophy skin care lines draw them in? Maybe it's the eye-catching T-shirts or the fab costume jewelry. 163 Cumberland St. ✆ 416/964-6751. Subway: Bay.

Japanese Paper Place The Japanese have elevated paper-making to an art form. In addition to being popular with artists, this shop has all the boxes, papers, and handmade cards you could ever need to create exquisite gift-wrappings. Better yet, it also stocks instruction books! 887 Queen St. W. ✆ 416/703-0089. Subway: Osgoode, then any streetcar west to Ossington Ave.

Legends of the Game This collectibles store, just 2 blocks north of SkyDome, houses memorabilia of Babe Ruth, Wayne Gretzky, Muhammad Ali, and Michael Jordan, among others. There are trading cards, team jerseys, and other souvenirs. 322A King St. W. ✆ 416/971-8848. Subway: St. Andrew.

Oh Yes, Toronto Looking for souvenirs for the folks back home? Oh Yes, Toronto stocks no end of Hogtown knickknacks, as well as quality T-shirts and sweatshirts. There's another outlet at Queens Quay West (✆ 416/203-0607). Eaton Centre. ✆ 416/593-6749. Subway: Dundas or Queen.

Pencraft If you take your writing implements seriously—and cringe at the thought of a disposable ballpoint—check out this small store. It carries top-of-the-line pens from Mont Blanc and Waterman, as well as secondhand fountain pens. 159 Yonge St. ✆ 416/364-8977. Subway: Dundas or Queen.

HEALTH & BEAUTY

Elizabeth Milan Hotel Day Spa ✪ Even if you don't have time for the spa, you will appreciate the well-stocked shop in its foyer. Elizabeth Milan carries one of the widest arrays of imported beauty products I've ever seen, including Dermologica, Yonka, Gehwol, and the perennial favorite from France, Decleor. Fairmont Royal York, 100 Front St. W. ✆ 416/350-7500. Subway: Union.

Lush This clever U.K.-based emporium looks like a gourmet grocery store. The heady scent of perfumes is the giveaway. Lush stocks a selection of fizzy bath bombs, skin lotions and potions, and aromatherapy-oriented items. All products are sold by weight. 312 Queen St. W. ✆ 416/599-5874. www.lush.com. Subway: Osgoode.

M.A.C. ✪ This makeup line used to be a trade secret among models and actors, though the word has been out for a while. (The company was founded in Toronto and is now owned by Estée Lauder.) M.A.C.'s flagship store is perpetually packed, especially on weekends, but if you call ahead you can schedule an appointment for a makeup lesson. The C$25 (US$18) charge is entirely redeemable in product. In addition to cosmetics, the store carries skin- and hair-care supplies. 89 Bloor St. W. © **416/929-7555.** Subway: Bay.

Noah's *(Value)* This is a mecca for health nuts. Noah's boasts aisle after aisle of vitamins and dietary supplements, organic foods and "natural" candies, skin care and bath products, and books and periodicals. The staff is well informed and helpful. There's a smaller but more centrally located outlet at 667 Yonge St. (at Bloor; © 416/969-0220). 322 Bloor St. W. © **416/968-7930.** Subway: Spadina.

Rubies Beauty Bar *(Finds)* This small shop is like a candy store for makeup junkies. You'll find an amazing array of products, many by Canadian brands you've never heard of before, such as Silk Road and Cake. 715 Queen St. W. © **416/601-6789.** Subway: Osgoode, then streetcar west to Bathurst.

Thompson's Homeopathic Supplies This is just like an old-fashioned apothecary, with endless rows of potions behind a wooden counter. It has a homeopathic remedy for everything from the common cold to dermatitis to conjunctivitis. The staff is friendly and knowledgeable. 844 Yonge St. © **416/922-2300.** Subway: Yonge/Bloor.

HOUSEWARES & FURNISHINGS

The Art Shoppe This is one of the prettiest stores in the city, with top-notch furniture arranged into suites of rooms. A wide range of styles is on display, from gilty baroque to streamlined Art Deco. The price tags are high, but the store is well worth browsing. 2131 Yonge St. © **416/487-3211.** Subway: Eglinton.

Caban Club Monaco's foray into the world of home decor has been a slam-dunk. This bi-level ode to loft living features clean-lined furnishings, table settings and accessories—all for reasonable prices. 262 Queen St. W. © **416/596-0386.** www.caban.com. Subway: Osgoode.

Elte Carpet & Home With 130,000 square feet of showroom space, Elte has room for a lot more than rugs. This megastore is divided into boutiques where big names like Ralph Lauren and Calvin Klein flog their home-design lines. History-spanning reproductions abound, and there are a few antiques finds, too. 80 Ronald Ave. (just west of Dufferin St.). © **416/785-7885.** Subway: Eglinton W., then any westbound bus to Ronald Ave.

En Provence Anyone who has been carried away by reading about the south of France—think of Peter Mayle's *A Year in Provence*—will feel right at home here. It stocks brightly colored dinnerware, printed bed linens, and wrought-iron furniture. 20 Hazelton Ave. © **416/975-9400.** Subway: Bay.

Kitchen Stuff Plus *(Value)* This housewares shop sells brand-name goods from the likes of Umbra at discount prices. It offers a good selection of picture frames, wine racks, area rugs, candles, painted ceramics, and kitchen accessories. 703 Yonge St. © **416/944-2718.** Subway: Yonge/Bloor.

Nestings *(Kids)* This terrific shop delivers comfort and style in equal measure. Many of the items, from ornate iron kettles to tassel-trimmed ottomans, hark back to a more glamorous age. There's also **Nestings Kids** at 418 Eglinton Ave. (© 416/322-0511; Subway: Eglinton, then walk west to Avenue Rd.). 1609 Bayview Ave. © **416/932-3704.** Subway: Eglinton, then no. 34 bus to Bayview.

Quasi-Modo Modern Furniture   With offerings for both home and office, this shop showcases some of the best of streamlined 20th-century design. Many of the items are European imports, like the tables and chairs by Sweden's Bruno Mathsson; other furnishings are from lines such as Knoll, Kartell, and Flou. 789 Queen St. W. © 416/366-8370. Subway: Osgoode.

Tap Phong Trading Co. *Finds*   If you have only a few minutes in Chinatown, spend them here. You'll find beautiful hand-painted ceramics, earthenware, decorative items, kitchen utensils, and small appliances. Best of all, just about everything is inexpensive and of reliable quality. 360 Spadina Ave. © 416/977-6364. Subway: Spadina, then LRT to Baldwin St.

Teatro Verde 🐾   Life is drama, so why shouldn't the items you fill your home with be dull? That seems to be the question at Teatro Verde, where even table coasters are things of great beauty. Hazelton Lanes. © 416/966-2227. www.teatroverde. com. Subway: Bay.

UpCountry 🐾   This Canadian company made its reputation with upscale Arts & Crafts and Mission-style home furnishings. The offerings at its flagship Toronto shop have expanded to include modern and contemporary furniture as well as vintage metal pieces. The sizable selection of decorative touches includes globes and pottery, and now inhabits a separate location at 16 Eastern Ave. (at Trinity St.; © 416/367-3906). 214 King St. E. © 416/777-1700. www.upcountry.ca. Subway: King.

JEWELRY

Birks 🐾   This Canadian institution, founded in 1879, is synonymous with top quality. Among the silver, crystal, and china is an extensive selection of top-quality jewelry, including exquisite pearls and knockout diamond engagement rings (the diamonds themselves were mined in northern Canada). There's even a children's section, filled with keepsake gifts like Royal Doulton Bunnykins china and whimsical picture frames by Nova Scotia's Seagull Pewter. My personal favorite is the showcase of antique estate jewelry. There's a smaller branch at the Eaton Centre (© 416/979-9311). Manulife Centre, 55 Bloor St. W. © 416/922-2266. www.birks.com Subway: Bay.

Experimetal   Some of proprietor Anne Sportun's sterling silver, gold, and platinum creations have won design awards. She will also fashion custom engagement and wedding bands. Also on display are pieces by other North American jewelers. 588 Markham St. (south of Bloor St. W.). © 416/538-3313. www.experimetal.com. Subway: Bathurst.

Mink *Finds*   In gangster-speak, a "mink" is a sexy woman—exactly the type who would love the fabulous fakes at this boutique. Many of the necklaces, bracelets, and rings are Canadian-designed, but a few are Euro imports. 550 College St. © 416/929-9214. Subway: Queen's Park, then streetcar west to Euclid Ave.

Peter Cullman   Cullman, who recently celebrated his 40th year as a goldsmith, studied and apprenticed in Europe, but his designs also show the influence of his travels to Africa and Mexico. You can watch him create his unique mini-masterpieces in his shop. Cumberland Court, 99 Yorkville Ave. © 416/964-2196. Subway: Bay.

Royal de Versailles Jewellers   This European-style shop carries an eye-catching assortment of pearls, gold, and platinum. The designs range from classic to funkier, playful styles. There are also watches by the likes of Piaget, Cartier, Rolex, and Tag Heuer, as well as a Bulgari boutique. 101 Bloor St. W. © 416/967-7201. Subway: Bay.

Silverbridge   Most of the necklaces, bracelets, rings, and earrings here are fashioned of silver, and the sensibility is modern. Most of the designs are the work of Costin Lazar, and they are produced in Toronto; Lazar will also take on custom work. There are also a few pieces in 18-karat gold and platinum, as well as watches by Georg Jensen and Ole Mathiesen. 162 Cumberland St. ✆ 416/923-2591. www.silverbridge.com. Subway: Bay.

Tiffany & Co.   Diamonds are still a girl's best friend at this Art Deco–style shop. Precious gems and designs by Elsa Peretti and Paloma Picasso are on the first level; the second floor holds silver jewelry, stationery, and housewares. 85 Bloor St. W. ✆ 416/921-3900. www.tiffany.com. Subway: Bay.

LEATHER GOODS

Danier *(Value)*   This Canadian chain carries suede and leather coats, suits, pants, and skirts at reasonable prices. Not-uncommon sales knock the prices down 20% to 50%. Eaton Centre. ✆ 416/598-1159. www.danier.com. Subway: Queen.

Taschen!   Exclusive designer handbags, luggage, wallets, and other accessories are mainstays here. Many are European imports, and quality is high. 162 Cumberland St. ✆ 416/961-3185. Subway: Bay.

LINGERIE

La Senza *(Value)*   This Montréal-based chain carries inexpensive but eye-catching bra-and-panty sets and naughty-looking nighties. There are also plush unisex robes and patterned boxers. An assortment of slippers, candles, bath mousse, and picture frames rounds out the offerings. Holt Renfrew Centre, 50 Bloor St. W. ✆ 416/972-1079. www.lasenza.com. Subway: Yonge/Bloor.

La Vie en Rose   You'll find quite the eclectic collection of undies here, from sensible cotton briefs to maribou-trimmed teddies, retro PJs to up-to-the-minute cleavage enhancers. The items at the front of the store are inexpensive; the farther back you go, the pricier it gets. Eaton Centre. ✆ 416/595-0898. Subway: Queen.

Linea Intima *(Finds)*   While there's no shortage of fabulous undergarments at this boutique, the real reason to visit is owner Liliana Mann's encyclopedic knowledge of what suits the female form. This extends to prosthetics and bras that are designed for women who have had mastectomies. 1925 Avenue Rd. ✆ 416/416-780-1726. www.lineaintima.com. Subway: York Mills, then bus west along Wilson Ave. to Avenue Rd. and walk 6 blocks south to Brooke Ave.

MAGAZINES & NEWSPAPERS

Great Canadian News Company   This small shop has a great selection, with more than 2,000 magazines filling its shelves, but not a comfortable place for a lengthy browse. BCE Place, 30 Yonge St. (at Front St.). ✆ 416/363-2242. Subway: Union.

Maison de la Presse Internationale ⭐   Although this store fills up fast on weekends, drawing expats and locals alike, it's still a great place to while away an hour. The many international magazines and newspapers are as current as you'll find. 124 Yorkville Ave. ✆ 416/928-2328. Subway: Bay.

MALLS & SHOPPING CENTERS

Atrium on Bay   This two-level complex has more than 60 shops selling clothing, jewelry, furniture, and more. Bay and Dundas sts. ✆ 416/980-2801. Subway: Dundas.

College Park   This shopping center has been under renovation forever, but some new sections are now complete, including the giant new Winner's store (see "The Best Bargains" on p. 180). 444 Yonge St. ✆ 416/597-1221. Subway: College.

Eaton Centre ☆ It's odd that one of urban Toronto's main attractions is a mall—but, oh, what a mall. More than 285 shops and restaurants spread over four levels in the Eaton Centre, which takes up 2 entire city blocks. 220 Yonge St. ✆ 416/598-2322. Subway: Dundas or Queen.

First Canadian Place ☆ A piece of the labyrinth of the underground city, this complex houses 120 shops and restaurants. It also stages free noontime events each week, with performances as diverse as Opera Atelier's Handel recital and the dancing monks of the Tibetan Drikung Monastery. There are also ongoing art exhibitions. King and Bay sts. ✆ 416/862-8138. Subway: King.

Hazelton Lanes ☆ A byword for elegance and extravagance, Hazelton is a two-level complex with about 90 shops. The charming courtyard at the center transforms into an ice-skating rink in winter. 55 Avenue Rd. ✆ 416/968-8602. Subway: Bay.

Holt Renfrew Centre Anchored by the chic Holt Renfrew department store, this small underground concourse is more down to earth. It connects with the Manulife Centre and the Hudson's Bay Centre. 50 Bloor St. W. ✆ 416/923-2255. Subway: Yonge/Bloor.

Manulife Centre ☆ More than 50 posh shops—including William Ashley, Indigo Books Music & More, and a top-notch LCBO outlet—occupy this complex. The Manulife connects to the Holt Renfrew Centre underground. 55 Bloor St. W. ✆ 416/923-9525. Subway: Bay.

Tips **Same Time Next Year**

In addition to the post-holiday sales at most shops, there are some don't-miss special sales that locals have penned into their calendars. Sale locations are often scattered around the city, so call each store for details and exact dates.

- **MAY:** The **Fashion Design Council of Canada** hosts a clearance sale of top-name Canadian designer wear at the Design Exchange, 234 Bay St. ✆ 416/977-6184.
- **JULY:** Many retailers host semi-annual sales that cut prices by as much as 50%. Some of the best are at the **Art Shoppe**, 2131 Yonge St., ✆ 416/487-3211 (p. 188); **Holt Renfrew**, 50 Bloor St. W., ✆ 416/922-2333 (p. 182); and **Elte Carpet & Home**, 80 Ronald Ave., ✆ 416/785-7885 (p. 188).
- **OCTOBER:** The **Old Clothing Show & Sale** should really be called the New *and* Old Clothing Show, because there's almost as much new clothing here as there is vintage wear. Exhibition Place; ✆ 416/410-1310.
- **NOVEMBER:** Fine china and crystal retailer **William Ashley's** (p. 180) annual warehouse sale is one of the season's most eagerly anticipated events; call ✆ 416/964-2900 for information. The **One-of-a-Kind Craft Show & Sale** brings about 400 craft artists under one roof at Exhibition Place, and the prices are often better than you'll find in shops; call ✆ 416/960-3680. The **Fashion Design Council of Canada** hosts another designer clearance sale this month, in case you missed the one in May (see above).

Queen's Quay Terminal　This is waterfront shopping at its best, with more than 30 shops and cafes. Queens Quay caters to tourists—you'll find some unique items, but the prices tend to be moderate to high. 207 Queens Quay W. © 416/203-0510. www.queens-quay-terminal.com. Subway: Union, then LRT to Queens Quay.

Royal Bank Plaza　Part of Toronto's underground city, the Royal Bank Plaza connects to Union Station and to the Royal York Hotel. Its 60-plus outlets include a variety of shops, two full-service restaurants, and a food court. The building above it is worth a look, too. Bay and Front sts. © 416/974-5570. Subway: Union.

Scarborough Town Centre　This is a megamall to rival the Eaton Centre; if you're staying on the city's eastern fringe, you can't miss it. It has more than 200 shops, including branches similar to those at the Eaton Centre. Hwy. 401 and McCowan Ave. © 416/296-0296. Subway: Scarborough Town Centre.

Village by the Grange　Cheek-by-jowl to the Art Gallery of Ontario, the Grange contains more than 40 shops. Its International Food Market has decent Middle Eastern and Asian selections. 122 St. Patrick St. © 416/598-1414. Subway: St. Patrick.

MARKETS
Kensington Market ⟨★⟩　This neighborhood has changed dramatically in the past 40 years. Originally a Jewish community, it now borders on Chinatown. It contains several Asian herbalists and grocers, as well as West Indian and Middle Eastern shops. Kensington Avenue has the greatest concentration of vintage clothing stores in the city. For a full description, see "Walking Tour: Chinatown & Kensington Market," in chapter 7. Along Baldwin, Kensington, and Augusta aves. No phone. Subway: Spadina, then LRT to Baldwin St. or Dundas St. W.

St. Lawrence Market　This market is a local favorite for fresh produce, and it even draws people who live a good distance away. Hours are Tuesday through Thursday from 9am to 7pm, Friday from 8am to 8pm, and Saturday from 5am (when the farmers arrive) to 5pm. See p. 141 in chapter 6 for a complete description. 92 Front St. E. © 416/392-7219. Subway: Union.

MUSIC
HMV　This is the flagship Toronto store of the British chain. (You'll find smaller outlets throughout the city.) The selection of pop, rock, jazz, and classical music is large. Best of all, you can listen to a CD before you buy it. 333 Yonge St. © 416/596-0333. Subway: Dundas.

The Music Store　On the Toronto Symphony Orchestra's home turf, this attractive shop includes several TSO CDs in its collection of classical and choral music. Roy Thomson Hall, 60 Simcoe St. © 416/593-4822. Subway: St. Andrew.

Sam the Record Man　I, like most Torontonians, still have a soft spot for Sam's, though it is but a shadow of its former glory. The store—beloved by Canadian artists like Joni Mitchell, Rush, Liona Boyd, and the Guess Who because it has always promoted homegrown talent—has gone through rough times of late, and large sections of the store now lie empty. 347 Yonge St. © 416/977-4650. Subway: Dundas.

SEX TOYS
Lovecraft ⟨★⟩　Believe it or not, Lovecraft—which marks its 32nd anniversary in 2004—is downright wholesome. Sure, there are the requisite bad-girl (and -boy) lingerie and toys, but much of the shop stocks joke gifts, T-shirts with suggestive slogans, and an impressive collection of erotic literature (no porn mags).

The staff is friendly and the atmosphere playful. 27 Yorkville Ave. ☎ 877/923-7331 or 416/923-7331. Subway: Bay.

SHOES

Browns 🏸 To treat your feet to fabulous footwear by Manolo Blahnik, Prada, or Ferragamo, beat a path to this newly renovated shop for men and women. There's also a selection of leather handbags. Browns has several branches around the city. Eaton Centre. ☎ 416/979-9270. Subway: Queen.

Capezio Whether you're looking for the perfect pair of ballet slippers or an up-to-the-minute design from Steve Madden or Guess, you'll find it here. All the shoes and other leather goods are for women. 70 Bloor St. W. ☎ 416/920-1006. Subway: Bay.

David's For serious shoppers only. This high-end store stocks elegant footwear for men and women—from Bruno Magli, Bally, and Sonia Rykiel, as well as the store's own collection—but prices are accordingly steep. 66 Bloor St. W. ☎ 416/920-1000. Subway: Bay.

Mephisto These shoes are made for walking—particularly because they're made from all natural materials. Devotees of this shop, now in its third decade, swear that it's impossible to wear out Mephisto footwear. 1177 Yonge St. ☎ 416/968-7026. Subway: Summerhill.

Petit Pied 🏸 For especially tiny tootsies, check out this elegant shop. Petit Pied carries children's shoes for newborns to adolescents. Many of the brands are European, including Minibel and Elefanten, but there are also sporty designs from Nike and Reebok. 890 Yonge St. ☎ 416/963-5925. Subway: Rosedale.

TOYS

George's Trains Everything the young (or young at heart) could want to spruce up a model train set is here, including tracks, stations, and scenic backdrops. There are wooden trains as well as train kits. 510 Mount Pleasant Rd. ☎ 416/489-9783. www.georgestrains.com. Subway: Davisville, then no. 11 or 28 bus to Mount Pleasant, and walk 1 block north.

Just Bears The name tells you all you need to know about this upscale shop. Anything that isn't a teddy has a bear motif. 29 Bellair St. ☎ 416/928-5963. Subway: Bay.

Kidding Awound *Finds* Wind-up gadgets are the specialty here—there are hundreds to choose from. There are also some antique toys (which you won't let the kids near) and gag gifts. 91 Cumberland St. ☎ 416/926-8996. Subway: Bay.

The Little Dollhouse Company 🏸 This toy store isn't really for kids. It's beloved by adults in search of miniature tea services and wicker furniture. It also sells nine different dollhouse kits, from a stately Victorian mansion to a ranch bungalow. 612 Mt. Pleasant Rd. ☎ 416/489-7180. www.littledollhousecompany.com. Subway: Eglinton, then no. 34 bus east to Mount Pleasant, and walk 2 blocks south.

Science City 🏸 Kids and adults alike will love this tiny store filled with games, puzzles, models, kits, and books—all related to science. Whether your interest is astronomy, biology, chemistry, archaeology, or physics, you'll find something here. Holt Renfrew Centre, 50 Bloor St. W. ☎ 416/968-2627. Subway: Yonge/Bloor.

Top Banana Fun for kids—and their parents. The toys range from Thomas the Tank Engine to Stomp Rockets. There are also games and books galore. 639 Mount Pleasant Rd. ☎ 416/440-0111. Subway: Eglinton, then no. 34 bus east to Mount Pleasant, and walk 2 blocks south.

The Toy Shop This double-decker shop carries toys, many of them educational, from around the world. It also stocks a good selection of books, games, and videos. 62 Cumberland St. ✆ 416/961-4870. Subway: Bay.

TRAVEL GOODS

Tilley Endurables *(Value)* The Tilley hat may not be Canada's greatest style moment, but it certainly is one of the most recognizable. The hats, belts, socks, and other travel gear are all well made, and they really will endure. Note that Tilley has branched out into travel underwear (they admit that "sexy they may not be," but claim that two sets of their underclothes will get you around the world—*now* I'm curious). Queens Quay, 207 Queens Quay W. ✆ 416/203-0463. www.tilley.com. Subway: Union, then LRT to Queens Quay.

The Travel Stop *(Finds)* If an item is made in travel size, The Travel Stop stocks it. Offerings include steamers and hair dryers, travel guides, and luggage. There's also a travel agency at the back of the store. 130 Cumberland St. ✆ 416/961-6088. www.thetravelstop.com. Subway: Bay.

VINTAGE CLOTHING

Asylum Secondhand jeans and vintage dresses line the racks in this Kensington Market stalwart. Bargains turn up in odd places, like the Anne Klein scarf at the bottom of a C$1 (US70¢) bin. There's also an assortment of toys and candy. 42 Kensington Ave. ✆ 416/595-7199. Subway: Spadina, then LRT to Baldwin St.

Brava *(Finds)* This shop is a favorite among local stylists, who pick up everything from cashmere sweaters to evening wraps for ladies, and printed shirts to golf pants for gents. 483 Queen St. W. ✆ 416/504-8742. Subway: Osgoode, then streetcar west to Spadina.

Courage My Love *(Value)* With its mix of vintage clothing and new silver jewelry, Courage is a Kensington Market favorite. Dresses run from '50s velvet numbers to '70s polyester, and almost everything costs less than C$25 (US$18). There's also a good selection of tweedy jackets and starchy white shirts. The owners' cat makes an occasional furtive appearance. 14 Kensington Ave. ✆ 416/979-1992. Subway: Spadina, then LRT to Dundas St. W.

Divine Decadence *(Finds)* Owner Carmelita Blondet has a unique line on vintage clothes: She imports them from her native Peru. Chic Peruvians had previously brought these glad rags in from Europe, so it's not unusual to find great French couture. The price tags are uniformly high, but so is the quality. 136 Cumberland St. ✆ 416/324-9759. Subway: Bay.

Ex-Toggery This is a consignment shop with outlets around the city. Items don't last long, particularly because the price drops every week. Scour the racks for designer names like Versace and Donna Karan. There are also a variety of vintage items on display, from clothing to accessories. 115 Merton St. ✆ 416/488-5393. www.extoggery.com. Subway: Davisville.

The Paper Bag Princess *(Finds)* Toronto isn't known as Hollywood North for nothing. L.A. has had a Paper Bag Princess boutique for several years, but only recently did its owner, Toronto native Elizabeth Mason, decide to open up a location in her hometown. This store is a treasure trove, and its boudoir-like setting makes it a sexy place to shop. The mint-condition Chanel and Pucci outfits cost a bundle, but what else would you expect? 287 Davenport Rd. ✆ 416/925-2603. www.paperbagprincess.com. Subway: Bay.

Preloved ⟨⟨ This isn't a traditional vintage store, because the classic here have been repurposed. The pieces really are one-of-a-kind: The shop's own ers breathe new life into cast-off jeans and T-shirts by adding unique details like vintage lace. The roster of celeb fans includes Alanis Morissette. 613 Queen St. W. ℂ 416/504-8704. Subway: Osgoode, then streetcar west to Bathurst.

WINE

In Ontario, Liquor Control Board of Ontario (LCBO) outlets and small boutiques at upscale grocery stores sell wine; no alcohol is sold at convenience stores. The best deals are on locally produced wines—especially the ice wine, a sweet dessert wine that has won awards the world over. There are LCBO outlets all over the city, and prices are the same at all of them. The loveliest shop is at the **Manulife Centre,** 55 Bloor St. W. (ℂ 416/925-5266). Other locations are at 20 Bloor St. E. (ℂ **416/368-0521**); the Eaton Centre (ℂ **416/979-9978**); and Union Station (ℂ **416/925-9644**). See www.lcbo.com for information about products and special in-store events.

Vintages stores have a different name, but they're still LCBO outlets. Check out the one at Hazelton Lanes (ℂ **416/924-9463**) and at Queens Quay (ℂ **416/864-6777**).

Toronto After Dark

Toronto may not have a reputation for being a city that never sleeps, but it does have a vital and varied nightlife scene. It's a mecca for top-notch theater—you can sometimes see Broadway shows before they reach Broadway. The Toronto Symphony Orchestra is world renowned, and the city's many dance and music venues host the crème de la crème of international performers. Some of the best entertainment is in Toronto's comedy clubs, which have served as training grounds for stars such as Jim Carrey, Mike Myers, Dan Aykroyd, and John Candy.

The nightclub scene moves at a frenetic pace. Martini bars are perennially popular, though lower-key pool bars are in vogue, too.

MAKING PLANS For listings of local performances and events, check out *Where Toronto* and *Toronto Life* (www.torontolife.com), as well as *The Globe & Mail* (www.globeandmail.

com), the *Toronto Star* (www.thestar. com), and the *National Post* (www. nationalpost.com). For up-to-the-minute lists of hot-ticket events, check out the free weeklies *Now* and *Eye,* available around town in newspaper boxes, and at bars, cafes, and bookstores. The city website **www.toronto. com** also boasts lengthy lists of performances. Events of particular interest to the gay and lesbian community are listed in *Xtra!* (www.xtra.ca), another free weekly available in newspaper boxes and many bookstores.

GETTING TICKETS For almost any theater, music, or dance event, you can buy tickets from **Ticketmaster** (*©* **416/870-8000;** www.ticketmaster. ca). There's a service charge on every ticket (not just every order) sold over the phone. To avoid the charge, head to a ticket center. They're scattered throughout the city; call the information line for the lengthy list of locations.

1 The Performing Arts

Toronto's arts scene offers something for everyone year-round. The city's arts institutions are widely renowned, and many top-notch international performers pass through town.

THEATER

While it may seem that Toronto favors big-budget musicals—*The Lion King* and *The Phantom of the Opera* both made a big splash here—there are many excellent smaller companies, too. Many of the smaller troupes have no permanent performance space, so they move from venue to venue.

The best time to capture the flavor of Toronto's theater life is during the **Fringe Festival** (*©* **416/534-5919;** fringeto@interlog.com), usually held for 10 days starting in early July. In July and August, try to catch the **Dream in High Park** (*©* **416/368-3110**). It mounts stunning productions of Shakespearean or Canadian plays from the CanStage company in an outdoor setting.

LANDMARK THEATERS & PERFORMANCE VENUES

The Distillery Historic District ✦   The year 2003 was an exciting one for the arts community in Toronto. Several performance venues opened up, including the Carlu (p. 203), the Yonge-Dundas Square (p. 203), and the Distillery Historic District. This was once the home of the Gooderham-Worts Distillery, which was Canada's largest distilling company in the 19th century. Now a historic district that houses three performing arts venues, the complex is an outstanding example of industrial design from the Victorian age. The Dancemakers and the Native Earth troupes now perform here. 55 Mill St. ✆ **416/367-1800**. www.thedistillery district.com. Tickets C$15–$40 (US$10.50–$28). Subway: King.

The Elgin and Winter Garden Theatre Centre ✦   These landmark theaters first opened their doors in 1913, and today they vie with the Royal Alex and the Princess of Wales Theatre for major shows and attention. Recent productions have included *The Full Monty.* Both book concerts and opera performances, and are favorite venues of the Toronto International Film Festival.

Both the Elgin and the Winter Garden have been restored to their original gilded glory at a cost of C$29 million (US$20 million). They are the only double-decker theaters in Toronto. The downstairs Elgin is larger, seating 1,500 and featuring a lavish domed ceiling and gilded decoration on the boxes and proscenium. Hand-painted frescoes adorn the striking interior of the 1,000-seat Winter Garden. Suspended from its ceiling and lit with lanterns are more than 5,000 branches of beech leaves, which have been preserved, painted, and fireproofed. Both theaters offer everything from Broadway musicals and dramas to concerts and opera performances. 189 Yonge St. ✆ **416/872-5555** for tickets, 416/314-2901 for tour info. Tickets C$20–$85 (US$14–$60). Subway: Queen.

Pantages Theatre   The Pantages is one of the theaters adversely affected by the collapse of the Livent production company; at the moment, the space is virtually empty. Livent had restored the glorious, glamorous building, which opened in 1920, to the tune of C$18 million (US$13 million). Originally a silent film house and vaudeville theater, the 2,250-seat Pantages was resurrected as a home for the splashy Andrew Lloyd Webber show *The Phantom of the Opera;* more recently, shows such as *Fosse* have played here. 244 Victoria St. ✆ **416/872-2222**. Tickets C$51–$92.50 (US$35–$65). Subway: Dundas.

Princess of Wales Theatre   This spectacular 2,000-seat state-of-the-art facility was built for the production of *Miss Saigon,* with a stage large enough to accommodate the landing of the helicopter in that production. More recently it was home to *The Lion King.* Frank Stella, who painted 10,000 square feet of colorful murals, decorated the exterior and interior walls. People in wheelchairs have access to all levels of the theater (not the norm in Toronto). 300 King St. W. ✆ **416/872-1212**. www.onstagenow.com. Tickets C$21–$116 (US$14–$80). Subway: St. Andrew.

Value Discount Tickets

Want to take in a show, but don't want to spend a bundle on it? Drop by the T.O. Tix booth ✦ (✆ **416/536-6468**, ext. 40), which sells half-price day-of-performance tickets. The booth is currently located in the Yonge-Dundas Square, which is just across the street from the Eaton Centre. T.O. Tix accepts cash, Visa and MasterCard, and all sales are final. The booth is open Tuesday through Saturday from noon to 7:30pm; it's closed Sunday and Monday (tickets for performances on those days are sold on Sat).

Downtown After Dark

PERFORMING ARTS

Air Canada Centre **34**
Buddies in Bad Times Theatre **38**
CanStage **60**
Carlu **37**
Cinematheque Ontario **3**
The Distillery Historic District **61**
The Elgin and Winter Garden
   Theatre Centre **52**
Factory Theatre **13**
Glenn Gould Studio **33**
Hummingbird Centre
   for the Performing Arts **55**
La Cage Dinner Theatre **50**
Lorraine Kimsa Theatre
   for Young People **58**
Maple Leaf Gardens **39**
Massey Hall **53**
Pantages Theatre **51**
Premiere Dance Theatre **35**
Princess of Wales Theatre **30**
Roy Thomson Hall **32**
Royal Alexandra Theatre **31**
St. James's Cathedral **57**
The St. Lawrence Centre
   for the Arts **55**
St. Patrick's Church **24**
Theatre Pass Muraille **4**
Yonge-Dundas Square **48**

CLUBS, MUSIC & BARS

Afterlife **27**
Al Frisco's **12**
Amsterdam **14**
BamBoo **10**
Bar 501 **44**
The Barn/The Stables **40**
Bauhaus **23**
The Bishop Belcher **11**
Byzantium **41**
Cameron House **7**
C'est What? **56**
Churchill's Cigar & Wine Bar **29**
Consort Bar **54**
Crews/Tango **45**
Crocodile Rock **28**
Easy & the Fifth **25**
El Mocambo **2**
Horseshoe Tavern **8**
Kit Kat Bar **19**
Laugh Resort **17**
Left Bank **6**
Library Bar **36**
Milano **18**
Mint et Menthe **16**
Montréal Bistro & Jazz Club **59**
NASA **5**
Phoenix Concert Theatre **47**
The Rivoli **9**
Sailor **42**
Second City **21**
Slack Alice **46**
Sneaky Dee's **1**
Top O' the Senator **49**
Vineyards Wine Bar & Bistro **20**
Wayne Gretzky's **22**
Wheat Sheaf Tavern **15**
Woody's **43**
Yuk Yuk's Supper Club **26**

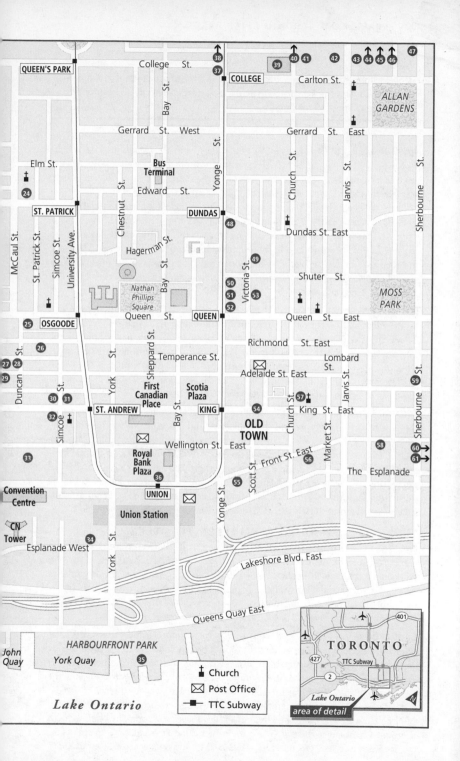

QUEEN'S PARK

College St.

COLLEGE

Carlton St.

ALLAN GARDENS

Bay St.

Elm St.

Gerrard St. West

Gerrard St. East

24

ST. PATRICK

Sherbourne St.

Jarvis St.

Church St.

Yonge St.

Bus Terminal

Edward St.

Chestnut St.

McCaul St.

St. Patrick St.

Simcoe St.

University Ave.

DUNDAS

48

Dundas St. East

Hagerman St.

Victoria St.

49

Nathan Phillips Square

Bay St.

50
51
52

53

Shuter St.

MOSS PARK

25 **OSGOODE**

Queen St.

QUEEN

Queen St. East

26

27 28

29

Duncan St.

Sheppard St.

York St.

Temperance St.

Richmond St. East

Lombard St.

Adelaide St. East

59 St.

30 31

Simcoe St.

32

ST. ANDREW

First Canadian Place

Bay St.

Scotia Plaza

KING

54

57

Church St.

King St. East

Sherbourne St.

33

OLD TOWN

58

60
61

Wellington St. East

Scott St.

Front St. East

Market St.

Convention Centre

Royal Bank Plaza

56

The Esplanade

CN Tower

36

UNION

Yonge St.

55

Union Station

34

York St.

Esplanade West

Lakeshore Blvd. East

Queens Quay East

HARBOURFRONT PARK

John Quay

York Quay

35

✝ Church

⊠ Post Office

■ TTC Subway

TORONTO

401

427

2

TTC Subway

Lake Ontario

area of detail

Lake Ontario

199

<hr>

Tips **Farther Afield**

Don't forget that two major theater festivals—the **Shaw Festival** in Niagara-on-the-Lake and the **Stratford Festival** in Stratford—are only an hour or two away. See chapter 10 for details.

<hr>

Royal Alexandra Theatre ✿   When shows from Broadway migrate north, they usually head for the Royal Alex. Subscription buyers often snap up tickets, so your best bet is to call or order tickets online ahead of time. Recent shows here have included *Mamma Mia!*, the ABBA-inspired musical.

The 1,495-seat Royal Alex is a magnificent spectacle. Constructed in 1907, it owes its current health to discount-store czar and impresario Ed Mirvish, who refurbished it (as well as the surrounding area) in the 1960s. Inside, it's a riot of plush reds, gold brocade, and baroque ornamentation. Avoid the second balcony and the seats "under the circle," which don't have the greatest sight lines. 260 King St. W. ✆ **800/461-3333** for tickets, or 416/872-1212. www.onstagenow.com. Tickets C$26–$94 (US$18–$66). Subway: St. Andrew.

The St. Lawrence Centre for the Arts   For 3 decades, the St. Lawrence Centre has presented top-notch theater, music, and dance performances. The Bluma Appel Theatre is home to the CanStage company, and the smaller Jane Mallet Theatre features the Toronto Operetta Theatre Company, among others. This is a popular spot for lectures, too. 27 Front St. E. ✆ **800/708-6754** or 416/366-7723. www.stlc.com. Tickets C$20–$70 (US$14–$49). Mon night pay what you can. Senior and student discounts may be available 30 min. before performance. Subway: Union.

Toronto Centre for the Arts   Built in 1993, this gigantic complex is home to the North York Symphony and the Amadeus Choir. It contains several performance venues. The 1,850-seat Apotex Theatre has featured award-winning musicals such as *Sunset Boulevard* and *Ragtime;* the 1,025-seat George Weston Recital Hall books music events. There are a 250-seat studio theater and an art gallery. Since the collapse of theater giant Livent, the Toronto Centre (formerly the Ford Centre for the Performing Arts) has been sadly underused. 5040 Yonge St. ✆ **416/733-9388.** www.tocentre.com. Tickets C$15–$75 (US$10–$53). Subway: North York Centre.

THEATER COMPANIES & SMALLER THEATERS

Buddies in Bad Times Theatre   Established in 1979, this gay, or queer (as the company prefers to be called), theater company produces radical new Canadian works that celebrate difference, and blur, as well as reinvent, the boundaries between gay and straight, gay and lesbian, male and female. American Sky Gilbert has built its cutting-edge reputation. 12 Alexander St. ✆ **416/975-8555.** www.buddiesinbadtimestheatre.com. Tickets C$12–$25 (US$8–$18). Subway: Wellesley.

CanStage ✿   The CanStage company performs an eclectic variety of Canadian and international plays. Recent productions include *The Shape of Things* by Neil LaBute and the late Pulitzer Prize–winning author Carol Shield's *Larry's Party.* They perform at the St. Lawrence Centre, seating 500 to 600, and the Berkeley Theatre, a more avant-garde, intimate space.

CanStage also presents open-air summer theater—traditionally Shakespeare—in High Park. It's known as the **Dream in High Park.** The company plans to focus more on Canadian-written works in the near future. Berkeley Theatre, 26 Berkeley St., and St. Lawrence Centre, 27 Front St. E. ✆ **416/368-3110.** www.canstage.com. Tickets C$20–$69

After Dark from Chinatown to Bloor Street

Bar Italia **3**
The Brunswick House **13**
Cafe Diplomatico **4**
Cinematheque Ontario **20**
The Corner Pocket **7**
El Convento Rico **1**
El Mocambo
  (Tequila Lounge) **10**
Insomnia **9**
La Serre at
  the Four Seasons **18**
Lee's Palace **12**

Madison **15**
The Roof at Park Hyatt **17**
Royal Conservatory
  of Music **16**
Sneaky Dee's **8**
Sottovoce **6**
Souz Dal **2**
St. Patrick's Church **19**
Tarragon Theatre **11**
Trinity-St. Paul's Church **14**
Wild Indigo **5**

(US\$14–\$48). Mon night pay what you can. Senior and student discounts may be available 30 min. before performance. Subway: Union for St. Lawrence Centre. King, then any streetcar east to Berkeley St. for Berkeley Theatre.

Factory Theatre   Since it opened in 1970, the Factory Theatre has focused on presenting Canadian plays, from political dramas to over-the-top comedies. Performances showcase up-and-coming scribes as well as established playwrights. George F. Walker started his career at the Factory, and the clown duo, Mump and Smoot, appears occasionally. 125 Bathurst St. ☎ **416/504-9971.** www.factorytheatre.ca. Tickets C\$10–\$30 (US\$7–\$21). Subway: St. Andrew, then any streetcar west.

Lorraine Kimsa Theatre for Young People ☆   Toronto's such a theater town that even tiny tots (and the rest of the family) get their own performance center. The always-enjoyable Lorraine Kimsa Theatre (formerly known as the Young Peoples Theatre) mounts whimsical productions such as *Jacob Two-Two's First Spy Case* (a musical by the late Mordecai Richler), and children's classics such as *Pinocchio* and *The Miracle Worker.* The theater company is committed to diversity in its programming and in its artists. 165 Front St. E. ℂ **416/862-2222.** www. lktyp.ca. Tickets C$14–$28 (US$10–$20). Subway: Union.

Native Earth Performing Arts Theatre   This small company is dedicated to performing works that express and dramatize the native Canadian experience. Playwright Thomson Highway, who authored *Dry Lips Oughta Move to Kapuskasing,* was one of the company's founders. Performing at the Case Goods Theatre in the Distillery Historic District, 55 Mill Street. ℂ **416/367-1800.** www.nativeearth.ca. Tickets C$10–$25 (US$7–$18).

Tarragon Theatre ⚜   The Tarragon Theatre opened in 1971. It produces original works by such famous Canadian literary figures as Michel Tremblay, Michael Ondaatje, and Judith Thompson, and an occasional classic or off-Broadway play. It's a small, intimate theater. 30 Bridgman Ave. (near Dupont and Bathurst sts.). ℂ **416/531-1827,** or 416/536-5018 for administration. www.tarragontheatre.com. Tickets C$15–$30 (US$11–$21). Sun pay what you can. Subway: Bathurst.

Theatre Passe Muraille   This theater started in the late 1960s, when a pool of actors began experimenting and improvising original Canadian material. It continues to produce innovative, provocative theater by such contemporary Canadian playwrights as John Mighton, Daniel David Moses, and Wajdi Mouawad. There are two stages—the Mainspace seats 220, the more intimate Backspace, 70. 16 Ryerson Ave. ℂ **416/504-7529.** www.passemuraille.on.ca. Tickets C$14–$28 (US$10–$20) Subway: Osgoode, then any streetcar west to Bathurst.

Toronto Truck Theatre   The Toronto Truck Theatre is the home of Agatha Christie's *The Mousetrap,* now in its 28th year. It's Canada's longest-running show—and it shows no signs of losing steam. 94 Belmont St. ℂ **416/922-0084.** Tickets C$15–$25 (US$11–$18). Subway: Rosedale.

DINNER THEATER

Famous People Players Dinner Theatre ⚜   This group mounts unique, visually fantastic "black light" shows. Famous People Players is renowned not just for the quality of its shows, but also for bringing out the creative potential in disabled performers. The price of the show includes a four-course dinner and backstage tour. 110 Sudbury St. ℂ **888/453-3385** or 416/532-1137. www.fpp.org. Dinner and show C$40 (US$28) adults, seniors and children 13 and over, C$27 (US$19) children 12 and under. Subway: Osgoode, then any streetcar west to Dovercourt.

La Cage Dinner Theatre   For the best in campy impersonations, head to La Cage. Buddy Holly, Roy Orbison, and Elvis may never have performed together, but their mimics get along famously here. 278 Yonge St. ℂ **416/364-5200.** Dinner and show C$39–$44 (US$27–$31); show only C$24–$28 (US$16–$20). Subway: Dundas.

Medieval Times Dinner & Tournament   Milord and Milady welcome you to their castle, where you'll be brought a cutlery-free meal by "serving wenches," view knights on horseback, and witness medieval games in the company of 1,000 of your closest friends. Adults may have trouble getting into the spirit of things, but it's always a hit with kids. Exhibition Place. ℂ **416/260-1234.** www.medievaltimes. com. Tickets C$57 (US$40) adults, C$39 (US$27) children 12 and under. Subway: Bathurst, then Bathurst streetcar south to Exhibition Place (last stop).

Mysteriously Yours   After 12 years at the Royal York, the show has gone uptown. The action at this interactive whodunit gets under way around dessert time. Actors are scattered at tables around the room, and guests try to solve the

crime with the aid of a detective who leads the investigation. 2026 Yonge St.
© **800-668-3323** or 416/486-7469. www.mysteriouslyyours.com. Dinner and show C$48–$75
(US$33–$51); show only C$35–$45 (US$24–$31). Subway: Davisville.

MAJOR CONCERT HALLS & AUDITORIUMS

In addition to the Elgin and Winter Garden Theatres, the Toronto Centre for the
Arts, and the St. Lawrence Centre, these are the city's top performance venues.

The Carlu ⭐   Toronto welcomed the return of the Carlu in 2003. Located on the
seventh floor of College Park, it was considered one of the grandest concert halls in
Canada when it opened in 1931; like so many other venues in Toronto, the Carlu
was shuttered in the 1970s. Now the 1,200-seat concert hall is back in favor, and
its architecture is believed to be one of the best surviving examples of Art Moderne
in the world. At press time no details of upcoming concerts were available, but
check the website for information. College Park, 444 Yonge St., 7th Floor. © **416/410-8727.**
www.thecarlu.com. Ticket information not available at press time. Subway: College.

Glenn Gould Studio ⭐   This 340-seat radio concert hall offers chamber, jazz,
and spoken-word performances. Its name celebrates the great, eccentric Toronto
pianist whose life was cut short by a stroke in 1982. 250 Front St. W. © **416/205-
5555.** www.glenngouldstudio.cbc.ca. Tickets C$20–$75 (US$14–$51). Subway: Union.

Hummingbird Centre for the Performing Arts   If you visited Toronto
before 1997, you might remember this as the O'Keefe Centre. It became famous
in 1974 when Mikhail Baryshnikov defected after performing here. Since then,
Hummingbird Communications has invested in renovations and refurbishing.
This 3,223-seat center is still the home of the National Ballet of Canada; the
Canadian Opera Company also performs here, though it has been trying to find
another home. 1 Front St. E. © **416/872-2262.** www.hummingbirdcentre.com. Tickets C$40–
$125 (US$28–$88). Subway: Union.

Massey Hall   This landmark building is one of Canada's premier music venues. The 2,800 seats aren't the most comfortable, but the flawless acoustics will
make you stop squirming. The music performances run from classical to pop to
rock to jazz, with recent stops by the likes of Diana Krall, Jewel, Prince, and
Pink. This is also a popular stop for lectures. 178 Victoria St. © **416/593-4822.** www.
masseyhall.com. Tickets C$25–$100 (US$18–$70). Subway: King.

Premiere Dance Theatre   This hall, specifically designed for dance performances, is where you can catch Toronto's leading contemporary dance companies.
Toronto Dance Theatre and the Danny Grossman Dance Company perform
here. Queen's Quay Terminal, 207 Queens Quay W. © **416/973-4000.** www.harbourfront.on.ca.
Tickets C$30–$95 (US$20–$65). Subway: Union, then LRT to York Quay.

Roy Thomson Hall ⭐   This stunning concert hall is home to the Toronto Symphony Orchestra, which performs here from September to June, and to the Toronto
Mendelssohn Choir. Since it opened in 1982, it has also played host to an array of
international musical artists, including Cecilia Bartoli, Ray Charles, Ravi Shankar,
and Aretha Franklin. The hall was designed to give the audience a feeling of unusual
intimacy with the performers—none of the 2,812 seats is more than 33m (107 ft.)
from the stage. The hall closed for 5 months in 2002 for an extensive acoustic
enhancement project that also increased the size of the stage. 60 Simcoe St. © **416/593-
4822.** www.roythomson.com. Tickets C$25–$120 (US$18–$84). Subway: St. Andrew.

Yonge-Dundas Square   I'm not sure what to say about this new outdoor
concert venue, located across the street from the Eaton Centre. Aside from a

splashy opening concert that drew 55,000 people in May 2003, little has happened here at the time of this writing. The plan is to host concerts and other interesting events in the Square, but at the moment the only reason to go there is the T.O. Tix discount tickets booth. Yonge & Dundas, southeast corner. © 416/979-9960. www.ydsquare.ca. Subway: Dundas.

CLASSICAL MUSIC & OPERA

In addition to the major musical venues mentioned above, visitors can check to see what's playing at churches around town. Possibilities include **Trinity-St. Paul's Church,** 427 Bloor St. W. (© **416/964-6337**), the home of the Toronto Consort, performers of early music; **St. Patrick's Church,** Dundas and McCaul streets (© **416/483-0559**); and **St. James' Cathedral,** King Street East and Jarvis Street, where the Orpheus Choir sings. The **University of Toronto** (© **416/978-3744** for the box office) offers a full range of instrumental and choral concerts and recitals in Walter Hall and the Macmillan Theatre. It's also worth checking out who's performing at the **Royal Conservatory of Music,** 273 Bloor St. W. (© **416/408-2825**).

If you're a fan of new music, look out for the **Sonic Boom concert series** (© **416/944-3100**), which produces new opera and other contemporary music.

Canadian Opera Company   Canada's largest opera company, the sixth largest in North America, was founded in 1950. At the moment, it is staging its productions at the Hummingbird Centre from September to April, but an opera house is in the works, so the company will have a new home soon. Recent productions include *Salome* and *Boris Godunov.* 227 Front St. E. © **416/872-2262** or 416/363-6671. www.coc.ca. Tickets C$38–$135 (US$27–$95). Subway: Union.

Tafelmusik Baroque Orchestra ⓖ   This internationally acclaimed group plays baroque compositions by the likes of Handel, Bach, and Mozart on authentic period instruments. Visiting musicians frequently join the 19 permanent performers. It gives a series of concerts at **Trinity/St. Paul's United Church,** 47 Bloor St. W., and stages other performances in Massey Hall and the Toronto Centre for the Arts (p. 200). 427 Bloor St. W. © **416/964-6337**. www.tafelmusik.org. Tickets C$20–$55 (US$14–$37). Subway: Yonge/Bloor for Trinity/St. Paul's; King for Massey Hall; North York Centre for Toronto Centre for the Arts.

Toronto Mendelssohn Choir ⓖ   This world-renowned group first performed in Massey Hall in 1895; it now calls Roy Thomson Hall home. Its repertoire ranges from Verdi's *Requiem,* Bach's *St. Matthew Passion,* and Handel's *Messiah* to the soundtrack of *Schindler's List.* 60 Simcoe St. © **416/598-0422**. www. tmchoir.org. Tickets C$25–$50 (US$18–$35). Subway: St. Andrew.

Toronto Symphony Orchestra   The symphony performs at Roy Thomson Hall from September to June. Its repertoire ranges from classics to jazzy Broadway tunes to new Canadian works. In June and July, the symphony puts on free concerts at outdoor venues throughout the city. 60 Simcoe St. © **416/593-4828**. www. tso.on.ca. Tickets C$15–$75 (US$11–$53). Subway: St. Andrew.

POP & ROCK MUSIC VENUES

Everyone comes to Toronto—even Madonna, who ran into some trouble with the obscenity police a while back. Tickets are available through **Ticketmaster** (© **416/870-8000**). In addition to the previously mentioned **Hummingbird Centre** and **Massey Hall,** these are the major pop and rock music venues.

Air Canada Centre   Better known as a sports venue (it's home to the Maple Leafs and the Raptors), the Air Canada Centre also hosts popular musical acts.

Neil Young has performed here, as have Ozzy Osbourne, Justin Timberlake, and Mariah Carey. 40 Bay St. (at Lakeshore Blvd). © **416/815-5500**. www.theaircanadacentre. com. Subway: Union, then LRT to Queens Quay.

Kingswood Music Theatre   From May to September, Kingswood's open-air theater plays host to diverse, top-notch talent. Don Henley, the Beach Boys, the Scorpions, Barry Manilow, and Public Enemy have all played here. The bandshell is covered, but the lawn seats aren't—so beware in bad weather. Paramount Canada's Wonderland, 9580 Jane St., Vaughn. © **905/832-8131**. Subway: Yorkdale or York Mills, then GO Express Bus to Wonderland. By car: Take Yonge St. north to Hwy. 401 and go west to Hwy. 400. Go north on Hwy. 400 to Rutherford Rd. exit and follow signs. From the north, exit at Major Mackenzie.

Maple Leaf Gardens   The good old Gardens just haven't been the same since the Leafs left. Nonetheless, this is a popular site for rock concerts. Don't expect cushy seats, but the sight lines are generally good. The exceptions are gray seats and green seats that bracket the stage (sections 94–97 and 76–77); avoid these if you care about seeing the show. 60 Carlton St. © **416/977-1641**. Subway: College.

Molson Amphitheatre 🐾   This is a favorite summer spot because you can listen to music by the side of Lake Ontario. Most of the seating is on the lawn, and it's usually dirt-cheap. Ontario Place, 955 Lakeshore Blvd. W. © **416/314-9900**. Subway: Bathurst, then Bathurst streetcar south to Exhibition Place (last stop).

SkyDome   The biggest venue in the city, SkyDome is where the biggest acts usually play. Ticket prices frequently rise into the stratosphere. This venue is about as intimate as a parking lot. If you're seated in the 400 (Upper SkyBox) or 500 (SkyDeck) levels, you'll be watching the show on the JumboTron, unless you bring your binoculars. And remember to steer clear of the seats next to the JumboTron, or you won't see anything at all. 1 Blue Jays Way. © **416/341-3663**. www. skydome.com. Subway: Union.

DANCE
Dancemakers   Artistic director Serge Bennathan's nine-person company has gained international recognition for its provocative mix of stylized physical movement and theater. One of the best known works in its repertoire is *Sable/Sand*, which won a Dora Award for choreography. Performing at the Case Goods Theatre in the Distillery Historic District, 55 Mill Street. © **416/367-1800**. www.dancemakers. org. Tickets C$20–$35 (US$14–$24).

Danny Grossman Dance Company   The choreography of this local dance favorite is noted for its athleticism, theatricality, humor, and passionate social vision. The company performs both new works and revivals of modern-dance classics. Refreshing, fun, and exuberant. Performing at Premiere Dance Theatre, Queen's Quay Terminal, 207 Queens Quay W. © **416/973-4000**. Office: 511 Bloor St. W. © 416/408-4543 or 416/531-5268. www.dgdance.org. Tickets C$22–$38 (US$15–$26).

National Ballet of Canada 🐾   Perhaps the most beloved and famous of Toronto's cultural icons is the National Ballet of Canada. English ballerina Celia Franca launched the company in Toronto in 1951, and served as director, principal dancer, choreographer, and teacher. Over the years, the company has achieved great renown.

The company performs at the Hummingbird Centre in the fall, winter, and spring; tours internationally; and makes summer appearances before enormous crowds at the open theater at Ontario Place. Its repertoire includes the classics and works by Glen Tetley *(Alice)*, Sir Frederick Ashton, and Jerome Robbins. James Kudelka, who has created *The Miraculous Mandarin, The Actress,* and

Spring Awakening, was appointed artist-in-residence in 1991. Performing at Hummingbird Centre for the Performing Arts, 1 Front St. E. (© 416/872-2262), and Ontario Place, 955 Lakeshore Blvd. W. Office: 157 King St. E. © 416/366-4846. www.national.ballet.ca. Tickets C$26–$114 (US$18–$78).

Toronto Dance Theatre   The city's leading contemporary dance company burst onto the scene in 1972, bringing an inventive spirit and original Canadian dance to the stage. Director Christopher House joined in 1979 and has contributed more than 35 new works to the repertoire, including *Severe Clear* and the critically acclaimed *Nest*. Performing at Premiere Dance Theatre, Queen's Quay Terminal, 207 Queens Quay W. © 416/973-4000. Office: 80 Winchester St. www.tdt.org. Tickets C$17–$38 (US$12–$26).

2 The Club & Music Scene
COMEDY CLUBS
Toronto must be one heck of a funny place. That would explain why a disproportionate number of comedians, including Jim Carrey and Mike Myers, hail from here. This is one true Toronto experience you shouldn't miss.

The Laugh Resort   If you get your kicks from incisive humor with occasional dashes of social commentary, this is your place. Gilbert Gottfried, Paula Poundstone, Ray Romano, and George Wallace have performed here. Most of the acts are stand-up solos, though there are sometimes inspired improvs, too. At the Holiday Inn on King, 370 King St. W. © 416/364-5233. Tickets C$7–$18 (US$4.75–$12). Subway: St. Andrew.

The Rivoli ⊛   While the Riv is well known for its music performances and poetry readings, the Monday night ALT.COMedy Lounge is its biggest draw. It features local and visiting stand-ups, and is best known as the place where the Kids in the Hall got their start. Shows take place in the intimate 125-seat back room. See p. 96 in chapter 5 for a restaurant review. 332 Queen St. W. © 416/597-0794. Pay what you can admission. Subway: Osgoode.

Second City ⊛   This was where Mike Myers, otherwise known as Austin Powers, received his formal—and improvisational—comic training. Over the years, the legendary Second City has nurtured the likes of John Candy, Dan Aykroyd, Bill Murray, Martin Short, Andrea Martin, and Eugene Levy. It continues to turn out talented young actors. The scenes are always funny and topical, though the outrageous post-show improvs usually get the biggest belly laughs. Next door is the **Tim Simms Playhouse** (© 416/343-0022), an intimate space that features fledgling local stand-up talent. 56 Blue Jays Way. © 800/263-4485 or 416/343-0011. www.secondcity.com. Dinner and show from C$35 (US$24); show only C$13–$25 (US$8.85–$17). Reservations required. Subway: St. Andrew.

Tips Good to Know: Nightlife
The drinking age in Ontario is 19, and most establishments enforce the law. Expect long queues on Friday and Saturday after 10pm at clubs in the downtown core. Bars and pubs that serve drinks only are open Monday through Saturday from 11am to 2am. Establishments that also serve food are open Sunday, too. If you're out at closing time, you'll find the subway shut down, but special late-night buses run along Yonge and Bloor streets. Major routes on streets such as College, Queen, and King operate all night. To find out what's on, see "Making Plans," earlier in this chapter.

Yuk Yuk's Superclub   Yuk Yuk's is Canada's original home of stand-up comedy. Comic Mark Breslin founded the place in 1976, inspired by New York's Catch a Rising Star and Los Angeles's Comedy Store. Some famous alumni include Jim Carrey, Harland Williams, Howie Mandel, and Norm MacDonald. Other headliners have included Jerry Seinfeld, Robin Williams, and Sandra Bernhard. Monday is new talent night, and Tuesday is all improv. There's another Yuk Yuk's in **Mississauga,** not far from Pearson International Airport (✆ 905/434-4985). 224 Richmond St. W. ✆ 416/967-6425. www.yukyuks.com. Dinner and show from C$25 (US$16); show only C$5–C$15 (US$3.40–$10). Subway: Osgoode.

COUNTRY, FOLK, ROCK & REGGAE
The BamBoo   Colorful confusion reigns here. The granddaddy of Toronto's reggae scene, the 'Boo also books calypso, salsa, jazz, soul, and R&B. Tables set for dinner surround the teensy dance floor, and the menu is as diverse as the music. Pad Thai, barbecued burgers, and jerk chicken are top choices. Forget quiet conversation, even if you score a seat on the rooftop patio—you're here for the music. 312 Queen St. W. ✆ 416/593-5771 (staffed 10am–5pm). Cover C$5–$10 (US$3.40–$6.80). Subway: Osgoode.

C'est What?   About as cozy as the basement of a historic warehouse can be, this casual spot attracts young and old alike. It offers 28 draft beers and a broad selection of single malts. Half pub and half performance space, C'est What? has played host to the likes of Jewel, the Barenaked Ladies, and Rufus Wainwright before they hit the big time. If the nightly acoustic music doesn't suit, check out the abundant board games. 67 Front St. E. ✆ 416/867-9499. www.cestwhat.com. Cover C$2–$10 (US$1.40–$7). Subway: Union.

El Mocambo ✪   This rock-and-roll institution was where the Rolling Stones rocked in the '70s, Elvis Costello jammed in the '80s, and Liz Phair mesmerized in the '90s. It has played peek-a-boo in recent years—it regularly closes and reopens. At the moment its usual Spadina Avenue digs have shut down, but the head of El Mocambo Productions has declared that the El Mo' is alive and well at the Tequila Lounge. In other words . . . El Mocambo is dead. Long live El Mocambo! At the Tequila Lounge, 794 Bathurst Ave. (at Bloor St. W.) ✆ 416/536-0346. Cover C$5–$15 (US$3.40–$10). Subway: Bathurst.

The Horseshoe Tavern   This old, traditional venue has showcased the sounds of the decades: blues in the '60s, punk in the '70s, New Wave in the '80s, and everything from ska to rockabilly to Celtic to alternative rock in the '90s. It's the place that launched Blue Rodeo, the Tragically Hip, the Band, and Prairie Oyster, and staged the Toronto debuts of the Police and Hootie & the Blowfish. It attracts a cross section of 20- to 40-year-olds. 368 Queen St. W. ✆ 416/598-4753. No cover; cover from C$10 (US$6.80) for special concerts. Subway: Osgoode.

Lee's Palace   Versailles this ain't. Still, that hasn't deterred the crème de la crème of the alternative music scene. The Red Hot Chili Peppers, the Tragically Hip, and Alanis have performed here. Despite the graffiti grunge, Lee's does boast the best sight lines in town. The audience is young and rarely tires of slam dancing in the mosh pit in front of the stage. 529 Bloor St. W. ✆ 416/532-1598. Cover C$10 (US$7) or less. Subway: Bathurst.

Phoenix Concert Theatre   One of the oldest dance halls in Toronto, the Phoenix attracts an all-ages, all-races crowd that includes straights and gays. As a rock venue, it showcases such artists as Screaming Headless Torsos and Patti Smith. On the weekends, it gets the crowds dancing with a mixture of retro,

Impressions

Toronto is known as Toronto the Good, because of its alleged piety. My guess is that there's more polygamy in Toronto than Baghdad, only it's not called that in Toronto.

—Austin F. Cross, *Cross Roads* (1936)

Latin, alternative, and funk. Thursday is gay night. 410 Sherbourne St. ℭ 416/323-1251. Cover C$5–$15 (US$3.40–$10). Subway: College, then any streetcar east to Sherbourne St.

The Rivoli ℛ   Currently this is the club for an eclectic mix of performances, including grunge, blues, rock, jazz, comedy, and poetry reading. Holly Cole launched her career here, Tori Amos made her Toronto debut in the back room, and the Kids in the Hall still consider it home (see "Comedy Clubs," above). Shows begin at 8pm and continue until 2am. People dance if they're inspired. Upstairs, there's a billiards room and espresso bar. 332 Queen St. W. ℭ 416/597-0794. Cover C$5–$15 (US$3.40–$10). Subway: Osgoode.

JAZZ, RHYTHM & BLUES

In addition to the clubs listed below, the **BamBoo** (p. 207) also offers some of the hottest jazz in town. Check out **www.tojazz.com** for the latest listings.

Montréal Bistro & Jazz Club ℛ   Here's a great two-for-one deal. Top performers like Oscar Peterson (still performing after his stroke in 1993), Molly Johnson, Ray McShann, and George Shearing perform in a small room lit by rose-tinted lamps; the neighboring room (see p. 99 in chapter 5) is a Quebecois eatery that features *tourtière* and smoked-meat sandwiches. 65 Sherbourne St. ℭ 416/363-0179. www.montrealbistro.com. Cover C$8–$20 (US$5.45–$14). Subway: King, then any streetcar east to Sherbourne St.

Reservoir Lounge   This perennial favorite is a modern-day speakeasy. The cramped space—it seats only 100—is below street level, and feels intimate rather than claustrophobic. Live jazz, whether Dixieland, New Orleans, or swing, belts out 6 nights a week. The epicenter for the swing dance craze in Toronto, this is still the place to watch glam hepcats groove. 52 Wellington St. E. ℭ 416/955-0887. Cover C$5–$7 (US$3.40–$4.75). Subway: King.

Rex Jazz and Blues Bar   This watering hole has been drawing jazz fans since it first opened in 1951. Admittedly the decor hasn't changed much since the old days, but the sounds you'll find here are cutting edge. The Rex lures top local and international talent; Tuesday is the weekly jam night. 194 Queen St. W. ℭ 416/598-2475. Cover up to C$8 (US$5.60). Subway: Osgoode.

Southern Po Boys   This new restaurant and club bills itself as the "Mardi Gras of the North." The menu is strictly rich Southern fare, and the sounds are bluesy and soulful. 159 Augusta St. ℭ 416/993-6768. Cover C$2–$5 (US$1.40–$3.50). Subway: Spadina, then LRT south to Dundas.

Top O' the Senator ℛ   Upstairs from the Torch Bistro (see p. 97 in chapter 5) and the Senator Diner, this is one of the classiest jazz joints in town. Top performers, such as vocalist Molly Johnson and sax goddess Jane Bunnett, have graced the long, narrow space. Leathery couches and banquettes add to the lounge-lizard ambience. For those who still care, the third-floor humidor has a premium collection of Cuban smokes. 249 Victoria St. ℭ 416/364-7517. www.thesenator.com. Cover C$10–$20 (US$7–$14). Subway: Dundas.

DANCE CLUBS

Dance clubs come and go at an alarming pace—the hottest spot can close or turn into a decidedly unhip place almost overnight—so keep in mind that some of the spots listed below may have disappeared or changed entirely by the time you visit. Some things stay constant, though. One is that, with few exceptions, everyone lines up to get into a club—so don't get the idea that charming the bouncer will get you in faster. Most clubs don't have much of a dress code, though "no jeans" rules are not uncommon. I have indicated what the current scene looks like, but it will almost certainly change, so be sure to call ahead. The club listings in the free weekly *Now* are consistently the best.

Several primarily gay and lesbian clubs attract a sizable hetero contingent; one notable destination is **El Convento Rico** (p. 214).

Afterlife Formerly the Limelight, this is truly the club that won't die. People have been coming in from the suburbs forever to dance, play pool, and lounge, and they show no signs of stopping. No jeans. 250 Adelaide St. W. (𝄞 416/593-6126. Cover C$5–$10 (US$3.50–$7). Subway: St. Andrew.

Bauhaus The unfinished metal-and-rivet decor gives this space an industrial feel. A young PVC-clad crowd dances to R&B and soul on the first floor, and to house and hip-hop on the second. 31 Mercer St. (𝄞 416/977-9813. www.bauhaus nightclub.com. Cover C$10–$15 (US$7–$10.50). Subway: St. Andrew.

Berlin As sophisticated and soigné as it tries to be—it has a smashing dining room and Tuesday-night salsa lessons—Berlin is best known as an upscale meat market. A perennial favorite in the Young and Eligible—oops, Yonge and Eglinton—neighborhood, the crowd is a little older (late 20s–mid 40s) than at most of the downtown clubs. As the club's cheesy but memorable ad goes, this is where "man meets woman, not boy meets girl." Consider yourself warned. 2335 Yonge St. (𝄞 416/489-7777. Cover C$10 (US$7). Subway: Eglinton.

The Docks 🔆 This vast waterfront party is a complex that books live entertainers like James Brown, Blue Rodeo, and the Pointer Sisters. The dance club boasts more than a dozen bars, the latest in lighting, and other party effects. Thursday night is foam fun (that is, beer). There's a restaurant and a full raft of sports facilities, too. 11 Polson St. (off Cherry St.). (𝄞 416/461-DOCKS. Subway: Union, then taxi (about C$7/US$4.90) to Lakeshore Blvd. E. and Cherry St.

Easy & the Fifth This is the place to come if you're looking for a sophisticated crowd. The music is less frenzied, and you might even manage a conversation. The dance area is a loft-like space. In the back, there's a cigar bar furnished with Oriental rugs and comfortable armchairs, plus two pool tables. The dress code in effect is "smart casual" (collared shirts, no jeans or caps). 225 Richmond St. W. (𝄞 416/979-3000. Cover C$10–$14 (US$7–$9.80). Subway: Osgoode.

Indian Motorcycle Café and Lounge It's got a bar, pool tables, and a dance floor—who could ask for anything more? When the 20- and 30-something patrons tire of dancing to R&B and rock, they take refuge on one of the several comfy couches in the bar. 355 King St. W. (𝄞 416/593-6996. No cover. Subway: St. Andrew.

NASA Space cadets, unite: house music plays in a "Jetsons"-like futuristic space. The crowd here is too young to have seen *2001: A Space Odyssey* the first time around, but video screens offer glimpses. If you think a theme bar sounds like fun, this is your place; if you've been there and done that, go elsewhere. 609 Queen St. W. (𝄞 416/504-8356. Cover C$10 (US$7). Subway: Osgoode.

Sneaky Dee's   Pool tables and Mexican food complement alternative rock spun by a DJ in the club upstairs until 1:30am. Downstairs, the bar is open until 3am on weekdays, 5am on weekends. 431 College St. © 416/603-3090. No cover. Subway: Queen's Park, then any streetcar west to Bathurst St.

3 The Bar Scene

The current night scene encompasses a flock of attractive bistros with billiard tables. You can enjoy cocktails, a reasonably priced meal, and a game of billiards in comfortable, aesthetically pleasing surroundings. The cigar bar is still in vogue, and most clubs have a humidor for the stogie set. Unlike dance clubs, the bars and lounges in Toronto are a pretty stable bunch.

BARS & LOUNGES

Al Frisco's   This is one of the few Toronto bars with its own microbrewery. Upstairs, people crowd around the pool tables or jam the dance floor, moving to retro sounds. Downstairs, cozy fireplaces enhance the gathering-spot atmosphere. The food is Mediterranean—pizza, pasta, salads, and antipasti. In summer, a mix

Cueing Up

It's not hard to find a bar or a restaurant with a token pool table—it's a must-have accessory in some quarters—but real shark shops aren't so easy to come by. If you have a serious pool habit, try one of the following clubs.

Academy of Spherical Arts   Okay, maybe this isn't your typical pool hall, but it has a great pedigree: The 5,000-sq.-ft. space used to house billiard manufacturer Brunswick. Now it looks more like a turn-of-the-20th-century gentlemen's club (there are even a few antique pool tables). This is a popular celebrity-sighting spot, and the likes of Kevin Bacon, Minnie Driver, Dennis Hopper, and Lennox Lewis have been known to drop by. (Because the Academy hosts private parties, always call to make sure it's open.) 38 Hanna St. © 416/532-2782. Subway: St. Andrew, then streetcar west along King St. to Atlantic Ave. and walk 1 block south.

Bar Italia & Billiards   Downstairs, a young, trendy, good-looking crowd quaffs drinks or coffee and snacks on Italian sandwiches. Upstairs, guys and gals gather 'round the six pool tables. This scene is strictly for the flirtatious—serious game-players should go elsewhere. 582 College St. © 416/535-3621. Subway: Queen's Park, then any streetcar west to Clinton St.

Charlotte Room   *Billiards Digest* has called the Charlotte Room one of the 10 best billiard rooms in North America. It feels like an old-boys' club. In addition to the 10 tables, there's a pub-grub menu and, on occasion, live jazz music. 19 Charlotte St. © 416/598-2882. Subway: St. Andrew.

The Corner Pocket   Smack-dab in the middle of trendy Little Italy, there's the Corner Pocket. Unpretentious and low-key, the hall has 17 billiard tables (and one foosball table, in case you're interested). The big-screen television is always tuned to sports. 722 College St. © 416/928-3540. Subway: Queen's Park, then any streetcar west to Crawford St.

of tourists, suits, and casual professionals in their late 20s and beyond jams the extra-large patio. 133 John St. © 416/595-8201. Subway: Osgoode.

Eau ⚘ As noted in the dining review in chapter 5, Eau is a stylish place. The bar is in super-nova mode at the moment, and this is definitely a see-and-be-seen spot. The cocktail menu is astonishingly overpriced for Toronto: One martini—"the-big-eau," which mixes vodka, champagne and ice wine—costs C$18 (US$13). Frankly, it wasn't one of the better martinis I've had. 609 King St. W. © 416/203-9399. Subway: St. Andrew.

Kit Kat Bar and Grill If you're interested in something a little more sophisticated than the usual bar scene, the Kit Kat is your place. The bar area is charmingly old-fashioned, albeit a little cramped. The selection of cocktails and fine wines is strictly for grownups. 297 King St. W. © 416/977-4461. Subway: St. Andrew.

Left Bank An over-25 crowd gathers in the lower-level bar at this restaurant. It's especially inviting in winter, when the fire warms folks playing billiards or lolling on the comfortable banquettes. 567 Queen St. W. © 416/504-1626. Subway: Osgoode, then any streetcar west to Bathurst.

Madison Madison has to be one of the city's most popular gathering places, with people (many of them students) jamming every floor and terrace. The newest development is the billiard room, with 10 tables. Everyone in the friendly crowd seems to know everyone else. 14 Madison Ave. © 416/927-1722. Subway: Spadina.

Milano Up front there's a bar, and beyond it stand several billiard tables. The dining area is off to the side. In summer, French doors open to the street, making for a pleasant Parisian atmosphere. The bistro-style food includes pizza, pasta, and sandwiches. 325 King St. W. © 416/599-9909. Subway: St. Andrew.

Mint et Menthe ⚘ Strictly for the been-there-done-that types, this lounge serves up excellent cocktails to a 30-something crowd. The setting is a little on the antiseptic side—white walls, white floors, white furniture—but the sexy music and communal couches give this bar some heat. 325 King St. W. © 416/599-9909. Subway: St. Andrew.

Panorama From this 51st-floor perch above Bloor and Bay, visitors can see north and south for 241km (150 miles)—at least on a clear day. Go for the lit skyline and the Latin ambience (check out the Rio Carnaval mural) and music. The seating is comfortable, and more than a dozen types of cigars are available. Arrive early if you want a window seat. In the Manulife Centre, 55 Bloor St. W. © 416/967-0000. Subway: Bloor/Yonge.

The Pilot This watering hole dates to the early years of the Second World War. Regulars who go way back mix with a suited-up after-work crowd. It's an unpretentious place with pool tables and a wonderful rooftop patio. 22 Cumberland St. © 416/923-5716. Subway: Yonge/Bloor.

The Real Jerk The original Real Jerk became so popular that it moved to this larger space. The hip crowd digs the hot background music, the lively ambience, and the moderately-priced, super-spiced Caribbean food—jerk chicken, curries, shrimp Creole, rotis, and patties. 709 Queen St. E. © 416/463-6055. www.therealjerk.com. Reservations only for parties of 8 or more. Subway: Queen, then any streetcar east.

Shark City Forget *Jaws*—the sharks here sport well-cut suits and smoke Havanas. When not busy striking a pose, the young, hip crowd shoots some pool at the basement tables. There's also a restaurant with basic pizza and pasta offerings and a small patio. 117 Eglinton Ave. E. © 416/488-7899. Subway: Eglinton.

Impressions
Returning to Toronto was like finding a Jaguar parked in front of the vic-
arage and the padre inside with a pitcher of vodka martinis reading Lolita.
                                    —Maclean's magazine, January 1959

Souz Dal ⚅   Located in Little Italy, Souz Dal stands out. It's dark and intimate, painted deep purple and mustard, and decorated in exotic Moroccan fashion. Kilims adorn the walls; the bar is fashioned out of copper. Candles light the
small, trellised patio. There's a great selection of martinis and margaritas, as well
as tropical drinks, like the Havana (rum, guava juice, and lime). Thursday is
acid-jazz night. 636 College St. ⓒ 416/537-1883. Subway: Queen's Park, then any streetcar
west to Grace St.

Wayne Gretzky's   Hockey fans will want to visit this shrine to the Great One,
who hails from the nearby town of Brantford. Several cases display memorabilia—
photos, uniforms, and equipment. They trace Gretzky's rise from the junior
leagues in Sault Ste. Marie, through his professional debut with the Indianapolis
Racers, to his career in the NHL. Forget the food, unless you simply have to say
that you dined at *his* place. Better to have a drink at the long bar or head upstairs
to the rooftop Oasis patio, with a fine view of the CN Tower. 99 Blue Jays Way.
ⓒ 416/979-PUCK. www.gretzkys.com. Subway: St. Andrew or Union.

Wild Indigo   This intimate Little Italy bar has a small, atmospheric patio in
the back. It attracts a youngish, intellectual crowd and features a DJ on weekends.
607 College St. ⓒ 416/536-8797. Subway: Queen's Park, then any streetcar west to Clinton St.

PUBS & TAVERNS
Allen's   Allen's sports a great bar that offers more than 80 beer selections and
164 single malts. Guinness is the drink of choice on Tuesday and Saturday
nights, when folks reel and jig to the Celtic-Irish entertainment. 143 Danforth Ave.
ⓒ 416/463-3086. Subway: Broadview.

The Amsterdam ⚅   This brewpub is a beer-drinker's heaven, serving more
than 200 labels as well as 30 types on draft. By 8pm the tables in the back are
filled, and the long bar is jammed. In summer the patio is fun, too. 600 King St.
W. (at Portland St.). ⓒ 416/504-6882. Subway: St. Andrew, then any streetcar west.

The Bishop and the Belcher   This British-style pub offers 14 drafts on tap
and a decent selection of single malts. The classic pub fare includes bangers and
mash, shepherd's pie, and a ploughman's lunch. 361 Queen St. W. ⓒ 416/591-2352.
Subway: Osgoode.

The Brunswick House   This cavernous room, affectionately known as the
Brunny House, is a favorite with University of Toronto students. Waiters carry
trays of frothy suds between the Formica tables. Impromptu dancing to background music and pool and shuffleboard playing drown out the sound of at least
two of the large-screen TVs, if not the other 18. This is an inexpensive place to
down some beer. Upstairs, there's live-broadcast thoroughbred and harness racing
from international tracks, including Hong Kong. 481 Bloor St. W. ⓒ 416/964-2242.
Subway: Spadina or Bathurst.

Cameron House   Old and new hippies hang in the front room, with its
rococo bar. Local bands try out in the back room. On Sunday, the Cameron
serves an amazingly good brunch. 408 Queen St. W. ⓒ 416/703-0811. Subway: Osgoode.

Dora Keogh Irish Pub ⟨⟩   Created by the same crew that devised the perennially popular Allen's, Dora Keogh is an unusually elegant pub. The evening brings music, with local fiddlers and vocalists strutting their stuff; famous fiddler Natalie McMaster has been known to join in, as have various members of the Irish group the Chieftains. 141 Danforth Ave. ℂ 416/778-1804. Subway: Broadview.

The Rebel House ⟨⟩   The youngish crowd here dresses in designer sportswear. This neighborhood pub draws them in with its impressive selection of microbrews and reasonably priced grub. 1068 Yonge St. ℂ **416/927-0704**. Subway: Rosedale.

Hotel Bars

Just as some of the best restaurants in the city are in hotels, so are some of the most charming watering holes. While I'm all for heading out and experiencing what a city has to offer, don't overlook these options in your home away from home.

Accents   This romantic wine bar offers many selections by the glass. The lighting is flattering, and a pianist provides jazz background music throughout the evening. Given how popular the Sutton Place is with the Hollywood glitterati, it's no surprise to see stars pass through the bar. At the Sutton Place Hotel, 955 Bay St. ℂ 416/924-9221. Subway: Museum or Wellesley.

The Consort Bar   This is a wonderfully clubby, old-fashioned bar. Not only does it boast comfortable wing chairs, but also its 2.5m-high (8-ft.) windows onto the street afford excellent people watching. The suited-up crowd is generally more corporate than romantic—with some sweet exceptions. At Le Royal Meridien King Edward, 37 King St. E. ℂ 416/863-9700. Subway: King.

La Serre   This piano bar offers a full range of single malts and martinis, and welcomes cigar aficionados. Located at street level, it's a great place to people-watch along Yorkville Avenue. One caveat: The live piano music refuses to remain in the background. It's so noisy that I find it impossible to talk—but the suits don't seem to mind. At the Four Seasons Hotel Toronto, 21 Avenue Rd. ℂ 416/964-0411. Subway: Bay.

The Library Bar   This intimate, wood-paneled bar is the best place in the city to order a top-quality martini, which is served in a generous "fishbowl" glass. With its leopard-print couches and wingback chairs, it has an old-fashioned, almost colonial feel. I think it's one of the most romantic settings in town. At the Fairmont Royal York, 100 Front St. W. ℂ 416/863-6333. Subway: Union.

The Roof   Author Mordecai Richler called this the only civilized spot in Toronto. It's an old literary haunt, with comfortable couches in front of a fireplace, and excellent drinks. The walls sport caricatures of members of Canada's literary establishment. The James Bond martini—vodka with a drop of lillet—is my personal favorite. The view from the outdoor terrace is one of the best in the city. At the Park Hyatt Toronto, 4 Avenue Rd. ℂ 416/924-5471. Subway: Museum or Bay.

The Unicorn   This Celtic pub is named for the Irish Rovers song. Along with the usual pub staples, there's Irish stew and a great list of imported dark ales. It's a fun, relaxed place to unwind. 175 Eglinton Ave. E. ℰ 416/482-0115. Subway: Eglinton.

Wheat Sheaf Tavern   Designated a historic landmark, this is the city's oldest tavern—it's been in operation since 1849. For fans, eight screens show great moments in sports. The jukebox features 1,200 choices, and there are two pool tables and an outdoor patio. 667 King St. W. ℰ 416/504-9912. Subway: St. Andrew, then any streetcar west to Bathurst St.

WINE BARS

Centro   Upstairs is the gorgeous dining room (see p. 110 in chapter 5); downstairs is the upscale wine bar. A well-dressed crowd drops by for the convivial atmosphere, the gourmet pizzas and pastas, and the extensive selection of wines, which includes more than 600 varieties from around the globe. 2472 Yonge St. ℰ 416/483-2211. Subway: Eglinton.

Sottovoce ℛ   The name (which translates as "very softly") must be an inside joke, because the decibel level here is outrageous. This wine bar is still a great find, not least because it serves truly inspired focaccia sandwiches and salads. 595 College St. ℰ 416/536-4564. Subway: Queen's Park, then any streetcar west to Clinton St.

4 The Gay & Lesbian Scene

Toronto's large, active gay and lesbian community has created a varied nightlife scene. At some nightspots, such as the **Phoenix Concert Theatre,** one night a week is gay night (in this case, Thursday). See "Dance Clubs," earlier in this chapter.

Bar 501   This bar is popular with gay men for its Sunday evening drag shows, which often attract crowds that watch from the sidewalk through the large front window. There's also Saturday afternoon bingo with the infamous Sister Bedelia. 501 Church St. ℰ 416/944-3272. Subway: Wellesley.

The Barn/The Stables   This is one of the city's oldest gay bars. The male-only crowd keeps the second-story dance floor jammed. There are afternoon underwear parties on Sunday, and sex videos, too. The favored look is denim with occasional ranch-style allusions (you'll see a few spurs). There's also an on-site leather shop selling fetish gear and clothing. 418 Church St. ℰ 416/977-4702. Subway: College.

Byzantium ℛ *Value*   An attractive bar-restaurant, Byzantium attracts an affable gay and straight crowd for cocktails, which are both excellent and reasonably priced (you must try either the Red Velvet or the Black Orchid; either is C$7/US$4.90). You can follow drinks with dinner in the adjacent dining room, where the cooking is top-notch. 499 Church St. ℰ 416/922-3859. Subway: Wellesley.

Crews/Tango   Located in a renovated Victorian house, this two-in-one club boasts a large outdoor patio. Crews is a gay bar for men, and it is known for its pubby atmosphere and its drag shows, which start at 11pm on Wednesday through Sunday. The adjoining Tango bar draws a lesbian crowd. It hosts Tuesday- and Thursday-night karaoke; on Friday and Saturday nights, the women head for the dance floor. 508 Church St. ℰ 416/972-1662. Subway: Wellesley.

El Convento Rico ℛ   The Latin beat beckons one and all—straight, gay, and otherwise—to this lively club. If you don't know how to samba, you can pick up the basics at the Friday- and Sunday-night dance lessons, but if you don't learn, no one on the jam-packed dance floor will notice. There's a substantial hetero contingent that comes out just to watch the fabulous drag queens. 750 College St. ℂ 416/588-7800. www.elconventorico.com. Cover C$5 ($3.50) or less. Subway: Queen's Park, then streetcar west.

Pope Joan This is the city's most popular lesbian bar. It has a pool table and a game room furnished with old, cozy couches downstairs, and a restaurant and dance area upstairs. On Saturday, there's a hearty buffet brunch. In summer, the fenced-in patio is the place to cool off. A group called the Drag Kings performs occasionally. 547 Parliament St. (at Winchester St.). ℂ 416/925-6662. Subway: Wellesley, then any streetcar east to Parliament St., and walk 2 blocks south.

Sailor This bar is attached to Woody's (see below), but has a livelier atmosphere; unlike Woody's, you won't see many women here. Every Thursday there's a Best Chest competition, and on Sunday the draw is the drag show. In the evening, a DJ spins an assortment of dance and alternative tunes. 465 Church St. ℂ 416/972-0887. Subway: Wellesley.

Slack Alice This incredibly popular bar draws a gay and lesbian crowd, with more than a few straights. The menu features home-style comfort food; on weekend evenings, a DJ gets the crowd on its feet. 562 Church St. ℂ 416/969-8742. Subway: Wellesley.

Woody's ℛ A friendly, popular local bar, Woody's attracts mainly men but welcomes women; the crowd is a mix of gay and hetero. It's a popular meeting spot, especially for weekend brunch. 467 Church St. (south of Wellesley St.). ℂ 416/972-0887. www.woodystoronto.com. Subway: Wellesley.

5 Cinemas & Movie Houses

There is no shortage of movie theaters—in fact, monster megaplexes are the rage at the moment. The largest theaters are at the Eaton Centre, St. Lawrence Market Square, and Yonge and Eglinton. Cinemas with a mere pair of screens can be found at the Sheraton Centre, Bloor and Yonge, and Yonge and St. Clair. Check *Now, Eye,* or one of the newspapers for listings.

Carlton Cinemas Home to the subtitled set, the Carlton plays films—many of them superb—that frequently don't see the light of day anywhere else. Many of the offerings originate in France, Italy, Russia, or China; there's also a smattering of independent North American films. Buy tickets early on weekends. 20 Carlton St. ℂ 416/964-2463. Tickets C$10 (US$7). Tues discounts. Subway: College.

Cinematheque Ontario This organization shows the best in contemporary cinema. The programs include directors' retrospectives, plus new films from France, Germany, Japan, Bulgaria, and other countries that you won't find in the first-run theaters around town. Screenings at Art Gallery of Ontario, 317 Dundas St. W. (between McCaul and Beverley sts.). Office: 2 Carlton St. ℂ 416/967-7371 or 416/923-3456 (box office). Tickets C$8 (US$5.60) adults, C$4.25 (US$3) seniors and students. Subway: St. Patrick.

6 Coffeehouses

While Starbucks has certainly staked out territory in Toronto, the Canadian chain the **Second Cup** is holding its ground. It offers a full range of flavored coffees and espresso varieties, plus cakes, muffins, croissants, and gift items. Another chain, **Timothy's,** invites you to pour your own selection from about 10 varieties. My favorite coffeehouses are all independents, though.

Sweet Treats: Toronto's Dessert Cafes

Nightlife doesn't have to mean high culture, barhopping, or anything in between. It doesn't even mean you have to stop eating. Here are some of the city's most agreeable places to satisfy a sweet tooth and do some people watching.

Demetre Caffe   In the heart of Greektown on the Danforth, Demetre is known for its Old World ambience as well as its sweets: Belgian waffles, oversized sundaes, cakes, tortes, and baklava. It's popular at all hours of the evening with a casual crowd, and on weekends it draws families. Closing time is midnight Sunday through Thursday, and 3am Friday and Saturday. 400 Danforth Ave. ✆ 416/778-6654. Subway: Broadview.

Desserts by Phipps   The cafe serves salads and sandwiches, but what really draw the crowds are the decadent desserts. Cappuccino chiffon cake is a direct hit, as are the moist but not gooey apple confections. 420 Eglinton Ave. W. ✆ 416/481-9111. Subway: Eglinton.

Dufflet Pastries   On menus around town, you'll sometimes see mention of "desserts by Dufflet." *Divine* is the word that best applies to these confections. Owner Dufflet Rosenberg bakes some of the most delectable tortes, tarts, and pastries in the city. The problem is deciding where to start. Chocolate raspberry truffle? Cappuccino dacquoise? Your call. There are a few selections for people with gluten or nut allergies, and the cafe also serves light fare. 787 Queen St. W. ✆ 416/504-2870. www.dufflet.com. Subway: Osgoode, then any streetcar west to Euclid Ave.

Greg's Ice Cream   One taste of Greg's homemade ice cream will turn you into an addict. (I should know—I've been one for years.) Different flavors are available each day, and the staff is generous about handing out samples. It's hard for me to pick one favorite flavor, but the roasted marshmallow would definitely be up there. 200 Bloor St. W. ✆ 416/961-4734. Subway: Museum or St. George.

Just Desserts   This cafe stays open practically around the clock on weekends for those in need of a sugar fix. Around 40 desserts are available—as many as 12 different cheesecakes, 10 or so pies, plus an array of gâteaux, tortes, and meringues. All cost around C$6 (US$4.20). 555 Yonge St. (at Wellesley). ✆ 416/963-8089. Subway: Wellesley.

Sicilian Ice Cream Company   This old-fashioned ice cream parlor is Toronto's top purveyor of Italian *gelati*. The wonderful patio is open in the summer. 712 College St. ✆ 416/531-7716. Subway: Queen's Park, then streetcar west.

Cafe Diplomatico ✿   One of the oldest cafes in Toronto, this Little Italy gem has mosaic marble floors, wrought-iron chairs, and an extra-large sidewalk patio. Many longtime area residents get their caffeine fix here in the morning; the patio attracts a trendier crowd. 594 College St. ✆ 416/534-4637. Subway: Queen's Park.

Daily Express Café   Near the student ghetto in the Annex neighborhood, this lively cafe draws most of its crowd from the nearby University of Toronto. 280 Bloor St. W. ✆ 416/944-3225. Subway: St. George.

Future Bakery This rambling cafe attracts an artsy crowd with fine breads and a selection of coffees. Would-be writers scribble away in well-lit corners. 483 Bloor St. W. ℂ 416/922-5875. Subway: Spadina.

Gypsy Co-op Coffee is not the only king here. Many teas and herbal infusions (for everything from stress to colds and flu) are available, as are super-rich brownies. 815 Queen St. W. ℂ 416/703-5069. Subway: Osgoode, then any streetcar west to Manning.

Lettieri ⊛ The house rule is that after 7 minutes, a pot of coffee is no longer fresh. This place takes the bean seriously. In addition to the wide range of coffees, there are focaccia sandwiches, tarts, cookies, and pastries. 94 Cumberland St. ℂ 416/515-8764. Subway: Bay.

10

Side Trips from Toronto

Here's a classic good news/bad news situation: Some of the greatest attractions in this region are within a 2-hour drive of Toronto. They're easily accessible, which is a good thing, but if you're trying to shoehorn all of the sights into a short stay . . . you've got some serious choices to make. This chapter describes the three best—the wine region of Niagara-on-the-Lake, the theater town of Stratford, and the golf/spa/sailing resort retreat of the Muskokas—as well as the less well-known city of Hamilton.

For information about the areas surrounding Toronto, contact **Tourism Ontario** (✆ **800/ONTARIO** or 416/314-0944; www.travelinx.com), or visit the travel center in the Eaton Centre on Level 1 at Yonge and Dundas streets. It's open Monday through Friday from 10am to 9pm, Saturday from 9:30am to 6pm, and Sunday from noon to 5pm.

1 Stratford ✯

145km (90 miles) NW of Toronto

The Stratford Festival has humble roots. The idea of a theater was launched in 1953 when director Tyrone Guthrie lured the great Sir Alec Guinness to the stage here. Whether Sir Alec knew the "stage" was set up in a makeshift tent is another question, but his acclaimed performance gave the festival the push—and press—it needed to become an annual tradition. Since then the Stratford Festival has grown to become one of the most famous in North America, and its four theaters (no more tents!) have put this charming and scenic town on the map. While visitors will notice the Avon River and other sights named in honor of the Bard, they may not realize that Stratford has another claim to fame. It's home to one of Canada's best cooking schools, which makes dining at many of the spots in town a delight.

ESSENTIALS

VISITOR INFORMATION For first-rate visitor information, go to the **Information Centre** (✆ **519/273-3352**) by the river on York Street at Erie. From May to early November, it's open Sunday through Wednesday from 9am to 5pm, and Thursday through Saturday from 9am to 8pm. At other times, contact **Tourism Stratford,** 47 Downie St., Stratford, ON N5A 1W7 (✆ **800/561-SWAN** or 519/271-5140; www.city.stratford.on.ca).

GETTING THERE Driving from Toronto, take Highway 401 west to Interchange 278 at Kitchener. Follow Highway 8 west onto Highway 7/8 to Stratford.

   Amtrak and **VIA Rail** (✆ **416/366-8411**) operate several trains daily along the Toronto–Kitchener–Stratford route. Call ✆ **800/361-1235** in Canada or **800/USA-RAIL** in the United States.

Tips **A Helpful Planning Tool**

Each week **Outside Toronto** (www.outsidetoronto.com) suggests things to see and do within a 2-hour drive of the city: antiques shows, farmers' markets, recreational events. The "Places to Go" section directs you to museums, festivals, and charming little towns. The site provides maps, too.

THE STRATFORD FESTIVAL ⓖ

On July 13, 1953, *Richard III,* starring Sir Alec Guinness, was staged in a huge tent. From that modest start, Stratford's artistic directors have built on the radical, but faithfully classic, base established by Tyrone Guthrie to create a repertory theater with a glowing international reputation.

Stratford has four theaters. The **Festival Theatre,** 55 Queen St., in Queen's Park, has a dynamic thrust stage (a modern re-creation of an Elizabethan stage). The recently renovated **Avon Theatre,** 99 Downie St., has a classic proscenium. The **Tom Patterson Theatre,** Lakeside Drive, is an intimate 500-seat theater. The newest venue—the **Studio Theatre** (attached to the Avon Theatre)—opened its doors in July 2002; the 278-seat space will be used for new and experimental works.

World famous for its Shakespearean productions, the festival also offers classic and modern theatrical masterpieces. Recent productions have included *My Fair Lady, The Hunchback of Notre Dame,* and *The King and I.* Offerings from the Bard have included *Romeo and Juliet, Richard III,* and *The Taming of the Shrew.* Sir Alec wasn't the company's only famous alumnus: The list of luminaries includes Dame Maggie Smith, Sir Peter Ustinov, Alan Bates, Christopher Plummer, Irene Worth, and Julie Harris. Present company members include Tom McCamus, Cynthia Dale, Colm Feore, and Lucy Peacock.

In addition to attending plays, visitors may enjoy the "Celebrated Writers Series," which features renowned authors (some of whom have penned works performed at the Stratford Festival). The list of speakers has included Margaret Atwood, Michael Ondaatje, Joyce Carol Oates, and Rohinton Mistry. All lectures take place on Sunday mornings at the Tom Patterson Theatre or the Studio Theatre, and they cost C$24 (US$17) per person; tickets are available from the box office.

The season usually begins in May and continues through October, with performances Tuesday through Sunday nights and matinees on Wednesday, Saturday, and Sunday. Ticket prices range from C$39 to $100 (US$27–$70), with special prices for students and seniors. For tickets, call ⓒ **800/567-1600;** visit www.stratfordfestival.ca; or write to the Stratford Festival, P.O. Box 520, Stratford, ON N5A 6V2. Tickets are also available in the United States and Canada at Ticketmaster outlets. The box office opens for mail and fax orders in late January; telephone and in-person sales begin in late February.

EXPLORING THE TOWN

Stratford has a wealth of attractions that complement the theater offerings. It's a compact town, easily negotiable on foot. Within sight of the Festival Theatre, **Queen's Park** has picnic spots beneath tall shade trees and by the Avon River. There are also some superb dining and good shopping prospects.

Past the Orr Dam and the 90-year-old stone bridge, through a rustic gate, lies a very special park, the **Shakespearean Garden.** In the formal English garden,

Stratford

0   1/2 mi
0   0.5 km

(i) Information
⊠ Post Office

Delamere Ave.
Mornington St.
Avon River
Queens Dr.
Romeo St.
Water St.
To Hwys. 7 & 8 → to Kitchener
Waterloo St. North
Cobourg St.
Ontario St.
Albert St.
Brunswick St.
King St.
Britannia St.
Mornington St.
Waterloo St. South
Bay St.
Queen St.
Avondale Ave.
Hibernia St.
Huron St.
Front St.
← To Hwy. 8 to Goderich
Douro St.
St. Patrick St.
George St.
Nile St.
■ Train Station
Avon St.
Shrewsbury St.
St.
David St.
Victoria St.
E. Gore St.
Downie St.
Norfolk St.
St. Vincent St.
Church St.
Erie St.
Cambria St.
Wellington St.
St.
W. Gore St.
Home St.
John St.
W. Gore St.
Easson St.
Brydges St.
Whitelock St.
Maple Ave.
Railway Ave.
Dufferin St.
Lorne Ave.

50 mi
50 km
✈ TORONTO
400 401
Lake Ontario
Stratford
Hamilton
401
Niagara Falls (Canada)
Buffalo
Lake Erie
N

8 To Hwys. 7 & 19 to London

ACCOMMODATIONS ■

Acrylic Dreams **21**
Albert Place **17**
Ambercroft **14**
Avonview Manor **6**
Bentley's **12**
Deacon House **15**
Festival Inn **8**
Queen's Inn **11**
Woods Villa **7**

DINING ◆

Bentley's **12**
The Church **16**
Keystone Alley Cafe **19**
The Old Prune **13**
Rundles **10**
York Street Kitchen **9**

ATTRACTIONS ●

Avon Boat Rentals **5**
Avon Theatre **20**
City Hall **18**
Festival Theatre **3**
Gallery Stratford **1**
Queen's Park **2**
Third Stage **4**

where a sundial measures the hours, you can relax and contemplate the herb and flower beds and the tranquil river lagoon, and muse on a bust of Shakespeare by Toronto sculptor Cleeve Horne.

If you turn right onto Romeo Street North from highways 7 and 8 as you come into Stratford, you'll find the **Gallery Stratford,** 54 Romeo St. (© **519/271-5271;** www.gallerystratford.on.ca). It's in a historic building on the fringes of Confederation Park. Since it opened in 1967, it has mounted fine Canadian-focused shows, often oriented to the theater arts. Its hours change with the seasons, but mid-May through late September it's open from 9am to 5pm (call ahead for hours for other times of year). Admission is approximately C$10 (US$7) for adults, C$8 (US$5.60) for seniors and students 12 and up, and free for children 11 and under. Admission prices change with the special exhibits on display.

Stratford is a historic town, dating to 1832. Ninety-minute **guided tours of Stratford** take place Monday through Saturday in July and August, and on Saturday only in May, June, September and October. They leave at 9:30am from the visitor's booth by the river, and are free of charge (call ahead to confirm). The visitor's booth also has maps available for self-guided tours.

Paddleboat, kayak and canoe rentals are available at the **Boathouse,** behind and below the information booth. It's open daily from 9am until dusk in summer. Contact **Avon Boat Rentals,** 40 York St. (© **519/271-7739**). There's also a boat, the **Juliet III,** which offers scenic half-hour tours.

A COUPLE OF EXCURSIONS FROM STRATFORD

Only half an hour or so away, the twin cities of **Kitchener** and **Waterloo** have two drawing cards: the **Farmer's Market** and the famous 9-day **Oktoberfest.** The cities still have a German-majority population (of German descent, and often German speaking), and many citizens are Mennonites. On Saturday starting at 6am, you can sample shoofly pie, apple butter, kochcase, and other Mennonite specialties at the market in the Market Square complex, at Duke and Frederick streets in Kitchener. For additional information, contact the **Kitchener–Waterloo Area Visitors and Convention Bureau,** 2848 King St. E., Kitchener, ON N2A 1A5 (© **519/748-0800;** www.kw-visitor.on.ca). It's open from 9am to 5pm weekdays only in winter, daily in summer. For Oktoberfest information, check out www.oktoberfest.ca; or write **K-W Oktoberfest,** P.O. Box 1053, 17 Benton St., Kitchener, ON N2G 4G1 (© **888/294-HANS** or 519/570-HANS).

Eight kilometers (5 miles) north of Kitchener is the town of **St. Jacobs.** It has close to 100 shops in venues such as a converted mill, silo, and other factory buildings. For those interested in learning more about the Amish-Mennonite way of life, the **Meetingplace,** 33 King St. (© **519/664-3518**), shows a short film about it (daily in summer, weekends only in winter). Ironically enough, there's also a **St. Jacobs Outlet Mall** (surely not run by the Amish!), filled with discounted Levi's jeans, Paderno cookware, Liz Claiborne and Jones New York clothing, Cadbury's chocolate, and Royal Doulton giftware. It's located at 25 Benjamin Road, and it's open Monday through Friday from 9:30am to 9pm, Saturday 8:30am to 6pm, and Sunday noon to 5pm (closed Jan 1 and Dec 25). Call © **519/888-0138** for more information.

WHERE TO STAY

When you book your theater tickets, you can book your accommodations at no extra charge. Options range from guest homes for as little as C$40 (US$28) to first-class hotels charging more than C$125 (US$88). Call the **Stratford Festival Accommodation Bureau** at ℭ **800/567-1600** for information (note that some accommodations are only open to festival-goers, and these can only be booked through the Accommodation Bureau). You can also get information about where to stay from **Tourism Stratford** at ℭ **800/561-SWAN.** Rooms in Stratford are most expensive in June, July and August; it's easier to get a discount from fall to spring.

HOTELS & MOTELS

Albert Place   Around the corner from the Avon Theatre, the Albert Place has large rooms with high ceilings. Furnishings are simple and modern. Some units have separate sitting rooms. Rates include coffee, tea, and doughnuts served in the lobby in the early morning.

23 Albert St., Stratford, ON N5A 3K2. ℭ **519/273-5800.** Fax 519/273-5008. 34 units. C$79–$105 (US$55–$74) double; C$165 (US$116) suite. Rates include small breakfast. MC, V. Pets accepted. **Amenities:** Restaurant; dry cleaning. *In room:* A/C, TV.

Bentley's ✿   This inn enjoys an excellent location at the center of town. The soundproofed rooms are luxurious duplex suites with efficiency kitchens. Period English furnishings and attractive drawings, paintings, and costume designs on the walls make for a pleasant ambience. Five units have skylights. The adjoining British-style pub, also called Bentley's, is popular with festival actors (see "Where to Dine," below).

99 Ontario St., Stratford, ON N5A 3H1. ℭ **800/361-5322** or 519/271-1121. www.bentleys-annex.com. 13 units. Apr–Nov C$150 (US$105) double; Nov–June C$95 (US$67) double. Extra person C$20 (US$14). AE, DC, MC, V. Free parking. **Amenities:** Pub. *In room:* A/C, TV, kitchen, fridge, coffeemaker, hair dryer.

Festival Inn   The Festival Inn sits outside town off highways 7 and 8, on 8 hectares (20 acres) of landscaped grounds. This is the largest full-service hotel in Stratford. The place has an Old English air, with stucco walls, Tudor-style beams, and high-backed red settees in the lobby. Tudor style prevails throughout the large, motel-style rooms. All have wall-to-wall carpeting, matching bedspreads, floor-to-ceiling drapes, and reproductions of old masters on the walls. Some units have charming bay windows with sheer curtains, and all rooms in the main building, north wing, and annex have refrigerators. The indoor pool has an outdoor patio.

1144 Ontario St. (P.O. Box 811), Stratford, ON N5A 6W1. ℭ **519/273-1150.** Fax 519/273-2111. www.festivalinnstratford.com. 182 units. C$140–$200 (US$98–$140) double. Extra person C$10 (US$7). Winter discounts (about 30%) available. AE, DC, MC, V. Free parking. **Amenities:** Dining room; coffee shop; indoor pool; Jacuzzi; sauna. *In room:* A/C, TV, fridge, coffeemaker.

The Queen's Inn   The Queen's Inn occupies one of the best locations in Stratford—it's right in the town center. The historic building is about a century and a half old, but the guest rooms have a fresh look every year, after the owners use the winter months for refurbishing. The English-style Boar's Head Pub is on the premises. Breakfast is included in the rates: From May to mid-November, it's a breakfast buffet Monday through Saturday; the rest of the year, it's a continental breakfast.

161 Ontario St., Stratford, ON N5A 3H3. ℭ **800/461-6450** or 519/271-1400. Fax 519/271-7373. www.queensinnstratford.ca. 31 units. May to mid-Nov 15 C$85–$130 (US$60–$91) double, C$165–$225 (US$116–$158) suite; mid-Nov to Apr 16 C$69 (US$48) double, from C$85 (US$60) suite. Rates include breakfast. AE, DC, MC, V. Free parking. Pets accepted. **Amenities:** Restaurant; pub; business center; limited room service; babysitting; same-day dry cleaning. *In room:* A/C, TV, hair dryer.

A PICK OF THE B&BS

For more information on the bed-and-breakfast scene, write to **Tourism Stratford,** P.O. Box 818, 88 Wellington St., Stratford, ON N5A 6W1 (© **519/271-5140**). It's open Monday through Friday from 9am to 5pm.

Acrylic Dreams   As its name suggests, the recently refurbished Acrylic Dreams has a fun, modern atmosphere, thanks to its artist owners. Cottage-style antiques furnish most of the house, but the living room is done in new wave style, with transparent acrylic furniture. Upstairs, a suite decorated in Provençal colors has a separate sitting room with TV and refrigerator. On the ground floor, two doubles share a refrigerator. The full breakfast varies, but might include peaches, peach yogurt, and homemade scones and preserves with ingredients from the garden (but no meat—the owners are vegetarians). There's a phone for guests' use. Co-owner Karen Zamara offers in-room reflexology treatments; guests are also welcome to attend yoga classes at her downtown studio (C$12/US$8.40 per class).

66 Bay St., Stratford, ON N5A 4K6. © and fax **519/271-7874.** www.bbcanada.com/3718.html. 4 units. C$90–$130 (US$63–$91) double; C$135 (US$95) suite. 3rd person in suite C$25 (US$18). Rates include full breakfast. 2-night minimum on weekends. No credit cards. Street parking. **Amenities:** In-room massage. *In room:* A/C, no phone.

Ambercroft   This inviting 1878 home in a quiet downtown area is convenient to the theaters and restaurants. The quirky, angular rooms are country cozy, and were refurbished recently. There's a comfy front parlor, a small TV room, and front and rear porches. Guests have the use of a refrigerator. The extended continental breakfast includes seasonal fruits, cereals, homemade baked goods, and more. No smoking; there is a spaniel in the house, but pets are not accepted.

129 Brunswick St., Stratford, ON N5A 3L9. © **519/271-5644.** Fax 519/272-0156. www.ambercroftbandb.com. 4 units. C$115–$135 (US$81–$95) double. Rates include breakfast. MC, V. *In room:* A/C, hair dryer, no phone.

Avonview Manor   In a 1916 Edwardian house on a quiet street, Avonview Manor offers attractive individually furnished rooms. Three have queen-size beds; the suite contains four singles, a sitting room, and a private bath. Breakfast is served in a bright dining room that overlooks the garden. Guests have the use of a kitchen. The living room is very comfortable, particularly in winter, when guests can cozy up in front of the stone fireplace. Smoking is allowed only on the porch. There's also an in-ground pool and Jacuzzi.

63 Avon St., Stratford, ON N5A 5N5. © **519/273-4603.** www.bbcanada.com/avonview. 4 units (3 w/private bathroom). C$90–$110 (US$63–$77) double; C$120–$160 (US$84–$112) suite. Rates include full breakfast. No credit cards; personal checks accepted. Street parking. **Amenities:** Outdoor pool; Jacuzzi; sauna. *In room:* A/C; no phone.

Deacon House ⊛   This is a great location, within walking distance of everything. Dianna Hrysko and Mary Allen have restored Deacon House, a shingle-style structure built in 1907. Rooms are decorated in country style, with iron-and-brass beds, quilts, pine hutches, oak rockers, and rope-style rugs. The comfortable living room holds a fireplace, TV, wingback chairs, and a sofa. The main-floor guest kitchen is a welcome convenience, as is the second-floor sitting and reading room. The entire house is nonsmoking, but allergy sufferers should know that there are pets in the house.

101 Brunswick St., Stratford, ON N5A 3L9. © **877/825-6374** or 519/273-2052. Fax 519/273-3784. www.bbcanada.com/1152.html. 6 units. C$110–$132 (US$77–$94) double. Extra person C$35 (US$25). Rates include full breakfast. Off-season packages available. MC, V. Free parking. *In room:* A/C, hair dryer, no phone.

Woods Villa This handsome 1870 house is home to Ken Vinen, who collects and restores early "musical amusement devices" from phonographs to vintage jukeboxes; the 30 pieces around the house are all in working order. Five rooms have fireplaces, and the handsome suite boasts a canopy bed. Rooms are large and offer excellent value. Morning coffee is delivered to your room, followed by breakfast prepared to order and served in the dining room. There's an attractively landscaped outdoor pool and terrace. House policies are no smoking, no children, and no pets.

62 John St. N., Stratford, ON N5A 6K7. (?) **519/271-4576**. www.woodsvilla.orc.ca. 6 units. C$145–$230 (US$102–$161) double. Rates include full breakfast. MC, V. Street parking. Children not allowed. **Amenities:** Outdoor pool. *In room:* A/C, TV, hair dryer, iron.

A NEARBY PLACE TO STAY & DINE
Langdon Hall 🏵🏵 This elegant house stands at the head of a curving, tree-lined drive. Eugene Langdon Wilks, a great-grandson of John Jacob Astor, completed it in 1902. It remained in the family until 1987, when its transformation into a small country-house hotel began. Today, its Langdon Hall is a Relais & Chateaux property, and its 81 hectares (200 acres) of lawns, gardens, and woodlands make for an ideal retreat. The main house, of red brick with classical pediment and Palladian-style windows, has a beautiful symmetry. Throughout, the emphasis is on comfort rather than grandiosity. The luxurious on-site spa offers a complete range of treatments. Most rooms surround the cloister garden. Each is individually decorated; most have fireplaces. The furnishings consist of handsome antiques reproductions, mahogany wardrobes, ginger-jar porcelain lamps, and armchairs upholstered with luxurious fabrics. The property has a croquet lawn and cross-country ski trails.

The light, airy dining room serves fine regional cuisine. Main courses run C$22 to $32 (US$15–$22). Tea is served on the veranda, and there's a bar.

RR #3, Cambridge, ON N3H 4R8. (?) **800/268-1898** or 519/740-2100. Fax 519/740-8161. www.langdonhall. ca. 49 units. C$259–$699 (US$181–$489) double. Rates include full breakfast. Spa packages from C$180 (US$126). AE, DC, MC, V. Free parking. From Hwy. 401, take exit 275 south, turn right onto Blair Rd., follow signs. Pets accepted. **Amenities:** Dining room; bar; outdoor pool; tennis courts; health club; spa; Jacuzzi; sauna; concierge; business center; 24-hr. room service; babysitting; dry cleaning; billiard room. *In room:* A/C, TV, dataport, coffeemaker, hair dryer, iron.

WHERE TO DINE
VERY EXPENSIVE
The Church 🏵🏵 CONTINENTAL The Church is simply stunning. The organ pipes and the altar of the 1873 structure are intact, along with the vaulted roof, carved woodwork, and stained-glass windows. You can sit in the nave or the side aisles and dine to appropriate sounds—usually Bach. Fresh flowers and elegant table settings further enhance the experience.

In summer, there's a special four-course prix-fixe dinner menu and an after-theater menu. Appetizers might include asparagus served hot with black morels in their juices, white wine, and cream; or sauté of duck foie gras with leeks and citron, mango, and ginger sauce. Among the selection of eight or so entrees, you might find Canadian caribou with port and blackberry sauce, cabbage braised in cream with shallots and glazed chestnuts, or lobster salad with green beans, new potatoes, and truffles scented with caraway. Desserts are equally exciting—try charlotte of white chocolate mousse with summer fruit and dark chocolate sauce.

To dine here during the festival, make reservations in March or April when you buy your tickets. In the off-season, call ahead; hours vary. The upstairs Belfry Bar is a popular pre- and post-theater gathering place.

70 Brunswick St. (at Waterloo St.). ℭ **519/273-3424.** www.churchrestaurant.com. Reservations strongly recommended. Prix-fixe dinner (summer only) C$59–$73 (US$41–$51); main courses C$33–$46 (US$23–$32). AE, DC, MC, V. Tues–Sat 11:30am–1am; Sun 11:30am–11pm. Off-season hours vary. Call for Mon hours during special events.

MODERATE

Bentley's CANADIAN/ENGLISH   Bentley's is *the* local watering hole, and a favorite theater company gathering spot. The popular pastime is darts, but you can also watch TV. In summer you can sit on the garden terrace and enjoy the light fare—grilled shrimp, burgers, gourmet pizza, fish and chips, shepherd's pie, and pasta dishes. The dinner menu features more substantial fare, including lamb curry, sirloin steak, and salmon baked in white wine with peppercorn-dill butter. The bar offers 16 drafts on tap.

99 Ontario St. ℭ **519/271-1121.** Reservations not accepted. Main courses C$8–$14 (US$5.60–$9.80). AE, DC, MC, V. Daily 11:30am–1am.

Keystone Alley Cafe ℛ CONTINENTAL   The food here is better than the fare at some pricier competitors. Theater actors often stop in for lunch—perhaps a sandwich, like the maple-grilled chicken and avocado club, or a main dish like cornmeal-crusted Mediterranean tart. At dinner, entrees range from breast of Muscovy duck with stir-fried Asian vegetables and egg noodles in honey-ginger sauce, to escalopes of calf's liver accompanied by garlic potato purée and creamed Savoy cabbage with bacon. The short wine list is reasonably priced.

34 Brunswick St. ℭ **519/271-5645.** www.keystonealley.com. Reservations recommended. Main courses C$17–$26.50 (US$12–$19). AE, DC, MC, V. Mon–Sat 11:30am–2:30pm; Tues–Sat 5–9pm.

The Old Prune ℛ CONTINENTAL   Two charming, whimsical women—Marion Isherwood and Eleanor Kane—run the Prune. In a lovely Edwardian home, it has three dining rooms and an enclosed garden patio. Former Montréalers, the proprietors demonstrate Québec flair in both decor and menu. Marion's inspired paintings grace the walls.

Chef Bryan Steele selects the freshest local ingredients, many from the region's organic farmers, and prepares them simply to reveal their abundant flavor. Appetizers might include outstanding house-smoked salmon with lobster potato salad topped with Sevruga caviar, or refreshing tomato consommé with saffron and sea scallops. Among the main courses, you might find Perth County pork loin grilled with tamari and honey glaze and served with shiitake mushrooms, pickled cucumbers, and sunflower sprouts; steamed bass in Napa cabbage with curry broth and lime leaves; or rack of Ontario lamb with smoky tomatillo-chipotle pepper sauce. Desserts, such as rhubarb strawberry Napoleon with vanilla mousse, are always inspired. The Old Prune is also lovely for lunch or a late supper.

151 Albert St. ℭ **519/271-5052.** www.oldprune.on.ca. Reservations required. 3-course prix-fixe dinner C$53 (US$37); lunch main courses C$7–$12 (US$4.90–$8.40), dinner main course C$7–$14 (US$4.90–$9.80). AE, MC, V. Wed–Sun 11:30am–1:30pm; Tues–Sat 5–9pm; Sun 5–7pm. After-theater menu Fri–Sat from 9pm. Call for winter hours.

Rundles ℛ INTERNATIONAL   Rundles provides a premier dining experience in a serene dining room overlooking the river. Proprietor Jim Morris eats, sleeps, thinks, and dreams food, and chef Neil Baxter delivers the exciting, exquisite cuisine to the table. The prix-fixe dinner offers palate-pleasing flavor combinations. Appetizers might include shaved fennel, arugula, artichoke, and Parmesan salad or warm seared Québec foie gras. Among the five main dishes might be poached Atlantic salmon garnished with Jerusalem artichokes, wilted arugula, and yellow peppers in a light carrot sauce, or pink roast rib-eye of lamb with ratatouille and rosemary aioli. My dessert choice would be glazed lemon tart and orange sorbet, but hot mango tart with pineapple sorbet is also a dream.

9 Cobourg St. (©) 519/271-6442. www.rundlesrestaurant.com. Reservations required. 3-course prix-fixe dinner C$59 (US$41). AE, DC, MC, V. Apr–Oct Wed and Sat–Sun 11:30am–1:30pm, Tues 5–7pm, Wed–Sat 5–8:30pm, Sun 5–7pm. Closed Nov–Mar.

INEXPENSIVE

York Street Kitchen ECLECTIC   This small restaurant is a fun, funky spot that serves reasonably priced, high-quality food. You can come here for breakfast burritos and other morning fare, and for lunch sandwiches, which you build yourself by choosing from a list of fillings. In the evenings, expect to find comfort foods like meatloaf and mashed potatoes or barbecued chicken and ribs.

41 York St. (©) 519/273-7041. www.yorkstreetkitchen.com. Reservations not accepted. Main courses C$8–$13 (US$5.60–$9.10). AE, V. Daily Apr to early Oct 8am–8pm; mid-Oct to Mar 8am–3pm. Closed Dec 24–Jan 5.

2 Niagara-on-the-Lake & Niagara Falls

130km (80 miles) SE of Toronto

Only 1½ hours from Toronto, Niagara-on-the-Lake is one of the best-preserved and prettiest 19th-century villages in North America. Handsome clapboard and brick period houses border the tree-lined streets. It's the setting for one of Canada's most famous events, the **Shaw Festival.** The town is the jewel of the **Ontario wine region.**

Less than a half-hour drive from Niagara-on-the-Lake is **Niagara Falls,** which was for decades the region's honeymoon capital (I say this in an attempt to explain its endless motels—each with at least one suite that has a heart-shaped pink bed). While the falls are a majestic sight, I have my reservations about the town, especially since the casino opened. My advice would be to stay at an inn in Niagara-on-the-Lake and come to Niagara Falls for a day trip. By the way, the drive along the **Niagara Parkway** is a delight: With its endless parks and gardens, it's an oasis for nature-lovers. (See "Along the Niagara Parkway," below.)

ESSENTIALS

VISITOR INFORMATION   The **Niagara-on-the-Lake Chamber of Commerce,** 153 King St. (P.O. Box 1043), Niagara-on-the-Lake, ON L0S 1J0 (© **905/468-4263;** www.niagara-on-the-lake.com/visit.html), provides information and can help you find accommodations. It's open Monday through Friday from 9am to 5pm, and Saturday and Sunday from 10am to 5pm.

For Niagara Falls travel information, contact **Niagara Falls Tourism** at (© **800/56-FALLS;** www.discoverniagara.com), or the **Niagara Parks Commission,** Box 150, 7400 Portage Rd. S., Niagara Falls, ON L2E 6T2 (© **905/ 356-2241;** www.niagaraparks.com). **Information centers** are open daily in summer from 9am to 6pm at Table Rock House and the Maid of the Mist Plaza.

GETTING THERE   Niagara-on-the-Lake is best seen by **car.** From Toronto, take the Queen Elizabeth Way (signs read QEW) to Niagara via Hamilton and St. Catharines, and exit at Highway 55. The trip takes about 1½ hours.

Amtrak and **VIA** (© **416/366-8411**) operate **trains** between Toronto and New York, but they only stop in Niagara Falls and St. Catharine's, not Niagara-on-the-Lake. Call © **800/361-1235** in Canada or **800/USA-RAIL** in the United States. From either place, you'll need to rent a car. Rental outlets in St. Catharines include **National Tilden,** 162 Church St. (© **905/682-8611**), and

Hertz, 404 Ontario St. (© 905/682-8695). In Niagara Falls, National Tilden is at 4523 Drummond Rd. (© 905/374-6700).

THE SHAW FESTIVAL

The Shaw celebrates the dramatic and comedic works of George Bernard Shaw and his contemporaries. From April to October, the festival offers a dozen plays in the historic Court House, the exquisite Shaw Festival Theatre, and the Royal George Theatre. Some recent performances have included *Hay Fever, The House of Bernarda Alba, Chaplin,* and Shaw's *Caesar and Cleopatra.*

Free chamber concerts take place Sunday at 11am. Chats introduce performances on Friday evenings in July and August, and question-and-answer sessions follow Tuesday evening performances.

The Shaw announces its festival program in mid-January. Tickets are difficult to obtain on short notice, so book in advance. Prices range from C$26 to $75 (US$18–$53). For more information, contact the Shaw Festival, P.O. Box 774, Niagara-on-the-Lake, ON L0S 1J0 (© 800/511-7429 or 905/468-2172; www.shawfest.com).

EXPLORING THE TOWN

Niagara-on-the Lake is small, and most of its attractions are along one main street, making it easy to explore on foot.

Touring Niagara-on-the-Lake Wineries

Visiting a local winery is one of the loveliest (and tastiest) ways to pass an hour or two in this region. For maps of the area and information about vintners, contact the Wine Council of Ontario, 110 Hanover Dr., Suite B-205, St. Catharines, ON L2W 1A4 (© 888/5-WINERY or 905/684-8070; www.wineroute.com). The wineries listed below are close to the town of Niagara-on-the-Lake. Tours are free. Prices for tastings vary with the winery and the wine you're sampling, and usually run C$3 to $10 (US$2.10–$7).

Take Highway 55 (Niagara Stone Rd.) out of Niagara-on-the-Lake, and you'll come to Hillebrand Estates Winery (© 905/468-7123; www.hillebrand.com), just outside Virgil. It's open year-round, plays host to a variety of special events (including a weekend concert series), and even offers bicycle tours. Hillebrand's Vineyard Café, with views of both the barrel-filled cellar and the Niagara Escarpment, is a delightful spot for lunch or dinner. Winery tours start on the hour daily from 10am to 6pm.

If you turn off Highway 55 and go down York Road, you'll reach Château des Charmes, west of St. David's (© 905/262-5202; www.chateaudescharmes.com). The winery was built to resemble a French manor house, and its architecture is unique in the region. One-hour tours are given daily. Open from 10am to 6pm year-round.

To reach the Konzelmann Winery, 1096 Lakeshore Rd. (© 905/935-2866; www.konzelmannwines.com), take Mary Street out of Niagara-on-the-Lake. This vintner is famous for its award-winning ice wines. It offers tours from May to late September, Monday through Saturday.

Niagara-on-the-Lake

Niagara River

Niagara Parkway

Lake Ontario

Melville St.

Ball St. St.

Wellington St.

Delatre St.

Ricardo St.

Byron St.

Picton St.

Davy

Platoff St.

St.

Castlereagh St.

Nelles St.

King St.

Regent St.

Victoria St.

Gage St.

Centre St.

Gate St.

Anne St.

John St.

Mary St.

William St.

Front St.

Prideaux St.

Queen St.

Johnson St.

Simcoe St.

Mississauga St.

Butler St.

Dorchester St.

TORONTO
Lake Ontario
Niagara-on-the-Lake
USA
CANADA
Hamilton
Niagara Falls

20 mi
20 km

1/4 mi
0.25 km

ACCOMMODATIONS ■
Gate House Hotel **3**
Moffat Inn **17**
Oban Inn **1**
The Old Bank House **15**
Pillar & Post Inn **7**
Prince of Wales Hotel **16**
Queen's Landing Inn **19**

DINING ◆
The Buttery **14**
Fans Court **2**
Ristorante Giardino **3**

ATTRACTIONS & SHOPPING ●
Court House/Court House Theatre **9**
Fort George National Historic Park **20**
Greaves Jam **6**
Loyalist Village **12**
Maple Leaf Fudge **11**
Niagara Apothecary Shop **13**
Niagara Historical Society Museum **8**
The Owl & the Pussycat **10**
Royal George Theatre **4**
Shaw Festival Theatre **18**
Shaw Shop **5**

SIGHTS

Fort George National Historic Park ✿ It's easy to imagine taking shelter behind Fort George's stockade fence and watching for the enemy from across the river—even though today there are only condominiums on the opposite riverbank.

The fort played a key role in the War of 1812, before the Americans invaded and destroyed it in May 1813. Although rebuilt by 1815, it was abandoned in 1828 and not reconstructed until the 1930s. You can view the guardroom (with its hard plank beds), the officers' quarters, the enlisted men's quarters, and the sentry posts. The self-guided tour includes interpretive films. Those who believe in ghosts, take note: The fort is one of Ontario's favorite "haunted" sites.

Niagara Pkwy. 📞 **905/468-6614.** Admission C$6 (US$4.20) adults, C$5 (US$3.50) seniors, C$4 (US$2.80) children 6–16, free for children 5 and under, C$20 ($14) family (2 adults, 2 children). Apr 1–Oct 31 Daily 10am–5pm.

Niagara Historical Society Museum More than 20,000 artifacts pertaining to local history make up this collection. They include many possessions of United Empire Loyalists who first settled the area at the end of the American Revolution. It's interesting, but then again I'm a history geek. If you're like me, allow 1½ hours for your visit.

43 Castlereagh St. (at Davy). 📞 **905/468-3912.** Admission C$6 (US$4.20) adults, C$4 (US$2.80) seniors, C$3 (US$2.10) students with ID, C$1 (US70¢) children 5–12. May–Oct daily 10am–5pm; Mar–Apr and Nov–Dec daily 1–5pm; Jan–Feb Sat–Sun 1–5pm.

A NOSTALGIC SHOPPING STROLL

A stroll along the town's main artery, Queen Street, will take you by some entertaining, albeit touristy, shops. The **Niagara Apothecary Shop,** at no. 5 (📞 **905/ 468-3845**), dates to 1866. Gold-leaf script marks its original black-walnut counters and the contents of the drawers, and the original glass and ceramic apothecary ware is on display. **Loyalist Village,** no. 12 (📞 **905/468-7331**), stocks Canadian clothes and crafts, including Inuit art, native Canadian decoys, and sheepskins. **Maple Leaf Fudge,** no. 14 (📞 **905/468-2211**), offers more than 20 varieties that you can watch being made on marble slabs. At no. 16 is a charming toy store, **The Owl and the Pussycat** (📞 **905/468-3081**). At no. 35 is **Greaves Jam** (📞 **905/ 468-7331**), run by fourth-generation jam makers. The **Shaw Shop** (📞 **800/511-7429**), no. 79, next to the Royal George Theatre, carries GBS memorabilia and more. There's also a Dansk outlet and several galleries selling contemporary Canadian and other ethnic crafts.

JET-BOATING THRILLS

Jet boat excursions leave from the dock across from 61 Melville St. at the King George III Inn. Don a rain suit, poncho, and life jacket, and climb aboard. The boat takes you out onto the Niagara River for a trip along the stonewalled canyon to the whirlpool downriver. The ride starts slow but gets into turbulent water. Trips, which operate from May to October, last an hour and cost C$54 (US$38) for adults, and C$44 (US$31) for children 13 and under. Reservations are required. Call the **Whirlpool Jet Boat Company** at 📞 **888/438-4444** or 905/468-4800, or visit www.whirlpooljet.com.

WHERE TO STAY

In summer, hotel space is in high demand, but don't despair if you're having trouble nailing down a room. Contact the Chamber of Commerce, which provides an accommodations-reservations service. Note that several of the hotels in town are owed by the same company, Vintage Inns (the company is famous for buying upscale properties and making them even more luxurious). However, there are 120 bed-and-breakfasts around town to choose from, too. The **Niagara-on-the-Lake Chamber of Commerce** (© **905/468-4263;** www.niagara-on-the-lake.com/visit.html) provides information about them and can help you find a place to stay.

IN TOWN
Expensive

Gate House Hotel *𝒢* Unlike many of the Canadiana-influenced lodgings in town, the Gate House Hotel is decorated in cool, clean-lined Milanese style. Guest rooms have a marbleized look, accented with ultramodern black lamps, block marble tables, leatherette couches, and bathrooms with sleek Italian fixtures. The effect is quite glamorous. Ristorante Giardino, one of the best places to dine in town, is in the hotel.

142 Queen St. (P.O. Box 1364), Niagara-on-the-Lake, ON L0S 1J0. © 905/468-3263. www.gatehouse-niagara. com. 10 units. C$170–$185 (US$119–$130) double. AE, MC, V. Free parking. **Amenities:** Restaurant; concierge. *In room:* A/C, TV, hair dryer.

Oban Inn *𝒢* In a prime location overlooking the lake, the Oban Inn is a lovely place to stay. It's in a charming white Victorian house with a green dormer-style roof and windows, plus a large veranda. (The house is a re-creation of the original 1824 structure, which burned down in 1992.) The gorgeous gardens are the source of the bouquets throughout the house. Downstairs is a piano bar with leather Windsor-style chairs and a fireplace.

Each of the comfortable rooms is unique. They are furnished with antique reproductions—cornhusk four-poster beds with candlewick spreads, ginger-jar lamps, and club-style sofas. It's all very homey and old-fashioned. Note that the inn no longer allows pets in the rooms.

160 Front St. (at Gate St.), Niagara-on-the-Lake, ON L0S 1J0. © 888/669-5566 or 905/468-2165. www.vintage inns.com. 22 units. From C$195 (US$137) double. Packages available. AE, DC, DISC, MC, V. Free parking. **Amenities:** Piano bar; lounge; access to nearby health club; bike rental; babysitting. *In room:* A/C, TV, dataport, hair dryer, iron.

Pillar & Post Inn The discreetly elegant Pillar & Post is a couple of blocks from the maddening crowds on Queen Street. In recent years it has been transformed into one of the most sophisticated accommodations in town, complete with a spa that offers the latest in deluxe treatments and a Japanese-style warm mineral-spring pool, complete with cascading waterfall (spa packages are available). The light, airy lobby boasts a fireplace, lush plantings, and comfortable seating. The style is classic Canadiana: The spacious rooms all contain old-fashioned furniture, Windsor-style chairs, a pine cabinet (with a color TV tucked inside), and historical engravings. In the back, there's a secluded pool. Some rooms facing the outdoor pool on the ground level have bay windows and window boxes.

48 John St. (at King St.), Niagara-on-the-Lake, ON L0S 1J0. © 888/669-5566 or 905/468-2123. Fax 905/ 468-1472. www.vintageinns.com. 123 units. From C$235 (US$165) double; from C$405 (US$284) suite. AE, DC, MC, V. Free parking. Pets accepted. **Amenities:** 2 dining rooms; wine bar; indoor pool; outdoor pool; spa; Jacuzzi; sauna; bike rental; children's programs; concierge; business center; dry cleaning. *In room:* A/C, TV, dataport, minibar, hair dryer, safe.

Prince of Wales Hotel *𝒢𝒢* The Prince of Wales is the most luxurious hotel in the district. This place has it all: a central location across from the lovely gardens of Simcoe Park; full recreational facilities, including an indoor pool;

lounges, bars, and restaurants; and attractive rooms, beautifully decorated with antiques or reproductions. It has a lively atmosphere yet retains the elegance and charm of a Victorian inn. Bathrooms have bidets, and most rooms have mini-bars. The hotel's original section was built in 1864; in 1999, the hotel was renovated and restored to its original glory. All rooms are nonsmoking.

6 Picton St., Niagara-on-the-Lake, ON L0S 1J0. © 888/669-5566 or 905/468-3246. Fax 905/468-5521. www. vintageinns.com. 114 units. From C$295 (US$207) double. Packages available. AE, DC, DISC, MC, V. Valet parking C$5 (US$3.50), free self-parking. Pets accepted. **Amenities:** Dining room; cafe; bar; lounge; indoor pool; health club; spa; Jacuzzi; bike rental; concierge; business center; 24-hr. room service; massage; dry cleaning. *In room:* A/C, TV, dataport, hair dryer, iron.

Queen's Landing Inn Overlooking the river and within walking distance of the theaters, the Queen's Landing Inn is a modern, Georgian-style mansion. Half the rooms have fireplaces, and 32 contain fireplaces and Jacuzzis. The spacious rooms are comfortably furnished with half-canopy or brass beds, wingback chairs, and large desks. This hotel attracts a business-oriented crowd, in part because of its excellent conference facilities, which include 20 meeting rooms.

155 Byron St., at Melville St., (P.O. Box 1180), Niagara-on-the-Lake, ON L0S 1J0. © 888/669-5566 or 905/ 468-2195. www.vintageinns.com. 144 units. From C$235 (US$165) double; from C$405 (US$284) suite. AE, DC, DISC, MC, V. Free parking. **Amenities:** Dining room; lounge; indoor pool; health club; Jacuzzi; sauna; bike rental; concierge; business center; 24-hr.room service; babysitting; dry cleaning. *In room:* A/C, TV, dataport, minibar, hair dryer, iron, safe.

White Oaks Conference Resort & Spa 🏈 Not far from Niagara-on-the-Lake, White Oaks is a sports enthusiast's paradise. Across from the resort is the Royal Niagara golf course, which consists of three 9-hole courses that are meant to be played in combinations (it's like having three different 18-hole courses). In 2000, the resort added a full-service luxury spa, which has become one of its main attractions. It's entirely possible to arrive here, be caught in a flurry of athletic activity all weekend, and not set foot outside the resort. The rooms are as good as the facilities, with oak furniture, vanity sinks, and niceties like a phone in the bathroom. Suites have brick fireplaces, marble-top desks, Jacuzzis (some heart-shaped), and bidets. All of the guest rooms have been soundproofed.

The long list of spa treatments for men and women includes facials, massages, body wraps, and manicures. Some of the less orthodox therapies include reiki (a Japanese massage to "align your energy field"), and Danse de la Mains, a massage choreographed to music and performed by two therapists.

Taylor Rd., Niagara-on-the-Lake, ON L0S 1J0. © 800/263-5766 or 905/688-2550. Fax 905/688-2220. www. whiteoaksresort.com. 220 units. July–Aug from C$160 (US$112) double; C$190 (US$133) suite. Off-season discounts available. AE, DC, MC, V. Free parking. From QEW, exit at Glendale Ave. **Amenities:** Restaurant/wine bar; outdoor terrace cafe; coffee shop; 8 tennis courts; 5 squash courts; 2 racquetball courts; health club; spa; sauna; bike rental; children's center; concierge; business center; massage. *In room:* A/C, TV, dataport, hair dryer.

Moderate
Moffat Inn This is a fine choice in a convenient location. Most rooms contain brass-framed beds and furnishings in traditional-style wood, wicker, and bamboo. Each has a teakettle and supplies. Eight rooms have fireplaces. Free coffee is available in the lobby. Smoking is allowed at the bar only.

60 Picton St. (at Queen St.), Niagara-on-the-Lake, ON L0S 1J0. © 905/468-4116. www.moffatinn.com. 22 units. Apr 15–Oct and late Dec C$95–$169 (US$67–$118) double; Nov to mid-Dec and Jan–Apr 14 C$69–$139 (US$48–$97) double. AE, MC, V. Free parking. **Amenities:** Restaurant; bar; access to nearby health club. *In room:* A/C, TV, dataport, coffeemaker, hair dryer.

The Old Bank House ⚅   Beautifully situated down by the river, this two-story Georgian was built in 1817 as the first branch of the Bank of Canada. All of the guest rooms and bathrooms were refurbished and redecorated in 2001. Several tastefully decorated units have private entrances; one is the charming Garden Room, which also has a private trellised deck. Eight units have a refrigerator and coffee or tea supplies. The most expensive suite accommodates four in two bedrooms. The extraordinarily comfortable sitting room (open to all guests) holds a fireplace and eclectic antique pieces.

10 Front St. (P.O. Box 1708), Niagara-on-the-Lake, ON L0S 1J0. ℂ **877-468-7136** or 905/468-7136; www.old bankhouse.com. 9 units. C$125–$195 (US$88–$137) double; C$230 (US$161) 2-bedroom suite. Rates include breakfast. AE, MC, V. Free parking. **Amenities:** Jacuzzi. *In room:* A/C, no phone.

ALONG THE WINE ROAD
Inn on the Twenty ⚅   In the village of Jordan, about 30km (18 miles) from Niagara-on-the-Lake, this modern accommodation consists entirely of handsome suites. Each has an elegantly furnished living room with a fireplace, and a Jacuzzi in the bathroom. Seven are duplexes—one of them, the deluxe loft, has two double beds on its second level—and five are single-level suites with high ceilings. All of the suites are non-smoking. The inn's eatery, On the Twenty Restaurant & Wine Bar (p. 235), is across the street.

3845 Main St., Jordan, ON L0R 1S0. ℂ **800/701-8074** or 905/562-5336. www.innonthetwenty.com. 30 units. From C$221 (US$155) suite. AE, DC, MC, V. Free parking. From QEW, take Jordan Rd. exit south; at first intersection, turn right onto 4th Ave., then right onto Main St. **Amenities:** Restaurant; nearby golf course; health club; concierge. *In room:* A/C, TV, dataport, coffeemaker, hair dryer, iron.

WHERE TO DINE
IN TOWN
In addition to the listings below, don't forget the dining rooms at the **Pillar & Post, Queen's Landing,** and the **Prince of Wales,** all listed above.

The stylish **Shaw Cafe and Wine Bar,** 92 Queen St. (ℂ **905/468-4772**), serves lunch and light meals, and has a patio. The **Epicurean,** 84 Queen St. (ℂ **905/468-3408**), offers hearty soups, quiches, sandwiches, and other fine dishes in a sunny Provence-inspired dining room. Service is cafeteria style. Half a block off Queen Street, the **Angel Inn,** 224 Regent St. (ℂ **905/468-3411**), is a delightfully authentic English pub. For an inexpensive down-home breakfast, go to the **Stagecoach Family Restaurant,** 45 Queen St. (ℂ **905/468-3133**). It also serves basic family fare, such as burgers, fries, and meatloaf, but doesn't accept credit cards. **Niagara Home Bakery,** 66 Queen St. (ℂ **905/468-3431**), is the place to stop for chocolate-date squares, cherry squares, croissants, cookies, and individual quiches.

The Buttery CANADIAN/ENGLISH/CONTINENTAL   The Buttery has been a dining landmark for years. At its weekend Henry VIII feasts, "serving wenches" bring food and wine while "jongleurs" and "musickers" entertain. The meal consists of "four removes"—courses involving broth, chicken, roast lamb, roast pig, sherry trifle, syllabub, and cheese, all washed down with a goodly amount of wine, ale, and mead.

The tavern menu features spareribs, 8-ounce New York strip, shrimp in garlic sauce, and such English pub fare as lamb curry and steak, kidney, and mushroom pie. On the dinner menu, I highly recommend rack of lamb or shrimp curry. Finish with mud pie or Grand Marnier chocolate cheesecake. You can take home fresh baked goods—pies, strudels, dumplings, cream puffs, or scones.

19 Queen St. ✆ **905/468-2564**. Reservations strongly recommended; required for Henry VIII feast. Henry VIII feast C$49 (US$34); tavern main courses (available Tues–Sun 11am–5pm, all day Mon) C$8–$15 (US$5.60–$11); dinner main courses C$14–$22 (US$9.80–$15). MC, V. Apr–Nov daily 11am–11pm; Dec–Mar Sun–Thurs 11am–7:30pm. Afternoon tea year-round daily 2–5pm.

Fans Court CHINESE   This comfortable spot, decorated with fans, cushioned bamboo chairs, and round tables spread with golden tablecloths, serves some of the best food in town. In summer, there's outdoor dining in the courtyard. The cuisine is primarily Cantonese and Szechwan. The menu includes Singapore beef, moo shu pork, Szechwan scallops, and lemon chicken.

135 Queen St. ✆ **905/468-4511**. Reservations recommended. Main courses C$13–$20 (US$9.10–$14). AE, MC, V. Tues–Sun noon–9pm.

Ristorante Giardino ✿ NORTHERN ITALIAN   On the ground floor of the Gate House Hotel is this sleek, ultramodern restaurant, with a gleaming marble-top bar and brass accents throughout. The food is Northern Italian with fresh American accents. Main courses might include baked salmon seasoned with olive paste and tomato concasse, veal tenderloin marinated with garlic and rosemary, and braised pheasant in juniper-berry-and-vegetable sauce. There are several pasta dishes, plus such appealing appetizers as medallions of langostine garnished with orange and fennel salad. Desserts include a fine tiramisu, and panna cotta with seasonal berries.

In the Gate House Hotel, 142 Queen St. ✆ **905/468-3263**. www.gatehouse-niagara.com. Main courses C$25–$40 (US$18–$28). AE, MC, V. May–Sept daily 11:30am–2:30pm and 5–10pm; Oct–Apr daily 5:30–9pm.

IN NEARBY VIRGIL, ST. CATHARINES & WELLAND

Café Garibaldi ✿ ITALIAN   This relaxed spot is a favorite among locals. It serves Italian staples such as zuppa di pesce and veal scalloppine; homemade lasagna is the most requested dish. The wine list features the local vintners' goods and some fine bottles from Italy.

375 St. Paul St., St. Catharines. ✆ **905/988-9033**. Reservations recommended for dinner. Main courses C$13–$27 (US$9.10–$19). AE, DC, MC, V. Tues–Sat 11:30am–2:30pm and 5–10pm. From QEW, exit at Ontario St., follow DOWNTOWN sign to St. Paul St. and turn left.

Hennepin's CONTEMPORARY   The region's first tapas bar, Hennepin's still stands out. The dining rooms display the works of local artists. The specialty of the house is Mediterranean- and Asian-inspired tapas—coconut shrimp, olive-stuffed meatballs, chicken satay, samosas—which are served all day. At dinner, starters always include such temptations as escargots in Pernod, and pan-seared game pâté with blueberry kirsch sauce. Game and serious meats dominate the main courses— venison bordelaise, liver in chausseur sauce, steak, and pork tenderloin with porto-bello Calvados sauce. The desserts are seriously rich—try the death by chocolate cake. The wine list is extensive; 28 selections are available by the glass.

1486 Niagara Stone Rd. (Hwy. 55), at Creek Rd., Virgil. ✆ **905/468-1555**. Tapas C$4–$8 (US$2.80–$5.60); main courses C$15–$28 (US$11–$20). AE, MC, V. Sun–Wed 11:30am–9pm; Fri–Sat 11:30am–11pm. From QEW, exit at York Rd., turn left, follow to Niagara Stone Rd., turn right.

Iseya ✿ JAPANESE   Chef Yasutoshi Hachoitori has had a virtual monopoly since he opened this eatery: Iseya is one of the region's few traditional Japanese restaurants. The restaurant attracts locals as well as out-of-towners. It serves fresh sushi and sashimi as well as teriyaki, tempura, and sukiyaki dishes. The classic Japanese cuisine doesn't offer a lot of surprises, but everything is beautifully done.

22 James St. (between St. Paul and King sts.), St. Catharines. ℭ **905/688-1141.** Reservations recommended for dinner. Main courses C$12–$27 (US$8.40–$19). AE, MC, V. Mon–Fri 11:30am–2:30pm; Mon–Sat 5–11pm. From QEW, exit at St. Paul St., turn right, follow to St. James St., turn right.

Rinderlin's CONTINENTAL   An intimate town-house restaurant, Rinderlin's has evolved from a traditional French restaurant to one with a Continental flair. On the dinner menu, you might find sautéed shrimps and scallops in medium-hot curry sauce on a bed of basmati rice; roast pork tenderloin with honey-mustard-bacon sauce; herb polenta with grilled bell pepper, eggplant and zucchini; and local venison with wild mushrooms and game sauce. There are also several vegetarian options. Desserts are seasonal—one favorite is the white chocolate torte flavored with brandy and served with raspberry sauce.

24 Burgar St., Welland. ℭ **905/735-4411.** Reservations recommended. Main courses C$21–$30 (US$15–$21). AE, DC, MC, V. Mon–Fri 11:30am–1:30pm; daily 6–8pm. From QEW, take Hwy. 406 to Burgar St. exit, turn left.

Wellington Court Restaurant CONTINENTAL   In an Edwardian town house with a flower trellis, the dining rooms here sport contemporary decor with modern lithographs and photographs. The menu features daily specials along with such items as beef tenderloin in shallot-and-red-wine reduction, roasted breast of chicken on gingered plum preserves, and grilled sea bass with cranberry vinaigrette.

11 Wellington St., St. Catharines. ℭ **905/682-5518.** Reservations recommended. Main courses C$20–$28 (US$14–$20). MC, V. Tues–Sat 11:30am–2:30pm and 5–9:30pm. From QEW, exit at St. Paul St., turn right, follow to Wellington Ave., turn left.

ALONG THE WINE ROAD

Hillebrand's Vineyard Café ⟡ CONTINENTAL   This dining room is light and airy, and its floor-to-ceiling windows offer views over the vineyards to the distant Niagara Escarpment, or of wine cellars bulging with oak barrels. The food is excellent. The seasonal menu might feature such dishes as poached Arctic char with shellfish ragout, or prosciutto-wrapped pheasant breast atop linguine tossed with mushrooms, roasted eggplant, and shallot. The starters are equally luxurious. Try roasted three-peppercorn pear served warm with salad greens, pine nuts, and Parmesan slivers, or spiced goat cheese and grilled portobello "sandwich" with walnuts and endive. My favorite among the irresistible desserts is chocolate tortellini.

Hwy. 55, between Niagara-on-the-Lake and Virgil. ℭ **905/468-7123.** www.hillebrand.com. Main courses C$24–$35 (US$17–$25). AE, MC, V. Daily 11:30am–11pm (closes earlier in winter).

On the Twenty Restaurant & Wine Bar ⟡ CANADIAN   This restaurant is a favorite among foodies. The gold-painted dining rooms cast a warm glow. The cuisine features ingredients from many producers, giving On the Twenty a small-town feel. Naturally, there's an extensive selection of Ontario wines, including some wonderful ice wines to accompany such desserts as lemon tart and fruit cobbler. Inn on the Twenty is associated with the Vintner's Inn (p. 233), across the street.

At Cave Spring Cellars, 3836 Main St., Jordan. ℭ **905/562-7313.** www.innonthetwenty.com. Reservations recommended. Main courses C$22–$40 (US$15–$28). AE, DC, MC, V. Daily 11:30am–3pm and 5–10pm.

Vineland Estates ⟡⟡ CONTINENTAL   This inspired eatery serves some of the most innovative food along the wine trail. On warm days you can dine on a deck under a spreading tree, or stay in the airy dining room. Start with a

plate of seasoned mussels in a ginger broth. Follow with a Canadian Angus tenderloin with a risotto of truffles and morel mushrooms, or go for pan-seared
sweetbreads with a celeriac and potato mash and confit of mushrooms glazed
with ice wine. For dessert, there's a wonderful tasting plate of Canadian farm
cheeses, including Abbey St. Benoit blue Ermite.

3620 Moyer Rd., Vineland. ☎ 888/846-3526 or 905/562-7088. www.vineland.com. Reservations recommended. Main courses C$20–$40 (US$14–$28). AE, MC, V. Daily noon–2:30pm and 5:30–9pm.

ALONG THE NIAGARA PARKWAY ☆

The Niagara Parkway, on the Canadian side of the falls, is a gem. Unlike the
American side, it abounds with natural wonders, including vast expanses of
parkland. You can drive along the 56km (35-mile) parkway all the way from
Niagara-on-the-Lake to Niagara Falls on the parkway, taking in attractions en
route. Here are the major ones, listed in the order that you'll encounter them:

- The **Great Gorge Adventure,** 4330 River Rd. (☎ **905/374-1221**): The scenic boardwalk runs beside the raging white waters of the Great Gorge
  Rapids. Stroll along and wonder how it must have felt to challenge this
  mighty torrent, where the river rushes through the narrow channel at an
  average speed of 35kmph (22 mph). Admission is C$5.75 (US$4) for
  adults, C$2.90 (US$2) for children 6 to 12, free for children 5 and under.

- The **Whirlpool Aero Car** (☎ **905/354-5711**): This red-and-yellow cable-
  car contraption that whisks you on a 1,097m (3,600-ft.) jaunt between two
  points in Canada. High above the Niagara Whirlpool, you'll enjoy excellent
  views of the surrounding landscape. Admission is C$6 (US$4.20) for adults,
  C$3 (US$2.10) for children 6 to 12, free for kids 5 and under. Open daily
  May to the third Sunday in October. Hours are from 9am to 6pm in May,
  9am to 8pm in June, 9am to 9pm in July and August, 10am to 7:30pm in
  September, and 9am to 5pm in October.

- The **School of Horticulture** (☎ **905/356-8119**): Stop here for a free view
  of the vast gardens and a look at the Floral Clock, which contains 25,000
  plants in its 12m-diameter (40-ft.) face. The new **Butterfly Conservatory**
  is also in the gardens. In this lush tropical setting, more than 2,000 butterflies (50 international species) float and flutter among such nectar-produc-
  ing flowers as lantanas and pentas. The large bright blue luminescent
  Morpho butterflies from Central and South America are particularly gorgeous. Interpretive programs and other presentations take place in the audi-
  torium and two smaller theaters. The native butterfly garden outside attracts
  the more familiar swallowtails, fritillaries, and painted ladies. Admission is
  C$8.50 (US$5.95) for adults, C$4 (US$2.80) for children 6 to 12, free for
  children 5 and under. The school opens at 9am daily. It closes at 8pm in
  May and June; 9pm in July and August; 6pm in March, April, September,
  and October; and 5pm from November through February. It's closed
  December 25.

- **Queenston Heights Park:** This is the site of a famous War of 1812 battle,
  and you can take a walking tour of the battlefield. Picnic or play tennis (for
  C$6/US$4.20 per hour) in the shaded arbor before moving to the **Laura
  Secord Homestead,** Partition Street, Queenston (☎ **905/262-4851**). This
  heroic woman threaded enemy lines to alert British authorities to a surprise
  attack by American soldiers during the War of 1812. Her home contains a
  fine collection of Upper Canada furniture from the period, plus artifacts
  recovered from an archaeological dig. Stop at the candy shop and ice-cream

---

Moments **The Falls by Night**

Don't miss seeing the falls after dark. Twenty-two xenon gas spotlights, each producing 250 million candlepower of light, illuminate them in shades of rose pink, red magenta, amber, blue, and green. Call ℂ **800/563-2557** (in the U.S.) or 905/356-6061 for schedules. The show starts around 5pm in winter, 8:30pm in spring and fall, and 9pm in summer. In addition, from July to early September, free fireworks start at 10pm every Friday.

---

parlor. Tours run every half hour. Admission is C$2 (US$1.40). Open late May through Labour Day daily from 10am to 6pm.

- Fruit farms, like **Kurtz Orchards** (ℂ **905/468-2937**), and wineries such as the **Inniskillin Winery,** Line 3, Service Road 66 (ℂ **905/468-3554** or 905/468-2187): You'll find peaches, apples, pears, nectarines, cherries, plums and strawberries at Kurtz; you can tour the 80 acres on a tractor-pulled tram. Inniskillin is open daily from 10am to 6pm June through October, and Monday through Saturday from 10am to 5pm November through May. The self-guided free tour has 20 stops that explain the wine-making process. A free guided tour, offered daily in summer and Saturday only in winter, begins at 2:30pm.

- **Historic Fort Erie,** 350 Lakeshore Rd., Fort Erie (ℂ **905/871-0540**): It's a reconstruction of the fort that was seized by the Americans in July 1814, besieged later by the British, and finally blown up as the Americans retreated across the river to Buffalo. Guards in period costume stand sentry duty, fire the cannons, and demonstrate drill and musket practice. Open daily from 10am to 6pm from the first Saturday in May to mid-September, and weekends only to Canadian Thanksgiving (U.S. Columbus Day). Admission is C$6.50 (US$4.55) for adults, C$4 (US$2.80) for children 6 to 16, free for children 5 and under.

SEEING NIAGARA FALLS

You simply cannot come this far and not see the falls, which are the seventh natural wonder of the world. The most exciting way to do that is from the decks of the **Maid of the Mist** ⟨⟩, 5920 River Rd. (ℂ **905/358-5781;** www.maid ofthemist.com). The sturdy boat takes you right in—through the turbulent waters around the American Falls, past the Rock of Ages, and to the foot of the Horseshoe Falls, where 34.5 million imperial gallons of water tumble over the 54m-high (176-ft.) cataract each minute. You'll get wet, and your glasses will mist, but that won't detract from the thrill. Boats leave from the dock on the parkway just down from the Rainbow Bridge. Trips operate daily from mid-May to mid-October. Fares are C$13 (US$9.10) for adults, and C$8 (US$5.60) for children 6 to 12, free for children 5 and under.

Go down under the falls using the elevator at Table Rock House, which drops you 46m (150 ft.) through solid rock to the tunnels and viewing portals of the **Journey Behind the Falls** (ℂ **905/354-1551**). You'll receive—and appreciate—a rain poncho. Admission is C$7.50 (US$5.25) for adults, C$3.75 (US$2.60) for children 6 to 12, free for children 5 and under.

You can ride the external glass-fronted elevators 159m (520 ft.) to the top of the **Skylon Tower Observation Deck,** 5200 Robinson St. (ℂ **905/356-2651;** www.skylon.com). The observation deck is open daily from 8am to midnight from June to Labour Day; hours vary in other seasons, so call ahead. Adults pay C$9.50 (US$6.65), seniors C$8.50 (US$5.95), children 12 and under C$5.50 (US$3.85). There is a revolving restaurant here but be warned that it's something of a tourist trap, with a C$20 (US$14) minimum per adult charge at lunch and a C$36.50 (US$26) minimum charge at dinner (there is a separate menu for kids). Also there's a C$2 (US$1.40) per person fee just for the elevator ride to the restaurant. Do the math and you'll see that it adds up to a pretty expensive proposition for a family to eat here.

For a different view of Niagara Falls, stop by the **IMAX Theater,** 6170 Buchanan Ave. (© **905/358-3611;** www.imaxniagara.com). You can view the raging, swirling waters in *Niagara: Miracles, Myths, and Magic,* shown on a six-story-high screen. Admission is C$12 (US$8.40) for adults and students, C$8.50 (US$5.95) for seniors, C$6.50 (US$4.55) for children 4 to 12; free for children 3 and under. I have to say that I consider this a lot of money to pay for a movie that is only 45 minutes long. Still, I'm an IMAX fan, and I have to admit the film looks great.

The falls are also exciting in winter, when the ice bridge and other formations are quite remarkable.

WHERE TO STAY & DINE NEAR THE FALLS

While Niagara-on-the-Lake is a far more scenic and charming option, you may find yourself staying overnight in Niagara Falls. One good hotel bet is the **Sheraton on the Falls,** 5875 Falls Ave. (© **888/229-9961** or 905/374-4445), which offers rooms with a truly gorgeous view; many have balconies. Rates start around

A Family Adventure

If you're looking for something to keep the kiddies amused, visit **MarineLand** 🐾, 7657 Portage Rd. (© **905/356-9565;** www.marineland canada.com). At the aquarium-theater, King Waldorf, the walrus mascot, presides over performances by killer whales, dolphins, and sea lions. Friendship Cove, a 4.5-million-gallon breeding and observation tank, lets the little ones see killer whales up close. Another aquarium features displays of freshwater fish. At the small wildlife display, kids enjoy petting and feeding the deer and seeing bears and Canadian elk.

Marineland also has theme-park rides, including a roller coaster, a Tivoli wheel (a fancy Ferris wheel), and Dragon Boat rides, and a fully equipped playground. The big thriller is Dragon Mountain, a roller coaster that loops, double-loops, and spirals through 305m (1,000 ft.) of tunnels. There are three restaurants, or you can picnic.

In summer, admission is C$33 (US$23) for adults and children 10 and over, C$28 (US$20) for seniors and children 5 to 9, and free for children 4 and under. Open daily July and August from 9am to 6pm; mid-April to mid-May and September to mid-October from 10am to 4pm; and mid-May to June from 10am to 5pm. Closed November through April. Rides open in late May and close the first Monday in October. In town, drive south on Stanley Street and follow the signs; from the QEW, take the McCleod Rd. exit.

Niagara Falls

To Toronto ↑

Thorold Stone Rd.

0   1/2 mi
0   0.5 km

N

Information (i)

Portage Rd.

Stanley Ave.

Victoria Ave.

① Heliport

② To Queenston

③

Whirlpool Bridge

④

Parkway

Bridge St.

Queen St.

420

Kitchener   St.

MacDonald Ave.

River Road

Niagara River

Robert Moses

Lundy's Lane

Buchanan Ave.

Ellen Ave.

Clark St.

Centre St.

Clifton Hill

Falls Ave.

⑤ Casino

⑥ Rainbow Bridge

⑨

Allendale

Robinson   St. ⑦

⑧

Murray St.

Niagara Falls, N.Y.

American Falls ⑩

Foot Bridge

Main St.

Goat Island

Oakes Dr.

(i)

⑪ ⑫

Horseshoe Falls (Canadian Falls)

UNITED STATES
CANADA

Portage Rd.

Fraser Hills

Niagara

⑬

McLeod Rd.

MarineLand Parkway

⑭

Niagara River

Rapids View Parking Lot

Parkway

Rapids Dr.

Stanley Ave.

⑮

MarineLand

Portage Rd.

0   20 mi
0   20 km

N

TORONTO

Lake Ontario

Niagara-on-the-Lake

Hamilton

USA

CANADA

Niagara Falls

To Fort Erie ↓

To Buffalo ↓

⑯ Village of Chippawa

American Falls **10**

Casino **5**

Dufferin Islands **14**

Great Gorge Adventure **3**

Heliport **1**

Horseshoe Falls **12**

IMAX Theater **8**

To King's Bridge Pk. & Fort Erie **16**

Maid of the Mist **9**

MarineLand **15**

Niagara Parks Greenhouse **13**

Rainbow Bridge **6**

Skylon Tower **7**

To Whirlpool Aero Car/
   Golf Club & Butterfly Conservatory **2**

Table Rock House **11**

Whirlpool Bridge **4**

Niagara Parkway Commission Restaurants

The Niagara Parkway Commission has commandeered the most spectacular scenic spots, where it operates reasonably priced dining outlets. They serve traditional family-style food at lunch and dinner, and do not accept reservations. **Table Rock Restaurant** (© **905/354-3631**) and **Victoria Park Restaurant** (© **905/356-2217**), on the parkway right by the falls, are both pleasant, if crowded. **Diner on the Green** (© **905/ 356-7221**) is also on the parkway, at the Whirlpool Golf Course near Queenston. It's very plain.

The star of the Niagara Parkway Commission's eateries is **Queenston Heights**, 14275 Niagara Pkwy. (© **905/262-4274**). Set in the park among firs, cypresses, silver birches, and maples, the open-air balcony affords a magnificent view of the lower Niagara River and the rich fruit-growing land through which it flows. Or you can sit under the cathedral ceiling in a room where the flue of the stone fireplace reaches to the roof. Dinner options might include fillet of Atlantic salmon with Riesling-chive hollandaise, prime rib, or grilled pork with apples and cider–Dijon mustard sauce. Afternoon tea is served from 3 to 5pm in the summer. If nothing else, go for a drink on the deck and enjoy the terrific view.

C$120 (US$84) in the winter and C$200 (US$140) in summer for a double room. If you're more interested in gambling than a view, check out **The Skyline Inn,** 5685 Falls Ave. (© **800/263-7135** or 905/374-4444), which is right by Casino Niagara. Rates here start at C$75 (US$53) per night.

Dining is not one of Niagara Falls' strengths. There are lots of options, but they tend to be overpriced. One interesting option is the **Pinnacle,** 6732 Oakes Dr. (© **905/356-1501**), which offers a Continental menu and a remarkable view from the top of the Minolta Tower. **Casa d'Oro,** 5875 Victoria Ave. (© **905/ 356-5646**), brings a wealth of kitsch (gilt busts of Caesar, Venetian-style lamps, statues of Roman gladiators) with its Italian cooking. **Betty's Restaurant & Tavern,** 8921 Sodom Rd. (© **905/295-4436**), is an inexpensive spot that serves up hearty portions of comfort food.

3 The Muskoka Lakes

Just a 90-minute drive north of Toronto, the Muskoka region has been a magnet for visitors since the 19th century. While the area proved futile for farming (it's located on the Canadian Shield, where you need only dig a foot or two in some places to come up against sheets of granite), its more than 1,600 lakes, unspoiled wilderness and laid-back attitude made it an excellent place for a retreat. In the past decade, Muskoka's charms have expanded to include excellent golf courses, soothing spas and top-notch restaurants. While the region is at its most popular in summer, when families congregate at the resorts and Hollywood celebrities like Goldie Hawn and Tom Hanks lounge at their lakefront "cottages," this is a great area to visit at any time of the year.

Once accessible only by the water, Muskoka is still a boater's dream. The region also has several towns of note: Gravenhurst, Bracebridge, Port Carling,

Huntsville and Bala. Located a few kilometers apart, these communities date back to the 1850s, when logging was Muskoka's primary industry. Filled with historic sites and more modern attractions, it's well worth devoting a day or two to explore them (fortunately, they are all easily reachable by car these days).

ESSENTIALS

GETTING THERE   You can drive from the south via Highway 400 to Highway 11, from the east via highways 12 and 169 to Highway 11, and from the north via Highway 11. It's about 160km (100 miles) from Toronto to Gravenhurst, 15km (9 miles) from Gravenhurst to Bracebridge, 25km (15½ miles) from Bracebridge to Port Carling, and 34km (21 miles) from Bracebridge to Huntsville. **VIA Rail** (*©* **416/366-8411;** www.viarail.ca) services Gravenhurst, Bracebridge, and Huntsville from Toronto's Union Station. There is also an airport about 18km (11 miles) from Gravenhurst, which is used mainly for small aircraft. There are several other landing strips, and a helicopter-landing pad at the Deerhurst Resort in Huntsville.

VISITOR INFORMATION   For information on the region, contact **Muskoka Tourism,** on Highway 11 at Severn Bridge, RR #2, Kilworthy, ON, P0E 1G0 (*©* **800/267-9700** or 705/689-0660; www.muskoka-tourism.on.ca).

GETTING AROUND   While you won't need a car if you plan to stay close to your resort while you're here (an entirely reasonable proposition), you will need a car if you're planning to do a lot of sightseeing in the area. You could take the train to Bracebridge, then rent a car at **Budget,** 1 Robert Dollar Dr. (© **705/ 645-2755**). There's also a **National** car rental center in Huntsville on Howland Dr. (© **705/787-1111**).

EXPLORING THE TOWNS

Both Gravenhurst and Huntsville are lovely towns that are well worth a visit. They are scenic but they also have enough shops, restaurants, and public spaces to make them interesting. Unless you have kids, there's not much of a reason to linger in Bracebridge.

GRAVENHURST

Gravenhurst is Muskoka's first town—the first you reach if you're driving from Toronto and the first to achieve town status (in 1887 at the height of the logging boom).

The **Norman Bethune Memorial House** is the restored 1890 birthplace of Dr. Norman Bethune, 235 John St. N. (© **705/687-4261**). In 1939, this surgeon, inventor, and humanitarian died tending the sick in China during the Chinese Revolution. Tours of the historic house include a modern exhibit on Bethune's life. A visitor center displays gifts from Chinese visitors and an orientation video is shown. In summer, the house is open daily from 10am to noon and from 1 to 5pm (weekdays only in winter). Admission is C$3.50 (US$2.45) adults and C$2 (US$1.40) for children 6 to 16; free for children 5 and under.

Sailing is one of Muskoka's greatest summer pleasures. Gravenhurst is home to the Muskoka Fleet, which includes a lovingly restored coal-powered 1887 steamship, the **RMS *Segwun.*** There are a variety of cruising options available, such as the 1-hour tour (C$11.50/US$8.05 adults, C$7.25/US$5.10 children), a 2-½-hour lunch cruise (C$44/US$30 adults, C$28/$19 children), and a 4-hour late-afternoon tour of **Millionaire's Row** (C$36/US$25 adults, $30/US$21 children), where you can be dazzled by the real estate as well as the natural beauty of the region. Advance reservations are required for all of the tours; call © **705/687-6667** or visit www.muskokafleet.com for more information.

Year-round, there are theater performances at the **Gravenhurst Opera House** (© **705/687-5550**), which celebrates its 103rd anniversary in 2004. In summer only, there are shows at the **Port Carling Community Hall** (© **705/765-5221**). For either, tickets usually cost between C$15 and C$30 (US$11–$21).

BRACEBRIDGE: SANTA'S WORKSHOP

Halfway between the equator and the North Pole, **Bracebridge** bills itself as Santa's summer home, and **Santa's Village** (© **705/645-2512;** www.santasvillage. ca) is an imaginatively designed fantasyland full of delights: pedal boats and bumper boats on the lagoon, a roller-coaster sleigh ride, a Candy Cane Express, a carousel, and a Ferris wheel. At Elves' Island, kids can crawl on a suspended net and over or through various modules—the Lunch Bag Forest, Cave Crawl, and Snake Tube Crawl. Rides, water attractions, and roving entertainers are all part of the fun. Mid-June through Labour Day, it's open daily from 10am to 6pm. Admission is C$17 (US$12) ages 5 and up and C$12 (US$8) for seniors and children 2 to 4; free for children under 2.

PORT CARLING

As waterways became the main means of transportation in the region, **Port Carling** grew into the hub of the lakes. It became a boat-building center when a lock was installed connecting Lakes Muskoka and Rosseau, and a canal between Lakes Rosseau and Joseph opened all three to navigation. The **Muskoka Lakes**

Museum on Joseph Street (© **705/765-5367**) captures the flavor of this era. July and August, it's open Monday through Saturday from 10am to 5pm and Sunday noon to 4pm; June, September, and October, hours are Tuesday through Saturday from 10am to 4pm and Sunday from noon to 4pm. Admission is C$3 (US$2.10) adults and C$2 (US$1.40) seniors and students.

HUNTSVILLE

Since the late 1800s, lumber has been the name of the game in Huntsville, and today it's Muskoka's biggest town, with major manufacturing companies. You can see some of the region's early history at the **Muskoka Heritage Place,** which includes **Muskoka Pioneer Village,** 88 Brunel Rd., Huntsville (© **705/789-7576;** www.muskokaheritageplace.org). It's open daily from 11am to 4pm from mid-May to mid-October. Admission is C$10 (US$7) adults and C$7 (US$4.90) children; children 2 and under are free. Muskoka Heritage Place also features the **Portage Flyer Steam Train.** Once part of the world's smallest commercial railway, it ran from 1904 till 1958. Now it has been reborn as a tourist attraction, and you can ride its scenic route from Tuesday through Saturday for C$5 (US$3.50) for adults and C$3 (US$2.10) for kids.

Robinson's General Store on Main Street in Dorset (© **705/766-2415**) is so popular it was voted Canada's best country store. Wood stoves, dry goods, hardware, pine goods, and moccasins—you name it, it's here.

WHERE TO STAY

Muskoka is famous for its lakes, but its resorts are renowned, too. While I normally like to wander from place to place when I travel to a particular area, I honestly think I could just stay put at one of the resorts here and be completely entertained for a week. There are also bed-and-breakfast and country inn choices aplenty. Contact **Muskoka Tourism** (© **800/267-9700** or 705/689-0660; www.muskoka-tourism.on.ca) or the **Muskoka Bed and Breakfast Association,** 175 Clairmont Rd., Gravenhurst, ON, P1P 1H9 (© **705/687-4511;** www.bbmuskoka.com).

RESORTS

Deerhurst Resort ★★★ *(Kids)*   The Deerhurst first opened its doors to guests in 1896, but its greatest expansion has occurred in the past 2 decades. Even more recently, a C$30 million renovation that ended in late 2002 really enhanced the property. This stunning resort complex now rambles over 800 acres, and it boasts an array of amenities that boggles the mind: two 18-hole golf courses (part of the Muskoka Golf Trail) and a golf academy; a full-service Aveda spa; seemingly endless miles of nature trails for hiking (or snowmobiling or cross-country skiing in winter); canoeing, kayaking, and all manner of water sports; an ambitious musical revue than runs all summer; and horseback riding. (Note that most of the activities, including golf, spa, and skiing, are available to visitors not staying at the resort.)

The accommodations here are spread out among several buildings on the property. They range from high-ceilinged hotel rooms in the Terrace and Bayshore buildings to fully-appointed one-, two-, or three-bedroom suites, many with fireplaces and/or whirlpools. The suites come with all the comforts, including CD players, TVs, and VCRs; some have full kitchens with microwaves, dishwashers, and washer/dryers. The most expensive suites are the three-bedroom units on the lake. One major draw is the top-notch Aveda spa, which has some of the most talented therapists I've ever encountered. The Deerhurst is an excellent spot for a family vacation, though it's also very popular with conference groups. The separate buildings make it easy to cater to cater to each.

1235 Deerhurst Dr., Huntsville, ON, P1H 2E8. (C) 800/461-4393 or 705/789-6411. Fax 705/789-2431. www. deerhurstresort.com. 388 units. Summer, from C$229 (US$160) double and from C$259 (US$181) suite; rest of the year, from C$139 (US$97) double and from C$169 (US$118) suite. AE, DC, DISC, MC, V. Free parking. Take Canal Rd. off Hwy. 60 to Deerhurst Rd. **Amenities:** 2 restaurants; 2 bars; 2 indoor pools, 3 outdoor pools; tennis courts; 2 18-hole golf courses; indoor sports complex, 3 squash courts, racquetball court; 11 Jacuzzi; sauna; spa; concierge; business center; limited room service; children's programs; laundry service; dry cleaning. In room: A/C, TV, dataport, minibar, hair dryer.

Grandview Inn & Resort ⭐ If the Deerhurst is for the folks on the fast track, the Grandview is for those looking for a more measured pace. This smaller resort retains the natural beauty and contours of the original farmstead even while providing the latest resort facilities. Eighty accommodations are traditional hotel-style rooms, but most units are suites in a series of buildings, some down beside the lake and others up on the hill with a lake view. All are spectacularly furnished. Each executive suite contains a kitchen, a dining area, a living room with a fireplace and access to an outside deck, a large bedroom, and a large bathroom with a whirlpool bath. The main dining room, in the old farmhouse, is decorated in paisleys and English chintz and has a patio that overlooks the gardens. Snacks are served in summer at the Dockside Restaurant right on the lake.

RR #4, Huntsville, ON, P0A 1K0. (C) 705/789-4417. Fax 705/789-6882. 200 units. Summer, from C$170 (US$119) double; rest of the year, from C$100 (US$70) double. AE, MC, V. Free parking. **Amenities:** 2 restaurants; indoor pool; outdoor pool; 9-hole golf course; 3 tennis courts; health club. In room: A/C, TV.

Taboo Resort ⭐⭐⭐ (Kids) Located near the town of Gravenhurst in the southern Muskoka region, Taboo stands out for its sleek sophistication in a bucolic setting. Known until May 2003 as Muskoka Sands, the resort's new name may conjure up images of a hedonistic adults-only retreat. The truth is anything but: Taboo is a family-friendly zone, with a kids' club that schedules activities for every day of the week during the high season in summer. But the fact that the resort is so willing to take care of the kiddies means that many adults can soak up spa treatments or dine at one of the on-site restaurants without a second thought.

Taboo is best known for its golf course, which Mike Weir (Canada's top PGA ranked golfer), named his home course in June 2002. The course is a major stop on the Muskoka Golf Trail. There's also the Golf Academy for those who want to improve their game. Another reason to come to Taboo is the excellent dining. The resort has indulged gourmets by creating two entirely different restaurants: Wildfire (p. 246), a serious innovator that pairs up Canadian ingredients and

Fun Fact The Shania Connection

The Deerhurst has many charms to recommend it, and whether or not you stay there you must check out its excellent song-and-dance stage show. Now in its 23rd year, it's famous in part because the phenomenally talented Shania Twain performed in it for 3 years (1988–1990). Twain has kept up her connection with the Deerhurst since, even having her wedding there. In 2002 she brought Katie Couric and a film crew from CNN to reminisce about her days on its stage. Twain continues to visit the resort—and when she does, she always checks out the show. Every summer the show is different, but it is always a pleasure to see.

Asian cooking techniques, and the Winewood, which elegantly serves up and more traditional fare.

One of my favorite things about Taboo is that every single room, large and small alike, has its own deck or balcony. While all of the sophisticated offerings at the resort are excellent, nothing beats taking in the utterly serene and beautiful setting it enjoys.

Muskoka Beach Rd, R.R.#1, Gravenhurst, ON P1P 1R1. © 800/461-0236 or 705/687-2233. Fax 705/687-7474. www.tabooresort.com. 157 units. Summer, from C$295 (US$207) double, from C$410 (US$287) suite; rest of the year, from C$150 (US$105) double, from C$210 (US$147) suite. AE, MC, V. Free parking. **Amenities:** 3 restaurants; bar; 3 outdoor pools, indoor pool; 2 golf courses (18-hole and 9-hole); 5 tennis courts; squash court; health club; sauna; spa (in-room treatments also available); Jacuzzi; children's program; game room; concierge; business center; limited room service; laundry service; dry cleaning. *In room:* A/C, TV, hair dryer.

Tamwood Resort ✷ A great choice for families, Tamwood Lodge is a moderate-size log lodge on Lake Muskoka, 10km (6 miles) west of town. The main lodge has 35 units, all simply but nicely decorated, and there are a few cottages. The four deluxe loft accommodations are stunningly appointed in pine, and each features two bedrooms with skylights, plus a loft area, two baths, an efficiency kitchen, and a living room with a Franklin stove and a balcony from which you can dive into Lake Muskoka. Three new waterfront units come with fireplaces. Knotty-pine furnishings and large granite fireplaces imbue the lounge and main dining room with character. The resort offers a wealth of activities, including fishing, tennis, volleyball, badminton, and shuffleboard, plus free waterskiing and boating, and all the winter sports imaginable. There's also lots of organized family fun, including baseball games, marshmallow roasts, and bingo.

Hwy 118, RR #1, Bracebridge, ON, P1L 1W8. © 800/465-9166 or 705/645-5172. www.tamwoodresort.com. 35 units. From C$180 (US$126) double. MC, V. Free parking. **Amenities:** Indoor pool; nearby golf course; 3 tennis courts; spa; watersports equipment rentals; children's programs; game room. *In room:* A/C, TV, fridge.

Windermere House Resort ✷ The appearance is a little bit deceiving: The Windermere looks like a striking 1870s stone-and-clapboard turreted mansion. In fact, the building was destroyed by fire in 1996 and rebuilt, according to its original design, in 1997. It overlooks well-manicured lawns that sweep down to Lake Rosseau. Out front stretches a broad veranda furnished with Adirondack chairs and geranium-filled window boxes. Rebuilding allowed the guest rooms to enjoy modern conveniences (including air-conditioning), while retaining a traditional, homey look. Most of the rooms have gorgeous views (the best look over the lake), and a few have balconies or walkout decks.

Off Muskoka Rte. 4 (P.O. Box 68), Windermere, ON, P0B 1P0. © 800/461-4283 or 705/769-3611. Fax 705/769-2168. www.windermerehouse.com. 78 units. From C$165 (US$116) per person. Rates include breakfast and dinner. Weekly rates and European Plan (no meals) also available. AE, MC, V. Free parking. **Amenities:** Restaurant; lounge; outdoor pool; tennis courts; golf; children's program; limited room service; laundry service; dry cleaning. *In room:* A/C, TV, minibar.

COUNTRY INNS

Inn at the Falls ✷ This attractive inn occupies a Victorian house on a quiet street overlooking Bracebridge Falls. The inviting gardens are filled with delphiniums, peonies, roses, and spring flowers, plus there's an outdoor heated pool. The guest rooms are individually decorated, with antiques and English chintz. Some units have fireplaces, Jacuzzis, and balconies; others have views of the falls. The Fox and Hounds is a popular local gathering place at lunch or dinner. In winter, the fire crackles and snaps, but in summer the terrace is filled with flowers and umbrella-shaded tables. The more elegant Victoria's serves upscale Continental fare.

1 Dominion St., P.O. Box 1139, Bracebridge, ON, P1L 1V3. © **877/645-9212** or 705/645-2245. Fax 705/645-5093. www.innatthefalls.net. 42 units. From C$90 (US$63) double; from C$195 (US$137) suite. Rates include breakfast. AE, DC, MC, V. Free parking. **Amenities:** 2 restaurants; outdoor pool; nearby golf course. *In room:* TV.

Severn River Inn   The Severn River Inn (19km/12 miles north of Orillia and 14km/9 miles south of Gravenhurst) occupies a 1906 building that has served as a general store, post office, telephone exchange, and boardinghouse. The guest rooms, which were refurbished in 2001, are individually furnished with pine and oak pieces, brass beds, flounce pillows, lace curtains, and quilts. The suite contains a sitting room and the original old bathtub and pedestal sink (this is the only room with a bathtub—the others all have showers only). The intimate restaurant, with a Victorian ambience, is candlelit at night. In summer, the screened-in porch and outdoor patio overlooking the river are favored dining spots. The menu features contemporary Continental cuisine.

Cowbell Lane off Hwy. 11 (P.O. Box 100), Severn Bridge, ON, P0E 1N0. © **705/689-6333.** Fax 705/689-2691. www.severnriverinn.com. 10 units. C$70–90 (US$49–$63) double; C$120–$200 (US$84–$140) suite. Rates include breakfast. MC, V. Free parking. **Amenities:** Restaurant; lounge; nearby golf course. *In room:* A/C.

WHERE TO DINE
VERY EXPENSIVE
Wildfire ★★★ *Finds* FUSION/INTERNATIONAL   It's strange to think that some Torontoans are coming to Muskoka to eat, given the big city's impressive culinary pedigree. But chef Michael Pataran has cooked at two of Toronto's best kitchens—Monsoon (p. 86) and Rain (p. 89)—so perhaps it's no wonder that this elegant and dramatic new restaurant is attracting gourmets from far and wide. Wildfire does have an a la carte menu, but roughly two-thirds of its diners choose one of the chef's "Faith" tasting menus. These 4-, 5-, and 11-course experiences put in the diner completely in the chef's capable hands: They don't list the beautifully presented dishes, in part because Pataran believes people shouldn't make blanket statements like "I don't eat seafood." Think that you could never enjoy caribou, salmon tartare, or eel? Think again, because it's almost impossible to resist these culinary masterpieces. Rest assured, you'll love 'em all. The restaurant's floor-to-ceiling windows face west, so that you can taste in the glorious sunset over the lake.

Muskoka Beach Rd., R.R.#1, Gravenhurst, ON P1P 1R1. © **705/687-2233.** www.tabooresort.com. Reservations strongly recommended. Main courses C$29–$41 (US$20–$29); tasting menus start at C$80 (US$56). AE, DC, MC, V. Daily 6–10pm.

EXPENSIVE
Ellipsis ★★ CANADIAN/INTERNATIONAL   Recently renovated and remodeled, Ellipsis remains a Muskoka favorite. With an expansive lake view, this spacious dining room with a soaring ceiling of Douglas fir beams is a blend of fine dining and casual Muskoka charm. Open for breakfast, lunch and dinner, the restaurant has a lengthy menu, so it's relatively easy to please different tastes; there are also many vegetarian options. My favorite appetizer is the baked phyllo pastry filled with forest mushrooms and goat cheese, but the Sizzle—the signature dish— is the most popular (tiger shrimp sautéed in garlic, dried chiles and white wine and baked under mozzarella). Entrees run the gamut from breast of pheasant filled with wild rice and cranberries, to a rack of lamb rubbed with fresh herbs and sourdough crumbs and served with apple-maple compote. The wine list is just as interesting as the menu. There are 175 selections, which sounds daunting, though the well-informed staff are ready to help you navigate through it.

1235 Deerhurst Dr., Huntsville, ON, P1H 2E8. © **705/789-6411.** www.deerhurstresort.com. Reservations recommended. Main courses C$25–$32 (US$18–$22). AE, DC, MC, V. Daily 7–11am and 5–11pm.

Rest, Relax, Recharge

Northern Ontario is deservedly famous for its outdoor activities, from skiing to boating, and from hiking to biking. But a growing segment of the tourist trade in these parts is coming for another reason altogether: spas. Getting away from it all in these parts no longer automatically means going on an ice fishing expedition; it could just as easily involve a hot rock massage (one of the latest trends). The spas listed below aren't targeted at women—the number of men going to spas has increased exponentially, so spas are offering almost all of their services to both sexes. For more information, including a free directory, contact the **Spas Ontario** association at ℭ **800/990-7702,** or visit the website at www.spasontario.com. Two of the best are at resorts:

Deerhurst Resort (p. 243): The Deerhurst thoughtfully provides children's programs, so you can drop off the tykes before you go for your aromatherapy massage or Ancient Dead Sea Mud Wrap (in fact, there is a special Couple's De-Stressor package . . .). The emphasis here is on total relaxation, and with all of the delicious Aveda products and scents, it's impossible to resist. The Deerhurst was one of the founding members of Spas Ontario, and the standards at the spa are excellent. The highly trained therapists are particularly talented at working out those inevitable golf-induced kinks.

Taboo Resort (p. 244): This is the choice for those who want to lie (and get a Swedish massage) in the lap of luxury. Because Taboo is in the middle of building a new top-of-the-line spa on their property, many of their spa treatments are done right in guests' rooms. And they don't just roll in with a massage table—the therapists put on soothing music and burn fragrant candles to set the scene. One of Taboo's best offerings is a chocolate wrap, which smells delicious and gives you perfectly soft skin (note to skeptics, the chocolate is mixed with lactic acid, which is a great exfoliator).

3 Guys and a Stove ℛ INTERNATIONAL   The name might sound casual—and the atmosphere is indeed unpretentious—but the cooking is very fine. This is a family restaurant (with a special menu for kids), but the gourmet quotient is high. The curried pumpkin and sweet potato soup is an absolute must-have when it's on the menu; the spicy chicken stew is another surefire winner.

Hwy 60, Huntsville. ℭ 705/789-1815. Main courses C$15–$25 (US$11–$18). AE, MC, V. Daily 11am–9:30pm.

MODERATE

Blondie's ℛ Finds   This family-run restaurant is a rare find in Muskoka. While the menu has plenty of comfort foods—think fish and chips, prime rib, eggs benedict, and smoked-meat sandwiches—there's also more exotic fare, such as sushi and a variety of seafood dishes. Blondie's is also the official caterer to the Gravenhurst Opera House. The setting is like a country kitchen, with its round wooden tables and cheery decorations, and the service is just as warm.

151 Brock St., Gravenhurst. ℭ 705/687-7756. Main courses C$10–$20 (US$7–$14). MC, V. Mon–Tues 9:30am–3pm; Wed–Sat 9:30am–8pm.

4 Hamilton

75km (47 miles) SW of Toronto

On a landlocked harbor spanned at its entrance by the Burlington Skyway's dramatic sweep, Hamilton has long been nicknamed "Steeltown" for its industrial roots. Since the early 1990s however, Hamilton has been making a name for itself with its ever-expanding list of attractions. It takes less than an hour to drive here from Toronto, and it's well worth a day trip for the whole family.

ESSENTIALS

VISITOR INFORMATION   The Hamilton Tourist Information Centre has been relocated to 1 James St. S., 8th Floor, Hamilton, ON L8P 4R5 (© **800/ 263-8590** or 905/546-2666; www.city.hamilton.on.ca). It has a wealth of information about what to see and do, as well as where to dine and sleep. Its year-round hours run from Monday through Friday from 9am to 5pm.

GETTING THERE   Hamilton is easy to get to by car. From Toronto, take the Queen Elizabeth Way (signs read QEW) to Hamilton. The drive will take about an hour.

GO (Government of Ontario) Transit is a commuter train that connects Toronto and Hamilton. Call © **800/438-6646** or 416/869-3200 for information. The **John C. Munro Hamilton International Airport** (© **905/679-8359;** www.hamiltonairport.com) has long been popular with cargo carriers and is now a hub for WestJet.

WHAT TO SEE & DO

Hamilton's downtown core is best explored on foot, though you may want a car to visit attractions in the outlying areas.

Canadian Warplane Heritage Museum   This interactive museum charts the course of Canadian aviation from the beginning of World War II to the present. Visitors can climb into the cockpits of WWII trainer crafts or a CF-100 jet fighter. The most popular attractions are the flight simulators, which allow aspiring pilots to test their flight skills. There are also short documentary films, photographs, and other memorabilia. The aircraft on display include rarities like the Avro Lancaster bomber and the deHavilland Vampire fighter jet. The collection also includes a variety of military and transport craft.

9280 Airport Rd. (at the John C. Munro Hamilton International Airport), Mount Hope. © 877/347-3359 or 905/670-3347. www.warplane.com. Admission C$10 (US$7) adults, C$8 (US$5.60) seniors and youths 8–18, free for children 7 and under, family admission for 2 adults and 2 youths is C$30 (US$21). Daily 9am–5pm; closed Jan 1, Dec 25.

Dundurn Castle   The castle affords a glimpse of the opulent life as it was lived in this part of southern Ontario in the mid-19th century. Sir Allan Napier MacNab, prime minister of the United Provinces of Canada in the mid-1850s and a founder of the Great Western Railway built it between 1832 and 1835; Queen Victoria knighted him for the part he played in the Rebellion of 1837. The 35-plus-room mansion has been restored and furnished in the style of 1855. The gray stucco exterior, with its classical Greek portico, is impressive enough, but inside, from the formal dining rooms to Lady MacNab's boudoir, the furnishings are rich. The museum contains a fascinating collection of Victoriana. In December, the castle is decorated splendidly for a Victorian Christmas.

The **Hamilton Military Museum** is on the grounds of Dundurn Castle. For those who are interested, it traces Canadian military history from the War of

ATTRACTIONS ●
African Lion Safari **1**
Dundurn Castle **3**
Royal Botanical Gardens **2**

DINING ◆
Canadian Warplane
  Heritage Museum **6**
La Cantina **5**
Perry's Restaurant **4**

1812 through World War I. Admission is included when you buy a ticket for Dundurn Castle.

Dundurn Park, York Blvd. ℂ **905/546-2872.** Admission C$10 (US$7) adults, C$8 (US$5.60) seniors and students with ID, C$5 (US$3.50) children 6–14, free for children 5 and under. Victoria Day to Labour Day daily 10am–4:30pm; the rest of the year, Tues–Sun noon–4pm. Closed Dec 25–26, Jan 1.

Royal Botanical Gardens ⚘   Situated just north of the city, the Royal Botanical Gardens spreads over 1,214 glorious hectares (3,000 acres). The Rock Garden features spring bulbs in May, summer flowers in June to September, and chrysanthemums in October. The Laking Garden blazes during June and July with irises, peonies, and lilies. The arboretum fills with the heady scent of lilac from the end of May to early June, and the exquisite color bursts of rhododendrons and azaleas thereafter. The Centennial Rose Garden is at its best late June through mid-September.

The gardens hosts many festivals during the year, including the Mediterranean Food & Wine Festival in February, the popular Ontario Garden Show in early April, the Tulip Festival in May, the Rose Society Show in June, and the Japanese Flower Society Show in September.

Should you work up an appetite while strolling the grounds, there are several on-site dining options, including the Gardens Café, which is open year-round, and the Rock Garden Tea House or the Turner Pavilion (both open throughout the summer).

680 Plains Rd. W., Burlington ℂ 905/527-1158. www.rbg.ca. Admission C$10 (US$7) adults, C$7(US$4.90) for seniors and children 13–17, C$2.50 (US$1.75) for children 5–12, free for children 4 and under. Daily 9:30am–dusk. Closed Jan 1, Dec 25.

African Lion Safari Just a half-hour drive northwest of Hamilton, you'll find a mirror image of a traditional zoo: At the African Lion Safari, visitors remain caged in their cars or in a tour bus while the animals roam wild and free. The 300-hectare (750-acre) wildlife park contains rhino, cheetah, lion, tiger, giraffe, zebra, vultures, and many other species. In addition to the safari, the cost of admission covers other attractions like the cruise aboard the African Queen, during which a tour guide will take you around the lake and point out local inhabitants like spider monkeys, crested macaques, and ring-tailed lemurs. There's also a train that will take you through a forest populated by snapping turtles, among other wildlife.

The park has three baby Asian elephants: Samson, Albert, and George. And the elephant-bathing event, which occurs daily, will particularly fascinate the kids. There's also a Pets' Corner filled with frisky otters and pot-bellied pigs. There are several play areas for children as well, including the Misumu Bay water park (bring bathing suits!).

Safari Rd, Cambridge. ℂ 800/461-WILD or 519/623-2620. www.lionsafari.com. Admission C$23 (US$16) adults, C$19 (US$13) seniors, C$17 (US$12) children 3–12, free for children 2 and under. Late June–Labour Day daily 10am–5:30pm; late Apr to mid-June and early Sept to early Oct, daily 9am–4pm; closed mid-Oct to mid-Apr.

WHERE TO STAY

Because Hamilton is so close to Toronto, it's easy to make a day trip here and back, rather than pulling up stakes and spending the night here. However, if you do want to stay in the area, several well-known chains have hotels here, including **Sheraton** (ℂ **800/514-7101** or 905/529-5515) and **Howard Johnson** (ℂ **800/ 263-8558** or 905/546-8111).

WHERE TO DINE

The suggested restaurants in St. Catharine's and Welland, such as Café Garibaldi, Iseya, and Rinderlin's, are just a short drive away from Hamilton. However, Hamilton has a few restaurants worth checking out, too.

La Cantina This is really two restaurants in one: There's a formal dining room, which serves up elegant plates like veal scaloppini in a dry Marsala sauce, and seared ostrich medallions cooked with Pinot Noir; equally elegant pasta plates include rotini with ham and peppers in a vodka sauce. Then there's the casual pizzeria, which serves up more than 20 varieties of pizza, ranging from the traditional Quattro Stagione (four seasons) with prosciutto, artichokes, olives and mozzarella, to the unusual Gamberi, which is topped with shrimp, smoked, salmon, olives, eggplant, and pesto. This is a very popular spot, so try to make a reservation or arrive early, especially at lunch. If you're very lucky, you might just secure a seat in the restaurant's garden patio.

60 Walnut St. S. ℂ 905/521-8989. Reservations recommended. Main courses C$10–$26 (US$7–$18). AE, MC, V.

Perry's Restaurant   This casual family-style restaurant has a large menu that has something for everyone. It borrows from a range of cuisines, including Italian, French, Mexican, Greek, and American. Offerings include chicken souvlaki, rack of ribs, hearty sandwiches, and fish and chips. There are also lighter options such as salads, soups, and chicken fingers. There's a sunny patio at the front of the restaurant, too.

1088 Main St. W. ℂ **905/527-3779.** Main courses C$6–$13 (US$4.20–$9.10). MC, V. Daily 11:30am–1am.

Appendix:
Toronto in Depth

In less than 300 years, Toronto has grown from a trading post to a vibrant international capital. Read on to get a sense of how it happened.

1 History 101

FROM FUR TRADING POST TO MUDDY YORK

As in most cities, the influences of geography, trade, and communications shaped Toronto and its history. Although the city today possesses a downtown core, it also sprawls across a large area—a gift of geography, for there are no physical barriers to stop it. When European settlement began, the broad plain rising from Lake Ontario to an inland ridge of hills (around today's St. Clair Ave.), and stretching between the Don River in the east and the Humber in the west, made the location ideal.

Native Canadians had long stopped here—at the entrance to the Toronto Trail, a short route between the Lower and Upper lakes. In 1615, French fur trader Etienne Brûleé was the first European to travel the trail. It wasn't until 1720 that the French established the first trading post, known as Fort Toronto, to intercept the furs that were being taken across Lake Ontario to New York State by English rivals. Fort Rouille, built on the site of today's CNE grounds, replaced the trading post in 1751. When the 1763 Treaty of Paris ended the Anglo-French War after the fall of Québec, French rule in North America effectively ended, and the city's French antecedents were all but forgotten.

Only 32km (20 miles) across the lake from the United States, Toronto has always been affected by what happens south of the border. When the

Dateline

- **1615** Etienne Brûleé travels the Toronto Trail. "Toronto" is derived from a Huron term for "place of meeting."
- **1720** France establishes post at Toronto.
- **1751** French build Fort Rouille.
- **1759** Fort Rouille burned during British conquest.
- **1763** Treaty of Paris effectively ends French rule in Canada.
- **1787** Lord Dorchester, British governor of Québec, purchases land from Scarborough to Etobicoke from the Mississauga tribe.
- **1793** Governor of Upper Canada, Col. John Simcoe, arrives and names settlement York. It becomes capital of Upper Canada.
- **1796** Yonge Street laid out, a 53km (33-mile) oxcart trail.
- **1812–15** War of 1812, between United States and England, uses Canada as a battleground. In 1813, Americans invade, blow up Fort York, and burn Parliament buildings. In 1814, U.S. troops are driven out of Canada.
- **1820s** Immigration of Nonconformists and Irish Catholics fosters reform politics.
- **1828** Erie Canal extended to Oswego on Lake Ontario.
- **1830s** Orange Order becomes prominent influence in politics.
- **1832–34** Cholera epidemics.
- **1834** City named Toronto; City Council replaces magistrates; William Lyon Mackenzie becomes first mayor.
- **1837** Former mayor Mackenzie leads rebellion sparked by economic downturn.

American Revolution established a powerful, potentially hostile new nation, Toronto's location became strategically more important, or so it seemed to John Graves Simcoe. He was lieutenant governor of the newly formed province of Upper Canada, which had been established in 1791 to administer the frontiers—from Kingston and Quinte's Isle to Windsor and beyond—settled largely by Loyalists fleeing the Revolution. To Simcoe, Toronto was more defensible than Fort Niagara and a natural arsenal for Lake Ontario, which also afforded easy access to Lake Huron and the interior.

The governor had already purchased a vast tract of land from the Mississauga tribe for the paltry sum of £1,700 (US$2,600), plus blankets, guns, rum, and tobacco. In 1793, Lieutenant Governor Simcoe, his wife, Elizabeth, and the Queen's Rangers arrived. Simcoe ordered a garrison built, renamed the settlement York, and laid it out in a 10-block rectangle around King, Front, George, Duke, and Berkeley streets. Beyond stretched a series of 40-hectare (100-acre) lots from Queen to Bloor, which were granted to mollify government officials, who resented having to move to the mosquito-plagued, marshy outpost. Its muddiness was prodigious, and in fact a story is told of a fellow who saw a hat lying in the middle of a street, went to pick it up, and found the head of a live man submerged below it! In 3 short years a small hamlet had grown, and Simcoe had laid out Yonge Street—then a 53km (33-mile) oxcart trail. Four years later the first Parliament meeting confirmed York as the capital of Upper Canada.

FROM MUDDY YORK TO THE FAMILY COMPACT

The officials were a more demanding and finicky lot than the sturdy frontier farmers, and businesses sprang up to serve them. By 1812, the population

- **1840s–50s** Mass Irish immigration.
- **1841** Act of Union establishes the United Province of Canada, with Kingston as ruling seat; Toronto loses status as a capital.
- **1843** The university, King's College, opens.
- **1844** City Hall built. George Brown founds the *Globe*.
- **1849** Great fire destroys much of city. Anglican King's College converts to secular University of Toronto.
- **1851** Population 30,000 (33% Irish). Anglican Trinity College founded. St. Lawrence Hall built.
- **1852** Toronto Stock Exchange opens. Grand Trunk Railroad charted, linking Québec, Montréal, Toronto, Guelph, and Sarnia.
- **1853** St. James Cathedral completed.
- **1858** Storm creates the Toronto Islands.
- **1861** Horse-powered street railway runs along Yonge to Yorkville.
- **1867** Canadian Confederation; Toronto becomes capital of new province of Ontario.
- **1868** Canada First movement begins.
- **1869** Eaton's department store opens.
- **1871** Population 56,000.
- **1872** Simpson's department store opens.
- **1876** John Ross Robertson starts *Evening Telegram*, which wields influence for next 90 years.
- **1886** Provincial parliament buildings erected in Queen's Park.
- **1893** First Stanley Cup played.
- **1896** *Maclean's* newsmagazine started.
- **1901** Population 208,000.
- **1903** The dramatic short film *Hiawatha* is the first movie made in Canada.
- **1904** Great Fire burns much of downtown.
- **1906** First autos produced by Canada Cycle and Motor Company. Toronto Symphony founded.
- **1907** Bell strike broken. Royal Alexandra opens. The Lord's Day Act forbids all public activity except churchgoing on Sunday.
- **1909** Florence Nightingale Graham drops out of nursing school in Toronto, changes her name to Elizabeth Arden, and founds the first cosmetics empire.

continues

had grown to 703 and included a brewer-baker, blacksmith, watch-maker, chair-maker, apothecary, hatter, and tailor.

During the War of 1812, despite initial victories at Queenston and Detroit, Canada was under siege. In April 1813, 14 ships carrying 1,700 American troops invaded York, blew up the incomplete fort, burned the Parliament buildings, and carried off the mace (which was not returned until 1934). The British general burned a 30-gun warship, the *Sir Isaac Brock,* which was under construction, and retreated, leaving young John Strachan to negotiate the capitulation. This event did much to reinforce the town's pro-British, anti-American attitude—a feeling that persists to some extent to this day. In retaliation for the burning of Fort York, some Canadians went to Washington and torched the American president's residence. (The Americans later whitewashed it to hide the charred wood—hence, the White House.)

A conservative pro-British outlook permeated the official political oligarchy that dominated York, a group dubbed the Family Compact. Many of the names on street signs, subway stops, and maps derive from this august group of early government officers and their families. Among them were William Jarvis, a New England Loyalist who became provincial secretary; John Beverley Robinson, son of a Virginia Loyalist, who became attorney general at age 22 and later chief justice of Upper Canada; and Scottish-educated Dr. John Strachan, a schoolmaster who became an Anglican rector and, eventually, the most powerful figure in York. Anglo-Irish Dr. William Warren Baldwin, doctor, lawyer, architect, judge, and parliamentarian, laid out Spadina Avenue as a thoroughfare leading to his country house; the Boultons were prominent

- **1911** Founding members of the Group of Seven meet at the Toronto Arts and Letters Club.
- **1912** Garment workers' strike broken. Royal Ontario Museum founded.
- **1914** New Union Station built.
- **1914–18** World War I; 70,000 Torontonians enlist, and 13,000 die.
- **1920** The Art Gallery of Toronto mounts the first Group of Seven exhibit.
- **1921** Population 521,893.
- **1922** University of Toronto researchers Frederick Banting and Charles Best discover insulin.
- **1923** Dr. Banting is awarded the Nobel Prize in medicine. Parliament passes the Chinese Exclusion Act. Ernest Hemingway moves to Toronto to become a reporter for the *Star.*
- **1930s** The Great Depression; thousands go on relief.
- **1931** Maple Leaf Gardens built as home base for the Maple Leafs.
- **1938** Toronto native Joseph Shuster creates *Superman.*
- **1939** Canada enters World War II; thousands of troops leave from Union Station.
- **1940–45** Toronto functions as war supplier.
- **1947** Cocktail lounges approved.
- **1950** Sunday sports allowed.
- **1951** Population 31% foreign-born.
- **1954** Metro created; Toronto becomes a model for urban consolidation. Toronto native Marilyn Bell, 16, becomes first person to swim across Lake Ontario. In October, Hurricane Hazel kills 83 people in Toronto.
- **1959** York University, Toronto's second major institution of higher education, opens.
- **1960** Movies are shown in Toronto on Sunday for the first time.
- **1961** Population 42% foreign-born.
- **1963** Ryerson Polytechnic University founded.
- **1965** New City Hall at Nathan Phillips Square is unveiled. Canada and the United States sign the Autopact, creating boom times in Toronto and nearby Oshawa.
- **1966** U.S. draft dodgers start fleeing to Canada; many settle in Toronto.

lawyers, judges, and politicians—
Judge D'Arcy Boulton built a mansion, the Grange, which later became
the core of the art museum and still
stands today.

These men, extremely conscious of
rank, were conformist, conservative,
pro-British, Tory, and Anglican. Their
power was broken only later in the
19th century, as a larger and more
diverse population gave reformers a
chance to challenge their control. But
even today, their influence lingers in
the corporate world, where a handful
of companies and individuals control
80% of the companies on the Toronto
Stock Exchange.

THE EARLY 1800S—CANAL, RAILROAD & IMMIGRATION

The changes that eventually diluted
their control began in the early 19th
century. During the 1820s, 1830s, and
1840s, immigrants—Irish Protestants
and Catholics, Scots, Presbyterians,
Methodists, and other Nonconformists—poured in to settle the frontier farmlands. By 1832 York had
become the largest urban community
in the province, with a population of
1,600. Already well established com-
mercially as a supply center, York
enjoyed another boost when the Erie
Canal was extended to Oswego on
Lake Ontario, giving it direct access to
New York, and the Welland Canal was
built across the Niagara Peninsula,
allowing access to Lake Erie and points
beyond. In 1834, the city was incorporated and York became Toronto, a city
bounded by Parliament Street to the
east, Bathurst to the west, the lakefront
to the south, and 400 yards north of
the current Queen Street (then called
Lot) to the north. Outside this area—
west to Dufferin Street, east to the Don
River, and north to Bloor Street—lay

- **1970s** Influx of immigration from Asia, Africa, India, Pakistan, the Caribbean, and Latin America.
- **1974** Mikhail Baryshnikov defects from the USSR during a trip to Toronto.
- **1975** Toronto International Film Festival founded. CN Tower becomes the world's tallest freestanding structure.
- **1980s** Creation and expansion of the Greater Toronto area, including nearby cities of Hamilton and Oshawa.
- **1981** Population 3,898,933.
- **1984** City's 150th anniversary.
- **1989** SkyDome opens, drawing wide criticism of its C$570 million (US$388 million) cost.
- **1992** Residents of Toronto Islands win 40-year struggle to retain their homes. Blue Jays win World Series for the first time.
- **1993** Blue Jays repeat as World Series champions.
- **1995** Progressive Conservative Government elected.
- **1996** Population 4,263,757. *Fortune* magazine names Toronto best city in the world to live and work in. University of Toronto professor John Polanyi wins Nobel Prize in Chemistry.
- **1997** Protests in Queen's Park target social service cuts and the passage of Bill 103, creating a megacity.
- **1998** Toronto becomes a megacity anyway.
- **1999** Researchers at McMaster University in Hamilton discover unusual characteristics of Einstein's brain. The new Air Canada Centre becomes home to the Maple Leafs and the Raptors.
- **2001** Toronto loses its bid to host the 2008 Olympics to Beijing.
- **2002** Toronto hosts the first World Youth Day ever held in Canada; the event includes a visit by Pope John Paul II.
- **2003** Toronto gains several new attractions, including the Distillery Historic District, the Yonge-Dundas Square, and the Carlu Theatre. Toronto tourism drops due to the SARS scare.

the "liberties," out of which the city would later carve new wards. North of Bloor, local brewer Joseph Bloor and Sheriff Jarvis were already drawing up plans for the village of Yorkville.

As more immigrants arrived, the population grew more diverse, and demands arose for democracy and reform. Among the reformers were such leaders as Francis Collins, who launched the radical paper *Canadian Freeman* in 1825; lawyer William Draper; and, perhaps most famous of all, fiery William Lyon Mackenzie, who was elected Toronto's first mayor in 1834.

Mackenzie had started his *Colonial Advocate* to crusade against the narrow-minded Family Compact, calling for reform and challenging their power to such an extent that some of them dumped his presses into the lake. By 1837, Mackenzie, undaunted, was calling for open rebellion.

A severe depression, financial turmoil, and the failure of some banks all contributed to the 1837 Rebellion, one of the most dramatic events in the city's history. On December 5, the rebels, a scruffy bunch of about 700, gathered at Montgomery's Tavern outside the city (near modern-day Eglinton Ave.). Led by Mackenzie on a white mare, they marched on the city. Two days later the city's militia, called out by Sheriff Jarvis, scattered the rebels at Carlton Street. Both sides then turned and ran. Reinforcements arrived, pursued the rebels, and bombarded the tavern with cannonballs. Mackenzie fled to the United States, and two other leaders—Lount and Matthews—were hanged. Their graves are in the Necropolis cemetery.

Between 1834 and 1884 the foundations of an industrial city were laid: Toronto gained water works, gas, and public transportation. Many municipal facilities were built, including a city hall, the Royal Lyceum Theatre (1848) on King near Bay, the Toronto Stock Exchange (1852), St. Lawrence Hall (1851), an asylum, and a jail.

During the 1850s the building of the railroads accelerated the economic pace. By 1860, Toronto was at the center of a railroad web. It became the trading hub for lumber and grain imports and exports. Merchant empires were founded, railroad magnates emerged, and institutions like the Bank of Toronto were established.

Despite its growth and wealth, Toronto still lagged behind Montréal, which had twice Toronto's population in 1861. But Toronto increasingly took advantage of its superior links to the south, and that edge eventually helped it overtake its rival. Under the Confederation of 1867, the city was guaranteed another advantage: As the capital of the newly created Ontario, Toronto, in effect, controlled the minerals and timber of the north.

During this mid-Victorian period the growth of a more diverse population continued. In 1847, Irish famine victims began flooding into Toronto, and by 1851 and 1852 the Irish-born were the city's largest single ethnic group. While many of them were Ulster Protestants who did not threaten the Anglo-Protestant ascendancy, the newcomers were not always welcomed—a pattern that repeated whenever a new immigrant group threatened to change the shape and order of society. As the gap between the number of Anglicans and Catholics closed, sectarian tensions increased, and the old-country Orange and Green conflicts flared into mob violence.

LATE- & HIGH-VICTORIAN TORONTO

Between 1871 and 1891 the city's population more than tripled, shooting from 56,000 to 181,000. The burgeoning urban market helped spawn two great Toronto retailers—Timothy Eaton and Robert Simpson—who moved to Toronto from Ontario towns to open stores at Queen and Yonge streets in 1869 and 1872, respectively. Eaton developed his reputation on fixed prices, cash sales only, and promises of refunds if the customer wasn't satisfied—all unique gambits at the time. Simpson copied Eaton and competed by providing better service, such as two telephones to take orders instead of one. Both enterprises developed into full-fledged department stores, and both entered the mail-order business, conquering the country with their catalogs.

The business of the city was business, and amassing wealth was the pastime of such figures as Henry Pellatt, stockbroker, president of the Electrical Development Company, and builder of Casa Loma; E. B. Osler; George Albertus Cox; and A. R. Ames. Although these men were self-made entrepreneurs, not Family Compact officials, they formed a traditional socially conservative elite, linked by money, taste, investments, and religious affiliation. And they were staunchly British. They and the rest of the citizens celebrated the Queen's Jubilee in 1897 with gusto, and gave Toronto boys a rousing send-off to fight in the Boer War in 1899. The prominent businessmen also had a fondness for clubs—the Albany Club for the Conservatives, and the National Club for the Liberals. As in England, their sports clubs (notably the Royal Yacht Club, the Toronto Cricket Club, the Toronto Golf Club, and the Lawn Tennis Club) carried a certain cachet.

The boom spurred new commercial and residential construction. Projects included the first steel-frame building—the Board of Trade Building (1889)—at Yonge and Front—George Gooderham's Romanesque-style mansion (1890) at St. George and Bloor (now the York Club), the provincial parliament buildings in Queen's Park (1886–92), and the city hall (1899) at Queen and Bay. Public transit improved, and by 1891 the city had 109km (68 miles) of tracks for horse-drawn cars. Electric lights, telephones, and electric streetcars appeared in the 1890s.

FROM 1900 TO 1933

Between 1901 and 1921 the population more than doubled, climbing from 208,000 to 521,893. The economy continued to expand, fueled by the lumber, mining, wholesale, and agricultural machinery industries, and after 1911 by hydroelectric power. Toronto began to seriously challenge Montréal. Much of the new wealth went into construction, and three marvelous buildings from this era can still be seen today: the Horticultural Building at the Exhibition Grounds (1907), the King Edward Hotel (1903), and Union Station (1914–19). Most of the earlier wooden structures had been destroyed in the Great Fire of 1904, which wiped out 5.6 hectares (14 acres) of downtown.

The booming economy and its factories attracted a wave of new immigrants—mostly Italians and Jews from Russia and Eastern Europe—who settled in the city's emerging ethnic enclaves. By 1912, Kensington Market was well established, and the garment center and Jewish community were firmly ensconced around King and Spadina. Little Italy clustered around College and Grace. By 1911 more than 30,000 Torontonians were foreign-born, and the slow march to change the English character of the city had begun.

It was still a city of churches worthy of the name "Toronto the Good," with a population of staunch religious conservatives, who barely voted for Sunday streetcar service in 1897 and in 1912 banned tobogganing on Sunday. As late as 1936, 30 men were arrested at the lakeshore resort of Sunnyside because they exposed their chests—even though the temperature was 105°F (41°C)! In 1947, cocktail lounges were approved, but it wasn't until 1950 that playing sports on Sunday became legal.

Increased industrialization brought social problems, largely concentrated in Cabbagetown and the Ward, a large area that stretched west of Yonge and north of Queen. Here, poor people lived in crowded, wretched conditions: Housing was inadequate, health conditions poor, and rag-picking or sweatshop labor the only employment.

As industry grew, unionism also increased, but the movement, as in the United States, failed to organize politically. Two major strikes—at Bell in 1907 and in the garment industry in 1912—were easily broken.

The larger, wealthier city also became an intellectual and cultural magnet. Artists like Charles Jefferys, J. H. MacDonald, Arthur Lismer, Tom Thomson, Lawren Harris, Frederick Varley, and A. Y. Jackson, most associated with the Group of Seven, set up studios in Toronto. Their first group show opened in 1920. Toronto also became the English-language publishing center of the nation, and national magazines like *Maclean's* (1896) and *Saturday Night* were launched. The Art Gallery of Ontario, the Royal Ontario Museum, the Toronto Symphony Orchestra, and the Royal Alexandra Theatre all opened before 1914.

Women advanced, too, at the turn of the century. In 1880, Emily Jennings Stowe became the first Canadian woman authorized to practice medicine. In 1886, the university admitted women. Clara Brett Martin was the first woman admitted to the law courts. The women's suffrage movement gained strength, led by Dr. Stowe, Flora McDonald Denison, and the Women's Christian Temperance Union.

During World War I, Toronto sent 70,000 men to the trenches; about 13,000 were killed. At home, the war had a great impact economically and socially: Toronto became Canada's chief aviation center; factories, shipyards, and power facilities expanded to meet the needs of war; and women entered the workforce in great numbers.

After the war the city took on much more of the aspect and tone that characterize it today. Automobiles appeared on the streets—the Canadian Cycle and Motor Company had begun manufacturing them in 1906 (the first parking ticket was given in 1908), and one or two skyscrapers appeared. Although 80% of the population was of British origin, ethnic enclaves were clearly defined.

The 1920s roared along, fueled by a mining boom that saw Bay Street turned into a veritable gold-rush alley where everyone was pushing something hot. The Great Depression followed, inflicting 30% unemployment in 1933. The only distraction from its bleakness was the opening of Maple Leaf Gardens in 1931. Besides being an ice-hockey center, it also was host to large protest rallies during the Depression, and later such diverse entities as the Jehovah's Witnesses, Billy Graham, the Ringling Bros. Circus, and the Metropolitan Opera.

As in the United States, hostility toward new immigrants was rife during the '20s. It reached a peak in 1923, when the Chinese Exclusion Act was passed, banning Chinese immigration. In the 1930s, antagonism toward Jews intensified. Signs such as NO JEWS, NIGGERS, OR DOGS were posted occasionally at Balmy and Kew beaches. In August 1933, the display of a swastika at Christie Pits caused a battle between Nazis and Jews.

AFTER WORLD WAR II

In 1939, Torontonians again rallied to the British cause, sending thousands to fight in Europe. At home, plants turned out fighter bombers and Bren guns, and people endured rationing—one bottle of liquor a month, and limited supplies of sugar and other staples—while they listened to the war-front news delivered by Lorne Greene.

Already prosperous by World War II, Toronto continued to expand during the 1940s. The suburbs alone added more than 200,000 to the population between 1940 and 1953. By the 1950s, the urban area had grown so large, disputes between city and suburbs were so frequent, and the need for social and other services was so great that an effective administrative solution was needed. In 1953, the Metro Council, composed of equal numbers of representatives from the city and the suburbs, was established.

Toronto became a major city in the 1950s, with Metro providing a structure for planning and growth. The Yonge subway opened, and a network of highways was constructed. It linked the city to the affluent suburbs. Don Mills, the first new town, was built between 1952 and 1962; Yorkdale Center, a mammoth shopping center, followed in 1964. American companies began locating branch plants in the area, fueling much of the growth.

The city also began to loosen up. While the old social elite (still traditionally educated at Upper Canada College, Ridley, and Trinity College) continued to dominate the boardrooms, politics, at least, had become more accessible and fluid. In 1954, Nathan Phillips became the first Jewish mayor, signifying how greatly the population had changed from the days when immigrants were primarily British, American, or French. In 1947, the Chinese Exclusion Act of 1923 was repealed, opening the door to relatives of Toronto's then-small Chinese community. After 1950, the door swung open further. Germans and Italians were allowed to enter, adding to the communities that were already established; then, under pressure from the United Nations, Poles, Ukrainians, Central European and Russian Jews, Yugoslavs, Estonians, Latvians, and other East Europeans poured in. Most arrived at Union Station, having journeyed from the ports of Halifax, Québec City, and Montréal. At the beginning of the 1950s, the foreign-born were 31% of the population; by 1961, they were 42%, and the number of people claiming British descent had fallen from 73% to 59%. The 1960s brought an even richer mix of people—Portuguese, Greeks, West Indians, South Asians, Chinese, Vietnamese, and Chilean refugees—changing the city's character forever.

In the 1960s, the focus shifted from the suburbs to the city. People moved back downtown, renovating the handsome brick Victorians so characteristic of today's downtown. Yorkville emerged briefly as the hippie capital—the Haight-Ashbury of Canada. Gordon Lightfoot and Joni Mitchell sang in the coffee-houses, and antiwar protests took over the streets. Perhaps the failure of the experimental, alternative Rochdale College in 1968 marked the demise of that era. By the mid-1970s, Yorkville had been transformed into a village of elegant boutiques and galleries and high-rent restaurants, and the funky village had moved to Queen Street West.

In the 1970s, Toronto became the fastest-growing city in North America. For years the city had competed with Montréal for first-city status, and now the separatist issue and the election of the Parti Quebecois in 1976 hastened Toronto's dash to the tape. It overtook Montréal as a financial center, boasting more corporate headquarters. Its stock market was more important, and it remained the country's prime publishing center. A dramatically different city hall opened in 1965, a symbol of the city's equally new dynamism. Toronto also began reclaiming its waterfront, with the development of Harbourfront. The city's new power and wealth came alive in new skyscrapers and civic buildings—the Toronto Dominion, the 72-story First Canadian Place, Royal Bank Plaza, Roy Thomson Hall, the Eaton Centre, the CN Tower—all of which transformed the 1930s skyline into an urban landscape worthy of world attention.

Unlike the rapid building of highways and other structures completed in the 1950s, these developments were achieved with some balance and attention to the city's heritage. From the late '60s to the early '80s, citizens fought to ensure that the city's heritage was saved and that development was not allowed to continue as wildly as it had in the '50s. The best examples of the reform movement's success were the stopping of the proposed Spadina Expressway in 1971 and the fight against several urban renewal plans.

During the 1970s, the provincial government also helped develop attractions that would polish Toronto's patina and lure visitors: Ontario Place in 1971, Harbourfront in 1972, and the Metro Zoo and the Ontario Science Centre in 1974. Government financing also supported the arts and helped turn Toronto from a city with four theaters in 1965 to one boasting more than 40 today.

2 Toronto Today

Toronto's growth has continued steadily since the 1970s, though the past several years have been a tumultuous time for the city. The merger of its separate municipalities, rapid population growth, and provincial government budget slashing have all had a serious impact on the life of the city. Toronto has few friends in the provincial government (perhaps because its citizens vote against it whenever given the opportunity). In addition to forcing the megacity merger through, the Conservative provincial government (or "Tories") cut social spending. The most frequent complaint heard in Toronto is that the city's municipal taxes aren't reinvested in its infrastructure, but end up being funneled to less populous parts of the province. Toronto is currently in a tumult over legislation passed by the city council in 2003 allowing emergency shelters for the homeless to be built in any ward in the city. Sadly the city's homeless problem only seems to be growing rather than improving.

But it has also been a boom time for Toronto, with the opening of new attractions such as the Distillery Historic District; the anticipated construction of a long-awaited opera house and a third subway line; and a burgeoning dining and entertainment scene. The downtown core is thriving, and the energy is driving its development west into previously neglected areas. Toronto is still the city of choice for arriving immigrants: 300,000 Hong Kong émigrés have joined Toronto's Chinese community, and there have been influxes from Somalia, Eastern Europe, India, Pakistan, and Central America. Neighborhoods around town preserve these cultures. While their influence is strong in many areas, it is perhaps most visible to a short-term visitor in the city's diverse dining options and in Toronto's many cultural festivals.

In 2001, Toronto made a Herculean effort to convince the International Olympic Committee that it would make the perfect host city for the 2008 Games, but it lost out to Beijing. Local wags claimed that Toronto was being "strongly encouraged" to go after the 2012 Games. However, the fact that Vancouver won the 2010 Winter Games has likely quashed that dream for now. Fortunately, the local government is considering the implementation of some of the terrific plans that were drawn up to win over the IOC. Watch for further development along the waterfront. Undoubtedly Toronto's energy will be channeled in new and interesting directions.

Index

See also Accommodations and Restaurant indexes, below.

GENERAL INDEX

A aroport, 40
AARP, 26
Abyssinia, 157
Academy of Spherical Arts, 210
Accents, 213
Access America, 24
Accommodations, 54–74.
  See also Accommodations Index
  at the airport, 72–74
  bed-and-breakfasts (B&Bs), 55
  best bets, 7–8
  Downtown East, 65–68
  Downtown West, 55–65
  East End, 71
  family-friendly, 66
  Hamilton, 250
  Midtown West, 68–71
  Niagara-on-the-Lake, 230–233
  in package tours, 37
  shopping online for, 29
  tipping, 53
  tips on, 38–39
  Uptown, 71
  what's new, 1
Addresses, finding, 44
Admiralty Point Condominiums, 159
African Lion Safari (Hamilton), 250
African Savanna, 131
Afterlife, 209
Afternoon tea, 10, 66, 170, 240
AIDS & Sexual Health InfoLine, 51
Air Canada, 1, 29, 33–34
Air Canada Centre, 6, 140, 152, 158
Airfares
  money-saving tips, 35–36
  shopping online for, 28–29
AirLine limo service, 40

Airlines, 1, 33–34
  bankruptcy and, 35
Airport Express bus, 40
Airports, 1
  accommodations at, 72–74
  arriving in, 40–41
  security procedures, 34
Air Tickets Direct, 35
Akropol, 135
Al Frisco's, 210–211
The Algonquians Sweet Grass Gallery, 181
Allan Gardens, 141
Allen's, 212
Alvand Food Mart, 158
American Airlines, 33
American Airlines Vacations, 37
American Express
  emergency number, 17
  traveler's checks, 15
American Foundation for the Blind, 26
The Amsterdam, 212
Amtrak, 36
  Niagara-on-the-Lake and Niagara Falls, 227
  Stratford, 218
Angus Glen Golf Club, 150
The Annex, 46
Another Man's Poison, 178
Antiques, 172, 174–176
The Archer (Moore), 124, 137
Architectural highlights, 135–138
Arctic Canada, 181
Area code, 50
Argonauts, 152
Aritzia, 184–185
Art galleries, 176
Art Gallery of Ontario, 6, 124, 143, 154, 166
  restaurants near, 130
Artists' Gardens, 119
Art museums
  Art Gallery of Ontario, 6, 124, 143, 154, 166
    restaurants near, 130

George R. Gardiner Museum of Ceramic Art, 2, 126–127
Henry Moore Sculpture Centre, 124–125
McMichael Canadian Art Collection, 128
Museum of Contemporary Canadian Art, 133
Royal Ontario Museum, 2, 127–128, 143, 146
  restaurants near, 130
Arts and crafts, 21
  Canadian Aboriginal Festival, 23
  shopping for, 135, 154, 159, 169, 181–182
  Winterfest, 19
The Art Shoppe, 188, 191
Arts on King, 182
Art Zone, 182
Ashbridge's Bay Park, 146
Assaulted Women's Help Line, 51
Asylum, 157, 194
AT&T Rogers Cup, 152
At Home, 172
ATMs (automated teller machines), 15
Atom Blaster, 119
Atrium on Bay, 190
Atticus Books, 178
Australia
  airlines from, 33–34
  Canadian High Commission in, 12
  Consulate-General, 50
  customs regulations, 14
  High Commission, 50
  passport information, 13
Australian Passport Information Service, 13
Auto racing, 151
Avis rental cars, 49
Avon Boat Rentals (Stratford), 222
Avon Theatre (Stratford), 220

B abysitting, 50
Ballenford Books on
  Architecture, 178
The BamBoo, 207
Bank of Montreal, 168
Bar 501, 214
Bar Italia & Billiards, 210
The Barn/The Stables, 214
Bars, 210–212
Baseball, 151
Basketball, 151–152
The Bata Shoe Museum,
  131–132
Bat Cave, 128
Bath and beauty products,
  187–188
Bauhaus, 209
Bau-Xi, 154, 176
The Bay, 165
Bay-Bloor Radio, 177
Bay of Spirits Gallery, 176
BCE Place, 168
The Beaches, 45, 146
  sights and attractions, 134
Beardmore Building, 169
Bed and Breakfast
  Canada, 55
Bed-and-breakfasts (B&Bs),
  55
  Stratford, 224–225
Beer Store, 51
Bell Canadian Open, 152
Belle Epoque, 174
Bellevue Park, 157
Berlin, 209
Bernardi's Antiques, 174
Better Business Bureau, 37
Bicycling, 147–148
  tours, 146
Bidding For Travel, 29
The Big Carrot, 186
Billiards, 210
Birks, 189
The Bishop and the Belcher,
  212
Bishop White Gallery, 127
Black Creek Pioneer Village,
  132, 143
Bloor Laundromat, 51
Bloor Street, 42
Bloor Street Viaduct, 126
Bloor Street West, 172
Blue Jays, 151
  Season Opener, 19
Blue Moon, 135
Boathouse (Stratford), 222
Boating, 147
Boat tours and cruises
  Muskoka region, 242
  Niagara-on-the-Lake,
    237–238

Stratford, 222
  Toronto, 145
Bob Miller Book Room, 178
Boingo, 31
The Bonnie Stern School,
  186
Book City, 178
Books, recommended, 39
Bookstores, 178–179
Boomer, 184
Bounty Contemporary
  Canadian Craft Shop, 119
Bracebridge, 242
Brava, 194
Bravo, 145
British Airways, 33, 34
Browns, 193
The Brunswick House, 212
Bucket shops, 35
Buddies in Bad Times
  Theatre, 200
Budget rental cars, 49, 242
Business hours, 50
Bus tours, 144–145
Bus travel, 36, 48
  to/from airport, 41
Butterfly Conservatory, 236
Byzantium, 214

C aban, 188
Cabbagetown, 46
Cabs, 48–49
  to/from airports, 40
  tipping, 53
Calendar of events, 18–23
Cameron House, 212
Campbell House, 138, 166
Canada Blooms, 19
Canada Customs and
  Revenue Agency, 13
Canada Day
  Celebrations, 20
Canada Life Assurance
  Building, 166
Canada Permanent Trust
  Building, 165
Canada's Sports Hall of
  Fame, 140
Canadian Aboriginal
  Festival, 23
Canadian Automobile
  Association (CAA), 37
Canadian Broadcasting
  Centre, 145
Canadian High
  Commission, 12
Canadian Imperial Bank
  of Commerce, 164
Canadian National
  Exhibition, 21

Canadian Opera Company,
  204
Canadian Tire, 177
Canadian Warplane Heritage
  Museum (Hamilton), 248
Canoeing, 147
CanStage, 200
Capezio, 193
Careful Hand Laundry & Dry
  Cleaners Ltd., 51
Care-on-Call, 50
Caribana, 21, 22
Carlton Cinemas, 215
The Carlu, 2, 203
Car rentals, 49
  shopping online for, 30
Car travel, 36–37, 49
Casa Acoreana, 157–158
Casa Loma, 126, 136–137,
  143
Cavalcade of Lights, 23
CBC Museum, 145
Cellphones, 32–33
Cemeteries, 142
Centre Island, 6, 124, 147
Centreville, 124
Centro, 214
C'est What?, 207
Chanel, 182
Chapters, 178
Charlotte Room Billiards
  Digest, 210
Château des Charmes, 228
Children, families with,
  26–27
  accommodations, 66
  Children's Film Festival,
    142
  entertainment, 201–202
  Lorraine Kimsa Theatre for
    Young People, 201–202
  Milk International
    Children's Festival,
    19, 142
  Paramount Canada's
    Wonderland, 129–131,
    143
  restaurants, 93
  shopping, 183, 188, 193
  sights and attractions,
    142–144
Children's Film Festival, 142
Chinatown, 45
  shopping, 171
  sights and attractions,
    133–134
  walking tour, 153–158
Chinese New Year
  Celebrations, 18
Chudleigh's, 143–144

ChumCity, 145
Church Street, 46
Cigars and tobacco, 180
Cinemas, 215
Cinematheque Ontario, 215
Cirrus ATM network, 15
City Hall
    New, 136, 137, 165
    Old, 136–137, 165
Citytv, 145
Classical music, 204
Climate, 18
Club and music scene,
    206–210
Club Monaco, 183
CN Tower, 6, 125, 143,
    160–161
    restaurants near, 130
Coffeehouses, 215–217
Colborne Lodge, 138
College Park, 190
Comedy clubs, 6–7, 206
Community Information
    Centre of Metropolitan
    Toronto, 25–26
Comrags, 185
Consolidators, 35
The Consort Bar, 213
Constantine, 174
Consulate General of Italy,
    154
Consulates, 50
Contemporary Canadian Art,
    Museum of, 133
Continental Airlines
    Vacations, 37
Contraception Museum,
    History of, 132
The Cookbook Store, 178
The Corner Pocket, 210–211
Council Travel, 27
Courage My Love, 141, 157,
    194
Crafts, 21
    Canadian Aboriginal
        Festival, 23
    shopping for, 135, 154,
        159, 169, 181–182
    Winterfest, 19
Craft Studio, 119
Credit cards, 16
    frequent-flier, 36
Crews/Tango, 214
Cross-country skiing, 147
Cullen Gardens & Miniature
    Village, 144
Currency and currency
    exchange, 14–16
    online currency con-
        verter, 32

Cushion concerts, 142
Customs regulations, 13–14

D ance clubs, 209
Dance companies, 205
Dancemakers, 205
Dancing Days, 157
The Danforth, 135
Danier, 190
Danny Grossman Dance
    Company, 205
David Mason, 178
David's, 193
Decibel, 184
Decorum Decorative Finds,
    174
Delphic, 184
Delta Airlines, 33, 34
Delta Vacations, 37
Dentists, 50
Department stores, 182
Design Exchange, 132–133
Dessert cafes, 216
Diamond taxi company, 49
Dinner theater, 202–203
Dinosaur Gallery, 128
Disabilities, travelers with,
    25–26
    accommodations, 8
The Distillery Historic
    District, 2, 197
Distress Centre, 51
Divine Decadence, 194
Dixie Outlet Mall, 180
The Docks, 209
Dock Shoppe, 159
Doctors, 50
Donald D. Summerville
    Olympic Pool, 146
Don Valley golf course, 149
Dora Keogh Irish Pub, 213
Down East Gifts and Gallery,
    187
Downtown
    shopping, 171–172
    sights and attractions,
        124–125
Downtown Association of
    Bed-and-Breakfast Guest
    Houses, 55
Downtown East, 42, 45
    accommodations, 65–68
    restaurants, 96–100
    sights and attractions, 134
Downtown Jazz Festival, 20
Downtown West, 42
    accommodations, 55–65
    restaurants, 84–96
    sights and attractions,
        133–134

Dragon City, 133, 156
Dream in High Park, 196,
    200–201
Driving rules, 49
Dry cleaning, 51
Du Maurier Theatre Centre,
    119
Dundurn Castle (Hamilton),
    248
Du Verre Glass, 179

E arl Bales Park, 151
The East End, 43, 46, 135.
    See also Midtown East
    accommodations, 71–72
    restaurants, 108–110
Easy & the Fifth, 209
The Eaton Centre, 137
    shopping, 171, 191
Eau, 211
Edwards Gardens, 142
Eglinton Avenue, 46
18 Karat, 154
El Convento Rico, 214–215
Elderhostel, 26
Electricity, 50
Electronic goods, 177–178
The Elgin and Winter Garden
    Theatre Centre, 197
Elizabeth Milan Hotel Day
    Spa, 148, 187
El Mocambo, 207
El Pipil, 135
Elte Carpet & Home,
    188, 191
Embassies and
    consulates, 50
Emergencies, 50
En Provence, 188
Enterprise rental cars, 49
Entertainment. See Nightlife
    and entertainment
Entry requirements, 13
Equifax, 17
Ernest Thompson Seton
    Park, 150
Eskimo Art Gallery, 176
Estée Lauder Spa, 148–149
Ewanika, 134, 185
Expedia, 28, 29, 37, 38
Experian, 17–18
Experimetal, 189
Ex-Toggery, 194
Eza Wear, 184

F actory Theatre, 201
Fairmont Royal York, 168
Fall, 18

Families with children,
26–27
    accommodations, 66
    Children's Film Festival,
    142
    entertainment, 201–202
    Lorraine Kimsa Theatre
    for Young People,
    201–202
    Milk International
    Children's Festival,
    19, 142
    Paramount Canada's
    Wonderland, 129–131,
    143
    restaurants, 93
    shopping, 183, 188, 193
    sights and attractions,
    142–144
Familyhostel, 26
Family Travel Files, 27
Family Travel Network, 26
Famous People Players
Dinner Theatre, 202
Fares, public
transportation, 48
Farmer's Market (Stratford),
222
Fashion Crimes, 185
Fashion Design Council
of Canada, 191
Fashions (clothing), 182–186
    children's, 183
    for kids, 183
    men's, 183–184
    vintage, 6, 194–195
    women's, 183–186
Feheley Fine Arts, 176
Femme De Carriere, 185
Ferries, 50
Festival of Beer, 21
Festivals and special events,
18–23
Festival Theatre (Stratford),
220
Film Festival, Toronto
International, 21
Financial District, 44–45
    walking tour, 160–166
First Canadian Place,
164, 191
First Hand Canadian Crafts,
159
First Night Toronto and New
Year's Eve at City Hall, 23
Fitness centers, 148–149
Five Potters Studio, 182
Flatiron or Gooderham
Building, 168–169
Flights.com, 35

Floral Clock, 236
Food stores and markets,
186–187, 192
Football, 152
Forest Hill, 46
Fort Erie, Historic, 237
Fort George National
Historic Park, 230
Fortune Housewares, 156
Fort York, 139, 143
French Country, 187
Frequent-flier clubs, 35
Frequent-flier credit
cards, 36
Fresh Baked Goods, 185
Frida, 182
Frida Crafts, 169
The Fringe—Toronto's
Theatre Festival,
20–21, 196
Frommers.com, 30
Frommer's favorite
experiences, 3, 6–7
F/X, 185

G alleria, 137
Gallery Moos, 176
Gallery Stratford, 222
Gardens
    Allan Gardens, 141
    Cullen Gardens &
    Miniature Village, 144
    Edwards, 142
    Royal Botanical Gardens
    (Hamilton), 249–250
    School of Horticulture
    (Niagara Falls), 236
Gardiner Museum of
Ceramic Art, 2, 126–127
Gay & Lesbian Pride
Celebration, 20
Gay and lesbian travelers
    accommodations, 8
    information and
    resources, 28
    marriage, 27
    nightlife, 214–215
Gay Toronto, 28
George R. Gardiner Museum
of Ceramic Art, 2, 126–127
George's Trains, 193
Gifts, 187
Girl Talk Toronto: A Mini City
Guide, 9
Glad Day Bookshop, 28,
178–179
Glen Abbey Golf Club,
150, 152
Glenn Gould Studio, 203

Global Cheese Shoppe,
141, 157, 186
Golf, 149–150
    tournaments, 152
Goods-and-services tax
(GST), 172
Gorilla Rainforest, 131
GoToMyPC, 31
GO (Government of Ontario)
Transit, 248
The Grange, 124–125
Gravenhurst, 242–247
Gravenhurst Opera House,
242
Gray Line, 144–145
Great Canadian Blues
Festival, 21
Great Canadian News
Company, 190
Greater Toronto Double
Decker Circle Tour,
144–145
Great Gorge Adventure, 236
Great Lakes Schooner
Company, 145
Great Library, 166
Greektown, 6, 46, 135
Green Tourism Association, 9
Greyhound, 36
Grreat Stuff, 180
Gucci, 182

H amilton, 248–251
Hamilton International
Airport, John C. Munro,
248
Hamilton Military Museum,
248–249
Hamilton Tourist Information
Centre, 248
Hanlan's Point, 147
Harbor and island tours, 145
Harbourfront Canoe and
Kayak School, 147
Harbourfront Centre, 6, 118
Harbourfront/Lakefront,
44, 142, 143, 150
    walking tour, 158–160
Harbourfront Reading Series,
20, 119
Harbourside Boating Centre,
147
Harry Rosen, 184
Hazelton Lanes, 150, 191
Health and beauty products,
187–188
Health concerns, 24–25
Health insurance, 24
Help! We've Got Kids, 143

Henry Moore Sculpture Centre, 124–125
Henry's, 177
Hermés, 183
Hertz rental cars
  Niagara-on-the-Lake, 228
  Toronto, 49
High Park, 141–142, 147
High Park Cycle and Sports, 148
Hillebrand Estates Winery, 228
Historic buildings, 138–140
Historic Fort Erie, 237
History of Contraception Museum, 132
History of Ontario and Toronto, 252–260
HMV, 192
Hoax Couture, 183
Hockey, 152
Hockey Hall of Fame, 140, 143, 168
  restaurants near, 130
Holidays, 18
Holt Renfrew Centre, 182, 191
Holt Renfrew Last Call, 180
Honest Ed's World Famous Shopping Centre, 180
Horsefeathers!, 174–175
Horse racing, 152
The Horseshoe Tavern, 207
Hospital for Sick Children, 51
Hospitals, 50
Hotels, 54–74. See also Accommodations Index
  at the airport, 72–74
  bed-and-breakfasts (B&Bs), 55
  best bets, 7–8
  Downtown East, 65–68
  Downtown West, 55–65
  East End, 71
  family-friendly, 66
  Hamilton, 250
  Midtown West, 68–71
  Niagara-on-the-Lake, 230–233
  in package tours, 37
  shopping online for, 29
  tipping, 53
  tips on, 38–39
  Uptown, 71
  what's new, 1
Hot lines, 51
Hotwire, 29–30
House of Tea, 186
Housewares and furnishings, 188–189

H2O Generation Station, 119
The Hudson's Bay Company, 182
Humber College, 151
Humber Valley golf course, 149
Hummingbird Centre for the Performing Arts, 169, 203
  restaurants near, 130
Huntsville, 243

IAMAT (International Association for Medical Assistance to Travelers), 25
Iberica Bakery, 158
Ice, 187
Ice-skating, 150
Identity theft or fraud, 17
IGLTA (International Gay & Lesbian Travel Association), 28
IMAX Theater (Niagara Falls), 238
Indian Motorcycle Café and Lounge, 209
Indigo Books Music & More, 179
Industrial tours, 145
Information sources, 12, 41–42. See also Websites
In-line skating, 150
Inniskillin Winery, 237
Insomnia, 51
Insurance, 23–24, 35
Intellicast, 32
International Association for Medical Assistance to Travelers (IAMAT), 25
International Dragon Boat Festival, 20
International Festival of Authors, 22, 119
International Gay & Lesbian Travel Association (IGLTA), 28
International Student Identity Card (ISIC), 27
International Youth Travel Card (IYTC), 27
Internet access, 30–32, 51
InTouch USA, 33
IPass network, 31
Ireland
  Canadian High Commission in, 12
  Embassy, 50
  Passport Office, 13

The Irish Shop, 183
ISIC (International Student Identity Card), 27
I2roam.com, 31

J & S Arts and Crafts, 154
Jane Corkin Gallery, 176
Japanese Paper Place, 187
Jazz, 20, 207–208
Jeanne Lottie, 185
Jet boat excursions, 230
JetsGo, 1
Jewelry, 189–190
Joe Rockhead's, 151
Jogging, 150
John C. Munro Hamilton International Airport, 248
John Quay, 159
Journey Behind the Falls, 237
Journeywoman, 28
Juliet III (boat), 222
Just Bears, 193

Kaleidoscope, 143
Kayaking, 147
Kensington Market, 6, 141, 156, 192
Kew Gardens Park, 146
Kidding Awound, 193
Kids Cats & Dogs, 183
Kids Help Phone, 51
Kiever Synagogue, 157
Kim Moon Bakery, 133, 154
Kingswood Music Theatre, 205
Kinko's, 51
Kinsman Robinson Galleries, 176
Kitchener, 222
Kitchener-Waterloo Area Visitors and Convention Bureau, 222
Kitchen Stuff Plus, 188
Kit Kat Bar and Grill, 211
Kiu Shun Trading, 154
Kol Kid, 183
Konzelmann Winery, 228
Koreatown, 46
Kurtz Orchards, 237
K-W Oktoberfest, 222

La Cage Dinner Theatre, 202
La Senza, 190
La Serre, 213
Last-minute.com, 29

L'Atelier, 175
The Laugh Resort, 206
Laundry and dry cleaning, 51
Laundry Lounge, 51
Laura Secord Homestead
    (Queenston), 236
La Vie en Rose, 190
Layout of Toronto, 42–44
Leather goods, 190
Lee's Palace, 207
Left Bank, 211
Legends of the Game,
    161, 187
The Library Bar, 213
Light rapid transit (LRT), 48
Limousine services, 40
Linda Lundstrom, 185
Linea Intima, 190
Lingerie, 190
Lionhead Golf Club, 150
Liquor Control Board of
    Ontario, 51
Liquor laws, 51
The Little Dollhouse
    Company, 193
Little Italy, 3, 6, 45, 134
Lorraine Kimsa Theatre for
    Young People, 201–202
Lost-luggage insurance, 24
Lost property, 16–17, 51
Louis Vuitton, 182
Lovechild, 183
Lovecraft, 192–193
Lower Don Valley bike
    trail, 147
LRT (light rapid transit), 48
Luggage, lost-luggage
    insurance, 24
Luggage storage and
    lockers, 51
Lululemon, 185
Lush, 187
Lynn Robinson, 182

M abel's Fables, 179
M.A.C., 187–188
Mackenzie House, 139
Madison, 211
Magazines and newspapers,
    190
Maid of the Mist, 237
Mail, 52
Mail2web.com, 31
Maison de la Presse
    Internationale, 190
Malls and shopping centers,
    190–192
Manulife Centre,
    51, 191, 195
Maple Leaf Gardens, 205

Maple Leaf Quay, 159
Maple Leafs, 152
    Opening Night, 22
Mapquest, 32
Marilyn's, 181
MarineLand (Niagara Falls),
    238
Mariposa Cruise Line, 145
Markets, 141, 192
Mark McLaine Collection,
    175
Martin Goodman Trail,
    147, 150
Massey Hall, 203
MasterCard
    emergency number, 17
    traveler's checks, 16
MasterCard ATM Locator, 32
Maxi Boutique, 185
McBride Cycle, 148
The McMichael Canadian
    Art Collection, 128
MEDEX International, 24
Medic Alert Identification
    Tag, 24
Medical insurance, 24
Medieval Times Dinner &
    Tournament, 202
Meetingplace (St. Jacobs),
    222
Melewa Bakery, 154
Mendels Creamery, 157
Mephisto, 193
Metro Central YMCA, 148
Metro Hall, 162
Metro Licensing
    Commission, 49
Metro taxi company, 49
Metro Toronto Convention &
    Visitors Association, 12
Michel Taschereau Antiques,
    175
MicroKids, 119
Midtown
    shopping, 172
    sights and attractions,
        126–128
Midtown East, 43, 46. See
    also The East End
Midtown West, 43
    accommodations, 68–71
    neighborhoods, 45–46
    restaurants, 100–107
    sights and attractions, 135
Milano, 211
Military Museum, Hamilton,
    248–249
Milk International Children's
    Festival, 19, 142
Millionaire's Row, 242
Mink, 134, 189

Mint et Menthe, 211
Mirvish Village, 135
Misdemeanors, 183
Mississauga, 207
Modrobes, 183
Molson Amphitheatre,
    119, 205
Molson Indy, 21, 151
Money matters, 14–18
Montréal Bistro & Jazz Club,
    208
Montréal/Toronto Tennis
    Masters Series, 152
Moore, Henry, 6
    The Archer, 124, 137
    Sculpture Centre, 124–125
Moores, 184
MossRehab, 26
Mostly Movables Inc, 175
Mountain Equipment Co-op,
    169
Mount Pleasant Cemetery,
    142, 147
Mount Sinai Hospital, 50–51
Movie houses, 215
MuchMusic, 145
Museum of Contemporary
    Canadian Art, 133
Music
    classical, 204
    clubs, 206–210
    pop and rock, 204–205
    stores, 192
The Music Store, 192
Muskoka Autumn Studio
    Tour, 22
Muskoka Bed and Breakfast
    Association, 243
Muskoka Heritage Place
    (Huntsville), 243
Muskoka Lakes Museum
    (Port Carling), 242–243
Muskoka Pioneer Village
    (Huntsville), 243
Muskoka region, 2, 22, 150,
    240–247
    accommodations, 243–246
    restaurants, 246–247
    transportation, 241–242
    traveling to, 241
    visitor information, 241
Muskoka Tourism, 241
Muti, 179
My Market Bakery, 157
Mysteriously Yours, 202–203

N ancy Poole's Studio, 177
NASA, 209
Nathan Phillips Square,
    137, 150

National Ballet of Canada, 205–206
National Club Building, 165
National Passport Agency, 13
National Passport Information Center, 13
National rental cars, 49, 242
National Tilden, 227
Native Canadians, 23, 128, 176, 181, 182, 185, 202, 230, 252
Eskimo Art Gallery, 176
shopping, 176, 181, 182, 185
Native Earth Performing Arts Theatre, 202
Native Stone Art, 182
Nautical Mind, 159
Necropolis, 142
Neighborhoods, 44–46
shopping, 171–172
sights and attractions, 133–135
Nestings, 188
Nestings Kids, 188
New Asia Supermarket, 133
New City Hall, 165
Newspapers and magazines, 41, 52, 190
New Zealand
airlines from, 34
Canadian High Commission in, 12
customs regulations, 14
High Commission, 50
Passports Office, 13
Niagara Falls, 227, 237–238
Niagara Falls Tourism, 227
Niagara Historical Society Museum, 230
Niagara-on-the-Lake, 7, 227–240
accommodations, 230–233
exploring, 228, 230
restaurants, 233–236
traveling to, 227
visitor information, 227
Niagara-on-the-Lake Chamber of Commerce, 227
Niagara Parks Commission, 227
Niagara Parkway, 227, 236–237
Nicholas Hoare, 169, 179
Nightlife and entertainment, 196–217
bars, 210–214
club and music scene, 206–210
current listings, 196

gay and lesbian, 214–215
movie theaters, 215
performing arts, 196–206
tickets, 196
what's new, 2
Noah's, 188
Norman Bethune Memorial House (Gravenhurst), 242
North by Northeast Festival, 20
North Toronto, 44
Northwest Airlines, 33

Oh Yes, Toronto, 158, 187
Oktoberfest (Kitchener-Waterloo), 22, 222
Old City Hall, 136–137, 165
Old Clothing Show & Sale, 22, 191
Old Navy, 183
Old Town/St. Lawrence Market, 45
Olga Korper Gallery, 177
One Front Street, 168
One-of-a-Kind Craft Show & Sale, 23, 191
Ontario College of Art & Design Gallery, 177
Ontario Cycling Association, 147
Ontario Legislature, 136, 138
Ontario Place, 119, 143
Ontario Science Centre, 6, 128–129, 143
restaurants near, 130
Ontario Travel, 53
Ontario Visitor Information Centre, 41
Opaque fare services, 29
Open Air Books & Maps, 179
Opera, 204, 242
Orbitz, 28, 37
Organized tours, 144–146
Osgoode Hall, 139, 166
Outdoor activities, 146–151
Outside Toronto (website), 220

Package tours, 37
Panorama, 211
Pantages Theatre, 197
The Paper Bag Princess, 194
Parachuting, 151
Paramount Canada's Wonderland, 129–131, 143
Paris Samples, 181
Parking, 49
Parks and gardens, 141–142

Patty King, 157
Peach Berserk, 185–186
Pearson International Airport, 40, 41
Pencraft, 187
Performing arts, 196–206
Perkins Building, 169
Perola Supermarket, 158
Peter Cullman, 189
Petit Pied, 193
PGA Tour Canadian Open, 21
Pharmacies, 52
Pharma Plus, 52
Phoenix Concert Theatre, 207
Picnic areas, 6, 118, 131, 146, 220, 236
The Pilot, 211
The Pineapple Room, 157
Pink Cobra, 186
Plaiter Place, 156
Planet Skate, 150
Playdium, 144
PLUS ATM network, 15
Po Chi Tong, 156
Poison Information Centre, 51
Police, 52
Pool and billiards, 210
Pop and rock music, 204–205
Pope Joan, 215
Portage Flyer Steam Train (Huntsville), 243
Port Carling, 242–243
Port Carling Community Hall, 242
Post offices, 52
Power Plant Contemporary Art Gallery, 119, 159
Prada, 182–183
Preloved, 195
Premiere Dance Theatre, 203
Prescription medications, 24–25
Priceline, 29
Price Roman, 186
Prime Gallery, 153
Princess of Wales Theatre, 161–162, 197
Provincial sales tax (PST), 172
Pubs and taverns, 212–214
Pusateri's, 186
Putti, 176

Quasi-Modo Modern Furniture, 134, 189
Queen's Park (Stratford), 220
Queen's Park (Toronto), 45, 150

Queen's Quay, 118
Queen's Quay Terminal,
   158, 192
Queenston Heights Park, 236
Queen Street West, 45
   restaurants, 134
   shopping, 172
   sights and attractions, 134

R a, 169
Radio, 52
Rape Crisis Line, 51
Raptors, 151–152
The Real Jerk, 211
The Rebel House, 213
Rental cars, 49
   shopping online for, 30
Reservoir Lounge, 208
Restaurants, 75–116. See
   also Restaurant Index
   alfresco, 3, 10
   best bets, 8–11
   by cuisine, 80–84
   Downtown East, 96–100
   Downtown West, 84–96
   East End, 108–110
   family-friendly, 93
   Hamilton, 250–251
   late-night, 109
   Midtown West, 100–107
   Niagara-on-the-Lake,
      233–236
   Niagara Parkway
      Commission, 240
   north of the city, 114–116
   smoking, 80
   taxes and tipping, 73, 75
   near top attractions, 130
   Uptown, 110–114
   vegetarian, 115–116
   websites, 98
   what's new, 1
Restrooms, 52
Rex Jazz and Blues Bar, 208
Rhonda Maternity, 186
Riverdale Farm, 6, 144
The Rivoli, 206, 208
Road-Post, 33
Robinson's General Store
   (Huntsville), 243
Rock-climbing, 151
ROMwalks, 136, 146
The Roof Lounge at the
   Park Hyatt, 126, 213
Roots, 183–184
Rosedale, 46
Royal Agricultural Winter
   Fair and Royal Horse
   Show, 22–23

Royal Alexandra Theatre,
   162, 200
Royal Bank Plaza,
   138, 168, 192
Royal Botanical Gardens
   (Hamilton), 249–250
Royal Conservatory of
   Music, 204
Royal de Versailles
   Jewellers, 189
Royal Food Centre, 157
Royal Ontario Museum,
   2, 127–128, 143, 146
   restaurants near, 130
Royal taxi company, 49
Roy Thomson Hall, 162, 203
Rubies Beauty Bar, 188

S able-Castelli, 177
Safety, 52
Sailor, 215
St. Andrew's Presbyterian
   Church, 162
St. Jacobs, 222
St. Jacobs Outlet Mall
   (St. Jacobs), 222
St. James Cathedral, 169,
   204
St. Lawrence Centre for
   the Arts, 200
St. Lawrence Hall, 169
St. Lawrence Market, 141,
   169, 192
St. Michael's Hospital, 50
St. Patrick's Church, 204
St. Patrick's Day Parade, 19
Sam the Record Man, 192
Samuel European Galleries,
   127
Sandra Ainsley, 177
Sandra Ainsley gallery, 164
Santa Claus Parade, 23
Santa's Village
   (Bracebridge), 242
Sante—The Bloor-Yorkville
   Wine Festival, 19
SARS, 13, 24, 25
Sasmart Smart Wear, 157
Scadding House, 137
Scarborough Town Centre,
   192
School of Horticulture
   (Niagara Falls), 236
Science Centre, Ontario,
   128–129
Science City, 193
Scotia Tower, 165
Seafood stores, 156–157

Sears, 137, 182
Seasons, 18
Second City, 206
Security, airport, 34
Seekers Books, 179
Senior travelers, 26
Senses Bakery, 186
72 First Canadian Place, 162
Sex toys, 192–193
Shakespearean Garden
   (Stratford), 220, 222
Shark City, 211
The Shaw Festival
   (Niagara-on-the-Lake),
   19, 227, 228
The Shoe Company, 181
Shoes, 193
Shopper's Drug Mart, 52
Shopping, 171–195
   best bargains, 180
   neighborhoods for,
      171–172
   sales, 191
   what's new, 2
Side-Step, 28
Side trips, 2
Sights and attractions,
   117–146
   architectural highlights,
      135–138
   Frommer's favorite
      experiences, 3, 6–7
   great views, 126
   historic buildings, 138–140
   for kids, 142–144
   suggested itineraries,
      117–118
   what's new, 2
Silverbridge, 190
The Silver Snail, 179
Sim & Jones, 184
Simone Marie Belgian
   Chocolate, 186
Site59.com, 29
Skiing, 151
SkyDome, 6, 140, 151, 205
   restaurants near, 130
Skylon Tower Observation
   Deck (Niagara Falls),
   237–238
Slack Alice, 215
Smarter Living, 29
Smoking, 54–55, 80
Sneaky Dee's, 210
Snowboarding, 151
Society for Accessible Travel
   and Hospitality, 26
Sonic Boom concert series,
   204

Sottovoce, 214
South Africa
   airlines from, 34
   Canadian High Commis-
      sion in, 12
   High Commission, 50
South African Airways, 34
Southern Po Boys, 208
Souz Dal, 212
Spadina Historic House &
   Gardens, 139–140
Spas, 1, 148–149
   Northern Ontario, 247
Speakers Corner, 145
Special events and festivals,
   18–23
Spectator sports, 140,
   151–170
Spring, 18
Spring Fever, 142
SpyTech, 178
STA Travel, 27, 35
Step Flight, 137
Stephen Bulger Gallery, 134,
   177
Steven Temple Books, 179
Stillwater Spa, 149
Stratford, 7, 218–227
   accommodations, 222–225
   excursions from, 222
   exploring, 220, 222
   restaurants, 225–227
   traveling to, 218
   visitor information, 218
The Stratford Festival,
   19–20, 218, 220
Stratford Festival
   Accommodation Bureau,
   223
Streetcars, 48
Student travelers, 27
Studio Theatre (Stratford),
   220
Subway, 46–48
   to/from airport, 41
   map, 47
Sugar Mountain
   Confectionery, 187
Summer, 18
Sun Life Centre's second
   tower, 162
Sunnybrook Hospital, 51
Sun protection, 19
Susan Hobbs Gallery, 177
Swimming, 151
Symphony of Fire, 20

T able of Contents, 159
Tafelmusik Baroque
   Orchestra, 204

Tai Kong Supermarket, 156
Tai Sun Co., 154
Talking yellow pages, 53
Tam O'Shanter golf course,
   150
Tango, 1
Tap Phong Trading Company,
   156, 189
Tarragon Theatre, 202
Taschen!, 190
Taste of Little Italy, 20
A Taste of the World
   Neighbourhood Bicycle
   Tours and Walks, 146
Taxes, 53, 172
Taxis, 48–49
   to/from airports, 40
   tipping, 53
Teatro Verde, 189
Telephone, 53
Tel-Xtra, 28
Temperatures, average, 18
Tennis, 151
   tournaments, 152
Tennis Masters Canada/
   Rogers AT&T Cup, 21
Ten Ren Tea, 154
Textile Museum of Canada,
   133
Theater, 6, 196–204
   The Fringe—Toronto's
      Theatre Festival,
      20–21, 196
   The Shaw Festival
      (Niagara-on-the-Lake),
      19, 227, 228
   The Stratford Festival,
      19–20, 220
Theater District, 45
Theatre Passe Muraille, 202
Thompson's Homeopathic
   Supplies, 188
Thrifty rental cars, 49
Ticketmaster, 119
Tiffany & Co., 190
Tilley Endurables, 159, 194
Time zone, 53
Tim Simms Playhouse, 206
Tipping, 53, 55
T-Mobile Hotspot, 31
TNT Man/TNT Woman, 184
Tommy Thompson Trail, 150
Tom Patterson Theatre
   (Stratford), 220
Tom's Place, 181
Top Banana, 193
Top O' the Senator, 208
TorDine, 98
Toronto Bed & Breakfast, 55
Toronto Bicycling Network,
   148

Toronto Blue Jays, 151
Toronto Centre for the Arts,
   200
Toronto Climbing Academy,
   151
Toronto.com, 9, 41–42, 98
Toronto Dance Theatre, 206
Toronto Dominion Centre,
   136, 164–165
Toronto Dominion Gallery
   of Inuit Art, 164
Toronto East General
   Hospital, 51
Toronto Exchange Tower,
   162, 164
Toronto Festival of
   Storytelling, 19
Toronto General Hospital, 50
Toronto Historical Board, 146
Toronto International
   Festival Caravan, 20
Toronto International Film
   Festival, 21
Toronto Island Airport, 40
Toronto Island Bicycle
   Rental, 148
The Toronto Islands,
   44, 119, 124, 143, 147
Toronto Life, 9
Toronto Life Online, 98
Toronto Maple Leafs, 152
Toronto Maple Leafs
   Opening Night, 22
Toronto Mendelssohn Choir,
   204
Toronto Music Garden,
   119, 159–160
Toronto Parks and
   Recreation, 147
Toronto Prayer Line, 51
Toronto Reference Library,
   135, 138
Toronto Sculpture Garden,
   170
Toronto Star, 9
Toronto Symphony
   Orchestra, 204
Toronto Transit Commission
   (TTC), 46
Toronto Truck Theatre, 202
Toronto Zoo, 131, 143
Tourism Ontario, 12
Tourism Stratford, 218, 223
Tourism Toronto, 12, 41, 55
Tourist information,
   12, 41–42
Tours. See also Boat tours
   and cruises
   organized, 144–146
      Stratford, 222
   package, 37

Toys, 193–194
The Toy Shop, 194
Train travel, 36, 41
Trakkers Cross Country
    Ski Club, 147
Transit information, 53
Transportation, 46–50
Transportation Security
    Administration (TSA), 34
Transport Canada
    Information Centre, 41
TransUnion, 18
Travel Assistance
    International, 24
TravelAxe, 29
Travel CUTS, 27
Traveler's checks, 15–16
Travelex Insurance
    Services, 24
Travel goods, 194
Travel Guard
    International, 24
Traveling Internationally
    with Your Kids, 26–27
Traveling to Toronto,
    33–37, 40–41
Travel insurance, 23–24, 35
Travel Insured
    International, 24
Travellers Aid Society
    of Toronto, 55
Travelocity, 28, 29, 37
The Travel Stop, 194
Travel Warnings, 32
Trillium Terminal 3, 40
Trinity Church, 137
Trinity/St. Paul's United
    Church, 204
Trinity Square, 137
Trip-cancellation insurance,
    23–24
TSX Broadcast & Conference
    Centre, 146
TTC Lost Articles Office, 51

Underground City, The, 44
    shopping, 172
The Unicorn, 214
Union Station, 158, 168
United Airlines, 33
United Kingdom
    airlines from, 33
    Canadian High
        Commission in, 12
    Consulate-General, 50
    customs regulations, 14
    High Commission, 50
United Kingdom Passport
    Service, 13

United Vacations, 37
University of Toronto,
    27, 45, 136
    Athletic Centre, 148, 151
    concerts, 204
UpCountry, 189
Uptown, 43, 46
    accommodations, 71
    restaurants, 110–114
US Airways, 33
USIT Campus, 27

Vegetarian restaurants,
    114–115
VIA Rail, 218, 227, 241
Victoria Spa, 149
Village by the Grange,
    154, 192
Vintage clothing, 194–195
Vintages, 195
Virgin Atlantic, 33
Visa
    ATM Locator, 32
    emergency number, 17
    traveler's checks, 16
Visitor information,
    12, 41–42. See also
    Websites
Visitor Rebate Program, 53

Walking tours
    guided, 146
    self-guided, 153–170
        Chinatown and
            Kensington,
            153–158
        Financial District,
            160–166
        Harbourfront,
            158–160
        St. Lawrence and
            Downtown East,
            166–170
Wards Island, 124, 147
Warplane Heritage Museum,
    Canadian (Hamilton), 248
Waterloo, 222
Wayne Gretzky's, 212
Wayport, 31
Weather, 18
    information, 53
Weather.com, 32
Websites (online resources)
    best, 9
    restaurants, 98
    traveler's toolbox, 32

travel-planning and
    booking, 28–30
visitor information,
    12, 41–42
Wenches & Rogues, 184
Western Union, 17
WestJet, 1
West Queen West,
    2, 45, 134
    shopping, 172
Wheat Sheaf Tavern, 214
Wheel Excitement,
    148, 150
Wheel-Trans, 25
Whim Antiques, 176
Whirlpool Aero Car, 236
Wild Indigo, 212
Wild Water Kingdom, 144
William Ashley's, 180,
    191
Wine bars, 214
Wine Rack, 51
Wineries, 228
Wines, 195
Winner's, 181
Win's Flowers, 157
Winter, 18
Winterfest, 19
Wired Seniors, 26
Wireless networks, 31–32
Women travelers, 28
Women Welcome Women
    World Wide (5W), 28
Wonderful & Whites, 169
Woodbine Beach, 146
Woodbine Racetrack, 152
Woody's, 215
Word on the Street,
    21–22
The World's Biggest
    Bookstore, 179
W Y Trading Co., Inc.,
    154, 156

Yahoo! Mail, 31
Ydessa Hendeles Art
    Foundation, 177
YMCA, pools at, 151
Yoga Studio, 148–149
Yonge-Dundas Square,
    2, 203–204
Yonge Street, 42
York Quay, 118
York Quay Centre, 159
Yorkville, 6, 45, 135
    shopping, 172
Young Peoples Theatre, 143
Yuk Yuk's Superclub, 207

Z ara, 184
Zig Zag, 176
Zoo, Toronto, 131, 143

ACCOMMODATIONS

Acrylic Dreams (Stratford), 224
Albert Place (Stratford), 223
Ambercroft (Stratford), 224
Avonmore Manor (Stratford), 224
Belaire Hotel Toronto Airport, 74
Bentley's (Stratford), 223
Best Western Roehampton Hotel & Suites, 71
Bond Place Hotel, 67
Cambridge Suites Hotel, 65
Courtyard Toronto Downtown, 67
Days Hotel—Toronto Airport, 74
Days Inn & Conference Centre Toronto Downtown, 67
Deacon House (Stratford), 224
Deerhurst Resort (Huntsville), 243–244, 247
Delta Chelsea, 7, 8, 64, 66
Delta Meadowvale Resort & Conference Centre, 74
Embassy Suites, 71
Fairmont Royal York, 8, 58
Festival Inn (Stratford), 223
Four Points Sheraton Toronto Airport, 74
Four Seasons Hotel Toronto, 8, 66, 68
Gate House Hotel (Niagara-on-the-Lake), 231
Grandview Inn & Resort (Huntsville), 244
Hilton Toronto, 55
Hilton Toronto Airport, 72
Holiday Inn on King, 64
Hôtel Le Germain, 1, 7, 55–56
Hotel Victoria, 65
Howard Johnson (Hamilton), 250
Howard Johnson Selby Hotel & Suites, 8, 70–71
Howard Johnson Yorkville, 70
Inn at the Falls (Bracebridge), 245–246

Inn on the Twenty (Jordan), 233
InterContinental Toronto, 68–69
Langdon Hall (Cambridge), 225
Le Royal Meridien King Edward Hotel, 7, 66–67
The Metropolitan Hotel, 7, 11, 58, 62
Moffat Inn (Niagara-on-the-Lake), 232
Neill-Wycik College Hotel, 67–68
Oban Inn (Niagara-on-the-Lake), 231
The Old Bank House (Niagara-on-the-Lake), 233
Park Hyatt Toronto, 7, 8, 69
Pillar & Post Inn (Niagara-on-the-Lake), 231
Prince of Wales Hotel (Niagara-on-the-Lake), 231–232
Quality Hotel Downtown, 68
Quality Hotel Midtown, 70
The Queen's Inn (Stratford), 223
Queen's Landing Inn (Niagara-on-the-Lake), 232
Radisson Plaza Hotel Admiral, 62, 71, 159
Ramada, 71
Regal Constellation Hotel, 73
Renaissance Toronto Hotel at SkyDome, 62
Severn River Inn (Severn Bridge), 246
Sheraton (Hamilton), 250
Sheraton (Scarborough), 71
The Sheraton Centre Toronto, 63, 66
Sheraton Gateway Hotel in Toronto International Airport, 72–73
Sheraton on the Falls, 238, 240
SoHo Metropolitan Hotel, 1, 7, 56
The Strathcona, 65
The Sutton Place Hotel, 8, 70
Taboo Resort (Gravenhurst), 244–245, 247
Tamwood Resort (Bracebridge), 245
Toronto Airport Marriott Hotel, 73–74

Toronto Marriott Eaton Centre, 63
University of Toronto at Scarborough, 72
Victoria University, 8, 71
Westin Harbour Castle, 63–64
Westin Prince Hotel, 72
White Oaks Conference Resort & Spa (Niagara-on-the-Lake), 232
Windermere House Resort, 245
Woods Villa (Stratford), 225
Wyndham Bristol Place, 73

RESTAURANTS

Acqua, 168
Agora, 11, 87, 130
Amore Trattoria, 113, 130
Angel Inn (Niagara-on-the-Lake), 233
Annapurna Vegetarian Restaurant, 114
Annona at the Park Hyatt, 10, 101
Astoria, 109
Auberge du Pommier, 110
Avalon, 84, 130
Avenue Coffee Shop, 107
Avli, 109–110
Barberian's, 10, 84–85
Bentley's (Stratford), 226
Betty's Restaurant & Tavern (Niagara Falls), 240
Biagio, 170
Biff's, 9, 10, 96–97, 130
Bistro 990, 10, 100
Blondie's (Gravenhurst), 247
Bloor Street Diner, 105
Blowfish Restaurant & Sake Bar, 1, 8, 10, 87–88
Boathouse Cafe, 159
Boba, 101
Brassaii, 1, 8, 10, 90–91
The Buttery (Niagara-on-the-Lake), 233–234
Bymark, 85
Café Brussel, 108
Cafe Diplomatico, 216
Café Garibaldi (St. Catharines), 234
Café Nervosa, 103
Café Societa, 91
Café Victoria., 170
Canoe Restaurant & Bar, 8, 85, 126

Caribbean Roti Corner, 109
Casa d'Oro (Niagara Falls),
    240
Centro, 9, 110–111
Chiado, 9–10, 88
Christina's, 108, 109
The Church (Stratford),
    225–226
Cities, 91
Citron, 91
Colony Kitchen, 1, 103, 130
Commodore's Dining Room,
    159
Courthouse Market Grille, 97
Co Yen, 156
Crush, 91–92
Daily Express Café, 216
Dante's, 116
Demetre Caffe, 216
Desserts by Phipps, 216
Diner on the Green
    (Niagara-on-the-Lake), 240
Dufflet Pastries, 11, 216
Eau, 85
Ecco La, 92
Ellipsis (Huntsville), 246
Epic, 8, 88
The Epicurean, 233
Fans Court (Niagara-on-the-
    Lake), 234
Far Niente, 88
The Fifth, 85–86
The Food Market, 154
Fortune Cookie, 92, 93
Fressen, 114
Future Bakery, 217
Gallery Café, 159
Goldfish, 103
Good Queen Bess, 166
The Goof, 107
Grand Yatt, 116
Grano, 93, 113, 130
Greg's Ice Cream, 216
Gus, 10, 103–104
Gypsy Co-op, 217
Hannah's Kitchen, 114, 130
Happy Seven, 95, 109,
    130, 156
Hello Toast, 99
Hennepin's (Virgil), 234
Hillebrand's Vineyard Café
    (between Niagara-on-the-
    Lake and Virgil), 235
Hiro Sushi, 10, 97
HotHouse Cafe, 98, 130, 169
Il Posto Nuovo, 9, 101–102
Indian Rice Factory, 105
Iseya (St. Catharines),
    234–235

Jacques Bistro du Parc,
    104, 130
Japan Deli, 106
Joso's, 104
Juice for Life, 114
Jump Café and Bar, 89, 164
Just Desserts, 216
Kalendar, 95, 115
Kensington Kitchen, 93, 106
Keystone Alley Cafe
    (Stratford), 226
La Bodega, 92, 130
La Bruschetta, 111–112
La Cantina (Hamilton), 250
Lai Wah Heen, 11, 89
Lakes, 112
Lalibela, 106
La Maquette, 170
Langdon Hall (Cambridge),
    225
La Palette, 92, 158
Lee Garden, 95, 130, 156
Le Papillon, 99, 130, 169
Le Royal Meridien King
    Edward Hotel, 10, 170
Le Sélect Bistro, 92–93
Lettieri, 217
Lolo, 1, 113
Lox, Stock & Bagel, 106
Mars, 107
Matignon, 104
Messis, 10, 104
Mezes, 110
Mezzetta, 113, 115
Mildred Pierce, 93
Millie's Bistro, 10, 93,
    112, 115
Mistura, 102
Monsoon, 8, 86
Montréal Bistro & Jazz
    Club, 99
Movenpick Marché, 168
Myth, 108, 109
Nataraj, 106, 130
Niagara Home Bakery
    (Niagara-on-the-Lake), 233
North 44, 10, 111
Octavia, 108, 109
The Old Prune (Stratford),
    226
On the Twenty Restaurant
    & Wine Bar (Jordan), 235
Opus, 100–101
Oro, 89
Ouzeri, 110
Pangaea, 102
Pan on the Danforth,
    10, 108–109
Patriot, 102

Pearl Harbourfront Chinese
    Cuisine, 159
Penelope, 95
Perry's Restaurant
    (Hamilton), 251
Peter Pan, 93
Pho Hung, 106–107
Pinnacle (Niagara Falls), 240
Pony, 94
Quartier, 112
Queen Mother Cafe, 95–96
Queenston Heights, 240
Radisson Plaza Hotel
    Admiral, 159
Rain, 9, 89–90, 130
Rebel House, 115
Rinderlin's (Welland), 235
Ristorante Giardino
    (Niagara-on-the-Lake), 234
The Rivoli, 96
Rodney's Oyster House, 94
Rosewater Supper Club,
    8, 97
Rouge, 104–105
Rundles (Stratford), 226–227
Sang Ho, 94, 130
Scaramouche, 9, 111
Senses, 90, 115, 130
Serra, 10, 107, 130
7 West Café, 109
Shaw Cafe and Wine Bar
    (Niagara-on-the-Lake), 233
Sheraton Centre, 166
Shopsy's, 10, 93, 100, 168
Sicilian Ice Cream Company,
    216
The Skyline Inn (Niagara
    Falls), 240
Sotto Sotto, 105
Sottovoce, 96
Soul of the Vine, 88
Southern Accent, 105
Spinnakers, 159
Splendido Bar and Grill, 102
SpringRolls, 107
Stagecoach Family
    Restaurant (Niagara-
    on-the-Lake), 233
Stork on the Roof, 113–114
Sun Lok, 154
Susur, 86
Swan, 94
Table Rock Restaurant
    (Niagara Falls), 240
Taro Grill, 94
Terra, 116
Terroni, 99
Thai Magic, 112
3 Guys and a Stove, 247

360 Revolving Restaurant,
 9, 86
Torch Bistro, 97
Tortilla Flats, 96
Truffles, 101, 115
Tundra, 8, 86–87
ZVanipha Lanna, 114
Veni Vidi Vici, 94–95

Victoria Park Restaurant
 (Niagara-on-the-Lake),
 240
Vineland Estates (Vineland),
 235–236
Wellington Court Restaurant
 (St. Catharines), 235
Wildfire (Gravenhurst),
 10, 246

Wish, 1, 99
Xacutti, 1, 90
York Street Kitchen
 (Stratford), 227
Young Thailand, 100, 130
YYZ, 87
ZooM Caffe & Bar, 98

Frommer's®

WITH KIDS

Traveling with kids ages 2 to 14 has never been this easy!

Frommer's Chicago with Kids
Frommer's Las Vegas with Kids
Frommer's New York City with Kids
Frommer's Ottawa with Kids

Frommer's San Francisco with Kids
Frommer's Toronto with Kids
Frommer's Vancouver with Kids
Frommer's Washington, D.C. with Kids

"Every page of this comprehensive book is full of tips."

—*Parenting*

Available at bookstores everywhere.

Discover America's National Parks with Frommer's

All the up-to-date, practical information and candid insider advice you need for the perfect park vacation

Available at bookstores everywhere.

FROMMER'S® COMPLETE TRAVEL GUIDES

Alaska
Alaska Cruises & Ports of Call
Amsterdam
Argentina & Chile
Arizona
Atlanta
Australia
Austria
Bahamas
Barcelona, Madrid & Seville
Beijing
Belgium, Holland & Luxembourg
Bermuda
Boston
Brazil
British Columbia & the Canadian
   Rockies
Brussels & Bruges
Budapest & the Best of Hungary
California
Canada
Cancún, Cozumel & the Yucatán
Cape Cod, Nantucket & Martha's
   Vineyard
Caribbean
Caribbean Cruises & Ports of Call
Caribbean Ports of Call
Carolinas & Georgia
Chicago
China
Colorado
Costa Rica
Cuba
Denmark
Denver, Boulder & Colorado Springs
England
Europe
European Cruises & Ports of Call

Florida
France
Germany
Great Britain
Greece
Greek Islands
Hawaii
Hong Kong
Honolulu, Waikiki & Oahu
Ireland
Israel
Italy
Jamaica
Japan
Las Vegas
London
Los Angeles
Maryland & Delaware
Maui
Mexico
Montana & Wyoming
Montréal & Québec City
Munich & the Bavarian Alps
Nashville & Memphis
New England
New Mexico
New Orleans
New York City
New Zealand
Northern Italy
Norway
Nova Scotia, New Brunswick &
   Prince Edward Island
Oregon
Paris
Peru
Philadelphia & the Amish Country
Portugal

Prague & the Best of the Czech
   Republic
Provence & the Riviera
Puerto Rico
Rome
San Antonio & Austin
San Diego
San Francisco
Santa Fe, Taos & Albuquerque
Scandinavia
Scotland
Seattle & Portland
Shanghai
Sicily
Singapore & Malaysia
South Africa
South America
South Florida
South Pacific
Southeast Asia
Spain
Sweden
Switzerland
Texas
Thailand
Tokyo
Toronto
Tuscany & Umbria
USA
Utah
Vancouver & Victoria
Vermont, New Hampshire & Maine
Vienna & the Danube Valley
Virgin Islands
Virginia
Walt Disney World® & Orlando
Washington, D.C.
Washington State

FROMMER'S® DOLLAR-A-DAY GUIDES

Australia from $50 a Day
California from $70 a Day
England from $75 a Day
Europe from $70 a Day
Florida from $70 a Day
Hawaii from $80 a Day

Ireland from $60 a Day
Italy from $70 a Day
London from $85 a Day
New York from $90 a Day
Paris from $80 a Day

San Francisco from $70 a Day
Washington, D.C. from $80 a Day
Portable London from $85 a Day
Portable New York City from $90
   a Day

FROMMER'S® PORTABLE GUIDES

Acapulco, Ixtapa & Zihuatanejo
Amsterdam
Aruba
Australia's Great Barrier Reef
Bahamas
Berlin
Big Island of Hawaii
Boston
California Wine Country
Cancún
Cayman Islands
Charleston
Chicago
Disneyland®
Dublin
Florence

Frankfurt
Hong Kong
Houston
Las Vegas
Las Vegas for Non-Gamblers
London
Los Angeles
Los Cabos & Baja
Maine Coast
Maui
Miami
Nantucket & Martha's Vineyard
New Orleans
New York City
Paris
Phoenix & Scottsdale

Portland
Puerto Rico
Puerto Vallarta, Manzanillo &
   Guadalajara
Rio de Janeiro
San Diego
San Francisco
Savannah
Seattle
Sydney
Tampa & St. Petersburg
Vancouver
Venice
Virgin Islands
Washington, D.C.

FROMMER'S® NATIONAL PARK GUIDES

Banff & Jasper
Family Vacations in the National
   Parks

Grand Canyon
National Parks of the American West
Rocky Mountain

Yellowstone & Grand Teton
Yosemite & Sequoia/Kings Canyon
Zion & Bryce Canyon

FROMMER'S® MEMORABLE WALKS

Chicago	New York	San Francisco
London	Paris	

FROMMER'S® WITH KIDS GUIDES

Chicago	Ottawa	Vancouver
Las Vegas	San Francisco	Washington, D.C.
New York City	Toronto	

SUZY GERSHMAN'S BORN TO SHOP GUIDES

Born to Shop: France	Born to Shop: Italy	Born to Shop: New York
Born to Shop: Hong Kong, Shanghai & Beijing	Born to Shop: London	Born to Shop: Paris

FROMMER'S® IRREVERENT GUIDES

Amsterdam	Los Angeles	San Francisco
Boston	Manhattan	Seattle & Portland
Chicago	New Orleans	Vancouver
Las Vegas	Paris	Walt Disney World®
London	Rome	Washington, D.C.

FROMMER'S® BEST-LOVED DRIVING TOURS

Britain	Germany	Northern Italy
California	Ireland	Scotland
Florida	Italy	Spain
France	New England	Tuscany & Umbria

HANGING OUT™ GUIDES

Hanging Out in England	Hanging Out in France	Hanging Out in Italy
Hanging Out in Europe	Hanging Out in Ireland	Hanging Out in Spain

THE UNOFFICIAL GUIDES®

Bed & Breakfasts and Country Inns in:	Southwest & South Central Plains	Mexio's Best Beach Resorts
California	U.S.A.	Mid-Atlantic with Kids
Great Lakes States	Beyond Disney	Mini Las Vegas
Mid-Atlantic	Branson, Missouri	Mini-Mickey
New England	California with Kids	New England & New York with Kids
Northwest	Central Italy	New Orleans
Rockies	Chicago	New York City
Southeast	Cruises	Paris
Southwest	Disneyland®	San Francisco
Best RV & Tent Campgrounds in:	Florida with Kids	Skiing & Snowboarding in the West
California & the West	Golf Vacations in the Eastern U.S.	Southeast with Kids
Florida & the Southeast	Great Smoky & Blue Ridge Region	Walt Disney World®
Great Lakes States	Inside Disney	Walt Disney World® for Grown-ups
Mid-Atlantic	Hawaii	Walt Disney World® with Kids
Northeast	Las Vegas	Washington, D.C.
Northwest & Central Plains	London	World's Best Diving Vacations
	Maui	

SPECIAL-INTEREST TITLES

Frommer's Adventure Guide to Australia & New Zealand
Frommer's Adventure Guide to Central America
Frommer's Adventure Guide to India & Pakistan
Frommer's Adventure Guide to South America
Frommer's Adventure Guide to Southeast Asia
Frommer's Adventure Guide to Southern Africa
Frommer's Britain's Best Bed & Breakfasts and Country Inns
Frommer's Caribbean Hideaways
Frommer's Exploring America by RV
Frommer's Fly Safe, Fly Smart

Frommer's France's Best Bed & Breakfasts and Country Inns
Frommer's Gay & Lesbian Europe
Frommer's Italy's Best Bed & Breakfasts and Country Inns
Frommer's Road Atlas Britain
Frommer's Road Atlas Europe
Frommer's Road Atlas France
The New York Times' Guide to Unforgettable Weekends
Places Rated Almanac
Retirement Places Rated
Rome Past & Present

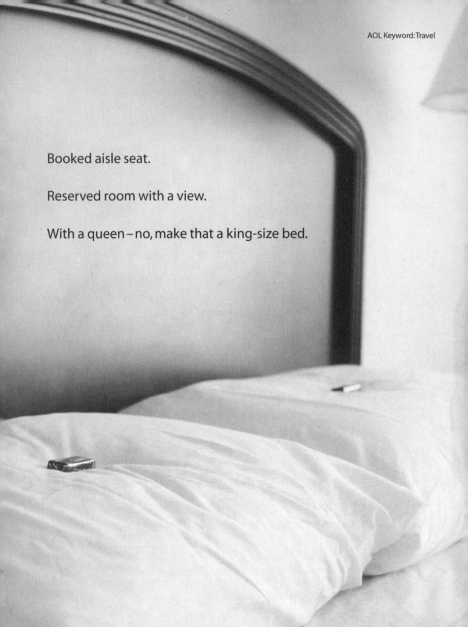

AOL Keyword: Travel

Booked aisle seat.

Reserved room with a view.

With a queen – no, make that a king-size bed.

'th Travelocity, you can book your flights and hotels together, so
u can get even better deals than if you booked them separately.
u'll save time and money without compromising the quality of your
p. Choose your airline seat, search for alternate airports, pick your
tel room type, even choose the neighborhood you'd like to stay in

Travelocity

Visit www.travelocity.com
or call 1-888-TRAVELOCITY

Fly.
Sleep.
Save.

Now you can book your flights and
hotels together, so you can get even better deals
than if you booked them separately.

Travelocity
Visit www.travelocity.com
or call 1-888-TRAVELOCITY

Travelocity,® Travelocity.com® and the Travelocity skyline logo are trademarks and/or service
marks of Travelocity.com L.P. © 2003 Travelocity.com L.P. All rights reserved.